MEALS THAT HEAL!

Three-Lesson Online Companion Course

with Julie Daniluk

LESSON 1: *The Anti-Inflammatory Live-It Plan*
Learn how to create a "Live-It" lifetime eating plan.

LESSON 2: *Hormone and Weight Balance*
Discover the right way to maintain nutritional balance.

LESSON 3: *Eating for Bliss*
Embrace the superfoods that work with your brain chemistry.

REPORTED RESULTS INCLUDE:

- Dramatic reduction in inflammatory pain
- Controlled cravings and emotional eating
- Balanced hormones
- Elevated mood
- Increased energy
- Natural weight balance

AS AN ADDED BONUS, WHEN YOU PURCHASE THIS COURSE, YOU'LL RECEIVE:

- A 21-day "Live-It" plan that includes daily healing affirmations
- An anti-inflammatory food chart
- A food-choice guide to put directly on your fridge
- An anti-inflammatory supplement guide
- Julie's recipe for hormone balance and stress reduction

Visit www.hayhouse.com to sign up today!

ALSO BY JULIE DANILUK, R.H.N.

Slimming Meals That Heal

MEALS THAT HEAL INFLAMMATION

Library of Congress Control Number: 2012932258

Tradepaper ISBN: 978-1-4019-4034-8
Digital ISBN: 978-1-4019-4035-5

15 14 13 12 11 10 9 8 7 6
1st Hay House edition, June 2012

Printed in the United States of America

JULIE DANILUK, R.H.N.

MEALS THAT HEAL INFLAMMATION

Embrace Healthy Living and Eliminate Pain, One Meal at a Time

HAY HOUSE, INC.

Carlsbad, California • New York City
London • Sydney • Johannesburg
Vancouver • Hong Kong • New Delhi

May this book be an inspiration to all those who seek a path to healing using food as their medicine. I would also like to dedicate this to the contributors who donated their knowledge so freely. This book was made possible by a community's collective contributions.

CONTENTS

AUTHOR'S PREFACE

After years of coping with pain caused by inflammation, I thought to myself, enough is enough! I decided to give everything I had to healing. I remember the moment clearly: I was sick for the fourth time in a month with symptoms of severe food poisoning. I was right in the middle of painful stomach cramps, nausea, vomiting, and diarrhea. Then it hit me: I had a small window of opportunity to turn my health crisis around. My husband brought me some water; he ran his hand over my hair and gently said, "Julie, when are you going to do what it takes to get to the bottom of these issues?"

This book is the culmination of my path to healing. I have had a chance to explore a world of nutritional theory. After studying radically different opinions, I have learned that there is no single perfect healing diet. Instead, you must examine what works for you, within you. I feel that if you tune in to what your body needs, then you will be capable of finding the power to heal. It takes commitment to create each meal in a way that will repair and replenish every cell in your body. I encourage you to use this book as a springboard for your own nutritional regime.

Reading this book shows that you're joining a revolution of people who are ready to reach their health potential. I understand that it takes courage to challenge our conventional Western diet. Many families and friends show their affection by sharing a meal, and it can be hard to convince them that healthy food can taste great. When you embrace your instinct to eat fulfilling whole foods, you'll start to prefer the boundless energy and fluid motion that they can give you. Compared to the few minutes of taste-bud exhilaration, a healthy pain-free body is worth the minor sacrifice of your favorite junk-food snack. It comes down to long-term happiness over short-term pleasure. The fun begins when your brain and body are free of the restrictions caused by your ailments. If you could return to the state of wellness you had as a child, you would probably return to laughing a hundred times a day.

You most likely don't fuel your car the way you fuel yourself. You wouldn't consider giving your car extra-rich oil for a treat, saying, "I know it might block up the engine, but it needs a naughty treat once in a while." Do you buy everything your car or pet needs to stay well, but put off feeling healthy yourself until another day? It's common to think that nutritious food is too expensive. In reality, it's likely you can afford to eat the best organic gourmet meals if you choose to cut back on the habits that don't nourish you.

This book offers you the best of my knowledge on systemic inflammation, which I have garnered over the years as a nutritionist and consultant. I hope the information will help you understand how easy it can be to heal yourself by changing your diet, lifestyle, and perspective on health.

Julie Daniluk

FOREWORD

BY DR. ZOLTAN RONA

Inflammation is the number-one reason that an individual consults any health care practitioner. Arthritis, gastritis, colitis, dermatitis, nephritis, neuritis, and cystitis are just some of the common inflammatory conditions that bring people to their doctors. If the doctor's diagnosis ends in the four letters "itis," by definition, inflammation is involved.

There are also numerous diseases or health challenges that are closely linked to inflammation. For example, heart disease, especially coronary artery disease, is thought to be directly associated with inflammation. Inflammation is now considered to be a more important risk factor for heart disease than high cholesterol levels. Laboratory tests showing elevated levels of ESR, hs-CRP, and fibrinogen indicate the presence of inflammation in the body and a higher risk for heart disease. Also noteworthy is that statin drugs such as Lipitor and Crestor routinely used by the medical profession to lower blood levels of cholesterol are anti-inflammatory in their mechanism of action.

Cancer spread is accelerated by inflammation, and many cancer therapies utilize anti-inflammatory drugs such as steroids to keep the symptoms of inflammation (swelling and pain) under control. As well, obesity, dementia, migraine headaches, and Alzheimer's disease involve inflammation. So do all infections, allergic conditions such as hives, and virtually all autoimmune diseases. To this list you can add asthma, diabetes, psoriasis and other skin disorders, and irritable bowel syndrome. The medical treatments for all these conditions use anti-inflammatory drugs as the main therapy. Sports injuries (for example, tendonitis and bursitis) and any musculoskeletal injury sustained in a motor vehicle accident involve inflammation. If you are alive, chances are high you are or have been inflamed in some way.

Conventional doctors have always treated inflammation with drugs and surgery. In some cases, interventions such as surgery for an inflamed appendix are lifesaving. So are short-term antibiotics for some infections such as pneumonitis (pneumonia). But while modern medicine is wonderful in treating acute illnesses, it fails miserably when it comes to chronic disease or prevention. In the majority of cases of chronic illness or inflammation, current medical treatments serve only to suppress symptoms without making any dent in the disease process itself.

For example, if you have osteoarthritis, doctors will prescribe NSAIDs (nonsteroidal anti-inflammatory drugs). Osteoarthritis is a lifelong illness, and most people who suffer from it are on NSAIDs for life. NSAIDs include drugs such as ibuprofen, naproxen, and numerous others. The trouble with all of these drugs is that they induce blood loss from the stomach or other areas of the gastrointestinal tract if taken for any extended period of time. One NSAID, Vioxx, was banned worldwide from the market a few years ago after it was proven to cause heart attacks and death in hundreds of users.

Other drugs prescribed for chronic illnesses such as rheumatoid arthritis or lupus are even worse. Drugs such as Imuran and Remicade suppress the immune system dramatically; drugs that are chemotherapeutic agents (methotrexate) and antimalarial drugs (Plaquinyl) can damage the liver, the bone marrow, and other organs. The horrendous side effects of these drugs are sometimes worse than the disease itself.

The one common denominator of all the current medical and

surgical treatments for chronic inflammatory conditions is that they do not address the underlying cause of the illness. Doctors say that the use of anti-inflammatory drugs addresses the cause but, if that were really true, why does the disease persist?

You do not make hives better by suppressing the immune system with steroids such as prednisone. You do not cure any form of arthritis by prescribing drugs that cause heart attacks, hemorrhage, and peptic ulcers. You do not reverse prostatitis with a year's prescription of broad-spectrum antibiotics that lead to chronic yeast infections. You can mask and suppress symptoms for years with powerful drugs, but you will never reverse the disease process. With symptom suppression, one pays a huge price in terms of side effects and, often, finances.

You cannot prevent inflammation in the body with any drug or surgical procedure. The fact that doctors and surgeons continue trying to do so without attempting a natural approach first is deplorable. Worse is the fact that many still tell their patients that diet has nothing to do with inflammation when there is overwhelming scientific evidence to the contrary.

There is a better way, and that is the subject of this book. As Julie Daniluk correctly points out and describes in great detail, you can prevent, control, reduce, and eliminate inflammation in the body by addressing the root causes of it in the first place. You do not need drugs in order to do this. Whether or not your doctor agrees, you can prevent or treat inflammation successfully through diet and lifestyle changes. This is not just folklore, herbalism, and old wives' tales— every bit of information in this book is backed up by scientific evidence, published studies, and clinical expertise.

What you will learn in this book is what all doctors and patients need to know about inflammation. My more than 33 years' experience as a medical doctor assessing people for deficiencies, toxins, and allergies and prescribing an anti-inflammatory diet and nutritional supplements has convinced me that anyone suffering from an "itis" can reverse the disease process naturally. With the help of this book, the reader will be guided step by step in exactly how to accomplish this.

The diet advice here is practical and easy for anyone to apply. There are numerous recipes and meals that truly do heal inflammation. It is indeed possible to improve health conditions without drugs and surgery. Certainly, in Julie Daniluk's good hands, one can be put well on the way to greater health naturally.

Zoltan P. Rona, M.D., M.Sc.,
author, *Vitamin D: The Sunshine Vitamin*

"He who has health has hope; and he who has hope has everything."

– ARABIAN PROVERB

INTRODUCTION

Let's face it: your pain may be directly affected by the foods you eat on a daily basis. Take white sugar, which I'll compare to a debit card. When you "insert" white sugar into your body, you have to cough up the funds in your account, such as B vitamins and chromium, to complete your transaction (that is, to metabolize it). Over time, your repeated consumption of white sugar depletes your account of nutrients. If you fail to continually replenish your vitamin and mineral reserves, you may end up with an overdrawn account. As a result, you will lack the necessary nutrients for keeping inflammation in check. There are other pro-inflammatory foods as well, and I will point them out to you as we go along.

This book is a catalyst for change. It will provide you with a systematized plan to reduce inflammation, while explaining how food works as a healing tool. The book is laid out in two parts. The first part is an introduction to the science of inflammation. If you don't read the book cover to cover, each chapter can be read as a stand-alone unit. I have repeated key concepts so that you won't miss the highlights. The second part of the book is packed with quick reference guides, delicious recipes, and tips on how to revamp your kitchen and cook with a new healing vision.

Meals That Heal Inflammation (MTHI) is a cutting-edge plan that steers clear of inflammatory choices such as white sugar, harmful fats, and processed foods, replacing them with healthy choices such as natural unrefined sweeteners, healing fats, and anti-inflammatory vegetables. For example, raw honey is a sweet ingredient frequently used in the recipes in this book. According to Dr. Aly M. Ezz El-Arab, honey works as a powerful antibiotic. It destroys the *Helicobacter pylori* (also referred to as *H. pylori*) bacteria that is sometimes the cause of gastric ulcers. When the bacteria are kept in check, inflammation of the stomach is reduced.

MTHI will inspire you to lead a healthier lifestyle. It may not be easy to start, especially since we're conditioned from birth to eat in a certain way. If we retrain our palates and taste buds and return to the diets of our ancestors, great rewards await. Remember, so much of our healing is in the mind. By eating healthy every day, you're giving yourself a beautiful affirmation: *I love myself enough to eat the things I need to heal.*

GETTING REAL: MY PERSONAL STORY

As you read this book you may wonder: How does Julie know what I'm really going through? Well, this may be hard to believe, but I've had a love-hate relationship with food from the get-go.

My struggle began as an infant. My mom had to take a medication that forced her to stop giving me breast milk and to switch to soy formula, which led to disastrous results. I had painful gas and diarrhea and started to get repeated infections soon after she switched to formula. I lived on a steady stream of antibiotics to treat pneumonia, and I had constant sinus and ear infections as a young child.

By grade two, I still couldn't read the alphabet because of a learning disability and attention deficit hyperactivity disorder. (It was simply called hyperactivity back then.) My mom started to believe that food allergies were the root of my problems. After discovering the book *Why Your Child Is Hyperactive* by Ben Feingold, M.D., she stopped giving me the foods, such as those containing sugar and red food dye, that my immune system and brain had become sensitive to. What was the result? I blossomed overnight. I slept eight hours in a row for the first time in my life. I was able to focus in school, and my grades went from D's to A's. The nagging infections in my sinuses, lungs, and ears started to clear up. As long as I stayed on a natural diet, I was a different person. I was happy, calm, and confident—until I discovered my secret passion: cookies and ice cream.

When I was sixteen and began making my own food choices, I started to eat refined foods. I was tired of food restrictions and wanted to rebel and assert my independence. I quickly found my grades slipping due to poor concentration. My skin broke out, and I became anxious and insecure. I started dieting, but then would lapse and start bingeing. My teachers would find me passed out in classes because my blood sugar was up and down like a roller coaster.

The cycles of antibiotics that I had taken for the respiratory infections had given the yeast in my intestines a huge advantage. As a result, I had to endure my first anti-candida diet. Restricting bread, pasta, and sugar from your diet is tough at any age, but as a sixteen-year-old, it felt like it was a life sentence—that is, until the yeast started to clear from my body and I could feel my excitement and energy return.

When I would let go of the five-minute thrill of enjoying a cookie, I had two hours of balanced blood sugar, which enabled me to function incredibly well in school. I wish the story ended there, but I found it very difficult to remain on an anti-candida diet. The moment I started eating like my friends, my symptoms rushed back. From sixteen to twenty-six years old I battled to stay on a healthy diet but often fell off the wagon to binge on refined carbohydrates. My stomach acid had become weak from years of eating inappropriately and, as a result, I started having more bouts of food poisoning (which happens when the environment in your stomach is not acidic enough to kill off the bacteria or mold in food). My gut inflammation progressed. Any simple carbohydrate would send my blood sugar soaring and then crashing. It started to feel like sugar was a drug, both addictive and punishing.

It was only when I met acupuncturist and therapist Kate Kent that I received the emotional and psychological support that put me on the path to healing my gut inflammation. I had two months of tough therapy. Kate taught me how to express my deepest feelings so that I didn't have to suppress them by eating. I began to discover the reasons for my self-abuse with food. I slowly assembled a toolbox of other coping methods that have helped me heal (many of which I will share in the chapter on emotional healing). I am forever grateful to Kate for leading me to the front door of food prison, supporting me as I broke out of jail!

With this newfound freedom and confidence, I left for a trip around the world when I turned thirty. Both the psychological guidance and change of diet helped heal my digestive inflammation, but I still wore the scars from my thirty years of allergies and a high-carbohydrate diet. While traveling, I learned to cook with the food I carried with me in my suitcase and created gourmet meals in the Australian Outback. I was having the time of my life when I arrived on a small island in Thailand. There were no roads large enough for a car, and my grass hut by the ocean seemed like true paradise. Little did I know that this part of the island had electricity for only twelve hours a day, meaning that frozen shellfish would be allowed to repeatedly thaw and freeze. Unfortunately, my vulnerability to food poisoning meant that when I had some of this shellfish, the result was swift and extremely violent.

I soon lost all control of my muscles. I was so ill that I could not walk or even control my bodily functions. I lay in bed with a fever of 108°F and could not even sip water without vomiting. My friend Shaun had to carry me to a four-wheel motorbike and rush me to the nursing station. I kept muttering that I did not want antibiotics because they would make my yeast issue come back. The nurse informed me that I could die if I did not take the strong antibiotics needed to kill the infection in my gut. I will never forget lying in the bed with an IV in my arm, praying that the needle was clean and that the very antibiotics I loathed would save my life.

The infection ravaged the lining of my gut. I was no longer able to digest starches and developed allergies to dozens of different proteins—dairy, wheat, rye, spelt, corn, peanut, and potato, to name a few. My boyfriend Alan, who would later become my husband, was a saint in our early relationship. This infection sent my immune system into red alert, and the result was chronic pain. My muscles became sore, my joints and stomach ached, and my life became miserable. After yet another inflammatory relapse around my thirty-third birthday, I remember Alan gently asking me what it would take for me to turn it all around.

The answer to that question is in this book: years of dedication to making every meal a chance to heal. I spent four years rebuilding my gut bacteria and repairing the lining of my digestive system. It only took that long because I did not have the guidebook to know how to heal. I had to eat to live instead of eating solely for pleasure. I learned to differentiate my food cravings: those for inflammatory foods and those for the soothing and healing foods I sought intuitively. You can crave a healthy food. But you have to strip away your addictions to feel your real intuition as to what your body needs. After a year on the MTHI plan, I honestly craved a bowl of blueberries over a piece of chocolate cake. I trained myself to remember the discomfort after eating the chocolate cake. The pain was not worth it, and I gravitated to the berries that left me feeling balanced and deeply nourished.

Every day that I choose a healthy option is one in which I can feel greater clarity, fluidity, energy, and happiness. Every day that I choose a healthy option is also one in which I can feel the gratitude of wellness.

PART ONE

WHY DO WE HURT?

"Pain adds rest unto pleasure and teaches the luxury of health."

– MARTIN TUPPER, WRITER

CHAPTER 1

THE SIX CAUSES OF INFLAMMATION

Every human will experience the pain of inflammation at some time in his or her life, so this book is for everyone. Inflammation is an immune response to injury, toxins, allergy, or infection, and causes pain, redness, heat, and swelling in the affected area. Since more than 70 percent of our immune system cells are found along the lining of our digestive tract, your immune response is hugely affected by the foods that interact with your gut. This book covers amazing research that describes how certain foods can put out the fire of inflammation, while other foods can promote it.

I don't believe that one diet works for everyone, since there is no single natural food that universally heals or harms; a comparison of the diets of two friends of mine illustrates this point. First, let's look at the diet of triathlete and best-selling author Brendan Brazier. He is a vegan, meaning he thrives on a plant-based diet that includes sprouted grains and beans, nuts, seeds, vegetables, and fruit. Despite going without meat, eggs, or dairy, he is able to run, bike, and swim hundreds of miles.

In sharp contrast, James Munro, who is a personal trainer and is studying osteopathy and nutrition, has a diet that consists mostly of fish, eggs, meat, and low-starch vegetables. James has a condition called ankylosing spondylitis (AS), which causes severe inflammation of the joints. He supports the theory suggesting that the presence of pathogenic bacteria in the gut, called *Klebsiella* spp., triggers AS. Reducing the amount of starch in the diet (which the bacteria require to grow) may benefit AS patients. In James's case, he noticed a huge improvement in his symptoms when he greatly reduced eating all forms of starch—even healthy starchy foods, like beans and whole grains. This makes a vegetarian diet impossible for him to follow. He has severe pain when he eats the very diet that is incredibly healthy and healing for Brendan.

The contrast between Brendan's and James's diets is perfectly encapsulated by Lucretius's (c. 99 B.C.–55 B.C.) belief that one man's food is another man's poison. Only you can figure out which foods heal your body. My goal is to offer you a balanced variety of foods that you can test and document in a systematic way over three months. Only then will you be able to see which foods increase your healing potential and which foods are your inflammation triggers. The longest-living humans on earth—the Sardinian citizens of Italy and the Okinawan islanders of Japan—have one thing in common: they all enjoy proteins, carbohydrates, and fats in a healthy balance and eat a lot of plants. The recipes in the MTHI plan focus on this balance. Vitality is attained when our body can absorb all the nutrients it needs to continuously regenerate itself. By healing the digestive lining with the anti-inflammatory food plan outlined in this book, you will be able to maximize the building blocks you need to prevent or heal many different forms of inflammation throughout the body. Whether you suffer joint pain or heart disease, skin disorders or asthma, your healing starts in the gut.

Throughout the book I will flag certain foods that may be problematic for people who suffer from certain conditions. As you read the chapters and experiment with the recipes, keep in mind your personal needs. To cater to as many preferences as possible, I have provided both a vegan and omnivore menu. I encourage you to explore whatever choices help you reach your potential. Your knowledge of your body is key, and the information in this book will help you understand your body even better.

Do you consistently get a stomachache after eating your favorite ice cream? Has your doctor diagnosed you with "runner's knee" even though you've never run past the corner store? If this sounds like you, you're part of a growing population that struggles with chronic pain long before old age. It's strange that North Americans over the age of thirty have started to accept pain as part of the aging process. With one in five people suffering from arthritis in Canada and the United States, fighting joint pain has become a top health care priority.

Food allergies, which are often a root cause of pain, are also becoming increasingly common across North America because many foods are heavily processed, and we don't have enough variety in our diet. We often choose the same popular menu items like wheat cereal for breakfast, wheat-bread sandwich for lunch, and wheat pasta for dinner. As a result, our immune system overreacts and we suffer the painful symptoms of allergies. Diagnosing a food allergy isn't always easy; symptoms can be diverse. Regardless of the signal our body sends us, inflammation is the ultimate consequence of an allergic reaction.

There are two basic types of pain: acute and chronic. Acute pain comes on quickly (for example, twisting an ankle), and lasts a relatively short period of time. The swelling, redness, heat, and inflamed nerve endings set off an alarm bell, warning the rest of the body that something is wrong. In this instance, inflammation serves a purpose and is a natural and necessary part of the healing process. However, when acute pain is not properly treated, it can develop into chronic pain (which stems from chronic inflammation).

Chronic pain occurs when an initial pain response won't go away, and the body continues to overreact long after the initial cause of pain has passed. Sadly, our views on chronic pain are all wrong. Chronic pain and discomfort should be rare at any age, and in each case it should be promptly addressed. Around the world, people who eat unprocessed nutritious foods all their lives remain limber and agile well into their senior years. Indigenous communities that have not adopted the processed foods prevalent in Western societies remain free from epidemics such as arthritis, cardiovascular disease, and other inflammatory conditions. It's high time we consider reducing inflammation. The ability to heal is within all of us.

In some ways, it's unfortunate that there are powerful analgesics (such as pharmaceutical painkillers) that effectively switch off the pain signal—after all, pain is supposed to warn you that something is wrong. Such medications allow you to continue functioning but prevent you from being able to keep in touch with your body's messages. If you can't feel pain, it will become more difficult to get to the root of your initial discomfort, and you won't know whether your body is healing properly. Have you ever seen the commercial where a woman injures her knee and, instead of resting, she runs up a hill while saying, "I don't let pain slow me down; I take [insert drug name] so I can continue with life"? Think about this for a second: if you ignore an injury and circumvent the pain response, you're working outside your natural limits. As a result, you could be on a path to more serious injury, or your current injury may eventually lead to chronic pain.

Although injuries and sore joints are hard to ignore, less severe symptoms of inflammation generally don't attract your attention in the same way. Symptoms such as indigestion after meals, bleeding gums, or a patch of eczema that won't clear up (despite using lots of anti-inflammatory creams) are easy to ignore for a long time. If left unchecked, these annoying little symptoms can lead to chronic inflammation and lifelong pain. In order to heal your pain, you need to understand how chronic inflammation occurs. The MTHI plan will teach you how to give your body the foods it needs to repair itself.

Inflammation plays a key role in the development of seemingly unrelated illnesses, including heart disease, diabetes, depression, eczema, psoriasis, and dementia. Conversely, as already mentioned, inflammation is also the natural result of the body's response to injury or infection, and it stimulates the healing process. Unfortunately, this protective response of the immune system, if prolonged, can result in damage to the body's organs. The World Health Organization reports that cardiovascular diseases, most of which are rooted in chronic inflammation, are the top causes of deaths internationally, and that "at least 80 percent of premature deaths from cardiovascular heart disease and strokes could be prevented through a healthy diet, regular physical activity and avoiding the use of tobacco."

Chronic inflammation can be extremely serious, but it can also be silent enough to ignore until it's too late. What's the safest way to prevent the process of painful inflammation? The answer is to avoid problem foods and consume specific foods that contain powerful phytonutrients including antioxidants, which can quell the inflammatory fire in the digestive tract, joints, heart, and skin. Phytonutrients are compounds found in plants that aren't classified as either vitamins or minerals and that aren't required for normal functioning of the human body, but that have a beneficial effect on health (the prefix "phyto" is derived from the Greek word for "plant").

GETTING TO THE ROOT OF INFLAMMATION

It is imperative that you figure out the origin of your inflammation. When did you first notice that you had irritation? For many people, it originates in the gut. For instance, I started having inflammation issues after a bout of food poisoning in Asia. It all started with a visit to a remote island that only had electricity for twelve hours a day.

I ate chicken and shellfish Pad Thai with ingredients that had been repeatedly frozen and thawed. The resulting bacterial infection was so severe that it damaged my small intestine, and I couldn't digest grains for over a year.

If you've picked up a parasite, fungus, or bacterial infection, it may have damaged the lining of your digestive tract. If it was left unchecked, it may have started a chain reaction throughout your entire body. Also, if you have IBS (irritable bowel syndrome), it is crucial that you not ignore it, especially since IBS can create serious inflammation.

Let's look at inflammation under a microscope: all inflammation occurs on a cellular level. Inflammation is a protective response that serves to destroy or dilute any injurious agent and is responsible for healing and repairing injured tissues by stimulating cell regeneration. The ensuing pain is an indicator that we should listen to. The initial inflammation is called "acute inflammation" and is supposed to be short-term and provides the environment for the body to heal. The danger comes when we suppress symptoms and push beyond our natural limits. When inflammation becomes chronic, it becomes destructive instead of healing.

Every cell in the human body functions within a narrow range of optimal environmental conditions called homeostasis. When these conditions change due to an external stimulus (such as physical strain or injury), the cell is stressed and may respond with what is called cellular adaptation. This means that the cell will try to adapt to newly imposed requirements in order to function at a high level. A perfect example of cellular adaptation that has a positive outcome is the increase in muscle mass following a significant increase in physical activity.

When the cell cannot adapt to the imposed stimulus, cell injury occurs. If the cell injury is not reversible, cell death may occur. This is why it's so important to stop repetitively stressing the body with harmful foods and to begin an eating program that sustains and builds the body.

THE UNDERLYING CAUSES OF CELL INJURY AND INFLAMMATION

The following table (page 8) is a brief overview of the six main underlying causes of inflammation. I am a nutritionist, so this book focuses on healing with food, but the MTHI program works best in conjunction with other complementary therapies. No matter what, I always recommend that you consult a physician to ensure a proper diagnosis of your personal symptoms—especially for pain management. Also, consider seeking out the services of a trained physiotherapist, osteopath, chiropractor, rehabilitation personal trainer, and/or emotional therapist to get to the root of your pain.

TOXICITY

I list toxicity as the first cause of inflammation because many other causes are connected to it. In fact, the extent to which your genes become damaged and mutated over your lifetime, the number and severity of infections you contract, and the severity of allergies you may suffer from are all affected or triggered by the amount and type of toxins that circulate throughout your system. Long-term exposure to toxins sustains inflammation in your body, and living in a state of chronic inflammation hinders your body's ability to properly rid itself of these toxins, creating a vicious cycle.

In today's environment, you are frequently exposed to thousands of toxic chemicals that your ancestors didn't have to contend with only a couple of hundred years ago. According to the USDA and FDA, in the U.S. alone, more than one million kids ages five and under with normal diets ingest a dangerous amount of organophosphate pesticides. A study by Terry M. Phillips in 2000 showed that the impact of these cancer-causing chemicals can overwhelm a child's

THE SIX MAIN CAUSES OF INFLAMMATION

TOXICITY	Cellular injury is caused by constant exposure to various irritants such as a chemical or physical agent (for example, radiation, cyanide, asbestos, pesticides, alcohol, drugs, and tobacco smoke). Inflammation ensues to heal and protect cells from these toxins.
INFECTION	A pathogenic organism, such as a yeast, fungus, virus, bacterium, or other parasite, attacks the body. The immune system responds with inflammation to fight the infection and heal infected tissues.
ALLERGY	During an allergic reaction, the immune system overreacts to a substance that may be harmless (such as natural food) or potentially harmful (such as synthetic chemicals) and creates an inflammatory response to protect the body. Immune reactions range from mild rashes to anaphylaxis and, if left unchecked, can contribute to autoimmune diseases.
NUTRITIONAL DEFICIENCY OR EXCESS	Nutritional imbalances may lead to hormone disturbances, a strained immune system, and chronic inflammation. A nutritional deficiency of proteins, fats, carbohydrates, vitamins, and minerals deprives the body of the materials required for proper repair. On the other hand, an excess of certain compounds or nutrients can cause an imbalance, which stresses the organs and tissues. Cell injury can be caused by genetic factors, but nutrition and lifestyle choices, as well as other environmental factors, play a key role in determining if and when these factors are expressed.
INJURY	Inflammation is part of the natural process of repairing cell or tissue damage caused by a physical injury.
EMOTIONAL TRAUMA	The body follows the mind: mental distress can affect human physiology. Elevated adrenaline and cortisol that are released during stress can lead to hormonal imbalance and unresolved inflammation.

body to the point where it stresses the immune system. If the child's immune system goes on red alert and becomes hypersensitive, it can start to see otherwise harmless substances, such as food, as an enemy. In this way, a food allergy is born. If a child's immune system is in a reactive state, eating a peanut butter sandwich can cause the immune system to launch an attack; as a result, the bronchial airways may become severely inflamed. This same type of immune system response occurs when a person has arthritis or IBS, except that in these latter conditions the inflammatory response is localized in the arthritic joints or irritable intestine.

As a person ages, the toxic load is usually more than his or her body can handle. Richard Dodd, N.D., explains the connection between toxicity and inflammation by using an analogy: think of yourself as a cup and of your contents as the toxins that you are exposed to or that you naturally generate in your body (as a result of normal daily metabolic processes). Depending on the size of your cup and the efficiency with which you empty it, you will have an individual capacity for tolerating and processing toxins. If your cup is continually filled more than it is emptied, you will overflow, and an imbalance or disease will manifest. Conversely, you will sustain good health if you are able to neutralize or remove toxins as quickly as they flow into your cup. Factors such as diet, lifestyle, exercise, mental and emotional health, genetics, and environmental exposure affect the size of your cup as well as your body's ability to detoxify.

By lowering the amount of toxins you're exposed to from the air you breathe, the water you drink and bathe in, and the food you eat, you are preventing your cup from overflowing. When your cup is kept half full, then you'll have lots of energy to keep your immune system balanced and your inflammation in check. Following the MTHI plan will help you empty your cup as well as increase your cup capacity.

INFECTION

Untreated infections can create conditions for chronic inflammation. Yeast, parasites, viruses, and bacteria inhabit the microscopic eco-system inside and outside your body. Entire populations of microbes use you as a planet on which to create their colonies. Like warring factions on Earth, yeast and bacteria battle for space in your body. Bacteria emit antifungal chemicals, and yeasts counterattack with antibacterial force. These creatures share a fluctuating and opposed relationship throughout your body, and, particularly in your gut, each species vies for control. If you're healthy, neither microorganism gains sole reign, so it's essential for your health that they're maintained in balance. In fact, when Dr. Alexander Fleming studied these microorganism relationships in 1928, he discovered penicillin. In Fleming's study, a spore from some moldy bread flew into a petri dish of bacteria. When he realized the bacteria were dead, he made the connection that something in the mold must have had the ability to kill bacteria; in this way, the modern age of antibiotics was born.

The great contribution of antibiotics to modern medicine is indisputable, but today their overuse has led to some serious concerns. Here are some examples you might be able to relate to:

- Your doctor may have put you on antibiotics to treat a misdiagnosed common cold. (Colds are caused by a virus and cannot be remedied by antibiotics.)

- The meat you consume from a conventional store contains antibiotics, which were used to prevent bacterial infections in the cows and chickens. These animals are more vulnerable to pathogens due to depressed immune systems, overcrowded living conditions, and lack of sunlight.

- You consistently use hand sanitizers and other cleaning agents that contain human-made antibiotic chemicals. Even if you don't use these products, there are tons of antibiotic sprays and gels applied to many surfaces in public places. Whenever possible, it's important to use natural soaps that are free of harmful chemicals.

- You drink municipal unfiltered tap water that is sanitized with chlorine to kill off infectious bacteria and other microorganisms. Unfortunately, this is a double-edged sword, since chlorine can kill our good bacteria just as easily as it kills the harmful bacteria present in the water supply. Whenever possible, you should filter your tap water.

One of the consequences of overusing antibiotics is that strains of resistant bacteria evolve quickly, rendering these drugs (especially those that are human-made) less effective. Moreover, there is a concern that this overprotection against bacteria has now tipped the balance in favor of yeast. Overuse of antibiotics encourages yeast to grow quickly as you're killing off its only natural predator: bacteria. When this imbalance occurs internally, yeast (often a type called *Candida* spp.) sets up camp in your digestive tract and digs holes into your gut lining. This not only weakens your digestive tract and compromises your digestion, but it also increases the ability of undigested food particles to pass across the gut lining into the blood. The result of this contamination is an allergic reaction that can set off an inflammatory pain response throughout the entire body (see page 12 for a more thorough description of what happens during an allergic reaction). This is why some people, no matter how hard they try, cannot reduce inflammation.

If you have a nagging case of athlete's foot or even a bit of gingivitis, you are living with a chronic infection that can have an impact on the degree and duration of inflammation in your body. The most important step to take to improve your quality of life is to improve the integrity and health of all your organs. This will strengthen your immune system, eliminate chronic infection, and subdue inflammation. Pay attention to all the signs your body gives you. Take care of the small pains because most often they are linked to, and are possibly the root of, your major pains.

ALLERGY

Have you ever felt like you gained five pounds in one day? After a night out for pizza with friends, perhaps you woke up to find you couldn't squeeze into your favorite pair of jeans? If so, you may be one of fourteen million North Americans who suffers from food allergies. Luckily, you can't gain five pounds of fat in twenty-four hours. What you were experiencing was extra water weight—that classic bloated feeling you get when you eat something that doesn't agree with your insides.

As you get older, your immune system becomes more sensitive and your digestive juices don't tear apart food as effectively. Poorly digested foods can become allergens. As a result, your body will often retain water in an attempt to flush the allergen out of your system. This usually results in excess inflammation.

An allergy may be defined as an immune reaction where antibodies flag and capture a substance that may be harmless (see page 54). Antibodies may sound like villains from a comic book, but, simply put, they're the security guards your body trains to apprehend anything they see as a potential hazard. Antibodies keep you safe from invaders. Unfortunately, if they're overly stimulated, they also hassle old friends (such as natural whole foods).

A food allergy is a type of hypersensitive immune reaction. It's not unlike an emergency light on the dashboard of your car that suddenly flashes red (even though the engine maintenance is up-to-date!). Food allergies and intolerances tell your body that the fuels you've enjoyed all your life are now dangerous intruders that must be fought off.

Two of the most common food allergens are the proteins found in wheat (gluten) and milk (casein). When these proteins try to pass through the gut, they often hit the security guards of the digestive tract. These guards flag the proteins, set off an alarm, and release histamine, which is a powerful messenger that sends a signal to the rest of the body to indicate a breach in defense. The body goes on red alert, telling you that something is wrong. What is the result? You experience pain caused by an inflammatory immune reaction.

NUTRITIONAL DEFICIENCY OR EXCESS

Many of your health problems may be eliminated not so much by what you add to your diet, but by what you take out. Excessive consumption of some foods can cause inflammation. The best example of this is how the body reacts when you eat a large amount of refined carbohydrates, such as sugar and grain flour. Refined carbohydrates are digested quickly and easily. This floods the blood with a deluge of fuel (in the form of the simple sugar glucose), which it's unable to cope with.

To clear out this large volume of glucose from your blood, your pancreas pumps out insulin. Insulin is the hormone responsible for shuttling sugar from the blood into your cells, where it is then converted into a usable form of energy. If your body is overwhelmed with high levels of sugar in the blood, then insulin cannot shuttle it into cells fast enough. Glucose remains in the blood for extended periods of time and causes damage to blood vessels as well as to other tissues. The body responds with an inflammatory reaction to heal the damaged tissues (see box on page 14.).

This type of blood sugar overload doesn't happen as quickly when you eat foods that take a relatively long time to digest (see the section that discusses the glycemic index of foods starting on page 91 to learn more about the foods that don't cause your blood sugar levels to spike rapidly). Whole foods are loaded with nutrients that support digestive function and pancreatic health. While refined foods may taste good to your tongue and brain, they are low in micronutrients, or lack them altogether. On the other hand, whole foods that contain many of the nutrients your body needs to maintain health or to heal may taste slightly bitter or sharp because they are not refined (sweet fruits are an exception, as they are very high in sugar yet are packed with nutrition). It may take some time to get used to the taste of whole foods, but it's important to remember that this is the way we were meant to eat.

When we return to the diet of our great-great-grandparents—who lived at a time when foods were less refined than they are today—we combat nutritional deficiencies that are the root of many inflammatory conditions. Your palate will develop a taste for what is healthy, and you will lose your cravings for refined and processed products. I used to crave sugar like crazy, but now that I focus on the natural sweetness of fruits and root vegetables such as yams and carrots, I find chocolate cake too much to handle. As you embrace healthy food, you will be able to distinguish the difference between a craving and something your body needs.

THE LINK BETWEEN GLUCOSE, AGE, AND AGING

AGE refers to advanced glycation end products. Glycation happens when sugar molecules floating in the blood attach to the protein molecules on the surface of cells, causing those proteins to lose some of their function. Normally, proteins that are embedded within cell membranes and that protrude to the outer surface of the cell have numerous vital functions, such as hormone reception, communication between cells, and cell identification. However, when a surface protein becomes incapacitated by glycation, it is changed into an AGE. Instead of helping cells communicate, the affected protein becomes a problem. Once an AGE is produced, it can actually speed up a chain reaction that furthers the damage to tissues (for example, by promoting the formation of free radicals, or by affecting how the cell reads its genetic code). AGE-induced tissue damage is especially noticeable in the following areas:

- Arteries: AGE can cause tears in blood vessels that the body then uses cholesterol to repair. The trouble comes when the cholesterol is oxidized or the tissue damage is too great. A plaque is created that can lead to a blood vessel blockage.

- Eyes: Excess blood glucose attaches to proteins in the lens. This causes crystallization of the lens, which may lead to the formation of cataracts.

- Skin and joints: Glucose in the blood attaches to collagen, thus causing the loss of elasticity in these tissues.

One of the secrets to aging gracefully comes down to how quickly the pancreas is able to produce the insulin necessary to shuttle sugar into the cells. It also depends on how sensitive your cells are to insulin (that is, how efficiently insulin can bind to your cells to escort glucose in), and how many minerals you have in storage, such as chromium and vanadium, which enhance insulin function. The longer blood sugar remains elevated, the more tissue damage results.

INJURY

Unless you plan to be a couch potato for the rest of your life, you will experience physical injuries from time to time. The body needs to be challenged to stay strong and balanced. A minor slip off a curb might cause severe pain for someone who doesn't exercise, whereas an athlete will typically spring back from such an accident within minutes. We need to learn how to handle an injury correctly so that it doesn't become chronic pain.

When you hurt yourself, your body raises a red flag, in the form of pain, to tell you the affected area needs immediate attention. This acute pain improves your quality of life by forcing you to check that everything is working properly. Essentially, it is a self-protective mechanism, helping you to look for ways to recover from a temporary injury before it becomes permanent or life threatening. When an injury is ignored and left untreated, it can develop into a chronic pain condition; an example of this is osteoarthritis.

The common healing protocol for acute physical injuries is the RICE routine (rest, ice, compression, elevation). When this doesn't seem to help, conventional medicine offers nonsteroidal anti-inflammatory drugs (NSAIDs), such as ibuprofen, for treatment of pain and inflammation. Unfortunately, this type of relief comes at a cost. NSAIDs can affect your stomach lining and increase your chances of developing a gastric ulcer. Your stomach must be strong enough to handle the stress caused by these drugs. However, anyone's stomach can be weakened or damaged by taking NSAIDs frequently or for extended periods of time.

People tend to take strong anti-inflammatory medications because they interpret inflammatory pain as an enemy. In reality, inflammation occurs when damaged tissue needs repair. Let's consider a twisted ankle: shortly after the injury, the ankle will likely become red, swollen, and slightly warm. The blood vessels in the injured tissue open wider to carry plasma proteins and leukocytes (white blood cells) into the surrounding tissue. This increased flow of fluid causes the swelling associated with inflammation, and the increased blood flow to the area causes reddening and more heat. Once the plasma proteins and leukocytes reach the site of injury, their function is to remove any substances that may hinder healing and to help repair the tissue. If this process is interrupted by drugs that stop the swelling or redness, thereby hindering the flow of these repairing cells to the site of injury, the body's ability to heal may be reduced.

Natural anti-inflammatory remedies like the ones described in MTHI reduce the pain without the side effects because whole foods and medicinal herbs don't contain just one active ingredient—they are loaded with nutrients that work synergistically to support the body's natural healing processes. This is why adopting a whole-food diet is a great long-term healing choice.

EMOTIONAL TRAUMA

Psychological stress can have quite the inflammatory effect. A 2005 report by Theodore F. Robles, Ronald Glaser, and Janice K. Kiecolt-Glaser suggested that stress and depression could enhance the production of pro-inflammatory substances (known as cytokines), which also regulate the body's immune response to infection and injury. This suggests that if you choose to ignore mental stress in your life, you may never be able to physically heal. Other studies have similarly indicated a relationship between psychological or emotional stress and overall health. Medical research exploring these phenomena has spawned a branch of science termed psychoneuroimmunology (PNI). PNI doctors and scientists explore how our thoughts and emotions affect the chemistry of our bodies.

The simple fact is that you must resolve emotional conflict and trauma to fully recover from inflammation. There are many paths to healing emotional health (such as meditation, support groups, and personal therapy, which are discussed in Chapter 2), but the one that I find particularly effective is International Experiential Dynamic Therapy. This method allowed me to fully express my feelings instead of trying to "eat them down" through bingeing or dieting. As therapist Kate Kent explains: "The counselor uses concrete situations to help the client to become more aware of the mechanisms or defenses he or she may use in order to avoid difficult feelings. Once the client has some awareness of this, the focus moves on to learning how to fully experience the whole range of emotions in a functional way without anxiety or guilt. Painful memories that surface are explored and worked through in order to find links to current issues. With this kind of approach, the counselor and client work actively together, each with his or her own set of tasks, to reach the therapeutic goal—namely, for the client to be able to recognize and understand his or her feelings and to have the ability to deal with them in a healthy and appropriate way."

The dynamic therapy approach was the key to a food prison I had locked myself into years ago. Where once I avoided many perfectly healthy foods, believing that they might be detrimental to my health, after a series of therapy sessions, I redeveloped a healthy relationship with food and learned that I could even eat treats without compromising my digestive health.

Now I *choose* to eat healthy without feeling anxious that I *must* eat healthy. This freedom to choose makes all the difference for long-term commitment. While step two of the MTHI plan is about restricting certain foods from your diet, it is important to remember that this is only a trial period for investigating which foods may be allergens for you. The ultimate goal, however, is to find foods that feel good for you and not to eliminate certain foods just because they are viewed by some as unhealthy.

WRAP-UP

- The underlying causes of inflammation are toxicity, infections, allergies, nutritional deficiencies or excess, injuries, and emotional trauma.
- Infections and allergies can be triggered by the amount of toxins you carry. A compromised immune system can lead to chronic infection and affect how your body regulates inflammation.
- Inflammation can result when allergens, such as gluten and casein, stimulate the immune system to release histamine.
- Eating too many simple carbohydrates can spike blood sugar and produce advanced glycation end products (AGE).
- Whole foods contain the right nutrients needed for healing, although they may taste unfamiliar at first.

"If we decide [the universe] is an unfriendly place, then we will build . . . weapons to destroy all that which is unfriendly. But if we decide that the universe is a friendly place, then we will . . . create tools for understanding."

—ALBERT EINSTEIN

CHAPTER 2

EMOTIONAL PAIN: LET'S TALK

This chapter is the most important one in the entire book. Some of you may disagree and might be tempted to skip over this section. After all, it's painful to deal with our feelings, and human beings tend to avoid painful experiences. However, you need to be mentally on board for the MTHI plan to work. If you're not committed emotionally, then you won't be willing to follow through with the necessary changes.

Full healing can take place only when the mental and emotional aspects of illness are addressed. Anger, fear, and anxiety are typically stored and expressed in the gut. This is clearly evident in our language—think about common sayings such as "his guts were churning with anxiety" and "her stomach clenched in fear."

As a nutritionist, I try to look at my own rituals to figure out how to help my clients beat old habits and shape new ones. As a teenager, I would hide cookies in my clothes hamper like a squirrel and eat them when I got upset. One day, at the age of twenty-eight, I realized this habit was self-destructive and I was able to stop hiding food. This was a decision only I could make—all the cajoling and threats from my family or boyfriends couldn't make me stop. Identifying what is destructive about the behavior, and understanding why a person might be forming a negative habit, helps to clarify how it can be stopped. Positive reinforcements are helpful for some people. For others, it doesn't matter if you offer them all the rewards in the world—they need to give up habits on their own terms.

THE SCIENCE BEHIND OUR FEELINGS

Emotional healing is the hardest thing to face because it isn't tangible or quantifiable. However, modern research has proven that stress does play a role in inflammation. According to a study by E. Clays published in the *Journal of Occupational and Environmental Medicine*, people with elevated job stress have increased inflammation. The study analyzed 892 male workers without cardiovascular disease. Those who believed they didn't have control over their work had high levels of a blood protein known as fibrinogen. Fibrinogen is a clotting protein produced by the liver and released into the blood when there is a tissue injury to repair. When blood vessels become damaged from high blood sugar, high cholesterol, alcohol, drugs, pathogenic infection, or food allergens, or when an inflammatory response is triggered by any one of these factors, fibrinogen is sent to the site of injury, where it combines with other proteins to form a blood clot. A wound scar remains as a result. A high level of fibrinogen in the blood is therefore a marker of inflammation, and it has been linked to an increased incidence of heart attacks. Many researchers are suggesting that high levels of inflammation are related to high stress and lead to an increased risk of cardiovascular disease.

Doctors and scientists understand that our minds play a huge role in healing ailments. For instance, in 1979 at the University of Massachusetts Medical Center, Dr. Jon Kabat-Zinn developed the Mindfulness Based Stress Reduction (MBSR) program, which teaches patients how to use meditation to manage pain and stress. Bodywork therapies, such as massage and acupuncture, also appear to help people resolve, or at least cope with, psychological and emotional stress.

Researchers continue to study bodywork therapies to better understand the physiological mechanisms by which stress affects health. Author Allan Walling writes that bodywork therapies do not change the number of stressors a person is subject to, but rather change one's physiological response to them. When a memory or feeling is uncovered and released through bodywork therapies, the catharsis that follows is particularly effective in stimulating healing. Given the emotional component inherent in bodywork, you should choose your practitioner with care—make sure she or he is an individual you feel comfortable with and has legitimate qualifications.

EATING FOR COMFORT VERSUS EATING TO HEAL

You may have to address the fact that you're eating extra food for comfort or out of boredom. Some foods may have seemingly addictive qualities. For example, when you eat tempting foods like chocolate, your body releases trace amounts of mood- and satisfaction-elevating hormones. This may reinforce a preference for foods that are closely associated with specific feelings. The pleasure of eating also briefly allows us to escape feelings of negativity.

According to Carl C. Pfeiffer, M.D., a huge part of mental wellness is balanced brain chemistry, which is related to whole body nutrition. You might be surprised to learn that the idea of eating more foods such as fresh veggies and fruits that grow *on* plants and eating fewer foods that are manufactured *in* plants holds a lot of truth—refined food lacks the hundreds of nutrients your brain needs to function correctly. Some people who suffer from anxiety, attention deficit disorder, and depression excrete high levels of substances once believed to be kryptopyrroles, but which are actually hydroxyhemopyrrolin-2-one (HPL), in their urine. HPL is naturally formed in the body as a by-product of red blood cell formation. It binds to vitamin B_6, zinc, and possibly biotin, increasing the urinary elimination of these nutrients. High levels of HPL in the urine are correlated with various mental and behavioral disorders that can be reversed with high dose, long-term supplementation of vitamin B_6 and zinc.

However, nutritional deficiencies aren't the only factors that can affect your mood and behavior. It's critical for you to also avoid foods that you are allergic to or intolerant of, such as wheat, sugar, or dairy. You have to remember that the brain uses 30 percent of your food energy. Pfeiffer writes, "Since the [brain] is perhaps the most delicate organ of the body, it should be no surprise that allergies to food can upset levels of hormones and other key chemicals in the brain, resulting in [mental and emotional] symptoms." These symptoms include anxiety, confusion, loss of memory, and depression.

You may be thinking that changing your eating habits will be too challenging. However, if you maintain a positive and confident perspective, you will succeed. Look beyond food for comfort and entertainment. Instead of unwrapping a candy bar, watch a movie, listen to music, or plan enjoyable events with family and friends. This behavior change is like getting into any new routine—it might be hard at first, but with time it will take root. Repetition is the key to maintaining any good or bad habit.

YOUR CRAVINGS ARE IN YOUR GENES

Anthropologists suggest that early humans were hunter-gatherers with diets high in protein, fat, and fiber, and for the most part, low in simple carbohydrates. It wasn't until the development of agriculture that the proportion of simple carbohydrates in the human diet began to increase. The modern age led to a particularly steep rise in consumption of refined carbohydrates, especially in Western societies.

Imagine living thousands of years ago: everything you ate would have been either gathered (such as berries and greens) or hunted (such as wild game). It would have been common for you to go days without food. When you had the strength, skill, and luck to kill a buffalo, you and your family would have gorged yourselves because eating such a substantial meal was a relatively unpredictable event. Seasonal fruits (or hives of honey) were rare feasting opportunities that provided the extra energy needed for a hunt. Eating them so infrequently allowed the pancreas to cope with the occasional indulgence in sugar.

It's estimated that *Homo sapiens* evolved about 200,000 years ago. We began to farm staple crops like roots and grains about 10,000 years ago. With the advent of modern industrial technology, we were able to refrigerate, can, or preserve food as never before. The problem with these practices is that our physiology has not evolved fast enough to keep up. Genetically, we remain very similar to our ancestors of 10,000 years ago. Yet, relatively suddenly, we have an endless supply of grains, sugar, corn, and potatoes, all of which overwhelm the pancreas and throw the hormones out of balance. Craving foods that are high in sugar and fat makes perfect biological sense, since up until about a century ago, our bodies still operated in a state of feast or famine. Foods high in sugar and fat guaranteed we would have had enough calories to survive. However, rather than expending thousands of calories hunting and gathering or cultivating our food the way our ancestors did, today we may only expend 75 calories driving to the store to pick up a fatty portion of ground-up cow and some white crusty buns to go along with it.

Cravings Are Not Your Fault

Your body craves sugary or starchy foods when it is lacking certain chemicals necessary for your body and emotions to function properly. When you indulge in carbohydrates, your blood sugar levels are quickly stabilized. Your brain receives a "quick fix" of energy, your taste buds stimulate the production of "feel-good" hormones (for example, serotonin and various endorphins) in your brain, and your entire nervous system feels soothed. Glucose, a type of simple sugar, is such an important fuel for your body that even your intestines can detect sugar the same way the taste buds on your tongue do!

Your mental and physical experiences from eating sweet foods tend to be so rewarding that it's understandable you crave sugar when you're hungry, cold, or stressed. Your appetite and cravings are regulated and influenced by a complex suite of factors. Serotonin is a chemical produced in your brain that helps to regulate appetite and satiation. It also plays a role in emotions. However, serotonin is also produced in your intestines, and as its levels in your blood rise, you feel satisfied and relaxed. Certain foods and pharmaceutical drugs will affect the production of serotonin in your gut, providing one direct link between food and mood.

If you have trouble sleeping at night and find yourself reaching for bread or sweets after 8 P.M., you may actually be looking for a way to soothe your nerves with serotonin. Dr. Judith Wurtman, cell biologist and nutritionist, explains: "In some people, the carbohydrate-serotonin mechanism may go awry and they develop frequent carbohydrate cravings that prompt them to eat when they're not hungry. Those with nighttime carbohydrate cravings may unconsciously be using carbohydrates as a sedative, capitalizing on serotonin's sleep-inducing property."

Cravings are a natural part of living and eating. In my experience, my cravings continued even after I committed to conscious eating. Instead of reaching for the refined foods I used to love, I gradually began to choose foods that were nourishing rather than depleting. The same is possible for you. Understanding how you can control your cravings instead of letting them control you can help you become aware of your actions and their consequences. Giving your body all the nutrients it needs in the right proportions and at the right times throughout the day will help you avoid drops in blood sugar that put you in sugar-craving mode. The recipes in the MTHI plan are powerful tools in gaining control over your cravings.

TRUE HUNGER VERSUS CRAVING

You need to recognize the difference between a true hunger pang and an emotional yearning for food. Emotional eating is an acquired habit. If you're angry, sad, happy, bored, or anxious, then food is not the answer. Food brings you temporary comfort and pleasure because this is how you've trained your brain to feel rewarded and soothed. With many other addictions, recovery programs focus on helping you eliminate the substance or behavior from your life. With food, you have no choice but to keep eating.

If you eat when you're feeling stressed, your body will be in a state of "fight-or-flight." It is not getting ready to digest food; it is getting ready to flee from possible danger or to protect itself from a physical attack. The food you eat will remain in your gut, largely ignored by your body, until the stress has passed. In the meantime, your gut flora starts to feast on whatever you've eaten. If you're like most people who eat for comfort, you likely reach for sweet and fatty refined foods, which is a perfect buffet for the not-so-friendly yeasts (such as candida) and bacteria that reside in your gut. These unfriendly yeasts and bacteria start to multiply as a result, and if you repeat this way of eating and of dealing with your problems, their numbers will increase exponentially, damaging your intestinal tissue in the process.

How do you avoid this vicious cycle? As I mentioned earlier, you must be able to distinguish between true physical hunger and a need for comfort. One way to do this is to keep track of how often you eat. If you ate a full meal a few hours ago and your stomach isn't rumbling, you are probably not hungry. Give the craving a few minutes to pass. This also means you need to know your triggers. You can use the food journal on page 208 to record what you eat; how much you eat; when you eat; how you're feeling before, during, and after you eat; as well as how hungry you are. Over time, you'll learn about your eating patterns, which will help you avoid triggers. If you feel blue and hungry, then munch on a protein-rich, healthy treat, such as a cup of

QUICK TIP

The fastest way to derail this program is to let yourself go hungry for a long period of time. The minute your brain is starving, it will start craving sugar (a quick fix). It tells your body to raise blood sugar levels by eating. When this happens, snack on healthy choices. If you feel the urge to eat between meals, choose fresh fruit, vegetables with bean dip, or a natural nut and seed bar. Also keep in mind that every meal should contain unrefined proteins, fats, and carbohydrates to ensure you maintain a balance in your body chemistry. If you're not getting enough calories to meet your energy needs, you may be more likely to give in to emotional eating. Try to eat at fairly regular times, and never skip breakfast.

edamame (young soybeans) or a trail mix combining one tablespoon each of hemp seeds and hazelnuts, and a few apple-juice-infused dried cranberries to sweeten the mix. Eating healthy treats such as these will help discourage you from making poor food-shopping decisions.

Following the meal and snack suggestions in the MTHI plan will help you learn what you can eat to feel physically and mentally satis-fied in a healthy way. Most of all, don't be shy about what you're doing. Get a friend to try this program with you, or ask your family or roommates to avoid keeping unhealthy foods around in order to support your brave move toward health. When stress nudges you toward the refrigerator, call up someone—anyone—to help you tune in to what you really need.

Once a week, make a cooking date with a friend, relative, or yourself. Whenever I hear people say they have no time to cook, I dig into their schedules and often find that, for instance, they are watching four to eight hours of TV a week. As you prepare soups, stews, and snacks on your cooking date, try listening to a recording of your favorite author reading his or her latest book. You'll be surprised to find just how relaxing this is.

TOOLS FOR EMOTIONAL HEALING

Taking care of your body isn't the only factor in achieving health; finding inner peace is also key. After sweeping your kitchen clean of inflammatory foods, you can use the following tools to help you succeed in the MTHI plan while you learn a thing or two about yourself.

Meditate

Commit to a meditative practice for at least fifteen minutes a day. Many studies have shown that meditation helps people cope with stress and get rid of negative emotions; improves immunity; increases energy levels; and enhances feelings of connection, satisfaction, and wholeness. The Dalai Lama has even encouraged neuroscientists to study how spiritual practices such as meditation affect the brain. In 1991, he asked Professor Richard Davidson of the University of Wisconsin to conduct a study on meditation. Davidson and his research teams have shown that meditation changes brain and body chemistry. According to Davidson, meditators experience reduced anxiety and depression. Their brain activity suggests a calmer state of being, and blood tests indicate increased immune system health.

There are innumerable books, CDs, and DVDs available to show you how to start a meditation practice. Many communities also have meditation centers or groups where you can meditate with other people. You can learn more about meditation from taking yoga or tai chi classe as well. Alternate nostril breathing, a breathing exercise that is often referred to as *pranayama,* is also an effective way of entering a meditative state. This exercise may seem intimidating at first, but is worthwhile. As my yoga instructor Shambunata Saraswati explains, "Through the practice of pranayama, an incision is made into the fabric of my life, and real experience comes rushing in. It is an experience that is so comforting, it slows down my mind so that I can walk between the spaces of my problems and directly interact with my true nature. The power and the joy of life has no choice but to pool in and flood my interactions with myself and the world, marinating me in grace."

Here's how you can practice the pranayama technique:*

1. Sit cross-legged on a cushion. If needed, look for a meditation stool that allows you to fold your feet comfortably without cutting off circulation. If you can't find a stool, you can lean against the wall for support and to help with relaxation. If you are uncomfortable, sit on a chair and rest one arm on the table to support your breathing. Make sure that your sitting bones (the bony protrusions) are at the base of your buttocks. Sit with your spine erect, without pushing your chest forward. Allow your chest to relax as the crown of your head reaches up.

2. Bring your right arm up and rest your index and middle finger on your forehead. Use your right thumb to block your right nostril while inhaling through your left nostril for five seconds. Gently hold your breath for five seconds. If this causes stress, then only hold for as long as you feel comfortable.

3. Then release your right nostril, close your left nostril with your right ring finger, and exhale through your right nostril for ten seconds.

4. Keep your position; inhale through your right nostril for five seconds. Next, close your right nostril with your thumb again, and gently hold your breath for five seconds. Then exhale through your left nostril for ten seconds. Inhale through the left nostril for five seconds.

5. Gently hold your breath for five seconds. Then release your right nostril, close your left nostril with your right ring finger, and exhale through your right nostril for ten seconds.

---

* (Note: Do not practice the retention of your breath if you have high blood pressure or if you're in the last trimester of pregnancy.)

6. Keep your position; inhale through your right nostril for five seconds. Next, close your right nostril with your thumb again, and gently hold your breath for five seconds. Then exhale through your left nostril for ten seconds.

7. You have just completed two rounds. Repeat the rounds for 5-15 minutes a day.

As your relaxation deepens, this exercise will become effortless. Once you grow accustomed to the technique, increase the number of repetitions. It helps you tune in to your true feelings and make peace with many irritants in your life. By performing this exercise, I find that I have more compassion for family and others whom I come in contact with. It helps me cultivate greater compassion, reminding me that others are just caught up in their own issues when they lash out.

Get Moving

Physical exercise bumps up the production of endorphins, your brain's feel-good chemicals. Although this is known as a "runner's high," a rousing game of tennis or a nature hike can also lead to the same feeling. Think of it as meditation in movement—after several laps in the pool, you'll often find that you've forgotten the day's dilemmas and irritations.

A 2005 study conducted by Andrea Dunn, Ph.D., and others showed that exercise helps reduce depression. As Dr. Madhukar Trivedi, one of the study's authors, explains, "The effect you find using aerobic exercise alone in treating clinical depression is similar to what you find with antidepressant medications . . . The key is the intensity of the exercise and continuing it for 30 to 35 minutes per day." You don't need to run a marathon in order to reap the benefits of exercise. Pick a physical activity that you enjoy—even if it's just a daily stroll—and you'll notice a difference. Remember to breathe deeply no matter what form of exercise you choose.

Know What You Want

When you wake up, set your intention for the day by completing the following statement: *My purpose is to* [fill in your goal]. The intentions you set out for yourself will define your life experiences. Your intentions and perspectives will shape how you see the world, other people, and yourself. Some people call this the "law of attraction," which states that a person's thoughts attract whatever the person is thinking of. To exploit this principle, practice these four things: know exactly what you want; ask for it; feel and behave as if the object or experience you desire is on its way; and be open to receiving it, letting go of any attachment to the outcome.

The same principle can apply to your health. While it may be necessary for you to get a proper diagnosis for a serious health concern, it is also equally important not to own and attach your entire identity to the diagnosis. So often many of us conflate who we are with the name of the disease.

Identifying with your illness can get in the way of working through a disease state and regaining health, since the healing process involves leaving this identity behind. The more anchored you are to a condition emotionally and mentally, the more challenging it may be to work toward a healthful state. Focus on healing and appreciate the many ways your body shows evidence of improving health.

Don't Take Yourself Seriously

Do things that bring you joy and laughter. Recently, P.D. Sorlie and other medical researchers at the University of Maryland found that emotional health can be further understood by studying the cells that line the inside (known as the endothelium) of blood vessels. These cells often reveal signs of inflammation in the early stages of heart disease. Healthy endothelial cells secrete chemicals, such as nitric oxide, that promote muscle relaxation and blood vessel dilation (as opposed to contraction). Activities and thoughts that bring you joy increase the amount of nitric oxide these cells produce and release. Hence, happiness and laughter can mimic the physiological effects of pain relief medication.

Humor is different for everyone. Making others happy is also important for one's own health. Try to make at least three people smile each day, and share laughter with your family and friends. It will do wonders and lift your spirits. Japanese researcher T. Hayashi and his team have found that laughter affects gene expression, decreases blood glucose levels, and boosts immunity. Laughing also changes brain chemistry. It stimulates the production of hormones that improve mental alertness. In turn, these hormones cause the release of endorphins in the same way that exercise does.

De-clutter

Feng shui, an ancient Chinese art, teaches us that our living space affects our physical, mental, and emotional well-being. According to this belief, clutter is a symptom and cause of "stuck" energy. When our homes or workplaces become cluttered and disordered, other aspects of our lives tend to feel uncomfortable, too. A chaotic space reflects a distracted mind and makes it difficult to focus on the task at hand. Feng shui experts Russ and Katherine Loader, who run the green design company Power of Place, explain that "over the last 20 years, research [has shown] that our lives have become increasingly stressful and this has now created a shift in our values." As a result, people are realizing that their homes can inspire positive changes. Clear the clutter around your house, in your car, and on your desk, and let new energy flow into your life. (Whenever I'm feeling blocked about something, I organize my closets.) Get rid of anything that is not useful, beautiful, or joyful.

Let Go

Find ways to relieve anger. Anger indicates that an important boundary has been crossed. The trouble is that few of us gracefully express our anger in the moment toward the person who is upsetting us. We've been taught to suppress our feelings, but in the end we take them out on the dog or cat, our loved ones, or ourselves.

Life is too short to waste time resenting anyone. Make peace with your past so that it doesn't spoil the present. For example, if your best friend missed an important celebration, it is easy to be hurt and shut down communication with her. However, if you're able to make peace with her, she might be the first person to support your next endeavor.

Don't Compare Your Life to Others

In Max Ehrmann's famous poem "Desiderata" he writes, "If you compare yourself to others you will become vain and bitter; there will always be greater and lesser persons than yourself." We often project onto others the life we believe they have, not actually knowing what their journey entails. Aside from anger, jealousy is the biggest way we inflict pain on ourselves. I used to waste so much energy thinking that other people had it easier, yet many times we do not know about the challenges others face. The illusion of perfection lasts only if we do not delve deeper. Concentrate instead on your achievements and the gifts you have to give.

No More Drama

Look at every crisis with this thought: In two years, will this matter? My sister Lynn taught me this tough lesson. Her beautiful son Kaydn was diagnosed with kidney failure when he was only eight years old. My mother, Elaine, gave Kaydn one of her kidneys, allowing him to grow, finish high school, and travel. The kidney recently was rejected by Kaydn's body; he now lives on dialysis, and is waiting for another kidney transplant. Lynn has faced life and death with her son so many times that she has no time for trivial dramas. Whenever I think life is annoying because someone was rude at the bank, I remember how little it will matter in the future. We can often stress ourselves in ways that are completely avoidable. We can choose to let go and remember that often we are just reacting automatically. When I remember that I have a choice about how I react, I am able to release a huge amount of tension and be more in the moment.

Don't waste your precious energy on gossip, issues in the past, or things you cannot control. Invest your energy in the positive present moment and on affirmations that make you stronger. I remind myself every day that the universe is a friendly place—even if that driver nearly did hit me with his car! Think of emotional health the same way you think of national defense. If you're at peace, you'll use your resources (whether they're in your body or within your country) to rebuild, repair, and look for alliances. If your mind is at war, then every bit of energy and resource is used to defend precious ground.

Build Your Relationships

It takes a community to strengthen one's health. Your job won't take care of you when you are sick, but your friends and family will. See friends you have lost touch with. Conversations are good for the soul not only because you are expressing your feelings, but also because you are listening and giving support to someone who may need you.

Adopt a philosophy of conducting random acts of kindness. Doing things for others is a great tonic when you're feeling down. Helping others makes you feel included and empowered. Importantly, don't hesitate to ask for help when you need support. We all feel this way from time to time, and it's the most natural feeling in the world. Trust yourself, your body, and your gut instincts. No one knows you better than you know yourself—just don't suffer in silence.

Go to Sleep

Sleep heals the body, clears the mind, and is the universal prerequisite to health and happiness. According to the National Sleep Foundation, it's estimated that North Americans get an average of about 6.7 hours of sleep per weekday. Sleep deprivation is a possible risk factor for heart disease, atherosclerosis, obesity, insulin resistance, diabetes, and immune system suppression. Therefore, establish a healthy bedtime routine that heals your whole body.

Note that sleeping in total darkness allows the maximum amount of healing melatonin to be released. Melatonin is the "sleep hormone." It is produced in the brain when your eyes are exposed to darkness. It signals the body to sleep, giving it the message that it is nighttime. When your eyes are exposed to light, melatonin is broken down and your body is given the message that it must awaken because it is daytime. Even while you're sleeping, light shining on your eyelids can affect the amount of melatonin your body produces and breaks down. Studies have shown that even dim light in the bedroom can decrease the amount of melatonin you make, thereby disrupting sleep patterns or preventing deep sleep. Melatonin also directly helps the body heal. It acts as an antioxidant (see page 101), boosts immune function (it has been used as part of cancer and HIV treatments), is an antidepressant, regulates the rhythms of bodily functions, including the synthesis and release of hormones, and is touted as the body's built-in antiaging hormone. If your bedroom has a window, buy blackout material to make the room completely dark (look for opaque fabric sold for curtains in most fabric stores). Place an object in front of your alarm clock to prevent light shining on your face.

To alleviate sleeping problems, also consider trying essential oils like lavender and chamomile in a hot bath. They both help relax the sympathetic nervous system, which is responsible for the fight-or-flight stress response. The calming smells of these oils also impact mood by directly affecting your brain chemistry.

Another very important habit to change is to stop staying up so late to watch your favorite TV shows! These days, there are many ways to time-shift your viewing, so make the effort to do that and go to sleep when your first wave of fatigue hits.

Write in a Journal

Jot down what you're thankful for. Each night before you go to bed, complete the following statement: *I am grateful for* [insert your items]. According to Robert Emmons, author of *Thanks!: How the New Science of Gratitude Can Make You Happier*, writing in a gratitude journal four times a week for as little as four weeks makes a difference in the level of happiness one feels. Another good exercise is to write a gratitude letter to a person who's had a positive influence on your life. Now is the perfect time to show appreciation—maybe you haven't properly thanked him or her in the past. Arrange to meet so that you can read your letter in person.

WRAP-UP

- We need to learn how to eat when we're hungry versus eating for comfort. Remember that your cravings are not your fault. You were genetically built to crave carbohydrates for survival.
- Part of the process is learning what triggers us to eat, the foods we choose to eat when we are triggered, and how it affects us. Keeping track of this in a food journal is beneficial.
- Emotional healing can strengthen the immune system and support good health.
- There are various tools for emotional healing that will allow us to succeed on the MTHI plan. If we are not on board emotionally, it will be more difficult for us to reap the benefits.
- Get lots of sleep to reduce cravings and promote healing.
- Thinking positively and letting go of the "small stuff" will help us emotionally heal; it will also make clear all we have to be grateful for, while boosting our self-esteem.
- Connect with friends or family members for support during the MTHI plan. Cultivate community in your life and trust that you're not alone in dealing with health imbalances or emotional pain.

*"The art of life is the art of avoiding pain;
and he is the best pilot, who steers clearest of
the rocks and shoals with which it is beset."*

—THOMAS JEFFERSON

CHAPTER 3

THE "OUCH" IN ALLERGY

Have you ever eaten something that makes you feel "off"? This reaction can be anything from mild sinus trouble, to full-blown hives, to a migraine headache. What you are experiencing is the connection between inflammation and allergy.

Many people don't realize that food allergies and inflammation are connected. Food allergens directly trigger an inflammatory response, irritating the intestinal lining and weakening the immune system. If your intestinal lining is inflamed, you cannot readily absorb the healing nutrients your body needs. When you maximize the flow of nutrients into cells and tissues, you enhance the body's healing mechanism.

GETTING GUTSY

Before we begin to look deeper at the relationship between food, allergies, and inflammation, it may help to generally understand the physiology of digestion and the anatomy of the gastrointestinal tract. The gastrointestinal tract includes all the tissues of the inner mouth, esophagus, stomach, small intestine, and large intestine through to the anus. When we eat, food is first chewed up by the grinding action of the teeth, then dissolved in a wet bath of saliva. It travels down the esophagus to the stomach, where acids and enzymes break down most of the food into a soft paste. This paste is then pushed through the small intestine, where it is digested further and most of the food nutrients are absorbed. The remaining material moves into the large intestine for the absorption of water and salts. After the long journey, which can take twenty-four to seventy-two hours (depending on your intestinal health), the resulting waste is excreted.

There are many stages of digestion in a healthy gastrointestinal tract. Your salivary glands secrete enzymes to begin the breakdown of carbohydrates and some fats; your stomach produces hydrochloric acid to break down proteins and fats; your pancreas produces enzymes to digest proteins, carbohydrates, and fats; your liver produces bile to help digest fats; and the lining of your small intestine produces enzymes to help digest carbohydrates. A healthy gastrointestinal tract also has a balanced population of friendly bacteria (probiotics), well-functioning cells along its inner lining, and good muscle tone and movement.

When all organs are in working order, the proteins you eat will be broken into single amino acids (the individual building blocks that link together to form new proteins), carbohydrates will disintegrate into simple sugars, and fats will be dismantled into smaller fatty acids such as monoglycerides. These elementary nutrients can then be absorbed into the bloodstream without eliciting an immune response because the body expects to receive them in this form.

ALLERGEN ATTACK! WHAT HAPPENS IN YOUR GUT WHEN YOU HAVE FOOD ALLERGIES?

If you have food allergies, the immune cells that line your gastrointestinal tract are hypersensitive. You may have low stomach acid, a pancreas that isn't working optimally, and possibly a congested liver and gallbladder. You may also have an imbalance in your gut flora. If this is the case, you will be unable to digest food properly.

What may surprise you is that food allergies are linked to seemingly unrelated conditions such as arthritis, asthma, eczema, or cardiovascular diseases. To understand how, let's consider what happens when an allergen is ingested. Your gut is lined with immune cells. In fact, more than 70 percent of your immune system cells are located in your gastrointestinal lining. The tissue lining the inside of your mouth down to the end of your bowels is composed of cells that help protect the rest of your body from parasites and other pathogens.

When you eat a food you're allergic to, intestinal immune cells perceive this food as a harmful invader. Your body goes into attack mode. Blood flow to the intestines increases so that leukocytes (white blood cells) can fight the allergen. The intestinal tissue becomes locally inflamed with a phalanx of cellular immune system soldiers. Inflammation causes the intestinal tissue and surrounding blood vessels to become more permeable. This increases the number of leukocytes that flood the areas initially exposed to the food allergen.

Each time you eat foods to which you are allergic, your body puts up a fight. Imagine what happens if you unknowingly consume a food allergen every day or even at each meal. Inflammation and increased permeability in the intestines are supposed to be a temporary condition to help your immune system remove the allergen. However, if the inflammation isn't subdued quickly enough or if you consistently eat foods that create this immune reaction, you don't give your intestines a chance to heal. A persistently inflamed intestinal wall suffers local damage and scarring that can lead to a number of detrimental consequences.

For example, intestinal inflammation hinders digestion. Undigested food becomes fuel for intestinal parasites, such as *Candida albicans*, *Escherichia coli* (*E. coli*), *Staphyloccocus aureus*, and other microorganisms that naturally exist in your intestines. This is partly why it is so important to maintain healthy populations of probiotics, including *Lactobacillus acidophilus* and *Bifidobacterium bifidus*, in your intestines. These organisms support digestion and are a part of your immune system defense (see Chapter 7 for more details). As parasites metabolize foods (via fermentation and putrefaction) that your own body should be digesting, waste products accumulate in your intestines. These wastes poison your body and cause the uncomfortable gas and bloating associated with indigestion. They also irritate, inflame, and erode your gut lining.

An inflamed and damaged gut is unable to produce enzymes that digest carbohydrates and fats. This is part of the reason why people with food allergies are particularly sensitive to refined carbohydrates. Inflammation decreases tissue integrity, so the intestines become a less effective barrier between your body and the toxins produced by gut parasites. This is one way a person can develop leaky gut syndrome (also known as malabsorption).

Leaky gut syndrome is a health disorder in which the intestinal lining has become more permeable than normal, and the body's ability to absorb nutrients is impaired (see page 40). This syndrome may also be caused by prescription hormones (for example, birth control pills or hormone replacement therapy), prescription corticosteroids (including hydrocortisone), nonsteroidal anti-inflammatory drugs (NSAIDs), and antibiotics, as well as a high intake of caffeine, alcohol, refined carbohydrates, and chemical-laden processed foods. A leaky gut has abnormally large spaces between cells in the gut wall. These gaps allow absorption of toxins, such as undigested foods, metabolic wastes, and microorganisms (especially yeasts and bacteria), into the bloodstream. Under normal circumstances, these substances would be excluded from the vascular system and eliminated in the stool.

The body works hard to keep the blood as clean as possible, as it is the life-supporting fluid that nourishes each cell and helps divert metabolic wastes from tissues. If the blood becomes encumbered with

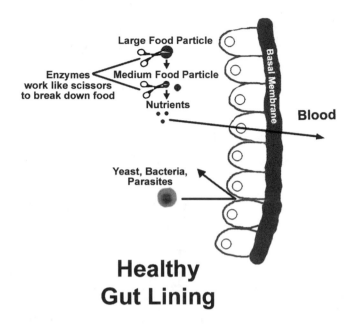

Healthy
Gut Lining

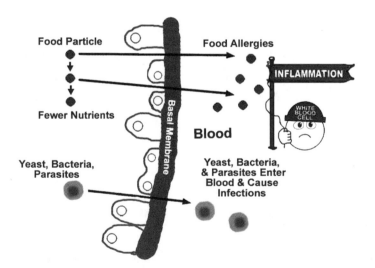

Compromised
Gut Lining

toxins absorbed across a weak intestinal lining, wastes may accumulate and become lodged within the cells of your body. Particularly vulnerable areas, such as the fluid-rich sacs that keep your bones and joints lubricated, become inflamed and painful. Furthermore, undigested food (particularly protein) that floats around in your blood causes an additional immune system response as the body tries to rid the blood of these unrecognized substances.

Recall that there are proteins embedded within the cell membranes of all your tissues (see page 14). Some of these proteins act as name tags for cells, letting the body know what is "self" versus "nonself." This is why a healthy body doesn't attack its own cells. However, when the immune system is continually put on alert by exposure to food allergens, the innate self-regulating and self-recognizing immune mechanisms sometimes go a little awry. The body may begin to confuse the protein name tags of its own cells with the undigested food proteins that are absorbed into the blood from a compromised intestinal lining. In other words, the body may begin to attack its own cells. This can be the starting point of an autoimmune disease.

Rheumatoid arthritis is an example of a disease that can originate from an autoimmune response. In particular, the synovium—the thin layer of tissue that lines the spaces within a joint—can become irritated and thickened. Inflammation of the synovial membrane is called synovitis. It's usually painful (particularly when you're moving) and characterized by swelling due to fluid accumulation in the synovial sac.

Often, people take NSAIDs such as aspirin and ibuprofen to relieve the discomfort. However, an excessive use of NSAIDs may result in a shortage of important enzymes that are involved in digestion. This can trigger a downward spiral of allergies or intolerances, spurring inflammation in areas that are weak or genetically vulnerable to tissue damage such as the joints.

The key to successful treatment is to minimize food allergies. You can enhance your digestion by chewing well, eating whole foods, improving hydration, and lowering stress, all of which will support the production and release of digestive juices. You can heal your gut by controlling harmful microorganisms such as yeasts, supporting immune and glandular functions, and supporting bowel regularity.

FOOD ALLERGIES IN ADULTS VERSUS CHILDREN

If food allergies develop after infancy, the hypersensitivity is most often caused by physical or chemical damage to the intestinal cells. For example, exposure to salmonella bacteria that your body and friendly intestinal bacteria are unable to control or eliminate results in "food poisoning" and some degree of intestinal damage. Food allergies in infants may also be caused by damage to the intestinal cells. For example, if an infant is fed infant formula in place of breast milk, or fed solid foods too early, food allergies may develop because the immune system and intestines aren't fully developed. However, hereditary factors and the fetus's environment during pregnancy may also play a significant role in the development of food allergies in young children.

Whether you acquired your food allergies early or late in life, the impact on your health is ultimately the same. Sadly, if you have had food allergies since childhood, your body will have suffered more damage than a person who developed allergies in adulthood. Triggering an immune response each time you expose your body to a food allergen creates inflammation in your intestines and possibly in your whole body (depending on the severity of your allergy and your frequency of exposure to the offending food). In the latter case, the weakest parts of your body generally suffer the most. Recurrent damage (inflammation) in a particular tissue or organ in the body may lead to a chronic imbalance in that tissue or organ. Therefore, the path to healing conditions such as heart disease, arthritis, skin disorders, and asthma often begins with repairing the gut.

FIX THE PLUMBING: OTHER CONSEQUENCES OF FOOD ALLERGIES

Another common symptom of food allergies is diarrhea or constipation. A healthy gut will digest food thoroughly, absorb nutrients efficiently, and eliminate wastes effortlessly every day. However, many North Americans may have only one bowel movement a day. Ideally, if you eat 35 grams of fiber and drink eight glasses of water each day, your bowels should move after every main meal. When you eat, the food should move smoothly through your digestive tract, functioning not unlike an internal conveyer belt. In essence, your digestive tract is one long hollow tube that stretches from top to bottom, processing food and drink without your conscious control. On average, it takes a healthy intestinal tract about twenty-four hours to move a meal from entry to exit. This means your body should easily move out a meal that was eaten the same time as the day before. Sadly, most of us drink so little water that our kidneys and bowels cannot flush out toxic material, such as the normal waste products of digestion, let alone food allergens and undigested substances. If the body cannot eliminate properly, it has to store toxic material within tissues, thereby creating additional waste storage sites.

Another serious problem caused by allergies is a lowered metabolism. Elson Haas, M.D., coauthor of *The False Fat Diet,* writes, "Allergies can increase production of hormones like insulin that cause weight gain and hypoglycemia. This will result in a reduction of energy and metabolic rate." This means that if you have an allergic reaction, your body invests massive amounts of energy and nutrients to fight off substances that may be harmless. Over time, your immune system shifts out of balance; you become malnourished due to the loss of valuable nutrients; and you increase your chances of becoming ill due to infectious organisms, such as viruses, yeasts, bacteria, or other parasites. Your metabolic rate will decrease due to your malnourished state and you will suffer from fatigue. If you're chronically tired, you're

THE FIVE CAUSES OF ALLERGIES

CAUSE	WHAT HAPPENS
FEEDING BABIES SOLID FOODS TOO EARLY	Several studies suggest that bottle-feeding formula to babies instead of breast-feeding may lead to allergies, possibly resulting in health problems. Cow's milk and baby formula contain large molecules that are difficult for an infant's gastrointestinal tract and immune system to properly digest and absorb. A gluten allergy can arise from the early feeding of grains, such as wheat, barley, and oats. The best ways to prevent allergies is to breast-feed exclusively for six months before introducing solid foods and to avoid feeding your infant gluten grains until she or he is at least one year old.
POOR DIGESTION	Poor digestion causes many food reactions. The problem starts with improper chewing and weak digestive organs. Incomplete digestion, together with a leaky gut, allows larger molecules of food to be absorbed into the bloodstream, where they cause an immune reaction. Low-level infections by pathogenic intestinal microorganisms, such as worms, yeasts, and certain bacteria, may also create allergic tendencies because of the damage they cause to the intestinal tissue.
ENVIRONMENTAL TOXINS AND CHEMICALS	External toxins have been shown to increase allergic reactions. While complete avoidance of these toxins is nearly impossible, measures should be taken to lighten the load by minimizing the consumption of refined and processed foods; choosing organic foods whenever possible (see page 156 for information on which foods are especially loaded with pesticides); and using chemical-free cleaners, detergents, and cosmetics.
STRESS	Stress disrupts immune functions and weakens the adrenal glands. Chronic stress also tends to hinder the function of digestive organs, thereby reducing your ability to break down food properly. Stress causes the intestinal lining to become more permeable, and therefore causes undigested proteins to enter the bloodstream.
GENETIC PREDISPOSITION	Genetics determine to some extent whether you suffer from hay fever, asthma, and eczema. If one parent has an allergy, the chance of the child having an allergy is 50 to 58 percent. If both parents have allergies, this figure rises to approximately 67 to 100 percent. However, diet and lifestyle modifications can help prevent the development of allergies despite a potential genetic predisposition.

less likely to be physically active. Your body becomes sluggish due to inactivity as well as malnourishment. The cycle is dangerous and destructive.

DO YOU SUFFER FROM FOOD ALLERGIES?

A food allergy is a hypersensitive reaction that occurs when the immune system overreacts to a substance that most other people find harmless (most often it's a protein, but even carbohydrates and lipids can effect an allergic response). It's like the emergency light on your car's dashboard that suddenly flashes red, even though the engine's maintenance is up-to-date. Food allergies and intolerances warn you that inflammatory foods aren't compatible with your body.

FOOD ALLERGY SYMPTOMS

Some food allergies affect only the gastrointestinal tract. They are often infant or early childhood conditions, and are persistent. For example, celiac disease is caused by an allergic reaction to gluten, a protein in wheat, barley, and other related cereal grains. Unlike some childhood food allergies, celiac disease stays with you throughout your lifetime, but it may not be diagnosed until later in life. The most common age of diagnosis is forty, and most patients have had at least ten years of symptoms before being diagnosed with the disease.

The following chart (page 46), prepared with information compiled from books written by Carolee Bateson-Koch, D.C., N.D., and Carl C. Pfeiffer, Ph.D., M.D., lists the most common (but not necessarily the most obvious) symptoms of food allergies. Everyone is unique, so each person's allergic reaction to food may be different. For example, my nephew had an allergy to potatoes when he was a baby; every time he ate them, he would have a tantrum. My mother is also sensitive to potatoes, but her reaction occurs in the joint tissue, causing swelling and pain in her fingers.

SOME OF THE SYMPTOMS OF COMMON FOOD ALLERGIES		
FOOD	PHYSICAL SYMPTOMS	MENTAL AND EMOTIONAL SYMPTOMS
FOOD COLORINGS	Eczema	Hyperactivity
MSG	Hives and skin rashes	Temper tantrums
PORK	Itchy eyes and nose	Aggression
SULFITES	Asthma	Inability to concentrate
PEANUTS	Chronic bronchitis and wheezing	Irritability
DAIRY	Chronic ear, sinus, and chest infections	Depression
COFFEE	Headaches	Food cravings (for allergy-inducing foods)
SOY	Gas and bloating	Personality change
GLUTEN GRAINS	Constipation and diarrhea	Excessive fatigue
WHEAT	Arthritis	Nonstop talking

If you suspect you are sensitive to certain foods, take this quiz to find out if you eat foods that have a high allergen potential. Using the grading system below, answer **A**, **B**, or **C** to the following statements:

A — I've never consumed this or I've never followed this pattern. **B — I've had or done this in the past, but not now.** **C — This is part of my diet all the time.**			
A	B	C	I eat prepackaged meals (take-out food, frozen meals, or boxed or canned goods) three or more times a week.
A	B	C	I eat dairy every day.
A	B	C	I eat wheat every day.
A	B	C	I drink coffee, black tea, or soda pop every day.
A	B	C	I eat fried food, such as chips, doughnuts, fries, fried fish, or spring rolls, more than once a week.
A	B	C	I crave or eat refined carbohydrates, such as cookies, cakes, candy, or bread, one or more times a day.
A	B	C	I use commercial salad dressing, cooking oils (vegetable, soy, canola, or peanut oil), margarine, or mayonnaise on a daily basis.

Now let's look at your symptoms.

A — I've never experienced this problem. **B — I've experienced this in the past, but not at the moment.** **C — I experience this now.**					
A	B	C	Bloated stomach	Yeast infections or athlete's foot	Embarrassing flatulence
A	B	C	Stomach pain	Nausea	Diarrhea
A	B	C	Constipation	Chronic tiredness	Persistent cough
A	B	C	Brain fog	Cravings	Moodiness
A	B	C	Severe headache	Mouth ulcer (canker sore)	Fluid retention
A	B	C	Asthma	Patchy-colored tongue	Hyperactivity
A	B	C	Sinus pain	Hives, flaking skin, or rash	Chronic postnasal drip

RESULTS

IF YOU ANSWERED MOSTLY:

A You're conscious about what you eat, and you're trying to avoid inflammatory foods. Keep making balanced and colorful food choices. If you're experiencing pain and you've never eaten allergy-causing or refined foods, investigate the problem with a health practitioner. For example, if your pain is from an accident, be sure to have it rehabilitated. If you suffer from chronic infections, focus on a low-sugar and low-starch diet to rebalance the immune system. Some people experience subtle allergies to unusual foods, so use the food journal on page 208 to identify items that could be reducing energy or weakening the immune system.

B Your old food habits may have caused inflammation. It is an emotional challenge to give up comfort foods such as pasta, cookies, and ice cream, but the rewards of a pain-free body are greater. Increase your intake of anti-inflammatory vegetables such as broccoli, Swiss chard, and celery to at least seven servings a day. Avoid spiking your blood sugar with refined starches and sugars. Also consider a deep detoxification cleanse, which will help remove toxins from your liver, kidneys, and bowel.

C Your inflammation is likely raging, even if you don't feel it yet. Some forms of inflammation, such as those of the arteries, are painless and yet damaging. Eating fried or damaged oils (see page 86) and potential allergy-triggering foods sets the right environment for degenerative illnesses such as heart disease, arthritis, and inflammatory bowel disease. This is why it's so important to cut back on refined flour, sugar, and fried foods while figuring out which foods could be sparking allergic reactions. Experiment with wholesome gluten-free grains, unrefined healing oils such as unrefined flax and chia seed oils, and the natural sweetness of whole fresh fruits.

HANDLING HIVES

Hives (also known by the medical term *urticaria*) are red, swollen, itchy bumps that form on the skin and are a symptom of inflammation. It's possible for hives to become a consistent problem once they appear unless you reduce the factors that cause them. Stress, skin irritants, food additives and preservatives, pesticides, chemicals in detergents and cleaning products, personal-care products, alcohol, nicotine, drugs, strenuous exercise, hot water, chlorinated pools, and most important, food allergens can cause hives to flare. Use the food journal on page 208 to determine whether food allergies are playing a role and try to remove as many of these harmful factors from your life as possible.

Certain foods can cause hives, yet they don't trigger a classic allergic reaction involving the immune system. In a classic allergic reaction, a substance such as a protein triggers immune system cells that can eventually stimulate the release of histamine from mast cells. Histamine causes much of the common symptoms of allergy such as congestion, fatigue, and swelling.

However, some foods contain compounds called biogenic amines, which include histamine, that can create all the symptoms of an allergic reaction without involving immune system cells such as macrophages and mast cells. A sensitive person who consumes biogenic amine-containing foods can experience symptoms like hives, a runny nose, and dilation of blood vessels.

The foods I've listed on page 50 contain amines that can trigger allergy-like symptoms, such as food-induced hives. Try to avoid eating more than one of these foods at any given meal and limit the amount you consume if you are prone to developing hives.

AMINES THAT ARE POTENTIAL HIVE TRIGGERS

- Beta-phenylethylamine: Chocolate, colas, and fermented foods

- Histamine: Berries, eggplant, fermented foods (including alcohol and especially wine, cheeses, fermented soy products, sauerkraut, vinegar, and yeast extract), improperly refrigerated fish, spinach, and sweet melons (cantaloupe, honeydew, watermelon)

- Octopamine: Fresh fruits (citrus has the highest amount)

- Tyramine: Baked foods such as bread and cake, chicken liver, dairy, eggs, fermented/pickled/marinated foods (alcohol, pickled vegetables and fish, sauerkraut, vinegar, and yeast extract), nuts, peanut butter, pork, and prepared or cured meats; smaller amounts are present in avocado, banana, eggplant, fig, red plum, and tomato

- Hydroxytryptamine: Avocado and banana

Other potential hive triggers that aren't amine related include spicy foods such as chili, cayenne pepper, and black pepper; aspirin and codeine; MSG (soup-stock cubes and bouillon cubes; condiments such as barbecue sauce and salad dressing; canned, frozen, or dried prepared food; snack foods such as flavored jerky and potato and tortilla chips); nitrates found in hotdogs, bacon, deli meats, sausages, processed meats, and soy-meat alternatives; sulfite-treated dried fruit, salad bar foods, balsamic vinegar, and wine; xanthines and related compounds such as caffeine (coffee and colas) and theobromine (tea and cocoa); and food coloring, especially tartrazine (FD&C yellow number 5) and allura red AC (FD&C red number 40). Avoid all alcoholic beverages if possible.

WHAT IS HISTAMINE?

Histamine plays an important role as a neurotransmitter, which is a type of naturally produced chemical involved in the communication

QUICK TIP

Physical stress from working too hard, lack of sleep, and emotional stress can also trigger hives. I recommend you counteract stress with the techniques found in Chapter 2 on page 27. Also, use perfume-free, 100 percent natural soap or detergent for your hands, body, and clothes to avoid skin irritants.

between cells. Neurotransmitters can be synthesized and released from a variety of cells, but they are most commonly produced by nerve cells, including those of the brain. Some neurotransmitters are produced only by specific cells and act upon a specialized region in the body, whereas other neurotransmitters are produced by various cells in different areas of the body. Histamine is one such neurotransmitter; it is manufactured and is active in the brain as well as in other tissues throughout the body. Even during orgasm, histamine is released—connections have been made between histamine and the "sex flush" that appears on women.

Most people think of histamine as "the allergy chemical." This is because specialized white blood cells, named mast cells, release histamine during an allergic reaction. Histamine is also released during an immune system "attack" on legitimately foreign and harmful pathogens, such as viruses, parasites, and bacteria. However, when the immune system overreacts to harmless elements in our environment, such as certain foods or plant pollen, then production and release of histamine can become a problem.

When histamine is released by mast cells, it elicits an inflammatory response. It increases the permeability of blood vessels to allow white blood cells and other immune substances to flood body tissues that are exposed to the allergen or pathogen. Even though this is an effective and essential part of histamine's role in protecting the body from harm, excessive and chronic release of histamine can cause the following problems:

- Swelling of skin, tongue, and throat

- Asthma

- Rhinitis (inflammation of inner nose tissues; causes runny nose)

- Excess stomach acid production (histamine also acts as a gastric hormone to stimulate the flow of hydrochloric acid)

- Allergic skin disorders

- Inflammation

- Tissue damage

- Excess saliva, tears, and nasal and bronchial secretions

- Vascular headaches

- Premature ejaculation

When a food allergen is ingested and histamine is released in the gastro-intestinal tract, the resulting inflammation and vascular permeability further increases the absorption of undigested proteins and toxins from the intestines. Continued intake of food allergens prevents the proper healing of intestinal tissues. In severe cases shock and anaphylaxis can occur. Anaphylaxis is a sudden, severe, and life-threatening allergic reaction involving the entire body, not just the localized region of the body that was directly exposed to the allergen.

Histamine also opposes the effects of adrenaline and can there-fore cause fatigue, which is why drowsiness and chronic fatigue are common symptoms of a food allergy. It's important to learn how to naturally lower and balance histamine production, stabilize mast cells, and minimize histamine-induced inflammation. Pharmaceutical anti-histamines have side effects with negative long-term consequences. There are two main types of pharmaceutical antihistamines: the older (sedating) varieties such as chlorphenamine (found in Naphcon,

Polaramine, Dimetapp, Drixoral, and Actifed) are more likely to make you feel sleepy, whereas the newer (non-sedating) varieties such as loratadine (the active ingredient in Claritin) rarely cause drowsiness. However, many prescription and over-the-counter antihistamines can also affect other tissues of the body that naturally produce or respond to histamine, including the gastrointestinal tract, spleen, thymus, smooth muscle, and nervous system.

Common side effects of antihistamine drugs include:

- Headaches

- Dizziness

- Dry mouth

- Constipation or diarrhea

- Topical irritation (from creams, lotions, and eye drops)

- High blood pressure

- Allergic reactions (such as swelling, rash, and breathing difficulties)

- Confusion

- Depression

- Disturbed sleep

- Blood and liver disorders

- Palpitations and abnormal heart rhythms (arrhythmia)

- Blurred vision

- Nausea or vomiting

- Difficulty in passing urine

These side effects are reason enough to reduce our allergy load so that we can avoid relying on antihistamines. Fortunately, many foods act as natural antihistamines without causing undesirable side effects. For example, the phytonutrient quercetin, which is a natural antihistamine and powerful antioxidant, is found in capers, apples, grapefruit and some other citrus fruits, cherries, raspberries, cranberries, red grapes, yellow and red onions, leafy vegetables, green tea, evening primrose, squash, blue-green algae, shallots, zucchini, tomato, and broccoli. Organically grown plants generally contain more quercetin (as well as other inflammation-fighting phytonutrients, minerals, and vitamins) than conventionally grown fruits and vegetables.

Many of the foods listed above also contain rich amounts of vitamin C, a powerful antioxidant and immune booster. In addition, some studies have shown that high doses of vitamin C can help reduce sensitivity to allergens and reduce inflammation, mucus production, and wheezing. Researchers at Arizona State University indicated that taking 2,000 mg of vitamin C per day reduces histamine levels in the blood by up to 40 percent. In order to act as a natural antihistamine, the recommended dose is usually greater than 1,000 mg per day. However, eating fresh whole foods rich in vitamin C provides you with all the other powerful phytonutrients not available in a supplement; these phytonutrients work synergistically to reduce inflammation, support immunity, and nourish tissues.

HOW THE IMMUNE SYSTEM RESPONDS TO ALLERGIES

Antibodies work by binding to an antigen, which is a substance (or part of a substance) that you've touched, ingested, injected, or inhaled. When you eat something you're allergic to, it acts as an antigen to which an antibody binds. The antibody and the antigen, now a single unit referred to as an immune complex (abbreviated IC), then bind to the immune mast cells and basophils. These are the cells responsible for releasing histamine.

There are five major families of antibodies: IgA, IgD, IgE, IgG, and IgM. (Antibodies are also called immunoglobulins, which is why they are abbreviated "Ig.") Blood tests are available to check which foods cause these antibodies to become active in your body.

- **IgA:** Found in the nose, breathing passages, ears, eyes, and digestive tract, IgA antibodies protect body surfaces that are exposed to external foreign substances. Unlike the immediate effects of IgE-mediated allergies, IgA-mediated reactions can take several days to appear.

- **IgD:** Small amounts are located in the tissues that line the belly or chest. How they work is still unclear.

- **IgE:** Found in the lungs, skin, and mucous membranes, these antibodies cause the body to react against foreign substances such as pollen, fungal spores, and animal dander. They may be active in allergic reactions to milk and some medicines and poisons.

- **IgG:** Located within all bodily fluids and small in size, they constitute up to 75 to 80 percent of all the antibodies in the body. IgG antibodies fight bacterial and viral infections. They're also associated with delayed food reactions, which can worsen or contribute to different health problems.

- **IgM:** This is the largest family of antibodies. IgM is found in blood and lymph fluids and is the first type of antibody that responds to an infection. IgM antibodies comprise 5 to 10 percent of all the antibodies in the body. The symptoms resulting from their response to an allergen can take several days to appear.

Below, I've highlighted three main types of reactions from food allergies. You will notice that you can experience allergic reactions without experiencing obvious or immediate symptoms such as stomach cramps, cough, or a swollen tongue.

Type I—Profound Allergies: Immediate Hypersensitivity Reactions

I have called this section "profound allergies" because the body reacts immediately or within two hours of ingesting an allergy–causing food. These reactions account for only 10 to 15 percent of food allergies, yet they are the ones most frequently tested for. They involve IgE and cause histamine release. Common symptoms include asthma (swelling and inflammation in the bronchioles), "brain fog," dermatitis, hay fever, and muscle fatigue. The food trigger also causes intestinal inflammation and malabsorption. This compromises the body's ability

QUICK TIP

Digestive enzymes improve digestion and nutrient absorption. Plant enzyme supplements help break down food in the digestive tract as well as any undigested food that may have been absorbed into the blood (due to a leaky gut). This immediately reduces the burden on the immune system—proteins or complex carbohydrates that were previously seen as foreign invaders are broken down into recognizable, immune-friendly single amino acids or simple carbohydrates. With the MTHI plan, I suggest taking two capsules of a broad-spectrum plant enzyme supplement with each meal for best results. However, if you're treating yourself to a serving of food that may cause a reaction, consider speaking to your health care practitioner about taking a higher dose. Keep in mind that supplements such as digestive enzymes are meant to be taken for short periods of time to support your body while it's healing. It's important to eat healing foods and herbs, such as those recommended in the MTHI plan, so that your digestive system regains the strength to naturally produce its own enzymes.

to digest and absorb nutrients properly. Your allergies will get worse if you're not able to absorb nutrients, which are necessary to balance the immune system.

Type II—Subtle Destruction: Cytotoxic Reactions

Subtle destruction is characterized by delayed cell damage without acute symptoms. These symptoms are classified as cytotoxic reactions ("cyto" meaning cell and "toxic" meaning harmful). It has been estimated that 75 percent of all food allergy reactions are accompanied by cell destruction. This type of reaction involves IgG and IgM antibodies, and it can take place anywhere in the body.

In the case of food allergies, the intestinal lining is often damaged. The lining of the intestine is the site where the food antigen and the immune system meet. When the intestinal lining is destroyed, one of the body's main protective barriers is broken down. If nutrients aren't properly absorbed, leaky gut can result.

Type III—Tissue Damage: Immune-Complex-Mediated Reactions

This type of allergic reaction is referred to as "tissue damage" because it involves immune complexes (ICs). ICs are formed when antigens bind to antibodies to which they have been previously exposed. They're involved in 80 percent of food reactions. ICs circulate in the blood and need to be cleaned out by white blood cells, a process that burdens the immune system and reduces your immune resistance. When ICs aren't cleaned out by white blood cells, they're deposited into tissues, where they cause damage. (In fact, conditions such as arthritis may develop from IC deposition in joints.) This tissue damage is why it's so critical to steer clear of foods that cause allergic reactions.

The connection between type I and type III allergic reactions is that they both result in tissue damage caused by increased levels of histamine. In type I reactions, you get immediate feedback, so you know you must avoid that food. However, type III food reactions are delayed and mediated by the IgG antibodies—they may not show up until two to seventy-two hours after having ingested the food. For example, when I eat chocolate, I get a little hyper and giddy. For years I enjoyed this treat without any concerns. However, it turned out that I had an IgG type III reaction to chocolate, and it was a major cause of acne breakouts on my chin. Because the breakouts happened two to three days after I ate chocolate, it took years for me to make the connection.

You can see why allergies are hard to diagnose. A peanut allergy may cause drowsiness in one child, while in another child it could close up his or her airways. We need to be open to the possibility that an unexplained symptom could be an allergy. In my years of practice, I've seen hundreds of clients reduce their pain by getting to the root of their individual allergies and by healing their gut.

Twelve million North Americans may be affected by allergies—and these numbers are increasing, especially among children. For many, the pain is silent until it becomes severe. You might be willing to put up with a stuffy nose or itchy skin in order to enjoy your favorite food, but on a cellular level, the allergen-induced inflammation is doing a lot of damage to your body.

ALLERGY VERSUS INTOLERANCE

Up to now, I have been talking exclusively about food allergies. Technically speaking, the diagnosis of an allergy must involve an antibody response. Before 1926, the medical community believed that only proteins could set off the inflammation alarm. However, many modern medical doctors are realizing that this definition may be limited. The alternative medical community has adopted a broader understanding that a starch, lipid, preservative, or additive can trigger an allergic reaction. This means that any type of food or chemical can provoke a response that looks and feels like an allergy—even if you haven't developed antibodies to it. Reactions that don't involve the mobilization of antibodies are called food intolerances or sensitivities.

Food intolerances are non–immune system responses that may be triggered by many factors. The most common reason for intolerance is an enzyme deficiency in the gut. For instance, certain people are lactose intolerant: their bodies no longer produce lactase, the enzyme that digests this type of milk sugar. If a lactose-intolerant person has too much milk or milk product, he or she may experience gas, bloating, and abdominal pain. Lactase is also made in our bodies by the friendly bacteria that live in the gut. In some cases, replacing the friendly bacteria can reverse this imbalance. Lactose intolerance can be caused by overexposure to antibiotics, so a high-dose probiotic supplement that contains billions of lactose-feeding bacteria (such as acidophilus) can help to turn the intolerance around.

A good example of sensitivity to a nonfood substance is the reaction many children have to artificial colors. Artificial colors are made out of petroleum, acetone, or coal tars, and are very hard on the brain and immune system. Children are the most vulnerable to artificial colors because their bodies are still developing. Symptoms of this sensitivity include hyperactivity, impaired learning, irritability, low motivation, and frustration. Unfortunately, conventional snacks and desserts are full of additives, which is a good reason to stay away from them as much as possible. You can avoid foods with artificial colors by reading food labels. Some bright colors are natural (such as deep purple from beets or vibrant orange from carrots), but if a snack is electric blue or fire-engine red, then artificial colors have been used.

IS AN ALLERGY-FREE DIET POSSIBLE?

An allergy-free diet is absolutely possible, but only on an individual basis. The problem with most diet plans is the assumption that one size fits all or, at best, that three or four diets fit all. In reality, there are as many "ideal" diets as there are fingerprints. It is impossible to create

TOP FOOD ADDITIVES TO AVOID

- Butylated hydroxyanisole (BHA) and butylated hydroxytoluene (BHT)

- Artificial sweeteners like saccharin, acesulfame-K, and aspartame

- Sulfites (sulfur dioxide, sodium sulfite, sodium and potassium bisulfate, sodium and potassium metabisulfite) and potassium bromate

- Artificial colors: FD&C blue #1 and #2, green #3, red #3 (erythrosine), red #40, yellow #5 (tartrazine), yellow #6

- Sodium nitrate

- Monosodium glutamate (MSG)

- Propylene glycol

- Parabens

a cookbook that eliminates all potential food allergies because the body can be allergic to anything. A number of people can't even tolerate some of the healthiest and supposedly most hypoallergenic foods such as hemp or amaranth. In this way, there are seven billion diets for seven billion people.

The first step in the MTHI plan is to eliminate the most common irritating foods and additives—all sugar, artificial sweeteners, artificial flavors, food preservatives and colors, MSG, alcohol, wheat and other gluten-containing grains, peanuts, nonfermented soy, corn, dairy, coffee, and nightshade vegetables—for a minimum of eight weeks (see page 149 for more details). You need to remove all of these foods from your diet to give your digestive system a true chance to recover and repair. Nightshade vegetables (eggplant, hot and sweet peppers, tomato, and white potato) can be inflammatory because they contain alkaloids that can affect nerve-muscle function, digestion, and joint flexibility in animals and humans. These alkaloids are especially high in the nightshade leaves, unripe fruit such as green tomatoes, and older potatoes. Tobacco is also a nightshade plant, so smokers may be more susceptible to a sensitivity.

Remember that this isn't a lifetime ban. In many cases, foods you aren't allergic to can be slowly reintroduced once the digestive system has healed and you've identified the foods that cause inflammation in your body. The second step in the plan incorporates healing foods such as flax seeds, chia seeds, burdock root, pineapple, pumpkin seeds, and kale into the diet. These foods can detoxify the body and help the immune system recover.

The beginning of the MTHI plan excludes dairy because you may not know whether or not you have an allergy to it. After step three is complete, you can test your tolerance for lactose-reduced fermented dairy items such as live organic yogurt or kefir (it's best to start off with goat or sheep dairy, which are generally easier to digest than cow dairy). If you find you can't tolerate these foods, you should use a probiotic supplement and try a second test a month or two later after your digestive tract has had a chance to rebuild its enzyme stores. Both allergies and intolerances can provoke symptoms anywhere in the body for up to five days after exposure. Keep a food journal to help track the items that are causing you health troubles.

While creating the recipes for this book, I tried to eliminate the most common offenders. However, I have included a few potentially allergy-causing foods because, if tolerated, they can be very healing. For example, almonds and sesame seeds contain minerals and plant fats, both of which can contribute to rebuilding tissue. Also, fish is one of the best sources of omega-3 fats and, if you tolerate it well, is excellent for healing inflammation. In addition, I've included organic free-range eggs as menu suggestions a few times a week, but you must watch for food reactions in your food journal and avoid any foods to which you may be reacting.

The only soy products included in the MTHI plan are edamame, which are young soybeans, and fermented soy, which includes miso, tamari (a wheat-free soy sauce), and tempeh. These are used occasionally, but if you are sensitive to soy, you should substitute edamame with

Peanut allergies constantly receive media attention due to their potentially deadly effects. There's also increasing awareness about the common incidence of allergies to corn, dairy, soy, and wheat (in particular the gluten protein it contains), although the symptoms caused by these reactions are usually less pronounced compared to peanut-induced anaphylaxis. Peanuts are a common and severe allergen largely due to the molds that grow on their shells. One particularly potent class of toxins produced by these molds is aflatoxins, which can induce severe immune reaction as well as directly cause damage to cells and genes. A recent study published by S. Peterson and others in *Food and Chemical Toxicology* suggests that foods from the carrot and parsley family, which also includes caraway, celery, cilantro/coriander, dill, fennel, and parsnip, help to protect the liver from the damaging effects of aflatoxins. Allergies to corn, dairy, soy, and wheat are becoming increasingly widespread because they are among the most commonly consumed foods in today's Western diets. What makes things worse is that these foods are often processed or refined, which increases their allergen potential. Moreover, many processed products contain substances isolated from one or more of these four foods (for example, corn starch in sauces; milk solids in crackers; soy lecithin in chocolate bars; and wheat flour in soups, cookies, and cakes), which makes avoiding them even more difficult. Aside from hereditary allergies, overconsumption of a specific food is one way your body may become sensitive to it. The unfortunate part of developing a food sensitivity in this way is that corn, dairy, soy, and wheat, when consumed in moderation and in whole form, are actually very nutritious. As a society, we are losing our ability to enjoy the benefits of whole foods because we refine and process them so widely.

whole nuts or seeds, soy miso with vegetable broth, tamari with vegetable broth or umeboshi plums, and tempeh with quinoa and black beans. Some people who experience allergy-related symptoms (such as digestive stress or sinus trouble) with nonfermented soy can generally tolerate miso, wheat-free tamari, and tempeh because the fermentation process reduces the trypsin-inhibiting compounds found in soy. Trypsin inhibitors are chemicals that reduce the digestive capacity of trypsin, which is a protein-digesting enzyme synthesized by the pancreas. If you find that you are sensitive or allergic to a food suggested in the menu plan, be sure to avoid it. Substitutions are suggested in the chart on page 209 wherever possible.

People who appear to have multiple food allergies may in fact be reacting to foods that are part of the same food family (taxonomically related). To avoid allergic reactions, you may have to avoid all foods that are part of the same family as the food to which you know you're allergic.

WRAP-UP

- Food allergies cause intestinal inflammation, malabsorption, and a weakened immune system. There are three main types of allergic reactions that involve five types of antibodies. Allergy symptoms vary between people and among different foods.
- A diet high in refined grains and sugars encourages overgrowth of intestinal bacteria and yeasts that may tunnel through the intestinal lining and contribute to leaky gut. This is why healing inflammation through improving digestion is imperative.
- If you're allergic to one type of food, you may react similarly to a food in the same taxonomic family.

- An allergy-free diet is possible, but it's an individual journey. The MTHI plan allows you to understand the types of foods your body reacts to, positively or negatively.

"Thought is an infection. In the case of certain thoughts, it becomes an epidemic."

—WALLACE STEVENS

CHAPTER 4

THE INFECTION CONNECTION

In the same way that allergies and stress work against your body, infections weaken the immune system. Regardless of how much you may try to avoid infections, many yeasts, parasites, and viruses dwell inside your body. Everybody harbors a host of microorganisms, but not everyone falls victim to these pathogens. When you allow your immune system to weaken or to drop its defenses, you become vulnerable to sickness and susceptible to inflammation.

You may be tempted to treat every infection you get with antibiotics, but authors Michael A. Schmidt and Theodore Dimon, Jr., Ph.D., say that antibiotics aren't always the answer. As I explained earlier, antibiotics can disturb intestinal health and kill health-promoting bacteria. The resulting overgrowth of yeast can further suppress friendly bacteria, which are your internal yeast killers. As a result, the intestinal tissue may become damaged (see page 36).

Here's a quiz that will help you assess how your body is reacting to any preexisting or recently diagnosed infections. The quiz results will not only teach you a thing or two about yourself, but will also show you how to use the MTHI plan to deal with nagging infections. Using the grading system below, answer A, B, or C to the following statements.

A — I've never experienced this problem. **B — I've experienced this in the past, but not at the moment.** **C — I experience this now.**			
A	B	C	I suffer from a chronic infection (for example, hepatitis, *H. pylori* infection, bowel parasites).
A	B	C	I suffer from an overgrowth of candida or other yeast (for example, persistent or recurring vaginal yeast infections, toenail fungal infection, athlete's foot).
A	B	C	I have respiratory problems (for example, asthma, runny or stuffy nose, sore throat, chronic cough).
A	B	C	I experience alternating constipation and diarrhea; I have irritable bowel syndrome (IBS) or an inflammatory bowel disease (for example, Crohn's disease, colitis).
A	B	C	I have frequent episodes of abdominal pain or discomfort (for example, bloating, gas, cramps).
A	B	C	I'm constipated.
A	B	C	I experience digestive problems when I'm under stress.
A	B	C	I have heart disease or high cholesterol.
A	B	C	I have rheumatoid arthritis or gout.
A	B	C	I have elevated blood sugar, hypoglycemia, or diabetes.
A	B	C	I suffer from eczema, psoriasis, or another chronic skin condition.
A	B	C	I have a stomach ulcer.
A	B	C	I smoke or I'm constantly around smoke.
A	B	C	I get a cold or flu more than once within each season.
A	B	C	I have seasonal allergies to pollen.
A	B	C	I'm allergic to mold.
A	B	C	I experience extreme stress.

RESULTS

IF YOU ANSWERED MOSTLY:

A Your immune system is functioning well, which means you fight infections quickly. If any of your tissues are inflamed, the condition will be easier to treat because it's in the early stages. Here's what you can do: stick with step three of the MTHI plan for eight weeks; this will help you figure out if you have food sensitivities that could trigger future inflammation. By increasing the amount of anti-inflammatory foods in your diet, you can reduce many potential health issues in your lifetime. When you finish steps one, two, and three of the program, try to include many of the suggestions on a long-term basis.

B You're beginning to have serious concerns with your health, and your symptoms are affecting the quality of your lifestyle. Continue step three of the MTHI plan for three to six months. (Staying on this step a little longer could reduce your food sensitivities, which are likely contributing to your inflammation.) By increasing your intake of anti-inflammatory foods, you can reduce the potential risk of your inflammation becoming a serious crisis in the future.

C The inflammation in your body is high, and you need to reduce it while simultaneously balancing your immune system. I recommend you follow step three of the plan for one year or longer to balance your immune system and reduce inflammation. Once you've reduced your food sensitivity, you might be able to occasionally enjoy your favorite foods without a reaction. By eating dark leafy green vegetables (such as Swiss chard and kale), enzyme-rich foods (such as parsley and papaya), and soothing anti-inflammatory oils (such as fish, algae, and omega-3-rich seed oils), you can provide your body with the healing nutrients it needs to reverse many of the health issues you're coping with.

Note: If you answered all or mostly all Cs, I highly recommend you seek advice from a professional health practitioner.

THE PROOF IS OUT THERE

Research has identified a correlation between infection, disease, and inflammation. Below are summaries of selected studies, particularly those that relate to irritable bowel syndrome (IBS), heart disease, diabetes, asthma, Alzheimer's disease, and psoriasis.

COMMON INFECTIONS

In 2001, the American Academy of Family Physicians reported the following as the most common infections among people ages 65 and older:

• Bacterial pneumonia

• Influenza

• Urinary tract infections (UTI)

• Herpes zoster (also known as shingles)

Irritable Bowel Syndrome
The Positive Aspects of Probiotics

Probiotics are the beneficial bacteria that reside in your intestines. They perform many functions and help to protect you from intestinal parasites such as yeasts, fungi, unfavorable bacteria, and worms (see Chapter 7 for more about how probiotics support your health). Recent studies have found that one type of probiotic, the "good" *Lactobacilli* bacteria, is found in lower numbers in the intestinal tracts of IBS-stricken people compared to people who don't suffer from the syndrome. One scientific review by R. Spiller, published in the journal *Alimentary Pharmacology and Therapeutics*, found that supplementing the diet with probiotic bacteria could inhibit pathogens from binding to the walls of the intestine. When a pathogen attaches itself to the intestine, the immune system reacts by creating inflammation. Therefore, keeping your intestine supplied with probiotics will prevent infection and the ensuing inflammatory response.

As noted in a 2008 review paper by E.M.M. Quigley, supplementing with various strains of probiotics improves intestinal gas and bloating. These promising results have left researchers wondering about the effects of specific probiotic strains, exact doses, and even the timing of dosages. Continued research will provide a deeper understanding of how probiotics support our health.

IBS After Infection

A British research team led by E.F. Verdu investigated the role of infection in the development of IBS. They found that 6 to 17 percent of people with IBS symptoms believed their gastrointestinal problems began with gastroenteritis (inflammation of the gastrointestinal tract) caused by a bacterial infection. This phenomenon, called postinfectious IBS, increases the inflammatory response in the gut. For about half the people who develop IBS after a bacterial infection, the resulting inflammation can persist for up to five years if appropriate measures aren't taken to heal the gut tissue.

Dr. B.A. Connor from the Weill Medical College of Cornell University reviewed the published literature that indicates IBS is linked to traveler's diarrhea. It's estimated that up to 3 percent of people with traveler's diarrhea have symptoms for more than thirty days. In these people, IBS is a common end result after a severe attack of gastroenteritis. Specifically, it's thought that chronic intestinal inflammation after an acute bacterial infection plays a role in the development of postinfectious IBS.

Heart Disease

Helicobacter pylori (*H. pylori*) Infection and Coronary Heart Disease

A 2004 report by R.F. Gillum at the U.S. Centers for Disease Control found that *H. pylori* infection was associated with a higher prevalence of heart disease in men with diabetes. These infectious bacteria thrive in the stomach and upper part of the gastrointestinal tract, where they produce a toxin that causes inflammation. People who suffer from an overgrowth of *H. pylori* may develop ulcers and are at a higher risk for certain cancers.

Periodontal Infection and Heart Diseases

Chicago researchers published an article in the *American Heart Journal* in 2007 that showed people with periodontal disease had more than double the risk of developing heart disease compared to those who didn't have a dental infection. When the scientists looked at the number of teeth a person had, they found that those with fewer than ten teeth were twice as likely to develop heart disease than those who had a full set of pearly whites. Why is there a link between dental health and heart disease? The theory is that elevated levels of pro-inflammatory immune substances in people who have periodontal disease may promote clot formation in the arteries and lead to coronary heart disease.

Furthermore, a person who has a lot of teeth removed also has more exposed gum tissue and therefore more exposed blood vessels. This makes the body more vulnerable to potential low-grade infections because it allows pathogens to enter into the bloodstream. Some of these pathogens may be deposited in the heart tissue and promote cardiovascular disease. While on this anti-inflammatory plan, it is critical that you brush and floss your teeth and gums regularly and see your dentist to deal with any gum infections.

Carbohydrates and Heart Diseases

In a 2002 Harvard study, S. Liu and others found that carbohydrates high on the glycemic index (or GI) could boost the risk of heart diseases by exacerbating pro-inflammatory processes such as insulin resistance. (The glycemic index is a system that measures how fast a particular carbohydrate affects blood sugar level. Learn more about it on page 90.) Having insulin resistance means that glucose from food isn't effectively cleared from the blood, and instead it lingers in the bloodstream, where it damages blood vessels. As a result, inflammation is triggered, and you'll be more prone to infections. Eating lots of rapidly digestible and absorbable high-GI carbohydrates increases the risk of heart diseases, particularly in overweight people who are already prone to insulin resistance.

Similar findings were reported by P. Kallio and others in 2008: a long-term intake of grains with different glycemic indexes affected the extent of inflammation in those with heart disease risk factors. For example, foods with a high glycemic index, such as white bread and white potatoes, cause a spike in blood sugar levels that leads to AGE (page 14). Eating these foods too often can harm your arteries and increase your risk of heart diseases.

Diabetes
Triggering Type 1 and Type 2 Diabetes

In March 2009, Dr. S. J. Richardson, together with a number of other researchers, found that a common family of viruses known as enteroviruses may play an important role in triggering the development of diabetes in kids. Enteroviruses usually cause symptoms similar to the common cold or, in more severe cases, vomiting and diarrhea. In this groundbreaking study, the researchers provided clear evidence that enteroviruses are frequently found in the pancreases of people who develop type 1 diabetes.

The researchers examined the pancreases of seventy-two young people who had died less than a year after being diagnosed with type 1 diabetes. More than 60 percent of the organs contained evidence of enteroviral infection of the beta-cells. (The beta-cells, located in the Islets of Langerhans of the pancreas, produce insulin.) By contrast, infected beta-cells were hardly seen in tissue samples from fifty children without the condition. (There are up to one hundred different strains of enteroviruses, and more research will be needed to identify which ones are associated with the development of diabetes.)

However, the way enteroviruses might contribute to the development of type 2 diabetes is still under investigation. Laboratory studies show that an enteroviral infection of beta-cells reduces their ability to release insulin. It is possible that in obese people (where there is a greatly increased demand for insulin secretion) a reduction of beta-cell function—secondary to enteroviral infection—may be sufficient to trigger type 2 diabetes. More research is required to confirm this theory.

Keep in mind that a pancreas weakened from a poor diet and lifestyle, alcoholism, drugs, nicotine, or overeating is more susceptible to viral infection. Therefore, the virus may be a consequence rather than a cause of diabetes. Being aware of your food and lifestyle is your best protection against infection and diseases.

Cytomegalovirus Infection and Type 2 Diabetes
Other viruses may also be implicated in diabetes. M. Guech-Ongey and his team explain the possible link between cytomegalovirus (CMV) in the blood, secondary cardiovascular events such as heart attacks, and diabetes. Cytomegalovirus is a common and widespread virus that may cause fatigue, prolonged fever, and soreness. For most adults, CMV is harmless, and many people carry it without even knowing. Nevertheless, the study, published in the *International Journal of Cardiology*, showed that people with diabetes and who are infected by CMV are at greater risk of having a serious cardiac event, since diabetics are already relatively immunocompromised.

Nutrients at a Young Age

In 2007, J.M. Norris and his team reported that kids with a family history of type 1 diabetes might be able to forestall the onset of the disease by eating more foods rich in omega-3 fats. The researchers examined 1,770 kids who were at a high risk for type 1 diabetes and asked their parents to complete annual surveys that recorded the frequency of omega-3 intake in the kids at ages three, six, and nine. Participants also received blood tests for autoantibodies, which are immune system cells that would mistakenly attack the body (in this case, autoantibodies attack pancreatic islet cells instead of foreign intruders, and this could cause enough damage to potentially trigger the onset of type 1 diabetes).

At the end of the six-year study, the data showed that each 800 mg increase in daily omega-3 fat intake was associated with a 55 percent drop in the risk of having autoantibodies. Interestingly, the most common sources of omega-3 fats for the young kids in this study were plant foods such as walnuts and flax seeds.

The Glycemic Index (GI) and Type 2 Diabetes

The glycemic index measures how foods affect blood sugar (see page 90). A study by Harvard researchers L. Qi and F.B. Hu showed that diets rich in low-GI whole grains and portion-controlled carbohydrates may protect against systemic inflammation in patients with diabetes. Portion control of carbohydrates—even of low-GI carbohydrates—can help regulate blood sugar levels. The report concluded that low-GI diets reduce cell damage and guard against system-wide inflammation, which may mark the beginning of type 2 diabetes.

Alzheimer's Disease
A Correlation with Cold Sores

The herpes simplex virus generally lies dormant in the nerve cells of an infected person. However, even if a person doesn't exhibit obvious herpes symptoms, this virus may be implicated in the development of some disorders of the nervous system.

Dr. R. Itzhaki and her team at the University of Manchester investigated the virus's role in Alzheimer's disease. In 2009, they discovered that 90 percent of beta-amyloid plaques present in the brains of Alzheimer's disease sufferers contain the herpes virus. Amyloid plaques are aggregations of protein that may abnormally accumulate in organs, where they contribute to neurodegenerative diseases. These researchers believe that the herpes simplex virus is a major contributor to Alzheimer's disease.

Infectious diseases and Alzheimer's are characterized by an increased frequency and intensity of immune responses. Interestingly, these conditions also change the way your body metabolizes cholesterol and fats. H.Y. Hsu and other researchers at Cornell University found that the herpes simplex virus infection leads to a significant buildup of cholesterol in the blood and a decreased removal of blood cholesterol from the body. This increase in blood cholesterol levels may explain why herpes simplex causes an increase in formation of beta-amyloid plaques in the brain. Therefore, eating foods that feed and protect the brain, such as the ones recommended in the MTHI plan, may help prevent diseases such as Alzheimer's.

Dental Infection and the Alzheimer's Connection

Similar to the relationship between heart disease and dental infections, Alzheimer's seems to be more prevalent in people with peridontitis. Recent studies suggest that infection or inflammation in the peripheries (that is, areas of the body external to the core) might affect the inflammatory state of the central nervous system (the brain is part of the central nervous system, and Alzheimer's disease is a consequence of chronic inflammation in the brain). Chronic peridontitis is a prevalent peripheral infection that is associated with elevated levels of infectious bacteria in the blood that continuously signal to the immune system to sustain inflammatory defenses. In 2008, dentists at New York University published an article in the journal *Alzheimer's & Dementia* proposing that treating chronic dental infection may reduce the risk of Alzheimer's.

Asthma

Respiratory Infection and Inflammation

Chronic coughs, colds, and the flu in early infancy are known to predispose people to asthma later in life. A report by S. Hashimoto and other Japanese physicians described how respiratory viruses replicate and start an infection in the surface cells of our airways. Local inflammation results from this infection, and the lungs remain prone to inflammatory conditions, such as asthma, long after the initial infection subsides.

People with asthma experience increased wheezing when they become infected with common cold viruses and influenza. Respiratory syncytial virus (RSV) appears to be the most important virus in producing more severe symptoms of the disease. In asthmatics, even a mild cold frequently causes more severe symptoms, while a severe cold may be associated with life-threatening asthma attacks. Other infectious agents that may trigger asthma attacks include the parainfluenza virus (which causes bronchiolitis and croup) and rhinoviruses (which cause inflammation of the nose and sinuses).

Some studies have suggested that this effect isn't only additive but also synergistic. Essentially, inflammation in the lungs is initially generated as a defense against the infectious pathogens. However, as the infection directly induces an asthma attack, the lung tissues become even more inflamed and damaged.

Nutrients and Asthma

Research from M. A. Biltagi and his team found that increasing dietary intake of zinc and vitamin C (two nutrients commonly used to fight colds), as well as anti-inflammatory omega-3 fat, significantly improved asthma in kids showing moderate symptoms of the respiratory condition. For the sixty kids involved in the study, lung function and sputum production (measured as a sign of inflammation) significantly improved when all three anti-inflammatory nutrients were combined.

Dietary studies suggest a link between oxidative stress, bronchial inflammation, and the development of asthmatic symptoms. Interventions may reduce oxidative stress and prevent or minimize asthmatic symptoms, but this conclusion isn't supported by many randomized, placebo-controlled studies. It appears that vitamin C and other antioxidants are most effective in preventing asthma induced by colds and lung infections.

Salt, Exercise, and Asthma

Dietary sodium chloride (common table salt) has been shown to increase the severity of exercise-induced asthma. T.D. Mickleborough and his team found that dietary salt loading increases airway inflammation following exercise in asthmatic subjects. Salt may exacerbate asthma by causing dehydration. Dehydration is known to increase the stress response in the body, which may induce an asthma attack and associated inflammation.

Psoriasis
Link Between Psoriasis and Bacterial Infections

Various microorganisms appear to provoke or aggravate psoriasis— including *Staphylococcus aureus* (which causes some staph infections) and *Candida albicans* (which causes some yeast infections). However, the strongest clinical evidence comes from the association between *Streptococcus pyogenes* throat infections and guttate psoriasis (also known as eruptive psoriasis). According to B.S. Baker and her team, strep throat infections in the tonsils may lead to psoriatic skin lesions as a result of the defensive immune response.

Dermatologists in Manchester, England, have also confirmed that people who previously had strep infections are at a greater risk for developing severe psoriasis flare-ups. In their study of people with sudden onset or worsening of psoriasis, 58 percent of those with severe flare-ups had overcome recent streptococcal infections. Strep infections had also recently occurred in over one-quarter of those with constant, milder psoriasis. Eating foods that support the health of your immune system not only helps to prevent these pathogens from affecting your body but also helps your body to subdue inflammation caused by any infections you may develop.

CANCER AND INFLAMMATION

Remember that inflammation is a natural part of the body's healing process—it tells you that tissue damage has occurred. According to the National Cancer Institute's Division of Cancer Biology, it can also help restrain the development of a cancerous tumor. When inflammatory processes in the body are functioning properly, they can stimulate an antitumor immune response to rid the body of cancerous and precancerous cells. However, when chronic inflammation goes unchecked, it appears to encourage tumor development.

Research indicates that chronic inflammation increases the risk of developing certain cancers. For example, studies such as the one by S.H. Itzkowitz and M. Yio published in the *American Journal of Physiology*, warn that, if left untreated, inflammatory bowel diseases (for example, ulcerative colitis and Crohn's) may develop into intestinal cancers such as colorectal cancer. When cancerous tumors are present, the cellular processes involved in inflammation are more likely to contribute to tumor growth, progression, and spread than to elicit an effective antitumor immune response.

TOP FIVE FOODS THAT FIGHT INFECTIONS

We bolster our resistance to illnesses when we provide our bodies with foods that are nutritious, unrefined, and rich in naturally occurring vitamins and minerals. These are my top five choices for beating infections.

Shiitake Mushrooms: These contain a substance called lentinan, which has immune-stimulating properties, and polysaccharides, which are a class of chemicals known to boost the immune system. In fact, several studies have shown that extracts of shiitake and other medicinal mushrooms are effective in the treatment of HIV and several types of cancer.

Garlic: As a powerful immune booster that stimulates infection-fighting white blood cells, garlic promotes the activity of natural killer cells (immune cells whose function is accurately described by their name) and increases the efficiency of antibody production. The immune-boosting properties of garlic come from its sulfur-containing compounds, such as allicin and sulfides (not to be confused with sulfates, which are additives used for preserving and extending the shelf life of prepared foods and wine). Garlic may also play a part in getting rid of potential carcinogens and other toxic substances that can dampen immune function.

Squash and Pumpkins: Both of these related vegetables are rich in beta-carotene, which the body converts into vitamin A. Vitamin A encourages rapid cell repair in lung and epithelial tissues, and increases the number of infection-fighting cells, natural killer cells, and helper T-cells.

Papaya: One cup of papaya has 87 mg of vitamin C, which tops the list of immune boosters for many reasons. Vitamin C increases the production of white blood cells and antibodies, while increasing levels of interferon (a class of antibodies that coats cell surfaces and prevents the entry of viruses).

Sesame Seeds: These tiny seeds are loaded with immune-balancing zinc and plant sterols. Zinc increases the number of infection-fighting T-cells, especially in the elderly, who are often deficient in zinc and have weakened immune systems. Vegetarians may need as much as 50 percent more of this essential mineral than do nonvegetarians because zinc may be absorbed less efficiently from plant foods. (It is very important for vegetarians to include good sources of zinc in their diet to obtain at least 25 mg a day.) Plant sterols are a type of immune-modulating fat that has been shown to help prevent autoimmune disorders, fight cancer, and lower cholesterol.

Cancer itself is a consequence of a stressed and unbalanced immune system. If a person's immune system is so weakened from years of infection, exposure to toxins, and poor diet that it can't keep inflammation at bay, it predisposes the individual to developing cancer (particularly in the tissues where inflammation continues to linger, unchecked). Think of it this way: improperly managed inflammation fans the flames of cancerous cell growth in a tissue that's already afflicted with cancer; then it spurs the development of tumors in tissues that are harboring precancerous cells.

At all three stages of tumor development (initiation, progression, and metastasis), inflammation increases DNA mutations, stimulates secretion of pro-inflammatory hormones, and is involved in a host of other damaging cellular processes. G.R. Smith and S. Missailidis wrote a review in 2004 explaining how chronic inflammation creates a cellular environment that encourages cells that already have a cancerous tendency to go haywire.

While chronic inflammation appears to increase the likelihood of developing several cancers, the exact mechanisms by which this happens remain to be determined. Infection is one plausible mechanism because it is a common cause of inflammation. Numerous studies show that microbial infections can exacerbate the already damaging effects of chronic inflammation to promote tumor growth. Johns Hopkins University teamed up with four other research centers to publish findings in the *Journal of Pathology* that showed that the human papillomavirus (HPV) infection is a risk factor in the development of nearly all cases of cervical cancer. Similarly, a study published in *Cancer Research* explains that *H. pylori* bacterial infection triggered colon cancer in 50 to 66 percent of the mice studied.

The National Cancer Institute explains that tumor cells also produce compounds that attract pro-inflammatory immune cells, which then secrete biological signals to further stimulate growth of cancerous cells. Once the cancer spreads to other parts of the body, inflammation supports tumor growth in metastatic sites; that is, the secondary areas of the body where the cancer cells cluster.

An understanding of the association between chronic inflammation and cancer has led to many clinical drug trials involving anti-inflammatory drugs. Unlike pharmaceutical remedies, which often alleviate one symptom but cause another, nutraceutical remedies from natural foods heal inflammatory damage without adverse side effects and with a smaller chance of toxicity. In their book *Foods to Fight Cancer*, Richard Béliveau and Denis Gingras explain the advantages of natural food remedies (also known as nutratherapy) over synthetic pharmaceutical remedies. Cancer-fighting compounds found in foods, which have been naturally selected over the course of evolution, target the same biological processes that anticancer drugs treat. One major advantage of using foods in cancer treatment is that the natural compounds they contain are synergistic—meaning they work together—to create a healing environment that soothes, rather than aggravates, inflammation.

NUTRITION AND PREVENTION

Lifestyle choices can influence whether or not a person develops cancer. Simple factors you can change, such as quitting or cutting down on smoking tobacco and drinking alcohol, can help protect you from this disease. Béliveau and Gingras tell us that researchers estimate 35 to 50 percent of potentially preventable cancers are triggered by foods we consume in our daily diet.

Cancer begins as a single abnormal cell that starts to multiply out of control. Groups of these rapidly multiplying cells form tumors that invade healthy tissue. Carcinogens from foods, the air, and even the substances made in our own bodies promote the development of tumors. It takes years for a noticeable tumor to develop. During this time, compounds known as inhibitors can keep the tumor cells from growing. Some vitamins and other nutrients in plant foods are known to be inhibitors. Dietary fat, particularly excessive intake of certain types of saturated fat, is known to encourage tumor cells to multiply quickly.

The latest research is pointing to our eating patterns—not specific nutrients or foods—as a contributing factor in cancer prevention. However, scientists are still trying to understand the benefits specific nutrients or foods may have in the fight against cancer. Those diagnosed with cancer can consider using the synergistic cancer-fighting compounds in foods to complement their anticancer drug therapy. Once the cancer is in remission, eating an anti-inflammatory diet may help prevent it from returning.

WRAP-UP

- We must prevent or treat infections, as they can wreak havoc on the immune system and cause chronic inflammation.
- There are many international studies that show a relationship between infections, diseases, and inflammation. This information can help us understand how our diets play a role in many inflammatory conditions.
- There is strong clinical evidence for association between the following:
  - Strep throat infections and outbreaks of eruptive psoriasis
  - Herpes virus and Alzheimer's disease
  - *H. pylori* infection and heart disease
  - Enteroviruses and type 1 diabetes
  - Cytomegalovirus (CMV) and risk of diabetes and heart attacks
  - IBS symptoms and foodborne pathogenic infections
- Studies have also shown that there is a higher chance of developing cancer in areas of chronic inflammation. Keeping "anticancer" foods in mind, we can learn how to help prevent cancer through improved nutrition.

"A false craving . . . is something we think we want but when we get it, it doesn't really satisfy us or enhance our lives."

—SHAKTI GAWAIN

CHAPTER 5

FINDING THE BALANCE

Does the following describe your life? Almost every day, you grab a coffee and something sweet as you head to the office, forgoing a proper breakfast. Lunch is whatever fast food is nearby, and it's wolfed down in twenty minutes while you answer e-mail. When you arrive home, take-out menus and frozen packaged foods are too often what's for dinner. If such patterns have become ingrained, it's likely you probably eat below the recommended daily servings of healthy food. Most of us eat fewer than five servings of vegetables and fruit a day. However, modern food guides recommend at least seven to ten daily servings of these foods. Many people don't eat this amount because they're ruled by cravings instead of being tuned in to the nutritional needs of their bodies.

When cravings control our lives, they become an addiction. We need to eat to live rather than live to eat—especially if we intend to break free from the food addictions we use to soothe ourselves. I'm not saying this is easy or that I've mastered this forever. It's a daily negotiation that I make with the two sides of my brain: the side that wants a little bit of fun by being part of a birthday party where everyone's eating cake, or the side of me that wants big fun, where I feel clear-headed and pain-free. Whatever temporary satisfaction I may feel from tasting sweet cake will be overshadowed by the pain I'll suffer hours later. Eating that small bit of cake just isn't worth it.

The MTHI plan involves restricting many of the refined foods that you crave and then reintroducing them one at a time to see if you feel a difference physically or emotionally. Remember that even though it's important to gradually eliminate the foods you're accustomed to, it's equally important for you to be fully committed to healing your body and supporting your overall health. Aim for eating as many vegetables as possible to balance out nutritional deficiencies caused by the refined treats you have eaten in the past. If you slip up on the plan, be gentle with yourself and get some help from a health practitioner to work on your goal. The MTHI plan will only work if your body is given a chance to heal and balance itself. Set yourself up to succeed by getting the support you need.

THE NECESSITIES

Nutritional imbalances can disrupt hormones and result in inflammation. A deficiency of vitamins, minerals, carbohydrates, fats, proteins, and water prevents the body from being able to repair itself, whereas an overload of nutrients can strain organs and tissues. Balance is essential. We need to look at the key nutrients our bodies require to help heal inflammation: macronutrients, micronutrients, and probiotics. Let's briefly consider probiotics first, and then look at nutrients.

PROBIOTICS

Probiotics are the beneficial bacteria that reside in your intestines that help digest food, increase nutrient absorption; contribute to immune defense against harmful (pathogenic) microorganisms; and that synthesize some vitamins, including folic acid, vitamin B_{12}, and vitamin K_2. For example, *Lactobacillus acidophilus* makes the enzyme lactase, which breaks down the lactose in milk into simple sugars, which the intestines can then easily absorb. *Bifidobacterium bifidus* resides in the colon, where it produces nutrients that support colon health and helps prevent colorectal cancer. It also helps to crowd out harmful bacteria, which increase toxicity and contribute to hormone imbalances by increasing blood concentration of estrogens and testosterone. We've developed a mutually beneficial relationship with probiotic bacteria to the extent that we become ill if we don't cultivate a good, strong population of these microorganisms. Probiotics are discussed in greater detail in Chapter 7.

MACRONUTRIENTS

Proteins, fats, and carbohydrates fuel our bodies. A balance of these three is necessary for cellular regeneration. Even water can be considered a macronutrient. It may boast zero calories, but it's as essential as the air we breathe. It has a different function in our bodies than proteins, fats, and carbohydrates because it doesn't provide energy or structural elements. Nonetheless, water is required in large quantities, and without it we would cease to exist. Whether water can be defined as a macronutrient isn't really important; I simply want to ensure that you understand how important proper hydration is in reducing inflammation. Now let's look at each macronutrient individually.

Protein

Amino acids are the building blocks of protein. Amino acids are critical elements for cell growth, metabolism, repair, and communication, as well as immune defense. Protein is therefore essential for healing, especially from physical injuries and inflammatory conditions. The human body requires twenty-two standard amino acids for life. While all of these are vital, they each have functions for which they are especially useful. For example, *L*-glutamine is an amino acid that is particularly effective in supporting cell rejuvenation because it promotes cell repair and recovery (especially in intestinal and muscle tissues) and helps boost the immune system. Several studies indicate that *L*-glutamine plays multiple roles in cells: it appears to function as a nutrient, chemical messenger, energy source, and building block for physical repair. It stimulates regeneration of intestinal mucosal and immune cells, therefore improving the intestine's resilience against infections.

L-glutamine is relatively abundant in foods, and the body is also able to synthesize it from other amino acids and nutrients, leading some people to assume that supplementation is unnecessary. However, when the body is under stress (for example, from a physical injury, emotional trauma, infection, or surgery), the adrenal glands release steroid hormones such as cortisol into the bloodstream. These adrenal hormones deplete *L*-glutamine fairly rapidly and therefore delay recovery. Studies have shown that supplementing with *L*-glutamine significantly increases the rate of the healing process.

Supplementing with *L*-glutamine powder may be a faster way to recover than to drastically increase your serving sizes of protein. Balance in protein intake is just as important as balancing every other nutrient. Eating an excess of protein (especially from animal sources) can strain your kidneys and acidify your body.

Fat

Increasingly, people are understanding the enormous differences among the types of fat—some fats are essential, some are extremely supportive of cell health, some are best consumed in small quantities, and some are downright detrimental to your body. The trick is knowing which is which, how much to ingest of the healthy ones, and which ones to avoid completely. Raw, fresh, unrefined oils taken daily in the appropriate doses can be anti-inflammatory and healing to every cell in your body.

Let's begin with the most important anti-inflammatory fats, which are the ones most commonly missing or too sparse in people's diets. Omega-3 and omega-6 fats are essential—they aren't produced in the human body and therefore must be acquired from the diet. Both fats, when consumed from high-quality sources, have powerful anti-inflammatory properties. They promote cardiovascular health, keep cell membranes fluid, lubricate joints and skin, boost metabolism, nourish the nervous and immune systems, and help keep hormones in balance. Essential fats are also important allies in preventing and healing cancer.

Omega-6 fats are more common in the typical Western diet. Omega-6 fats are found in corn, peanut, soybean, and various seeds: grape, rape (canola), safflower, and sunflower. All these foods are common sources of the oils used in everyday cooking. However, the poor quality of omega-6s in the Standard American Diet (often abbreviated, rather appropriately, as "SAD") not only decreases their anti-inflammatory power but also makes them pro-inflammatory! This is because omega-3 and omega-6 fats are extremely sensitive to light, heat, oxygen, and free radicals. When these oils are fried, cooked at high temperatures, hydrogenated (a process that produces transfats), commercially refined, or used in processed foods, the omega-6 fats become damaged. Damaged essential fats can actually wreak havoc in your cells, especially the liver.

If damaged oils make up a substantial part of your fat intake, the best thing you can do for your health is to work toward eliminating these completely. Go to a health-food store and buy healthy oils such as unrefined avocado, olive, or sesame seed oils to replace the refined vegetable oils in your kitchen. If you already avoid these damaged oils, then it's time to take it one step further. Having an unbalanced ratio of omega-6 to omega-3 fats is also not ideal for optimal health. The reason for this is due to the way your body metabolizes these essential nutrients.

For example, in a person who is prone to inflammation or who lacks the nutrients required for the healthy metabolism of fats, the body tends to metabolize omega-6 fats through a biochemical pathway that promotes inflammation. Here's how: the body usually converts dietary omega-6s into other types of fat. One of these fats is arachidonic acid (abbreviated AA). AA may be used by the body directly, or it may be converted into various hormone-like substances (some of which are pro-inflammatory and some of which are anti-inflammatory). AA is essential to human health. However, when it is converted into pro-inflammatory compounds, and when the body is unable to control this inflammation, AA can be an undesirable nutrient. A high consumption of simple carbohydrates and processed foods increases the conversion of AA into pro-inflammatory compounds.

Alternatively, omega-6s can also be converted into the anti-inflammatory and hormone-balancing gamma-linolenic acid (abbreviated GLA). Your diet and lifestyle affects which omega-6-derived fat your body produces. Omega-3 fats are heroic fats that reduce inflammation in joints, nerves (including the brain), blood vessels, and the heart. Omega-3 deficiency can lead to excess inflammation and contribute to a variety of conditions, including asthma, diabetes, colitis, cardiovascular diseases, nervous and mental disorders, cancer and other immune disorders, arthritis, hormone imbalances, and skin conditions such as eczema and psoriasis.

It almost seems far-fetched that one type of fat can do so much, but innumerable studies have shown how important omega-3s are to health. For example, by reducing stickiness in the blood and helping the blood flow freely, these healthy fats help prevent cardiovascular diseases. Omega-3s directly nourish nervous tissue, particularly the brain. According to a 2007 study, underdeveloped brains in newborns have been linked to a lack of omega-3s in their mothers' diets. When pregnant women have a higher intake of omega-3s, their babies are more mentally developed than other babies.

QUICK TIP 📌

How can you prevent omega-6 fats from promoting inflammation?

• Consume only raw, fresh, unrefined omega-6 fats and balance these with raw, fresh, unrefined omega-3 fats.

• Improve your gut flora: eat fermented foods and take a high-quality probiotic supplement (see Chapter 7).

• Increase your intake of anti-inflammatory foods, such as those featured in the MTHI plan.

• Boost your intake of micronutrients by eating whole foods and taking a high-quality multivitamin/mineral supplement.

• Avoid spiking your blood sugar (and therefore insulin) levels.

• Perhaps most important, drink adequate amounts of water each day.

When you eat too many omega-3s and not enough omega-3s, you reduce the ability of omega-3s to do their job properly. Omega-6 fats compete with omega-3 fats for the enzymes that metabolize them because the enzymes that metabolize omega-6s are some of the same ones that metabolize omega-3s. If your body is using these enzymes to metabolize omega-6s, the omega-3s you eat will be less effective. An ideal ratio of omega-6s to omega-3s ranges from 1:1 to 4:1, depending on the individual's needs. People healing from an illness or inflammatory condition should take a higher amount of omega-3s.

What about all the other types of fat? Most people have heard that saturated fats are not good for you. That's partially true—a high intake of saturated fats is unhealthy. For example, consuming excessive amounts of saturated fat from grain-fed farm animals can contribute to inflammation. Saturated fats compete with omega-3s and omega-6s for metabolic enzymes, directly increase levels of pro-inflammatory chemicals, make our blood vessels and cell membranes more rigid and stiff, and increase liver congestion. When eaten in moderate doses, a healthy body can process saturated fats well and is able to find great uses for these nutrients, such as hormone production.

Keep in mind that a well-functioning liver and gallbladder are essential for fat digestion. Excessive intake of any fat can be detrimental if your liver and gallbladder are congested, so be mindful of how much fat you consume at every meal. Once again, balancing your intake is key.

Carbohydrates

Carbohydrates are the most digestible sources of energy. They are present in some form or another in every food (although insignificant amounts are present in animal flesh and organs). The best sources of carbohydrates are whole plant foods. You may know that whole grains are excellent sources of complex carbohydrates (for example, starches and fibers) and that refined sugars are classic examples of simple carbohydrates. However, you may not know that the body metabolizes refined grains (for example, flour) and sugars similarly. Both are digested quickly. They cause your blood sugar to skyrocket and then drop just as quickly, often to levels below your initial blood sugar level before eating.

If you continually eat foods that spike your blood sugar levels, you run the risk of decreasing your cells' sensitivity to insulin. Insulin's job is to shuttle sugar from your blood into your cells. If your cells aren't responding to insulin's "message," sugar will remain in the blood for too long, which in turn makes your body prone to inflammation. Over time this pattern may lead to insulin resistance, which means your body doesn't respond to the normal amounts of insulin your pancreas produces. Consequently, you'll require higher amounts of insulin for your cells to take up glucose from the blood. Insulin resistance may lead to conditions related to chronic inflammation, especially obesity, cardiovascular diseases, type 2 diabetes, and certain types of cancers (for example, breast, colon, and prostate).

The glycemic index (GI) was developed by researchers at the University of Toronto to quantify the effects of different foods on blood sugar levels. Foods with a high GI cause a rapid spike in blood sugar and should not be eaten alone on an empty stomach. Foods with a low GI are digested slowly. They create a gradual, more sustained elevation in blood sugar level, and can be eaten alone on an empty stomach or in combination with high-GI foods to help moderate the blood sugar spike that high-GI foods cause. By avoiding wild fluctuations in blood sugar levels, you'll be kind not only to your pancreas but also to your liver (which breaks down insulin and works hard to help regulate blood sugar levels) and all your cells. Spikes in blood insulin levels change the way your body metabolizes certain nutrients. For example, high levels of insulin stimulate the conversion of AA into pro-inflammatory substances.

To help plan your anti-inflammatory meals, refer to the following GI chart created by the world authority on the glycemic index, Dr. Jennie Brand-Miller at the University of Sydney. The chart highlights food choices taken from *The New Glucose Revolution Shopper's Guide to GI Values 2008*, which lists more than one thousand foods and includes carbohydrate and fiber measurements. This book explains how to control blood sugar, and thereby inflammation, by eating mostly foods that have a GI score of 55 or less.

GLYCEMIC INDEX CHART

The following has been reprinted with permission from *The New Glucose Revolution Shopper's Guide to GI Values 2008* by Dr. Jennie Brand-Miller and Kaye Foster-Powell (Da Capo Press).

FOOD BEANS AND LEGUMES	SERVING SIZE	MEASUREMENT	CALORIES	GI	LOW-MED-HIGH
Black beans, boiled	2¼ oz	⅓ cup	86	30	Low
Chickpeas, dried, boiled	3 oz	½ cup	115	28	Low
Hummus (chickpea dip)	1 oz	1½ tbsp	73	22	Low
Lentils, red, dried, boiled	4½ oz	⅔ cup	96	26	Low
Lentil soup, canned	9 oz	1 cup	98	44	Low
Peas, frozen, boiled	5½ oz	1 cup	113	48	Low
Split peas, yellow, boiled	6¼ oz	1 cup	118	32	Low
FOOD BEVERAGES	SERVING SIZE	MEASUREMENT	CALORIES	GI	LOW-MED-HIGH
Apple juice, no sugar added	4 fl oz	½ cup	50	40	Low
Tomato juice	12 fl oz	1 bottle	75	33	Low
Carrot juice	8 fl oz	1 cup	71	43	Low
Coffee, black	8 fl oz	1 cup	3	8	Low
Orange, soda	4 fl oz	½ cup	64	68	Med
Gatorade	8 fl oz	1 cup	63	78	High
Orange juice, unsweetened, fresh	8 fl oz	1 cup	86	50	Low
Pineapple juice, unsweetened	4 fl oz	½ cup	52	46	Low
Prune juice	4 fl oz	½ cup	72	43	Low
Smoothie, mango	8 fl oz	1 cup	215	32	Low
FOOD BREAD	SERVING SIZE	MEASUREMENT	CALORIES	GI	LOW-MED-HIGH
3 grain, sprouted	1 oz	2 slices	120	55	Low
Italian	1¼ oz	1 slice	98	73	High
Wonder White	1 oz	1 slice	69	80	High
Country Life, gluten-free, multigrain	1 oz	1 slice	81	79	High

FOOD BREAKFAST CEREALS	SERVING SIZE	MEASUREMENT	CALORIES	GI	LOW-MED-HIGH
All Bran, Kelloggs	1 oz	½ cup	80	49	Low
Cheerios, General Mills	1 oz	1 cup	110	74	High
Corn flakes, Kelloggs	1 oz	1 cup	100	86	High
Gluten-free Muesli	1½ oz	½ cup	183	39	Low
Oatmeal, regular, made from oats with water	6 oz	¾ cup	101	58	Med
Shredded Wheat, Nabisco	1½ oz	2 biscuits	160	83	High

FOOD CAKES AND MUFFINS	SERVING SIZE	MEASUREMENT	CALORIES	GI	LOW-MED-HIGH
Carrot cake	1 oz	1 small piece	103	36	Low
Cupcake, strawberry-iced	1 oz	⅓ cupcake	84	73	High
Bran muffin, commercially made	1½ oz	¾ average	120	60	Med
Doughnuts, cinnamon sugar	1½ oz	1 small	168	76	High
Macaroon, coconut	1 oz	1 cookie	115	32	Low

FOOD CEREAL GRAINS	SERVING SIZE	MEASUREMENT	CALORIES	GI	LOW-MED-HIGH
Buckwheat, boiled	3 oz	½ cup	89	54	Low
Quinoa, raw	1 oz	2 tbsp	84	53	Low
Muesli breakfast bar, gluten free	¾ oz	½ bar	97	50	Low
Calrose rice, white, medium grain, boiled	2 oz	⅓ cup	92	83	High
SunRice medium grain brown rice	2 oz	⅓ cup	92	59	Med
Rice pasta, enriched (gluten-, maize-, wheat-, and soy-free), Freedom Foods	¾ oz	⅙ cup	80	51	Low
Wild rice, boiled	2½ oz	½ cup	70	57	Med
Premium soda cracker	1 oz	3 crackers	80	74	High
Puffed rice cake, white	¾ oz	2 cakes	75	82	High

FOOD DAIRY AND ALTERNATIVES	SERVING SIZE	MEASUREMENT	CALORIES	GI	LOW-MED-HIGH
Cheddar cheese	1 oz	1½ slices	122	***	Low
Parmesan	1 oz	⅓ cup	133	***	Low
Wildberry, nondairy, frozen fruit dessert	1¾ fl oz	1 scoop	48	59	Med
Milk, 3.6% fat	8 fl oz	1 cup	127	30	Low
VitaSoy***, light original, soy milk	8 fl oz	1 cup	89	32	Low
Yogurt, low-fat, natural	12 fl oz	1½ cups	106	45	Low
Yogurt, full-fat, natural	7 oz	1 container	111	35	Low
FOOD FRUIT AND SWEETENERS	SERVING SIZE	MEASUREMENT	CALORIES	GI	LOW-MED-HIGH
Agave nectar, premium, Sweet Cactus Farms	¾ oz	4 tsp	64	19	Low
Apple	4 oz	1 small	58	38	Low
Apricot and apple fruit strips	¾ oz	1 strip	75	29	Low
Apricots, dried	1 oz	1 piece	75	30	Low
Avocado	2¾ oz	⅓ average	171	***	Low
Banana	3 oz	1 small	73	52	Low
Blueberries	3½ oz	½ cup	45	53	Low
Cherries, raw, sour	5 oz	1 cup	78	22	Low
Cranberries, dried, sweetened	¾ oz	3 tbsp	62	64	Med
Dates, pitted	1 oz	5 average	72	45	Low
Figs, dried, tenderized, dessert-made	1 oz	1½ figs	78	61	Med
Fruit and nut mix	1½ oz	¼ cup	178	15	Low
Glucose syrup	¾ oz	3 tsp	65	100	High
Grapefruit	11 oz	1 large	86	25	Low
Grapes	3½ oz	25 grapes	63	53	Low
Honey, general	¾ oz	3 tsp	70	52	Low
Kiwi	6¾ oz	2 small	108	53	Low
Maple syrup, pure, Canadian	¾ oz	3 tsp	52	54	Low
Mango	3½ oz	½ average	60	51	Low
Mulberries	2½ oz	½ cup	23	***	Low
Nectarine, fresh	4 oz	1 average	50	43	Low
Orange	7 oz	1 large	78	42	Low

Food	Serving Size	Measurement	Calories	GI	Low-Med-High
Papaya	7 oz	1 small	66	59	Med
Peach	7 oz	2 small	69	42	Low
Pear	4 oz	1 small	68	38	Low
Pineapple	6 oz	1 large slice	69	59	Med
Plum	9 oz	2 large	103	39	Low
Prune, pitted, Sunsweet	1 oz	4 prunes	65	29	Low
Raspberries	2 oz	½ cup	29	***	Low
Strawberries	17 oz	3 cups	115	40	Low
Sugar, white	½ oz	6 tsp	65	68	Med
Watermelon	10 oz	1 large slice	69	76	High

FOOD MEAT	SERVING SIZE	MEASUREMENT	CALORIES	GI	LOW-MED-HIGH
Beef, roast	1 oz	2 slices	44	***	Low
Chicken breast, grilled without skin	3 oz	⅓ small	150	***	Low
Chicken curry and rice, prepared convenience meal	10½ oz	1 meal	640	45	Low
Egg, whole, raw	2 fl oz	1 average	77	***	Low
Sardines, canned in oil, drained	2 oz	⅔ small can	137	***	Low
Salmon, red, no salt added, drained	2 oz	⅔ small can	119	***	Low
Sushi, salmon	2¾ oz	3 pieces	102	48	Low
Trout, cooked	4 oz	1 fillet	164	***	Low
Tuna, cooked	4 oz	1 fillet	213	***	Low

FOOD NUTS, SEEDS, AND DRESSINGS	SERVING SIZE	MEASUREMENT	CALORIES	GI	LOW-MED-HIGH
Cashew nuts, raw	½ oz	1 tbsp	76	22	Low
Coconut, fresh	½ oz	1 tbsp	37	***	Low
Hazelnuts	½ oz	1 tbsp	84	***	Low
Linseeds (flax seeds)	½ oz	1 tbsp	46	***	Low
Pumpkin/sunflower seeds, raw	½ oz	1 tbsp	75	***	Low
Tahini (sesame butter)	¾ oz	1 tbsp	86	***	Low
Walnuts	½ oz	1 tbsp	90	***	Low
Salad dressing, homemade oil and vinegar	1 fl oz	1½ tbsp	178	***	Low

FOOD CONVENTIONAL SNACKS	SERVING SIZE	MEASUREMENT	CALORIES	GI	LOW-MED-HIGH
Chocolate, dark, plain, regular	1 oz	1 row family-sized block	144	41	Low
Gummy confectionary, based on glucose syrup	¾ oz	5 pieces	63	94	High
Licorice, soft	1 oz	2 pieces	61	78	High
Popcorn, plain, cooked in microwave	1 oz	3 cups	89	72	High
Pretzels, oven-baked, traditional wheat flavor	¾ oz	1 small packet	76	83	High
FOOD VEGETABLES	SERVING SIZE	MEASUREMENT	CALORIES	GI	LOW-MED-HIGH
Asparagus	3 oz	8 small spears	20	***	Low
Beans, green	1¾ oz	10 average	14	***	Low
Beets, canned	6 oz	1 cup sliced	82	64	Med
Broccoli	3½ oz	1 cup	34	***	Low
Cabbage, green, raw	3 oz	1 cup	23	***	Low
Carrots, peeled, boiled	9 oz	1½ cups	84	41	Low
Celery, raw	1 oz	2 small stalks	5	***	Low
Lettuce, iceberg	¾ oz	3 medium leaves	2	***	Low
Peas, green	7 oz	1½ cups	129	45	Low
Pepper, green, raw	1½ oz	4 rings	7	***	Low
Potato, peeled, boiled 35 minutes	4 oz	1 medium	82	101	High
Potato, Ontario, white, baked in skin	5¾ oz	1 medium	161	60	Med
Squash, butternut, boiled	2¾ oz	½ cup	30	51	Low
Sweet corn, on the cob, boiled	2¾ oz	1 medium	84	48	Low
Sweet potato, baked	3 oz	½ large	79	46	Low
Zucchini, raw	2 oz	½ medium	2	***	Low

*** Contains little or no carbohydrates

Note: You can eat foods with a GI of 56 to 69 as long as you slow down the absorption of carbohydrates they contain. Eat small portions of high-GI foods; avoid eating them on an empty stomach; and combine them with foods high in fiber, protein, or good fats. Foods with a GI of 70 or more should be avoided because they increase your blood sugar too rapidly and are common inflammation triggers. Low-GI foods are recommended, as they help reduce inflammation. Medium-GI foods can be reintroduced one at a time once you're sure that you're not allergic to them.

Another consequence of eating highly refined carbohydrates is the disruption to your gut flora. Yeasts and pathogenic bacteria thrive on simple carbohydrates, so support your friendly bacteria by consuming complex carbohydrates instead. Among the best complex carbohydrates for supporting probiotics are inulin and FOS (fructooligosaccharides). These are naturally occurring complex sugars that are not broken down by human digestive enzymes. Inulin and FOS are considered "prebiotic" nutrients because they serve as food for probiotic bacteria. These carbohydrates therefore help to support overall gastrointestinal health. Both are plentiful in chicory root, garlic, asparagus, jicama, Jerusalem artichoke, burdock root, and leeks. M. Levrat and others report in the *Journal of Nutrition* that inulin and FOS also promote calcium absorption in the human gut. When healthy intestinal bacteria metabolize these carbohydrates, they create a more acidic environment in the gut. Calcium is more soluble in acid, and therefore prebiotics increase absorption into the bloodstream.

If you consume prebiotics, make sure to simultaneously supplement with probiotic supplements or lacto-fermented foods (see page 126). Inulin and FOS may also be metabolized by pathogenic bacteria and yeasts, so it's important to keep your intestinal flora in check. Prebiotics may cause discomfort in people who suffer from IBS, IBD, ankylosing spondylitis, or carbohydrate intolerance.

Fiber is another type of complex carbohydrate that supports healthy gut bacteria. It is also essential for providing bulk to stool, maintaining regular bowel movements, and supporting good intestinal muscle tone. Fiber also binds toxins and cholesterol in the intestines to prevent their absorption into the blood. In a randomized, double-blind, placebo-controlled trial led by Dr. C. Shimizu, subjects experienced a 15 percent reduction in LDL cholesterol after six weeks on a high-fiber diet. Naturopathic doctor and nutritional consultant Brenda Watson recommends that we eat 30 to 40 grams of fiber per day. Vegetables, grains, legumes, and fruits are rich sources of soluble and insoluble fiber. Diets low in fiber cause constipation, hemorrhoids, IBS, varicose veins, and diverticulitis. All these conditions are either a consequence or a cause of chronic inflammation.

The fiber, minerals, and vitamins in whole-food sources of complex carbohydrates help you feel full faster than if you were to eat refined carbohydrates, making it less likely that you will overeat. However, it is possible to eat too many carbohydrate-rich foods, and the consequences can be very uncomfortable. For example, grains and legumes (especially peanuts and soybeans) contain compounds called lectins. While lectins can be very beneficial when consumed in moderation, they tend to aggravate inflammatory and digestive diseases such as IBD and IBS. Symptoms improve when these potentially irritating foods are either completely avoided or eaten in smaller quantities. Research by L. Cordain, Ph.D., and others suggests that "lectins may effectively serve as a 'Trojan horse' allowing intact or nearly intact foreign proteins to invade our natural gut defences and . . . cause damage well beyond the gut, commonly in joints, brain, and skin of affected individuals." Once damage occurs to the gut and the defense system is breached, "leaky gut" results.

What's the take-home message? Balance your intake of complex carbohydrates with other macronutrients, avoid fads that tout either high-protein/low-carbohydrate or high-carbohydrate/low-fat diets, eat an adequate amount of high-fiber foods every day, and eliminate or minimize your intake of refined carbohydrates.

Water

Water literally bathes each cell in your body. When you are well hydrated, your body as a whole is made up of approximately 75 percent water and your brain is made up of approximately 85 percent water. Water is vital for maintaining balance of every physiological process, yet most people are dehydrated. Dehydration sets in long before your mouth feels dry. This is the most common signal people use to gauge their thirst, yet it is one of the last signals your body gives you to ask for water. You can actually decrease your sensitivity to the signs of dehydration and to your sensation of thirst so that over time, you become less aware of the level of water in your body. Acute dehydration will slow your digestion, increase your heart rate and blood pressure, slow your metabolism, cause fatigue, and slow your mental and physical abilities. Chronic dehydration is much more serious, and because so many people become increasingly dehydrated as the years go by, most people are severely dehydrated by the time they reach their senior years.

Chronic dehydration increases inflammation in your body. Some health practitioners believe that dehydration is at the root of almost every chronic condition. (See Dr. F. Batmanghelidj's book, *Your Body's Many Cries for Water*, for an in-depth look at the link between dehydration and disease.)

Let's look at how disease conditions may come about when water is scarce in the body. It is important to understand that there is no substitute for water. When short on water, the body is forced to either put its needs on "pause" or to find an alternative source of water (that is, tap into its own reserves). Your brain immediately alerts your kidneys to decrease the production of urine and save as much water as possible. This makes it more difficult for your kidneys to filter toxins from your blood. Your urine becomes more concentrated, and you urinate less frequently. Your brain also tells your bowels to extract as much water as possible from the stool. This makes your stools harder, and it also increases the amount of toxins you draw out from your digestive wastes. Dehydration is the number-one cause of constipation.

Your brain signals to the skin and sweat glands that water is in short supply, so you sweat less. Without water, your digestive organs produce fewer enzymes and digestive juices, so this sets up a prime scenario for intestinal bacteria and yeasts to take over the job. Dehydration is also the number-one cause of indigestion. Your stomach needs water to make hydrochloric acid (see page 145 for more about this digestive juice), and you need hydrochloric acid to digest your food properly. Pancreatic juices and bile also become more concentrated, lower in volume, and more difficult to secrete without water. Your intestines will move less easily and less frequently, keeping undigested food in your gut for longer periods. This increases the chances that you will develop food allergies, and it also makes it more difficult for your intestines to absorb nutrients. Local inflammation may begin to develop along the gastrointestinal tract.

Over time, your blood becomes relatively thicker, and your heart needs to pump a little harder to move it though the fine capillaries that nourish your cells. Your muscles are less able to effectively convert fuel from food into energy that cells can use. With decreased circulation to the area, fewer nutrients will reach the muscles, and fewer toxins (especially lactic acid) will be flushed out. The result is physical fatigue and weakness, as well as local inflammation, where lactic acid and other toxins start to build up. Your joints, which are lubricated and kept mobile by the water-rich synovial fluid, dry up a little more each time you let your body go thirsty. As a result, you lose flexibility, feel stiff and sore, and increase your chances of injury and of developing arthritis or osteoporosis.

Collagen in your skin, joints, bone, tendons, ligaments, muscles, and the inner matrix of all cells (known as cytoplasm) holds a high volume of water. Before your mouth gets pasty, your body will tap into this water reserve. Your brain's plan is to compensate for what it perceives as a temporary period of dryness. It essentially tries to prevent water loss as much as possible, redirects water from tissues rich in collagen to areas of the body that need it more, and reserves its water stores for the most essential processes. If you don't satisfy your needs for water, more and more chemical reactions are slowed down or stopped altogether. The most vital organs are spared this water shunt, so your brain, heart, liver, and lungs are among the last organs to be given water-sparing instructions. Nevertheless, the water shortage still makes their job a little more difficult. Eventually, these organs will also suffer from water deprivation if you fail to meet your body's water needs.

One of the most common symptoms of early dehydration is mental or physical fatigue. Unfortunately, most people reach for a coffee, black tea, cola, or sugary drink to relieve the brain fog and physical weakness. All of these beverages are diuretics—they actually promote water loss by increasing the production of urine. The body is also forced to use precious water and minerals to metabolize these drinks, so they dehydrate you even further.

What's the solution? Drinking six to twelve full glasses of water each day is certainly a good start. Decreasing your intake of diuretics, table salt, refined sugars, and processed foods loaded with preservatives is equally important. Balance your mineral and vitamin intake with a high-quality multivitamin supplement, use unrefined sea salt instead of table salt, and eat whole foods with a high water content such as vegetables and fruits to nourish all your cells and flush out toxins. Drinking mineral-rich spring water is your best option, but filtered tap water is also good. Remember that drinking from any clean water source is better than drinking no water at all.

MICRONUTRIENTS

A diet low in micronutrients can weaken your tissues because you lack the nutrients required for proper repair. Processed and refined foods are deficient in many critical nutrients such as magnesium, selenium, potassium, chromium, zinc, all the vitamins A through K, and fiber. The most abundant essential mineral in processed foods is sodium. Sodium is essential for life. However, it must be balanced with other minerals, especially potassium.

In ancient times, we ate seven parts potassium for every part of sodium; we now have this ratio in reverse, eating seven parts sodium for every part of potassium. In 2000, a study in the *European Journal of*

Nutrition showed that the average U.S. diet contains four times less potassium and five times more sodium than the paleolithic diet (the presumed diet of our ancestors). Packaged foods are loaded with refined salt, which contains sodium but no potassium. If we don't balance our diet with potassium-rich vegetables and fruits, we increase our risk of developing inflammatory conditions. One part of the DASH (Dietary Approaches to Stop Hypertension) study published in 2000 by P.R. Conlin and others confirmed that a high-sodium and low-potassium diet could increase the risk of hypertension. It also plays a role in the incidence of kidney stones, osteoporosis, gastrointestinal cancers, asthma, and tinnitus. Inadequate potassium intake can result in the accumulation of free radicals, which leads to increased inflammation.

ANTIOXIDANTS

Micronutrients include more than just your standard vitamins and minerals. There's a whole world of other, less commonly known nutrients that support whole body health. For example, antioxidants prevent oxidants (popularly known as free radicals) from damaging your cells and tissues. To understand what a free radical does, consider what happens to an iron pipe when it's exposed to salt—it rusts! The salts erode the pipe, and the iron becomes a free radical. When our cells are exposed to free radicals, they essentially "rust" from the inside out. Once formed, free radicals tend to start a chain reaction of events that leads to the formation of new free radicals. Due to the cellular damage they may cause, free radicals can promote a state of inflammation. It's imperative that these reactive chemicals are neutralized quickly.

The production of free radicals is an inevitable and necessary part of life because free radicals help to initiate chemical reactions such as those involved in metabolism. Thankfully, our bodies have evolved independent means of making their own antioxidants (for example, the hormone melatonin and various antioxidant enzymes) to ensure that free radicals don't wreak havoc inside cells. Our bodies require specific essential nutrients to manufacture in-house anti-oxidants. A diet with few vitamins and minerals compromises your body's ability to protect itself from free radicals.

Many external substances also act as free radicals, increasing the load our bodies have to cope with. For example, chemicals such as the pesticides sprayed on conventionally grown foods, the toxins produced by pathogenic intestinal organisms, cigarette smoke, vehicle exhaust, and the by-products of alcohol metabolism are all sources of free radicals that use up the body's naturally produced antioxidants. X-rays, radiation therapy, microwaves, and UV light also generate free radicals in our bodies. Luckily, nutrients (such as vitamins, minerals, and phytonutrients) found in whole fresh foods act as powerful antioxidants. By consuming whole fresh foods, we give our bodies the materials they need to heal. Let's look at some examples of antioxidant nutrients.

ACE the Race

"ACE" stands for provitamin A (beta-carotene) plus vitamins C and E. These powerhouse vitamins can neutralize the free radicals formed inside the body. They put the brakes on the chain reaction of free radical synthesis and halt inflammation. Studies have shown that these vitamins help reduce or counteract the carcinogenic effects of smoking, stress, and illness, all of which promote inflammation, while depleting the body's vital anti-inflammatory nutrients.

Mine Your Minerals

Minerals also provide impressive antioxidant protection. For example, many minerals function as cofactors for various classes of antioxidant enzymes that your body produces. A cofactor is a nonprotein compound that binds to a protein and is essential for that protein's function (enzymes are a type of protein). Selenium is a mineral cofactor for glutathione peroxidases, a family of enzymes that protect fats (for example, the fats that make up cell membranes) from free radical damage. Zinc is a mineral cofactor for one type of superoxide dismutase (abbreviated SOD; these make up another family of antioxidant enzymes) that protects every cell from free radicals. Zinc also directly protects cells from free radicals (that is, zinc acts as an antioxidant on its own in addition to being a necessary cofactor for a SOD). Zinc is especially abundant in brain tissue where it may help strengthen the blood–brain barrier (which protects the brain from heavy metals, toxins, and pathogens); it also helps prevent free radical damage to proteins and DNA.

Deep Purple

Phytonutrients can also be potent antioxidants. One of my favorite examples of antioxidant-rich foods is a powerhouse berry, the black currant (*Ribes nigrum*). This fruit is a phenomenal source of vitamin C and is also loaded with various anthocyanins. Anthocyanins are a class of antioxidant phytonutrient that contributes to the red, purple, or blue pigment of some flowers and fruits. In plants the anthocyanins seem to act as a kind of sunscreen for plant tissues, shielding cells from constant exposure to the sun's ultraviolet rays. Studies on human tissues suggest that anthocyanins seem to play a similar function, providing shield-like protection that prevents oxidation of cells throughout the body.

In a study published in 2002 in the *Journal of Agriculture and Food Chemistry,* Dr. Jan Frank and colleagues found that black currants helped to protect vitamin E from free radical damage in the blood vessels of rats. Vitamin E, in turn, acts as a cardiovascular protective antioxidant that supports heart health and helps to keep blood vessels healthy, supple, and free of plaques. (As you can see, even antioxidants need antioxidants! This is why it is best to obtain dietary antioxidants from whole foods rather than synthetic supplements.) In 2001, Dr. César Ramírez-Tortosa and others found that black currant extract helped to protect fats as well as DNA from free radical damage, and a trio of Japanese scientists showed that black currant concentrate dilated blood vessels in rats (thereby improving blood flow).

(Note that black currants are tart and astringent, so when you add them to meals, it's good to blend them with sweet fruits to balance the flavors and textures.)

Whatever your preferred source of antioxidants is, make sure you have an ample amount each day—especially if you're very active, have a relatively poor diet, or are exposed to a lot of environmental free radicals. You need higher doses of antioxidants when you are fighting an infection or if you are healing from chronic inflammation. Like a hurricane relief crew, antioxidants mop up what's left behind from the whirlwind of an active immune system, keeping your cells and tissues healthy.

Crazy Diets

You may have noticed how I've focused on the importance of avoiding extremes. Balance is of the utmost importance. When studying diet theories, it's easy to jump onto the latest craze. In the mid-1800s, protein was seen as the master nutrient. In 1923, Dr. John Harvey Kellogg wrote *The Natural Diet of Man*, in which he insisted that carbohydrates were the most important nutrient and that animal protein was the villain. By the 1980s, fat became the bad guy, and by the year 2000, carbohydrates took their turn in the black hat.

What's the truth? None of these macronutrients are evil, and we need all of them for a balanced diet. Eating all foods raw, as suggested by the latest raw-food craze, can be irritating for certain people and may leave a person vulnerable to food poisoning. After studying and trying many diet theories, I have come to one conclusion: cookie-cutter diets don't work. One size cannot fit all. You have to be intuitive about the foods that feel good in your system and focus on variety and balance for true healing. Your individual diet will also change throughout your life, reflecting your different stages of growth, activity, and healing.

"GOOD" VERSUS "BAD" SOURCES OF MACRONUTRIENTS

PROTEINS–"GOOD SOURCES"	"BAD SOURCES"
• Unprocessed and unrefined foods • Raw, soaked, or sprouted nuts and seeds • Legumes • Fermented beans (for example, tempeh and natto) • Cooked seed grains (for example, quinoa and amaranth) • Sprouted grains and beans • Eggs and meat from seed-fed, free-range organic poultry • Wild-caught (ecologically sustainable) fish • Edible jellyfish • Fermented dairy from organic, free-range and grass-fed goats, sheep, and cows (after MTHI step 3) • Organic, free-range, grass-fed beef, lamb, goat, and wild game	• Processed and refined foods • Deli meats, luncheon meats, hotdogs, and commercial sausages • Cuts of meat with large amounts of fat such as bacon • Smoked meats and fish • Dairy desserts (for example, conventional ice cream, canned whipped cream, etc.)

FATS–"GOOD SOURCES"	"BAD SOURCES"
• Unprocessed and unrefined foods • Dark leafy greens rich in omega oils such as purslane (eaten raw, juiced, or steamed) • Sea vegetables and edible algae • Raw, soaked, or sprouted nuts and seeds • Avocado, durian fruit, sea buckthorn berry, and açai fruit • Wild-caught (ecologically sustainable) fish (especially coldwater and deep-sea fish) • Eggs and meat from seed-fed, free-range organic poultry • Organic, free-range, grass-fed beef, lamb, goat, and wild game • Cold-pressed raw oils stored in dark glass jars	• Processed and refined foods • Deep-fried foods • Oils cooked to smoking point • Chemically extracted and bleached oils • Oils stored in plastic containers • Modified oils such as trans-fats, hydrogenated oils, fractionated oils, shortening, monoglycerides, and diglycerides

CARBOHYDRATES–"GOOD SOURCES"	"BAD SOURCES"
• Unprocessed and unrefined foods • Dark leafy greens • Root vegetables (raw or cooked) • Whole, well-cooked grains • Whole, well-cooked legumes • Raw, dried, or cooked fruit	• Processed and refined foods • Refined sugars • White flour (stripped of grain bran and germ); also cake flour, bread flour, and baker's flour • Commercially baked products such as cookies, pastries, muffins, crackers, and cakes • Commercial bread

SERVING SIZES

It may seem overwhelming to think about all the "rules" you need to follow to maintain good health. In reality, it's quite simple once you understand how whole foods already contain balanced proportions of essential minerals and vitamins. Your job is simply to enjoy a combination of different foods at each meal to obtain the nutrients your body needs. For suggestions on serving sizes, refer to the MTHI food pyramid (page 178). I also highly recommend Sam Graci's book, *The Food Connection: The Right Food at the Right Time*, to learn how to personalize your nutrient intake, portion sizes, and eating schedule.

All nutrients must be eaten in balanced quantities and from high-quality sources. I've compiled a chart (see page 105) to summarize "good" versus "bad" sources of specific macronutrients. If all your meals comprise selections from the "good sources" column, you will get the vitamins and micronutrients you need (however, I still highly recommend taking a high-quality multivitamin and mineral supplement because mineral levels in soils around the world are becoming depleted).

EATING FOR BALANCE

In his book *In Defense of Food*, Michael Pollan suggests that we "eat food, not too much, mostly plants." These seven simple words sum up a method of eating that creates the conditions for pain-free living. When we overconsume food (even the healthy kinds), we can create an imbalance that taxes the body's ability to process the abundance of nutrients.

Avoid the food coma! I empathize with the notion that avoiding a binge is easier said than done. Instead of eating until you're so stuffed that your belly is swollen and you feel tired, pack unfinished food away in the fridge as leftovers for another meal. Even though eating freshly made food is the ideal because it always contains more nutrients, eating leftovers is vastly better than forcing down the last bits of food on your plate and using your stomach as a human compost bin. I find that parents often feel they need to finish their children's unfinished food, which creates an incredibly destructive habit.

Eating small, frequent, well-chewed meals will maintain a steady blood sugar level, support digestion and digestive organ health, increase absorption of nutrients, and decrease inflammation in the gut. Steady blood sugar levels and balanced micronutrient absorption will stabilize your moods, support brain function and mental alertness, and give you lasting energy. You will feel mentally and physically satisfied, which will decrease emotional eating. It's hard to have happy thoughts with a toxic intestine. Treat your belly well and your mind will be joyful.

Follow these recommendations for balancing your eating patterns and decreasing inflammation:

Reduce your intake of caffeine. Caffeine may disrupt sleep. It works as a diuretic, and contributes to dehydration. It will increase the loss of minerals such as calcium, and water-soluble nutrients such as B vitamins. If you feel you must have coffee, then I recommend one espresso in the morning taken separately from your multivitamin. It contains less caffeine than the regular cup of joe and is often freshly ground. Espresso can be watered down to create an Americano. It's important that any coffee be freshly roasted to ensure it contains more antioxidants. Stale coffee beans that have been roasted more than a week ago or ground more than a day ago can contain pro-inflammatory rancid oils that are hard on the digestive tract and liver. An even better choice is green tea: it contains only 33 mg of caffeine per cup, is packed with antioxidants, and has anti-inflammatory properties. Green and black teas naturally contain fluoride that can disrupt thyroid function, so be mindful if you have a family history of hypothyroidism.

Watch out for sugary or refined foods. Refined carbohydrates cause the pancreas to overproduce insulin, which then stokes the production of pro-inflammatory substances. Refined foods usually contain trans-fats, which interfere with the body's metabolism of other fats, including essential fats.

Maintain a healthy weight. Fat cells are not simply storage sites for extra sources of energy. Fat cells actually produce a variety of substances, including pro-inflammatory compounds and even some hormones, including estrogen. High levels of body fat increase blood levels of estrogen, which can lead to a relative hormone imbalance. Hormone imbalances can have profound effects on whole body metabolism, even though the first symptoms you notice might not appear to be very serious, such as premenstrual syndrome (PMS) or perimenopausal hot flashes. Men must also maintain hormone balance to protect against hormone-sensitive cancers such as prostate cancer.

Eat organic and free-range animal foods and products whenever possible. This will help decrease your exposure to the antibiotics, hormones, and genetically modified feed given to livestock. These toxins may negatively affect your intestinal bacteria, hormone balance, and immune system health, and thus promote inflammation.

Get into an exercise routine. Weight-bearing, such as climbing stairs and weight training, and cardiovascular exercises are crucial for preventing bone loss and helping you avoid fractures. According to the National Institute of Arthritis and Musculoskeletal and Skin Diseases, swimming and riding your bike aren't considered weight-bearing exercises. "Although these activities help build and maintain strong muscles and have excellent cardiovascular benefits," says the institute, "they are not the best way to exercise your bones." Cardio exercises can indirectly support bone health by improving circulation and nutrition to bone cells and to the muscles that support joint movements.

Sleep and reduce stress. Insufficient sleep increases levels of stress hormones, which promote inflammation. Find ways to handle daily stressors, especially if you're experiencing PMS or if you have perimenopausal symptoms. Based on their 2003 study, R. Seguin and M.E. Nelson explain that "with the aging population, physical activity represents one way for women to stay mentally healthy. Physical activity can help throughout the menopausal transition and afterwards." This study revealed that after female participants walked five days a week for an hour and a half at 4 miles (6.5 kilometers) per hour, they experienced less stress and a positive attitude. Exercise is equally important for men.

Stay hydrated with water. Drink half of your body weight in ounces on a daily basis. (Consider a 130-pound person: 130 divided by 2 equals 65 ounces or 8 cups.) Staying hydrated is essential for every metabolic process in your body. Water will also help you eliminate toxins in your stool, decrease inflammation in your intestines, and keep your bowel movements regular.

Moderate alcohol intake. When consumed in excess, alcohol can put a lot of strain on all your organs, particularly your liver, stomach, and cardiovascular system. If you enjoy having an occasional drink, it will not cause irreparable damage, but please be mindful of the frequency of your indulgences as well as the amount you drink each time. Excessive alcohol intake directly increases inflammation and dehydration, which in turn stokes inflammation further. Everyone's tolerance level is different, so what may be a manageable amount of alcohol for one person can be severely damaging for someone else. Know and respect your body's limits.

WRAP-UP

- We need balanced amounts of macronutrients and micronutrients. Nutritional deficiencies and excesses can occur when we eat too much refined or processed food. Overconsuming healthy foods can also create an imbalance because it overwhelms the body's capacity to digest and metabolize nutrients. To rebalance this discrepancy, supplement your diet with antioxidants, vitamins, macronutrients, minerals, and probiotics.

- Water is an essential macronutrient for keeping our cells healthy and free of unmanageable inflammation. Boost your water intake and eliminate diuretics while on the MTHI plan. Moderate amounts of green tea are okay for people who aren't sensitive to caffeine.

- Nourish your body with "good" sources of all macronutrients and avoid fad diets that promote extreme eliminations of specific macronutrients.

- Use the glycemic index as a tool to avoid spiking blood sugar and insulin production. High-GI foods promote inflammation.

"The great art of life is sensation, to feel that we exist, even in pain."

—LORD BYRON

CHAPTER 6

INJURY RECOVERY: MOVING TO HEAL

In some ways, even pain can be considered desirable because it is a sensation, and feelings are what tell us we are alive. Pain can be an appropriate sort of discomfort when, for example, it comes from building new tissue; destructive pain, on the other hand, comes from injurious old habits. This is why you need to take your pain seriously; the earlier you catch it, the better is your chance for healing effectively.

Many people who find an anti-inflammatory diet to be ineffective in alleviating their pain may have a structural imbalance that needs to be addressed. Even though I had initially followed the MTHI plan for years, I was still experiencing pain from an old shoulder injury. Once I went through physical rehabilitation and strength training and continued with the MTHI plan, my shoulder healed and I attained a pain-free body. The MTHI program is especially effective in combination with other therapies.

REASONS FOR INJURIES RELATED TO PHYSICAL ACTIVITIES

CAUSE	WHAT HAPPENS
INAPPROPRIATE FOOTWEAR	Wearing casual shoes for running or performing other sports will not provide enough support. As a result, you can strain the knees, ankles, hips, and joints.
LACK OF FLEXIBILITY/ STRENGTH	Inflexible muscles could tear, which is why it's necessary to stretch. Stretching "trains" your muscle fibers to get used to new positions. Performing new activities without the appropriate strength can also cause sprains.
NOT WARMING UP BEFORE PERFORMING A PHYSICAL ACTIVITY	According to Ben E. Benjamin, author of *Listen to Your Pain,* warming up should be a priority; otherwise, Benjamin writes, "nerve impulses are sluggish, reaction time is far below what it could be, heart and breathing apparatus fatigue easily, and cold, stiff muscles have no resilience."
MUSCLE TENSION	It's normal to have some muscle tension, but it can become excessive and chronic from past traumas. Too much tension makes movements stiff; the muscles become fragile, unable to absorb pressure and more vulnerable to injury.
MUSCLE IMBALANCE	If the sides of the body are developed unequally, movements that require muscle balance become unstable; paired muscles can become unstable, causing one side to be stronger than the other.
FATIGUE	When your muscles get tired and you continue to work them, other parts take on the pressure. For instance, Benjamin explains that "when ligaments . . . are asked to do the work of muscles, they often strain and tear."
POOR BONE ALIGNMENT	Improper alignment, such as knees that turn in while the feet turn out, causes stress on body parts that are accustomed to accommodating strain.

LET'S GET PHYSICAL

According to Bill Pearl and Gary T. Moran, Ph.D., authors of *Getting Stronger,* we must learn when to seek expert help for dealing with physical pain. In order to do this, we need to listen to our symptoms during and after an injury. For common and not-so-severe injuries, the RICE (rest, ice, compression, elevation) method is appropriate. This involves giving the injured body part a pause from activity, applying ice after the injury, wrapping the body part with a tensor bandage, and elevating it to reduce swelling. "In the case of any acute injury," says Toronto-based chiropractor Dr. Patricia McCord, "the more immediately ice is applied to the injured area, the quicker the inflammatory reaction can be curtailed." Icing an injury within forty-eight to seventy-two hours reduces inflammatory reactions such as swelling. After the swelling decreases, apply ice for ten minutes. Follow with a hot water compress for another ten minutes. "The more repetitions completed, the better the overall effect. The ice temporarily slows the circulation to the area and the heat increases the local circulation," McCord explains. Alternating between the two temperature extremes stimulates recovery and clears toxins.

Seek the help of a health care practitioner if your pain or swelling is severe, you're not able to move the injured area, or it continues longer than seven to ten days. If your pain affects your daily living, then it's reducing your quality of life.

The following review of modalities will give you an idea of whom to seek help from for a new or lingering injury. You'll notice that each physical treatment is effective in reducing pain and inflammation in a different way.

PHYSIOTHERAPY (PHYSICAL THERAPY)

Many common movements, such as lifting or twisting, can add stress to our bodies and may lead to unforeseen injuries. What can a physiotherapist (also known as a physical therapist) do to help this situation? "There is an ideal way that our bodies were designed to move—whether it's bending forward to tie our shoes, reaching overhead, or pushing off with each step as we walk—and achieving these optimal movement patterns can alleviate sources of pain. This is where a physiotherapist can help," says Lindsey Davey, a Toronto-based physiotherapist.

MODALITY SUMMARY CHART

MODALITY	HOW IT WORKS
PHYSIOTHERAPY	Uses a variety of techniques, such as balance retraining, learning specialized exercises for certain muscles, and learning how to adjust to a physical activity or your return to work.
MASSAGE THERAPY	Reduces tension through massage. This stimulates the nervous system, improves blood circulation, removes toxins and lactic acid buildup in tissues, and alleviates muscle soreness.
OSTEOPATHY	Manipulates joints and soft tissue by analyzing and correcting structure, function, and motion of the whole body.
CHIROPRACTIC CARE	Predominantly focuses on the relationship between the manipulations of joints, spine, and nerves to regain structural balance.
ACUPUNCTURE	Encourages the flow of energy using needles, which relieve "blockages" surrounding injured areas.
STRENGTH TRAINING	Uses exercises to retrain muscles, while increasing flexibility and balance; prevents future injuries from occurring.

Physiotherapists have the skills to assess and manage many conditions that impact the musculoskeletal, circulatory, respiratory, and nervous systems. Davey explains, "There are many reasons why individuals experience chronic pain. In addition to certain whole body conditions such as fibromyalgia, chronic pain can result when secondary issues arise following an acute injury. Degenerative changes that occur with the natural aging process, such as osteoarthritis in the joints or disc changes in the spine, can also lead to chronic pain."

Moreover, Davey emphasizes that physiotherapists "are trained to treat not only their patients' symptoms, but also the underlying cause of the problem."

Overall, physiotherapists have many techniques in their toolbox to relieve pain, decrease inflammation, and promote optimal tissue healing. This treatment is an option for people who are itching to get back on their feet after experiencing back pain, repetitive strain injury, or even surgery.

MASSAGE THERAPY AND OSTEOPATHY

While massage therapy and osteopathy are two separate modalities, they do share some similarities. "From a musculoskeletal perspective," says Ursula Buck, "pain often arises from a lack of mobility or over-mobility in the soft tissue and joints." Buck, a registered massage therapist and osteopath, believes the body is constantly seeking balance for better function. "When we have weakness or inflammation in an area, local and distant joints and soft tissue will compensate to provide the body with as much stability and flexibility as possible." However, she notes that "there are only so many compensations the body can create without symptoms beginning to arise. Over time, as we remain in our favored postures and actions, these systems get tired and begin to lose their potential range—inflammation will likely be associated with the resulting dysfunction, pain, and discomfort."

As stated by the Massage Therapist Association of Alberta, massage therapy is successful because of "the movement of the therapist's hands over the body, physically stretching the muscles, encouraging circulation, inhibiting muscle spasm, and sedating . . . the nerves." In this way, osteopathy provides an effect similar to massage therapy. "The restoration of proper circulation is one of the . . . guiding principles of osteopathy," says Buck. Treatment is based on the connection between the body's structure, function, and motion, which "encourages the body to re-establish proper function to tissue, increasing range and reducing pain and inflammation, while healing injury. When structural imbalances are left to their own devices, our bodies will continue to develop compensations," says Buck. "These compensations are the main cause of musculoskeletal pain, discomfort, and inflammation. This is why manual therapies play an important role in encouraging the body to return to structural balance."

CHIROPRACTIC CARE

Chiropractors are principally concerned with the neuromusculoskeletal system; that is, "they diagnose and treat disorders of the spine and other body joints by adjusting the spinal column or through other corrective manipulation," states the Canadian Chiropractic Association.

"We must first diagnose the origin of a patient's complaint to ensure that it's in fact a chiropractic problem," adds chiropractic doctor Patricia McCord. "If the joints aren't able to move normally within their natural range of motion, this creates stress in the surrounding tissues, causing a myriad of ill effects. These include, but aren't limited to, back pain, tendonitis, headaches, carpal tunnel syndrome, sciatica, plantar fasciitis, and early degenerative change."

At Dr. McCord's clinic, her approach involves the evaluation of the entire physical structure, because injury, regardless of its cause, can result in negative compensations involving related regions of the body. The correction of subluxations (which are partial dislocations of a joint) and other imbalances in the biomechanics of the patient's area of concern will result in the restoration of normal function. This allows the body to heal itself, unimpeded, through its own natural processes.

McCord gives a good example of how important it is to treat the entire body. "A mild ankle sprain can often lead to dysfunctional joints in the foot. Once the natural shock absorption of the foot is altered, the body may attempt to compensate by involving the knee, the hip, the pelvis, and so on. Only then does the pain become apparent and appear to 'come out of nowhere' weeks or months later. Especially in cases of long-existing, chronic problems, you can receive treatment again and again for your lower-back pain without lasting results if the original problem, the immobile foot, has not been addressed as well." Whether your condition is old or new, or the result of athletics, a work-related injury, poor posture, or trauma, addressing the pain as well as the original cause of that pain will optimize and restore normal function.

Chiropractic care is suitable for acute and chronic pain, though Dr. McCord clarifies that "only a small percentage of complaints presented at chiropractic offices are caused by an obvious trauma. A much larger proportion is caused by poor posture, poor ergonomics at work, and inappropriate exercise techniques. These bad habits or postures are often years in the making, causing cumulative and repetitive abnormal stress and strain on the body."

ACUPUNCTURE

As a component of traditional Chinese medicine (TCM), acupuncture is a physical treatment that involves inserting thin needles into specific parts of the body. Acupuncture is an art, and it's important to seek a well-experienced and knowledgeable practitioner if you want to gain the most out of your treatments. Depending on the patient's health issue, an acupuncturist may move the needles, add an herbal mixture to the point (known as moxibustion), or use cupping, wherein suction cups help stimulate channels through which energy travels. "Six people coming in with stomach problems can be treated in six different ways," explains acupuncturist Kate Kent.

According to acupuncture theory, a healthy person should have an adequate amount of life energy or *qi* (pronounced *chee*). Qi is a concept in TCM that describes the intangible essence (energy) that is inherent to all living beings; it's the force that gives life and that ignites physical and metaphysical biological processes. The concept of qi is equivalent to the concepts of *prana* in Ayurvedic medicine and of the vital force in traditional Western medicine.

Our qi is supposed to be balanced and flow freely through our body. Acupuncture encourages qi to flow through the organ systems, which are also known as qi meridians. "Where there is pain, there is blockage of either the qi or blood. It's like a highway at rush hour and everyone is zipping along. If there's an accident, there is a backup because the cars can't get through. Once the emergency vehicles come and clear the scene, then they can get through," Kent explains. "Acupuncture takes away the blockage that is causing the pain. If there is no blockage, there is no pain. The acupuncture points have more energy than the other parts of the body, and so they can be used to either bring more energy or bring down energy" to a specific area, or throughout the entire body, depending on the need of the individual.

Unlike many other modalities, acupuncture blends the mind and body together. "You've got to have your emotions and immune system working in tandem," says Kent. "Emotional energy, trauma, and pent-up feelings can also stop energy from circulating properly. Hence, people get painful headaches from being stressed. Premenstrual tension, rheumatoid arthritis, and any kind of autoimmune disease has what I believe to be an emotional component. I do think that arthritis has been linked to pent-up anger. The energy can't get through and then the joints swell because the energy can't go past the joint."

If you experience an injury, Kent advises to "always listen to your pain, from a stubbed toe to a headache . . . If there's a lot of inflammation at the beginning, use a little bit of ice—but you have to use hot and cold temperatures to get things moving. Ice alone just constricts it. If you injure your feet, take hot and cold footbaths. For your knee, hot and cold compresses. These will help get things moving, just like an acupuncture treatment."

Overall, Kent believes that acupuncture is suitable for any type of injury; just get it treated as soon as you can. "Pain from ten years ago is kind of stuck," explains Kent, "and the body has a memory of it."

YOGA

Yoga comes from the sanskrit word *yuj* that means to connect, join, or balance. It's a complete system that can help heal the mind, body, and spirit. Jon Kabat-Zinn, Ph.D., author of *Full Catastrophe Living: Using the Wisdom of Your Body and Mind to Face Stress, Pain, and Illness*, explains that practicing hatha yoga on a regular basis can counteract neuromuscular atrophy. Just make sure you find a yoga instructor who will safely guide you. "Some yoga poses are too advanced and they can create further injury," explains yogi Shambunata Saraswati. "If you suffer from hypermobility, such as too much flexibility, you may damage the joint by overstretching. Damage to soft tissue can occur over time, even if you aren't aware of it. You may not know that you're exceeding your limits until you experience physical pain or injury."

STRENGTH TRAINING

From the perspective of strength training, it's normal to have some pain. However, according to personal trainer Colin Campbell, "what's really important is the ability to distinguish between injury pain and recovery pain. If we were to discuss where it's appropriate to feel pain, the joints are most likely not the appropriate places to feel pain on a regular basis. Pain within the joints, ligaments, and tendons, particularly when it comes with an undue amount of swelling, isn't good. If you avoid moving the joint, there shouldn't be joint pain when at rest. If you do have joint pain without movement, it's likely that you've injured the joint."

However, if your muscles ache for long periods of time, this could indicate physical damage. Campbell explains: "In this case, if it's so severe that it lingers for more than seventy-two hours after working out, chances are you've strained or sprained the muscle—which is a more serious injury."

Researchers Rebecca Seguin and Miriam Nelson at Tufts University completed a strength-training program with older men and women who had moderate to severe osteoarthritis in their knees. The results of this sixteen-week program indicated that strength training decreased pain by 43 percent, increased muscle strength and general physical performance, improved clinical signs and symptoms of the disease, and decreased disability. The study also showed that strength training was just as effective as medications in easing osteoarthritic pain, and in some cases it was even more effective. Similar results have been seen in patients with rheumatoid arthritis who engaged in strength training.

It's also essential to learn from a personal trainer when you should rest after an injury. If you don't allow your muscles to rest between training sessions, explains Brad Walker, author of *The Anatomy of Sports Injuries,* you could face overtraining. In this case, your body won't be able to repair properly from injuries, which leads to even more damage.

WRAP-UP

- You will need to address a lingering injury to ensure that the MTHI plan will meet your expectations of pain reduction.
- It is always better to be physically active, as sedentary individuals can experience more structural imbalances due to a lack of muscle tone. Everyone experiences injuries for a number of reasons, including a lack of strength and not warming up. However, it's not uncommon to be injured from an everyday task due to poor posture.
- For pain that isn't severe, you can practice RICE. However, seek the help of a professional if the pain continues for more than seven to ten days and you notice swelling.
- There are many treatments to choose from in dealing with pain. Some of these include physiotherapy, massage therapy, osteopathy, chiropractic care, acupuncture, and strength training.
- Everyone has a different experience with treating injuries. The modalities I've featured have similarities and differences, so it's always best to get your questions answered by certified professionals in their respective fields.

"Everything I eat has been proved by some doctor or other to be a deadly poison, and everything I don't eat has been proved to be indispensable to life . . . But I go marching on."

—GEORGE BERNARD SHAW

CHAPTER 7

HEALING STARTS WITH THE GUT

YOUR STOMACH IS ON GUARD!

More than 110 million people in North America have digestive problems. If you are one of those people, you may tolerate the symptoms because you tend to think the discomfort will pass. However, when a digestive problem becomes chronic and serious, it can wreak havoc in the entire body.

I strongly feel that fixing the gut can help all chronic health problems. The health of your gut determines which nutrients are absorbed and which toxins, allergens, and microbes are kept out. Poor digestion is found to be the root cause in many diseases, ranging from allergies to arthritis, and acne to autoimmune disorders, because the gut plays a large role in our immune system.

The paper-thin intestinal lining protects your entire body from the toxic environment in your gut. Imagine your body as a fortress that's separated from the rest of the world by an enormous winding wall (your intestinal lining). Guards keep watch along the exterior and especially at each entrance. Your intestines have millions of portals to absorb nutrients, so it's important that nothing else is allowed to enter your bloodstream. Your gut is lined with "guard" immune cells (see page 37) that communicate with the rest of your body's immune organs and cells. The intestines are the largest interface we have with the external environment. It makes perfect sense to have your strongest guards protecting the largest gateway into your body. The immune guards are very selective about what substances are considered safe enough to enter the fortress.

If any area of this lining barrier is damaged, your local defenses are weakened and the rest of your immune system is warned that there's an exposed area. Your gut will become inflamed in that area, and your body will attempt to repair the damage. However, while it's being repaired, this area remains weak and vulnerable to toxins and parasites. Immune cells surrounding the damaged tissue remain hypersensitive to foreign substances to prevent your blood from being poisoned.

If the damaged area is relatively small, you probably wouldn't feel very much other than temporary indigestion, nausea, or bloating. You may not even notice anything at all. If the damage is a little more severe or if it's persistent enough that the body cannot heal itself properly after each assault, you will very likely develop some sort of intestinal or digestive imbalance. For example, you may start to notice that you burp a lot after a meal or perhaps you don't digest meat as well as you used to. You feel full after eating a small meal; you experience diarrhea or constipation more frequently than before; or certain foods start to make you feel uncomfortable, bloated, or tired. These are important signs alerting you that there's deeper trouble ahead unless you pay attention and fix the problem. You may be at risk of developing food allergies or leaky gut syndrome.

In Chapter 3, I described how exposure to food allergens can cause damage to the intestinal lining and contribute to leaky gut. However, how do food allergies develop in the first place? It's not always easy to trace the origin and find the answer because food allergies may develop for numerous reasons in different people. It's like deciding which came first—the chicken or the egg. Food allergens can cause damage to the gut lining, and damage to the gut lining can cause food allergies to develop. Ultimately, the end result is the same: local injury and subsequent inflammation in the intestines cause immune cell hypersensitivity, which makes your immune system more likely to attack food substances that are usually harmless. Damage to the intestines, by whatever cause, makes it more likely that toxins and pathogens from the gut are able to penetrate the lining (causing more damage) and seep into the bloodstream.

Once toxins start to seep into the blood, your problem becomes systemic. Your entire immune system becomes involved in the battle to keep your body clean and safe. If the body remains on hyperalert for a long period of time (weeks, months, or years) because the intestines don't have a chance or the right nutrients to heal properly, your immune system will remain hypersensitive. As time goes on, you will have allergic reactions to more and more foods, chemicals, and environments; you may begin to feel pain, stiffness, or soreness in different parts of your body; you may develop skin tags or notice hard lumps of tissue (known as granulomas) under your skin; your veins and arteries may become more visible or bulging in different areas of your body; you may become bloated easily and find it difficult to return to a more stable weight; or your body shape may change rather suddenly, and your metabolism may seem to grind to a halt overnight. These are some signs of systemic inflammation, and they all start with weakness in your digestive system.

Every cell in your body contributes to immune protection. All play different roles—some play a bigger part in immune defense than do others—but each cell has the ability to send an SOS message and warn immune guards that an invader is in their midst. You want to make sure that there are no false alarms—that each time your immune guards are pulled into action, they are eliminating a real intruder and not a harmless substance.

Immune defense requires a lot of resources: energy, vitamins, minerals, antioxidants, and other nutrients. If you are always fighting, you divert your body's resources from other functions such as metabolism, growth, and repair. When there's constant inflammation raging in your tissues, you literally deplete yourself, and your immune system is unable to regulate itself. Generating a temporary and healing inflammatory response is supposed to be followed by a termination of this inflammation. The body must be allowed to return to a normal and balanced state, known as homeostasis. However, with constant inflammation, your immune system isn't able to "turn off" the inflammatory response in one region of the body before it's alerted once more that there has been a breach in defenses elsewhere. A state of chronic, low-grade systemic inflammation develops, and eventually a name (for example, arthritis, cardiovascular disease, clinical depression, diabetes, fibromyalgia, tinnitus, or cancer) can be given to the definable set of symptoms you begin to show. A study published by C. Cuvelier and others reported that arthritis patients examined by colonoscopy had chronic intestinal inflammation, even if they were unaware of the distress in their gut!

Canker sores in your mouth and ulcers in your stomach and small intestines are signs of a damaged gastrointestinal lining. Polyps are a sign that when your body attempted to heal this damaged tissue, its healing mechanisms weren't well regulated. These are early signs of an immune system that is depleted, imbalanced, and in need of your attention.

CONSIDER THE "PROS"

We have over one hundred trillion bacteria living in our digestive system. That's four pounds of healthy "bugs" hanging out all along the digestive tract from the mouth to the stomach, small intestines, and colon! We need these bacteria to be healthy; it's quite a symbiotic

MAJOR CULPRITS THAT DAMAGE THE GASTROINTESTINAL LINING

- A low-fiber, high-sugar diet of processed foods that causes the wrong bacteria and yeast to grow in your gut

- Excess consumption of acidic foods, such as coffee, alcohol, white vinegar, soft drinks, citrus fruits, and tomatoes, as well as very spicy foods, especially when eaten in combination with sugar and other refined carbohydrates

- Eating or drinking very hot foods or drinks that literally burn your gut lining

- Overuse of medications that damage the gut or block normal digestive function; for example, acid blockers (Prilosec, Nexium, etc.), anti-inflammatory medication (Aspirin, Advil, and Aleve), antibiotics, steroids, hormones (oral contraceptives, hormone replacement therapy, and in vitro fertilization–supporting drugs) and antihistamines

- Undetected gluten intolerance; celiac disease; or low-grade allergies to foods such as dairy, eggs, corn, soy, or nuts

- Unbalanced gut flora, with inadequate amounts of beneficial bacteria relative to pathogenic bacteria, yeasts, and fungi

- Toxins such as heavy metals (especially mercury that has leached from dental amalgams) and those produced from molds or intestinal pathogens

- Lack of adequate digestive enzyme function, which can result from using acid-blocking medication, having a poor diet, inadequately chewing food, overeating, or being deficient in zinc

- Stress, which can alter intestinal nerve activity, cause a leaky gut, and change the normal bacteria in the gut

- Intestinal parasites, such as worms, amoebas, *Giardia* spp., etc.

125

relationship. (Symbiosis describes the relationship between two or more different organisms that live together.)

People with inflammatory bowel diseases have lower numbers of friendly bacteria, so increasing probiotics is essential to healing intestinal inflammation. I was once one of the people who ignored nagging digestive complaints—I'm asking you to make a wiser choice. If you can stop inflammation early, you'll be able to repair

PROBIOTICS: CERTAIN SPECIES AND STRAINS OF BENEFICIAL BACTERIA THAT SUPPORT YOUR HEALTH	
SOURCE	**HEALTH BENEFIT**
• Probiotic supplements **Fermented foods:** • Buttermilk • Cheese • Kefir • Yogurt • Quark • Kimchi (cabbage, radish/daikon, scallion, cucumber; or brined anchovy, brined shrimp) • Vinegar-free pickle (carrot, beet, cucumber) • Poi (taro root) • Sauerkraut (cabbage) • Douchi (black bean) • Miso (soy, red bean) • Natto (soy) • Amazake (rice) • Injera (teff flour) • Miso (barley, rice) • Pao cai (rice congee) • Sourdough (grain flour) • Nata de coco (coconut) • Sicilian green olives • Rakfisk (Arctic char, trout)	• Produce enzymes to digest food • Make vitamins B_1, B_2, B_3, B_5, B_6, B_{12}, and K_2 and folic acid and biotin • Increase the absorption of nutrients through the intestines • Act as a critical component of the intestinal immune system • Support health of intestinal mucosa • Produce antibacterial, antiyeast, and antifungal compounds to kill off pathogenic (bad) bacteria, yeasts, and fungi • Physically crowd out intestinal pathogens • Decrease the level of toxins in the intestines
PREBIOTICS: NUTRIENTS THAT FEED PROBIOTICS, INCLUDING INULIN, FRUCTOOLIGOSACCHARIDES (FOS), AND ARABINOGALACTAN	
SOURCE	**HEALTH BENEFIT**
Artichokes • bananas • burdock root • chicory root • garlic • honey • leeks • onions • whole grains	• Provide food for probiotics • Improve mineral absorption

your gut, increase absorption of nutrients, and overcome many health challenges.

Lacto-fermented foods contain beneficial bacteria that assist in immune defense and the digestion of food. The table above lists various foods that, once fermented, are excellent sources of probiotics. Eat a selection of these daily to help replenish your gut. Avoid dairy until you have completed steps one to three of the MTHI plan.

GETTING FRIENDLY WITH BACTERIA

While we are armed with a brigade of beneficial bacteria, we are also home to various other yeasts (for example, candida), bacteria (for example, various strains of *E. coli*), and fungi that constantly vie for more living space in our bodies. Probiotics are the soldiers we want to keep in command. If their populations remain strong, then the other microorganisms are relatively harmless living on the sidelines. If our legion of probiotics ever starts to wane in number or strength, the "bad" yeasts, bacteria, and fungi are ready to take advantage of the opportunity to increase their numbers and rise in power. When our probiotics are pushed out of their territory, we may suffer dysbiosis (an imbalance in the healthy microflora) in the digestive tract, infectious diarrhea, and vaginal yeast infections.

Even though probiotics permanently reside in our intestines, our food and lifestyle choices will affect how well they thrive. All the culprits that have the potential to directly damage our intestinal lining may also harm our friendly probiotics. Excessive use of antiseptic sprays or soaps, and exposure to toxins in our food and environment, can also alter the populations of microorganisms in our intestines.

How do you prevent an imbalance between the probiotics and other microorganisms in your gut? Replenish your probiotics with good dietary sources and maintain a diet and lifestyle that supports their health. When you see probiotic foods advertised, it's easy to think that they are all the same. Sadly, they aren't. Some products dazzle you with the enormous numbers of bacteria they contain. However, the number of bacteria in a product like yogurt can be misleading. If the yogurt doesn't contain a strain of bacteria that has the ability to permanently colonize and easily reproduce in your intestines, then it will be less effective at healing and protecting your body.

Even more important is the kind of environment that you have in your intestines. If your intestinal tissues are inflamed, ulcerated, or infected with parasites, then you'll need to take very high doses of specific probiotic strains for an extended period of time. Different probiotic strains are required to deal with different intestinal needs.

The most extensively researched probiotics are *Lactobacillus* and *Bifidobacterium* species. These probiotics produce and release lactic acid when they digest carbohydrates. This lactic acid helps to increase the bioavailability of nutrients (that is, the amount of minerals, vitamins, and other nutrients that are available for your body to absorb) that require an acidic environment to be properly absorbed by the intestinal tissues (for example, calcium). Without a healthy population of beneficial bacteria, the environment in your intestines may not be optimal for nutrients to be properly assimilated.

WHAT IS A STRAIN, AND WHY DOES IT MATTER?

As far as probiotics are concerned, different strains or subtypes are differentiated based on their genetic variation. Just as different breeds of horses have distinguishing attributes, so too do different strains of even the same species of bacteria. There are over four hundred species of microorganisms in the human digestive tract. Each strain has different functions, inhabits different regions of the body, is useful in the treatment of specific ailments, and can be particularly effective in killing off or controlling the population of different parasites.

WHEN FOOD IS CARRYING BAGGAGE!

Food poisoning is actually more common than you think. You may think you have the stomach flu when, in fact, you have a mild form of foodborne infection that is causing your stomach major distress. What people commonly call the stomach flu is actually a form of gastroenteritis or inflammation of the stomach and intestines (the gastrointestinal tract). Gastroenteritis may be caused by a virus, bacteria, or parasite contracted from spoiled food or unclean water. Keeping a healthy and robust population of probiotics in your gut will

RECOMMENDATIONS FOR KEEPING THE PROS IN YOUR GUT

To maintain the good bacteria in your gut, follow these recommendations:

- Cut out refined sugars and processed carbohydrates, as they tend to feed the harmful bacteria and yeasts in your body.

- Avoid antibiotics whenever possible. If you have a serious infection that requires antibiotics, be sure to follow up your course of treatment with a month of probiotic supplements. This will help your gut recover from having lost the good bacteria (which are killed off along with the infectious bacteria the antibiotics were intended to eliminate).

- Avoid drinking chlorinated water because it kills good bacteria in your gut. Filter your drinking water whenever possible. If you don't have a water filter system, you can boil water prior to drinking or leave an uncovered glass bottle of tap water on a countertop overnight to allow chlorine to evaporate.

- If you are sensitive to milk, you may find that you can tolerate a bit of unsweetened organic goat or sheep yogurt after step three of the MTHI plan. Good bacteria create lactase, which helps break down the lactose in milk products.

- Consume lacto-fermented foods, such as those listed in the table on page 126.

- Take a high-quality probiotic supplement (some of the most effective ones require refrigeration, but if you are traveling, bring some that will stay fresh without refrigeration). Increase your dose when your immune system is down and you feel an infection starting to develop, and when you eat out or travel.

increase your ability to fight off such harmful invaders. It's nearly impossible to completely avoid exposure to pathogens and parasites; the more important and realistic strategies are to support your immune system and keep your digestive system strong. The following table (page 131) provides information about common food pathogens and ways you can prevent bacterial food poisoning.

Symptoms of food poisoning can vary. One individual may experience different symptoms from being infected by the same bacteria at different times. Common symptoms include upset stomach or nausea, intestinal or abdominal muscle cramps, diarrhea (which may contain blood), fever, or headache. Symptoms of food poisoning can show up within hours of consuming the contaminated food or after several days, making it hard to isolate which food caused the infection. With mild cases of food poisoning, you likely won't feel sick for very long unless you already suffer from a weak or chronically inflamed gut. However, even a mild case of food poisoning will kill off important good bacteria in the gut, so each foodborne infection should be taken seriously. Increasing your intake of probiotics usually suffices to rebalance your gut.

As I explained in Chapter 1, one of the main culprits behind inflammation is an infection that originates in the intestines. I think that my serious intestinal problems started when I was backpacking through Asia. I ate some bad seafood that was stored in a freezer that had electricity for only twelve hours a day due to power shortages. I got such a bad case of bloody dysentery that I couldn't digest food properly for six months and developed a profound allergy to gluten. If you feel unusually ill after consuming pork, beef, chicken, mushrooms, shellfish, sprouts, or food from a salad bar or buffet, you may need immediate medical attention. It's important to flush out the toxins produced by infectious bacteria and other parasites. When I had food poisoning in Thailand, I waited too long before going to a clinic and, as a result, put myself in danger. I couldn't hold down water without vomiting, I became dehydrated, and I developed a dangerously high fever. If you have even the slightest concern, seek medical attention. You may require intravenous fluids to compensate for the electrolytes and fluids you lose due to nausea, vomiting, or diarrhea.

If you have only a mild case of food poisoning and you can drink fluids without vomiting, then rehydrate with a basic electrolyte blend

FOOD POISONING: AN OUTLINE OF BACTERIA

TYPE OF BACTERIA	SOURCES	SOURCES OF CONTAMINATION	PREVENTION
Staphylococcus spp.	Meats; prepared salads such as tuna, egg, and potato; cheese and other milk products	Staph is transferred to food from the hands and nose of food handlers during preparation, or from consuming tainted foods. Symptoms develop 1 to 8 hours after exposure and last for 1 to 2 days.	Normal cooking temperatures won't kill it. Cooks should wash their hands with soap and hot water for 30 seconds before handling food.
Salmonella spp.	Meat, poultry, and raw eggs	Spread through contact with an infected person (for example, by kissing) or eating infected food such as eggs, leafy greens, and meat. Symptoms arise 1 to 3 days after exposure and last 4 to 7 days.	Wash hands thoroughly. Avoid raw eggs. Cook meats to an internal temperature of 180°F (82°C).
E. coli 0157: H7	Undercooked ground meat; some raw produce such as spinach and strawberries	Undercooked meats, contaminated berries and spinach, poor sanitation, and contaminated water can be sources of infection. Symptoms can arise within 3 days of exposure and cause gastrointestinal distress for up to 3 days. It's known to cause kidney failure in people with compromised immune systems.	Cook meat to an internal temperature of 160°F (70°C). Thoroughly wash produce with food-grade hydrogen peroxide. Clean hands and cooking surfaces. Boil questionable sources of water.
Listeria spp.	Deli meats, hotdogs, and soft cheeses	These bacteria can live in home refrigerators and can contaminate foods stored nearby. It's hard to connect the infection to the symptoms, as it can incubate in your body for about 3 weeks before symptoms occur.	Keep potential sources of listeria separate from other foods in the fridge. Toss meats after their expiration dates.

(powder or liquid) from a health-food store or drugstore. This will replace important minerals you may have lost. Other excellent sources of electrolytes are coconut water (it has a very pleasant taste, and it's packed with potassium); simple broth made from vegetables or animal bones; or a homemade electrolyte drink made by adding a pinch of unrefined sea salt, a dash of maple syrup, and a squeeze of lemon or lime juice.

Don't eat solid foods until the diarrhea has passed, and get plenty of rest. It's also best to avoid dairy products, which can worsen diarrhea; food poisoning can cause a temporary state of lactose intolerance. You'll usually recover from the most common types of food poisoning within a couple of days. The goal is to keep yourself well hydrated to ease your symptoms and help you recover faster.

When you feel you have a good appetite and are ready to try food again, eat small, bland meals. Steamed rice or millet and boiled yams are an ideal first venture into solid food; make sure to chew each bite into a liquid paste. Eat only fresh food that has been boiled and is served promptly—bacteria can grow even in rice. If light grains such as rice or millet are in short supply, then unleavened (yeast-free), gluten-free bread that's chewed slowly will do.

At this point, your digestive tract will still be inflamed from the infection, so avoid spices, fats, roughage, raw foods, and heavy protein until you have completely recovered. All are too stimulating or difficult to digest after you've suffered from food poisoning, so it's best to avoid them for the first few days after your nausea and diarrhea subside. You need to consume enough starchy carbohydrates for energy, but avoid burdening your digestive system with large meals.

This may sound contradictory to the MTHI plan because I ask you to eat well-balanced meals that include protein, fiber, and essential fatty acids. However, when you're just starting to recover from an acute pathogenic infection, I suggest you avoid fiber and other foods that are difficult to digest until the digestive tract can tolerate them again. Until your symptoms subside, stick to overcooked, bland, and moist or soupy food. Take a whole-food form multivitamin/mineral supplement to help support your metabolism and immune system.

In an emergency, drink a strong cup of black or green tea (two to four tea bags per cup) to treat severe diarrhea. The tannins in tea are natural antibiotics, and they tighten (astringe) your intestinal tissue, helping to prevent intestinal pathogens and toxins from being absorbed into the bloodstream. However, too much caffeine and tannins may irritate your gut, so it's best not to rely on this quick fix frequently, especially if you are sensitive to caffeine. Follow with charcoal tablets or food-grade hydrated bentonite clay. Both are sold in many health-food stores and drugstores. Take three capsules of charcoal, two to three times a day, or two tablespoons of bentonite clay away from food and supplements, for up to a week. Charcoal and clay will soak up toxins plus the offending bacteria or parasites and help your body eliminate them. After taking either remedy, make sure to drink at least two to three glasses of warm water to avoid dehydrating your intestines further.

DINING OUT AND TRAVELING

When you're eating out, hold the starch (this includes bread, pasta, and potato) and substitute with steamed vegetables, such as broccoli or green beans. Depending on what you order, you may find the best restaurants to dine at are Japanese, Thai, Korean, Greek, Russian, Polish, Italian, Ethiopian, Indian, or vegetarian restaurants that serve healthier choices than the standard North American cuisine. Ask your server to hold the sauce so you'll avoid dairy, poor-quality fats, sugar, and white vinegar. Dress your greens with olive oil and lemon juice.

When you travel, especially to exotic destinations, bringing probiotics with you is essential. Make sure you bring a good-quality probiotic supplement that doesn't require refrigeration. While the locals have been acclimated to the bacteria in their food and water, travelers may find it causes diarrhea. When you return home from your travels, make sure to buy a high-dose probiotic and take it daily for at least one month. See the chart on page 135 for some guidelines to help you make safe food choices while you travel.

Many people find that becoming vegetarian is the safest plan when traveling abroad. If you do want to eat meat, ask for it to be prepared well done. There should be no visible blood in steaks or pink meat in chicken, as that's when microbes are at their highest concentrations. If any food smells sour or off, don't risk it. Chai (spiced tea from India) is an ideal beverage to have when suffering digestive distress, as the tea tannins can help slow diarrhea and the spices are antimicrobial and support digestion. If possible, ask for it black to avoid the dairy.

DIARRHEA AND CONSTIPATION: TWO SIDES OF THE SAME COIN

If your digestive tract is irritated, then you might experience diarrhea, constipation, or both. Ideally, the bowels should move and empty two or three times a day; the stool should be bulky and soft so that it can be eliminated without the need to push. When stool stays in the bowels for too long, some toxins are reabsorbed into the blood and circulated throughout the body. Toxins from the blood will eventually deposit in your tissues if your liver, kidney, and bowels are not able to flush them from your body quickly enough. Feces will become compacted into hard, dry, pellet-like stools that are difficult to eliminate.

TRAVEL GUIDELINES

SAFE FOODS TO EAT	FOODS TO AVOID
Boiled or baked greens and root vegetables such as sweet potatoes or yams	Salad or raw vegetables because the water used to wash them can be the greatest source of contamination. Potato salad with mayonnaise because of the high risk of bacterial contamination.
Peeled fruit such as pineapple (if cut with a clean knife) Stewed fruit (if stored properly)	Berries or thin-skinned fruit such as pears, especially if the skin is bruised. It's impossible to wash away microbes once they burrow through the skin into the fruit. Precut melon or melon drinks. These can harbor high mold and bacteria counts. Fresh fruit drinks or juices because they can be made with contaminated water. Strawberry or berry bar drinks because they can contain bacteria, even if frozen.
Freshly cooked whole grains (whole rice, millet, etc.) and crackers or flatbreads made from these grains	Leftover cooked grains. Left out in the heat, these can form mold. Cook rice and other grains fresh for each meal.
Eggs (boiled, scrambled, or as an omelet)	Raw eggs, liquid yolk, and sunny-side-up eggs (could cause salmonella poisoning).
Freshly cooked soups and stews	Reheated meat soups, unless refrigerated properly and boiled. Make sure that soups and stews are always kept hot. If soups are boiled well, microbes are killed. However, if they're left at room temperature and then reheated, you can still get sick from the toxins that the microbes created—even after they are reboiled.
Fish that's freshly caught (same day) or frozen once Well-cooked fresh meat	Old, smelly fish. Avoid animal foods if electricity is sporadic, as refrozen meat, fish, or dairy can cause food poisoning. All shellfish because of the high risk of allergies and parasites. Raw or rare meats and fish.
Well-cooked beans stored cold to avoid mold	Bean dip and other bean dishes from a salad bar, as they could be fermenting in the heat.

The flip side of the coin is watery, loose stools that may beg to be eliminated a dozen times a day. Diarrhea can lead to severe dehydration, weight loss (which is mostly water, not fat), and an electrolyte imbalance (especially of sodium and potassium) in the blood. Some people who suffer from chronic diarrhea for several years begin to lose muscle tone in their intestines and may experience prolapse of their transverse colon (the part of the large intestine that stretches from the upper right to the upper left of your abdominal area, just below your diaphragm). Dr. Bernard Jensen's classic book, *Guide to Better Bowel Care,* provides more information about the consequences of bowel irregularity.

In both cases of diarrhea and constipation, the intestines are irritated and inflamed. You can see from the chart below that some factors

DIARRHEA MAY BE CAUSED BY:	CONSTIPATION MAY BE CAUSED BY:
• stress • spicy food • excessive peristaltic movements (for example, IBS patients) • osmotic diarrhea* • imbalanced intestinal flora (such as candida infections) • fruits with inedible or unchewed seeds • exposure to a food allergen • food poisoning • some medications • extremely hot weather • high consumption of alcohol or coffee • too much fiber • irritability or emotional stress	• dehydration • insufficient dietary fiber • high-fat foods • reduced peristalsis • foods that are astringent or spicy • low physical activity • overeating • not eating enough • some medications • irritability or emotional stress • exposure to a food allergen • liver congestion (which causes a decrease in the amount of bile produced) • cholecystitis (inflammation of the gallbladder) • ignoring the urge to evacuate the bowels • imbalanced intestinal flora (such as candida infections) • stress • physical obstruction

*Occurs when a high amount of water is drawn into the large intestines. This can happen when there's an excessive amount of a food or substance in the intestines that can't be completely digested or absorbed; for example, lactose, vitamin C, magnesium salts, improperly digested foods, or sugar alcohols such as sorbitol and mannitol. Some intestinal parasites may also cause osmotic diarrhea, as can an overgrowth of unfriendly bacteria or consuming a high amount of probiotics.

overlap—they may cause either diarrhea or constipation. Your diet and hydration, level of physical activity, lifestyle, personal history, emotions, and personality will determine whether your gut responds to these factors with loose bowel movements or with none at all.

To help prevent and treat diarrhea or constipation, I suggest that every day you drink at least six to twelve glasses of fluid such as water, diluted and unsweetened fruit or vegetable juices (except prune juice, which naturally contains high amounts of sorbitol and other compounds that have a laxative effect), veggie broth, diluted plain gelatin or bone broth, and herbal teas such as ginger root. These fluids will help to replace electrolytes and water-soluble nutrients in people who suffer from diarrhea, while helping to flush toxins and soften stools in people who suffer from constipation. In both cases, drinking these fluids throughout the day will help to soothe and alleviate intestinal inflammation.

Supporting your liver and gallbladder with vegetables such as beet root, broccoli, burdock root, carrot, daikon, dandelion leaf and root, garlic, kale, onion, and radish will help to regulate your bowel movements. Lemon and lime juice also help stimulate bile production. Liver bile is a natural lubricant and nature's best in-house laxative for the bowels.

Some people with chronic diarrhea or constipation may be suffering from an inability to break down simple carbohydrates such as fructose, sucrose, lactose, or complex carbohydrates such as those found in grains and beans. Most often, this type of intolerance is caused by insufficient amounts of enzymes, which are required to properly digest these nutrients. If you're not experiencing positive results with increasing and moderating your fluid intake, consult the Specific Carbohydrate Diet™ in the book *Breaking the Vicious Cycle,* by biochemist Elaine Gottschall. I've compiled a short reference chart with recommendations that may also help soothe your intestinal troubles.

DIARRHEA VERSUS CONSTIPATION

FOODS TO AVOID

DIARRHEA	CONSTIPATION
Eliminate foods high in insoluble fiber, which can irritate the intestines and worsen diarrhea. These foods include bran cereals, unrefined grains, isolated grain bran (for example, wheat bran, oat bran, etc.), and granola; raw vegetables; whole-kernel corn; whole, unsoaked nuts and seeds; dried fruit; and fruit with small seeds (such as strawberries).	Avoid processed foods, as these are most often devoid of fiber and nutrients.
Remove the skins, seeds, and membranes from fruits and vegetables to make these foods easier to digest.	Minimize or avoid refined carbohydrates that imbalance intestinal bacteria. Constipation will already contribute to overgrowth of unfavorable yeasts (such as candida) and bacteria, so take extra care to avoid yeast-promoting foods.
Fat (especially cooked fats) may irritate the gut; avoid fried or greasy foods, and remove visible fat on meat.	Eliminate foods high in hydrogenated oils and animal fats, as they stress the digestive organs.
Eliminate milk and milk products.	Eliminate milk and milk products, which can cause constipation.
Very spicy foods may also cause diarrhea and inflame the gut; minimize or avoid these altogether.	Refrain from eating foods that are very astringent, such as citrus, unripe fruits, and tea.
Avoid all allergy foods.	Avoid all allergy foods.

LIQUIDS TO AVOID

DIARRHEA	CONSTIPATION
Limit or avoid caffeinated beverages, such as coffee, colas, soft drinks, and energy drinks. Limit strongly brewed caffeinated teas.	Refrain from consuming drinks that are high in sugar, caffeine, or other stimulants; astringent tannins or citrus; ice-cold fluids; and non-nutritional drinks because all can irritate your intestines.

LIQUIDS TO DRINK

DIARRHEA	CONSTIPATION
Filtered water, vegetable broth, herbal teas, and fresh unsweetened or diluted fruit and vegetable juices are the best fluids to consume. Decaf teas and black, oolong, or green tea (which contain tannins) may help control diarrhea.	Drink warm or room-temperature water, vegetable broth, fresh unsweetened or diluted fruit and vegetable juices, and gentle herbal teas that promote bile flow, such as dandelion root and yellow dock root mixed with ginger root. (Avoid senna, as it's habit forming.)

NUTRIENTS YOU NEED	
DIARRHEA	**CONSTIPATION**
Replace minerals such as sodium and potassium, which are lost through bouts of diarrhea. Eat mineral-rich foods. Foods loaded with potassium include spinach and other leafy greens, apricot (fresh), avocado, squash, all melons, coconut, coconut water, sea vegetables, and vegetable or bone broth. Also take a vitamin and mineral supplement to replace the nutrients you're losing.	Vitamin B complex, vitamin C, and magnesium found in fruits, vegetables, whole grains, seeds, and beans have been shown to support bowel function.

FOODS TO EAT	
DIARRHEA	**CONSTIPATION**
Focus on easy-to-digest foods high in soluble fiber, such as quinoa porridge; applesauce; cooked peas; mashed beans; peeled root vegetables such as squash and sweet potato; brown rice or millet; brown rice pasta; gluten-free crackers; and ready-to-eat, soft, sugar-free cereals (for example, brown rice crisps, puffed quinoa, and puffed amaranth). Eat well-cooked leafy greens if you can tolerate them. Bake, broil, or steam food instead of frying or sautéing. Eat eggs, fish, lean meats, and poultry. Unheated omega-3-rich oils (especially fish or algae oil) will help to decrease intestinal inflammation and heal the gut tissue. Mixing small amounts (from 1 teaspoon/5 mL to 1 tablespoon/15 mL, depending on your tolerance) of raw flax seed oil with your meals may help to minimize your discomfort.	Increase high-fiber foods such as root vegetables with their skins; teff, amaranth, quinoa, and buckwheat porridge; brown rice and other whole grains; beans, lentils, and peas; fresh or dried fruits (particularly if the skins are eaten; make sure to thoroughly soak dried fruits in warm water before eating); leafy green vegetables (raw or steamed); sea vegetables; and soaked nuts and seeds. Bake, broil, or steam food instead of frying or sautéing. Eat moderate amounts of eggs, fish, and poultry. Limit lean meat intake. Raw oils rich in essential fatty acids (especially omega-3s) will help decrease intestinal inflammation and heal the gut tissue.

Note: If you experience constipation or diarrhea for more than one week, you should consult your healthcare provider to determine the cause of your problem.

QUICK TIP

People who eat plenty of high-fiber foods usually don't have constipation problems. While the recommendation is 25 to 40 grams of fiber a day, the National Center for Health Statistics reveals that North Americans get only 5 to 14 grams per day.

HOW MUCH FIBER IS TOO MUCH?

People who suffer from irritable bowel syndrome (IBS) or inflammatory bowel disease (IBD, which includes ulcerative colitis, diverticulitis, and Crohn's disease) may be advised by their doctors or dieticians to avoid whole foods high in insoluble fiber. There are two kinds of fiber: soluble fiber (such as inulin, pectin, and mucilage), which breaks down in water and can slip through the digestive tract fairly easily, and the rough and bulky insoluble fiber (for example, the bran of whole grains and the skins of beans, seeds, nuts, and fruit), which doesn't dissolve in water and therefore scrapes through the digestive tract. Most raw foods are high in both soluble and insoluble fiber, which is why not every person can tolerate them.

If you have zero digestive irritation, then moderate amounts of insoluble fiber can be an effective nutrient for eliminating waste. However, if you have serious digestive inflammation such as IBS or IBD, then the otherwise cleansing action of insoluble fiber can act more like sandpaper. In this case, you may be better off consuming foods that contain gentle fibers like the soothing and healing mucilage of seeds such as ground flax, chia, and cooked amaranth or teff. Fiber is an incredible nutrient for cleaning out toxins, balancing hormones, and regulating blood cholesterol.

If you're planning to increase the amount of fiber in your diet, you must do it slowly. Whether you have an intestinal condition or not, the inner lining of the gastrointestinal tract is tender and can be easily irritated by a sudden increase in fiber (especially the insoluble kind). Also make sure to drink plenty of warm or room-temperature water throughout the day to soften the fiber. Avoid very cold fluids because they can cause intestinal muscles to spasm, become immobile, or contract out of sync. If your symptoms improve or bowel movements become more frequent, softer, and easier to pass, then you can gradually increase your intake. If your symptoms worsen or you experience bloating or cramps, decrease your intake of fiber and/or increase your intake of fluids (especially warm water or herbal tea) throughout the day.

If you have a digestive illness, it's imperative that you know the quantity and type of fiber you can handle. You may need to make slight modifications to some recipes in the MTHI food plan to suit your tolerance. For example, some people are particularly sensitive to whole seeds, such as those found in berries, because unchewed seeds can be abrasive or get stuck in the folds of the intestine. If the digestive tract is inflamed and overwhelmed with rough fiber, then the valve separating the small and large intestines may swell. The result can be a nagging condition called ileocecal valve syndrome.

The ileocecal valve is located where the small and large intestines meet. It allows digested food to pass from the small intestine into the large intestine, and it blocks waste from backing into the small intestine. It's supposed to be a one-way valve. However, when it's stuck open (for example, if this area of the intestines becomes inflamed), waste products can remain in the small intestine, disturbing digestion and causing toxins to accumulate.

The underlying causes of ileocecal valve syndrome may be eating too much dietary fiber, dehydration, overeating, emotional distress, food allergens, and unchewed food. To recover from this syndrome, avoid the allergy-inducing and irritating foods outlined in the MTHI plan, such as alcohol, chocolate, coffee, refined sugar, and cayenne peppers. For some people, avoiding raw foods is necessary to help the valve recover because cooking softens plant fiber.

The medical profession may overlook ileocecal valve syndrome. If you have digestive symptoms that are relieved by avoiding the foods I listed, consider seeing a naturopath or a holistic nutritionist who can advise you how to adapt the MTHI plan to suit your needs. For fast pain relief, a chiropractor or osteopath can provide temporary relief from symptoms. Acupuncture treatments may help to correct the problem.

RELIEVING DIGESTIVE STRESS

Perhaps you don't suffer from ileocecal valve syndrome, but you may still experience occasional or frequent intestinal distress. How many times have we eaten and drunk so much that it actually hurt to move? The redefinition of indulgence starts with embracing the dictum we become what we eat. Brad J. King, a fitness and nutrition expert, explains, "We may be making food choices unconsciously in an effort to satisfy a need that is not tangible at the time." For that reason, we need to plan ahead in order to avoid cravings that may appear to be the body's cries for certain nutrients but are, in fact, false intuitions.

There are so many natural, healthy, and easy ways you can relieve the pain in your gut. Here's the simplest method: take your time when you're tasting your food. According to Leslie Beck, R.D., it's best to "chew foods thoroughly . . . poorly chewed foods are more difficult to digest and may lead to intestinal discomfort."

Chewing your food slowly also relaxes your entire nervous system so you won't be in "fight-or-flight" mode while you're eating. Chewing rapidly and swallowing quickly signals to your body that you're in a rush and have no time to eat (or digest) properly, or that you're anxious and nervous. Either way, you're stimulating your adrenals to secrete adrenaline. This hormone literally shuts down your digestion by shunting blood away from your gastrointestinal tract. Chewing thoroughly also helps you to enjoy flavors and avoid overeating. Keep your mind and your thoughts calm; eat in a relaxed and inviting environment.

Food temperature will also affect your digestion. Enzyme function is affected by temperature—some enzymes stop working at very

MODIFICATIONS TO THE MTHI PLAN

If you suffer from ileocecal valve syndrome, ankylosing spondylitis or any inflammatory bowel disease such as ulcerative colitis, diverticulitis or Crohn's disease, you'll have to make food modifications to the MTHI plan. I suggest you reduce or completely eliminate (depending on the severity of your condition) foods high in roughage: raw foods, nuts, seeds and whole grains. Eat fruits and vegetables lightly cooked to soften them and avoid swallowing inedible seeds such as those in berries, cucumber, grape, watermelon, tomato, pepper and eggplant (eat nightshade vegetables only after step three). You may need to avoid strawberries, raspberries, blueberries and related fruits in their whole form. By removing the seeds through a strainer, you may be able to enjoy the health benefits without their seeds. Eat soupy *dal* (split beans and peas with the outer skins removed) instead of whole legumes. Eliminate spicy foods and avoid stimulants such as alcohol, cocoa, and caffeine. Blending your food into a hearty soup may help improve your digestion, soothe your intestines and calm inflamed areas.

high or very low temperatures. Very hot foods and drinks can also scald your intestinal lining, making you vulnerable to pathogens and toxins, and to developing ulcers.

Ice-cold food and beverages can cause your intestinal muscles to spasm and cramp. This may either stimulate peristalsis (potentially causing diarrhea) or make the smooth wave-like action of peristalsis grind to a halt (contributing to gas and constipation).

FOODS THAT COMPLEMENT

Sometimes chewing well and eating warm foods isn't enough. You may need to pack digestive enzyme supplements the next time your family gets together for a potluck or buffet! Eating a mixture of different foods can overwhelm your enzyme reserves—a recipe for bloating and gas. If your stomach is sensitive, try to minimize your number of food choices in a single meal to enable your digestive organs to respond adequately. Try consuming ginger root, turmeric, or raw parsley with meals since these contain natural enzymes that can soothe an upset stomach. Eating a small serving of fresh ripe papaya or pineapple approximately one hour after a meal will also help support digestion, soothe inflammation, and promote peristalsis.

If you suffer digestive distress such as heartburn or nausea after a meal, or if you suffer from diarrhea, constipation, or ileocecal valve syndrome, then separating food types can help your body digest properly. By following the guidelines set out in the following chart, you can prevent unnecessary stress on your digestive system and allow your gut tissue to heal.

Here's how to use the chart:

• You can combine the foods listed under columns A and B.
• You can combine the foods listed under columns B and C.
• Don't combine the foods listed under A and C, unless you have excellent digestion. Even then, it's best to maintain awareness of food combinations to avoid straining your digestive organs too often. No one is superhuman, and every person's organs have different levels of tolerance.
• Avoid combining foods within column A in a single meal.

AVOID MIXING A AND C (UNLESS YOU HAVE EXCELLENT DIGESTION)	MIX ANYTHING FROM LIST A WITH LIST B	MIX ANYTHING FROM LIST B WITH LIST C
A	B	C
PROTEINS	NEUTRAL FOODS	STARCHES AND SUGARS
Beans	All leafy greens	Whole grains
Fish	Herbs	Starchy vegetables such as roots
Eggs	Nuts and seeds	Refined carbohydrates (sugar and flour)*
All poultry	Healthy oils	Best Eaten Alone
All red meats	Berries	Sweet fruits
Milk and milk products	Most (nonstarchy) vegetables	Sweet juices

* I don't recommend these foods, but I know that some people may still want to indulge in an occasional treat after they finish the MTHI plan.

FOOD-COMBINING SUCCESS TIPS

These food-combining guidelines aren't meant to be restrictive. Proportions are important—you may be able to occasionally tolerate combining a small serving of foods from column A with those from column C. Use your judgment and keep serving sizes within the limits of your digestive capacity. By keeping a food diary, you'll be able determine the best combinations for you.

Those with fairly healthy digestive systems may be able to handle bean and grain combinations. Many people also find that sweet potato or brown rice can be eaten with fish or poultry because they're all relatively easy to digest. Make sure to complement these meals with leafy green vegetables, herbs, and spices to support your digestion.

Some foods in column C are best eaten alone. Their high sugar content will decrease transit time through the intestines, affect enzyme function, and halt the proper digestion of other foods. Combining simple carbohydrates with other foods will promote putrefaction and yeast fermentation. Eat dessert (this includes sweet fruits) an hour or more after a meal to avoid indigestion.

If you have good digestion, I suggest that you combine carbohydrates with some form of protein, fat, or fiber to reduce the glycemic index of a food, especially when your blood sugar is low and you're reaching for a sweet snack. If you combine foods, you'll avoid an insulin spike; however, this trick comes at a cost. Proteins must churn in the stomach for one to five hours to be completely digested. Eating protein with fruits and sugary or floury foods can cause putrefaction, gas, and bloating because sugars can hinder protein digestibility by human enzymes. As your digestive health improves, your organ health improves, and this will allow you to bend these food-combining rules more in the future. For now, avoid eating refined flour and sugar at any time to maximize your healing potential. Berries are generally low in sugar, so they don't contribute to protein putrefaction the way other sweet fruits do. If you have weak digestion, eat berries alone as you would all other fruits.

If you have weak digestion, you may be producing too little stomach acid. Avoid eating foods such as ice cream, milk, yogurt, dairy, raw tomato, cucumber, melon, raw lettuce, seaweed, and cold beverages, as these will further reduce your production of hydrochloric acid and cause indigestion or irritable bowel.

To minimize bloating or gas, spice up your meals with anise or fennel seed, cinnamon, cumin, dill, and turmeric. These and other digestive herbs will stimulate the secretion of digestive juices, as well as settle upset stomachs. You can also drink a cup of peppermint, chamomile, ginger root, or dandelion tea 30 minutes after a meal for similar relief.

Avoid drinking ice-cold drinks during your meal. These will cramp your intestines and also decrease your enzyme power. Limit drinks to short sips for hydration during your meal. Drink a glass of warm or room-temperature water 10 to 15 minutes before a meal and 30 to 60 minutes after a meal to support secretion of gastric acid and digestive enzymes.

If you followed these guidelines and still have gas or nausea after a meal, look closely at the ingredients of what you just ate. Try to assess what you may be sensitive to and avoid it next time.

WRAP-UP

- The gut plays a large role in our immune system because 70 percent of our immune cells are located along the digestive lining.
- The health of your digestive lining (gut) determines which nutrients are absorbed and which toxins, allergens, and microbes are kept out. Poor digestion has been found to be the root cause of many diseases, ranging from allergies to arthritis, and acne to autoimmune disorders.
- Food allergens can cause damage to the gut lining and contribute to leaky gut. If the damage to your digestive lining is severe, the body cannot heal itself properly. Damage to the intestines makes it more likely that toxins and pathogens from the gut will penetrate the lining.
- If the body remains on hyperalert for a long period of time, the intestines don't have a chance or the right nutrients to heal properly, and your immune system will remain hypersensitive. As time goes on, you will have allergic reactions to more and more foods, chemicals, and environments; you may begin to feel pain, stiffness, or soreness in different parts of your body.

- Probiotics are the good bacteria that work like soldiers in the body. If their populations are strong, other microorganisms are relatively harmless living on the sidelines. When our probiotics are pushed out of their territory, we may suffer dysbiosis, infectious diarrhea, and vaginal yeast infections. Yeasts such as candida, and pathogenic bacteria such as various strains of *E. coli*, constantly vie for more living space in our bodies.
- Food poisoning is more common than you think. You may believe that you have the stomach flu when in fact, you have a mild form of foodborne infection, which is causing your stomach major distress.
- Inflammatory bowel disease patients will need to alter the MTHI plan to reduce the insoluble fiber and starch contained in some of the recipes. Sometimes chewing well and eating warm foods isn't enough. If you are experiencing an active flare-up, be sure to follow the food-combining guidelines on page 144.
- Major culprits that damage the gastrointestinal lining include:
  - low-fiber, high-sugar, processed diets
  - excess consumption of acidic and spicy foods
  - undetected gluten intolerance; celiac disease; or low-grade allergies to foods such as dairy, eggs, corn, soy, or nuts
  - yeasts, parasites, and pathogenic bacteria, including chronic low-grade infections and overgrowth of these microbes
  - heavy metals
  - stress

PART TWO

THE ANTI-INFLAMMATORY MENU PLAN

"The task ahead of us is never as great as the power behind us."

—RALPH WALDO EMERSON

CHAPTER 8

THE FIVE-STEP PLAN

The best way to understand the MTHI plan is to imagine being taken back in time to when everyone ate whole foods. Unlike fad diets, especially those that eliminate entire food groups such as carbohydrates or fats, this program simply asks you to eat as your ancestors did, before refined foods were formulated.

Just like a child taking his first steps, it's important to ease into an anti-inflammatory program—and when I say *ease,* I mean it. I know not everyone feels comfortable on a limited meal plan—after all, it's hard to resist a slice of chocolate cake at a birthday party! The purpose of the MTHI five-step plan is to guide you into a lifestyle shift as painlessly as possible. As you look through steps one to five, you'll notice that this program is safe to follow for the rest of your life, but you need to have your mind, body, and soul on board. Who knows? You might find that a treat sweetened with only raw honey will eventually satisfy your daily craving for jelly beans! If you're ready to start a new way of eating and living, the following step-by-step plan will help guide you on your healing path.

Note: I recommend that you get dietary clearance from a medical doctor (M.D.) or a naturopathic doctor (N.D.) before you start the program. The information in the MTHI plan is cutting-edge, and may be outside the knowledge base of some practitioners. If you don't feel comfortable with your practitioner, it truly is worth finding someone you'll feel more at ease with.

I also ask that you seek professional advice to get a diagnosis for whatever is causing your pain. You must know the root of your pain in order to heal yourself properly. A lot of people self-diagnose, but it's important to get a full medical examination, along with blood work, and to have your serious questions answered.

STEP ONE—GEARING UP

Duration: 2 weeks

I'm a firm believer in the importance of setting yourself up for success. You must prepare for a lifestyle shift before you undergo it—this will prevent you from being overwhelmed by new food choices. Here's a good example: the worst thing you can do after you've learned that you have heart disease is to stop eating regularly because you're at a loss as to what you should or shouldn't eat. As a nutritionist, I've had so many people in my office in tears because they didn't know what to eat!

It's important not to shock your body by going from one extreme diet to another. If you always eat burgers and fries and then try a dramatic fasting cleanse, you'll be disappointed—your system will fight the rapid change, sabotaging your efforts. Despite your best efforts, you could slip back into the habit of double-fisting pastries and bread after a week of strict cleansing.

A big part of this step is to psych yourself up. To do this effectively, clean out your kitchen cupboards. Yes, you heard me—just toss out the unhealthy items. Refer to the following charts to see which foods to keep, which to eliminate, and what you should replace these items with. And get rid of any items with ingredients that you don't understand, such as unpronounceable chemicals. Take up to two weeks to cut these foods out of your diet. To make things easier, start by eliminating the foods that you can part with easily so you don't feel like you're making an unbearable sacrifice in starting the MTHI plan.

Now, when I tell you to toss out your food, I don't necessarily mean for you to throw it in the garbage. If it's a healthy food that you may want to reintroduce after the eight weeks, then put it out of sight or on an upper shelf. If it's a refined food that's included on the red-light list of the Anti-Inflammatory Food Chart (p. 166), then it's time to get rid of it so you can make room for healing choices.

If you feel uncomfortable throwing away food, consider donating unopened food to a food bank. I don't expect you to give away your wine collection or toss the contents of your pantry; just remember to avoid consuming these items in the first eight weeks of the plan. Don't worry. We'll fill up the cupboard with tasty, nutritious alternatives—I promise!

Step one encourages you to try this plan for eight to ten weeks (which is equivalent to steps two and three combined). If you're going into this program without the right frame of mind (that is, if you don't faithfully follow the plan), you won't see enough of a difference to stick with it long-term and truly reap the benefits.

WHAT TO TOSS

ITEM	WHY TOSS IT?
ARTIFICIAL ADDITIVES	Get rid of any boxed or processed food that contains additives and preservatives, such as MSG (the full name is monosodium glutamate; related substances that may also cause reactions include autolyzed yeast and hydrolyzed vegetable protein); BHA (butylhydroxyanisole) and BHT (butylhydroxytoluene); food coloring (which may be listed by a complete name such as tartrazine or by a food dye and color number such as FD&C Yellow No. 5); glutamate; glutamic acid; parabens; sodium caseinate; and mineral oil. Many of these additives cause reactions including headaches and skin rashes.
SUGAR AND ARTIFICIAL SWEETENERS	These include aspartame (also an ingredient in Canderel, Equal, EqualSweet, and NutraSweet), acesulfame-K, glucose, high-fructose corn syrup, lactose, maltose, mannitol, raw sugar, sorbitol, sucrose, and turbinado sugar. These can all dampen immune system function and feed candida and other unfavorable yeasts in your digestive system. People with irritable bowel syndrome (IBS) and inflammatory bowel disorder (IBD) should stick to raw honey, as its peroxide content is beneficial in healing ulcers. Check the ingredients in chewable and liquid supplements to ensure they don't contain any of the sweeteners listed above.
MOLDY OR OLD FRUIT	Grapes, melons, raspberries, and strawberries harbor the highest amount of mold, so always keep them in the fridge. Avoid eating bananas and oranges until you know you're not sensitive to them. Candied fruit and prepared fruit juice are too concentrated with sugar, so it's best to eliminate them.
ALCOHOLIC BEVERAGES	Beer, spirits, and wine are laden with yeast and are hard on the liver, which is a key detoxifying organ in the body.
SOFT DRINKS AND CARBONATED BEVERAGES	Soft drinks can leach calcium out of bones. The effects of carbonated beverages on digestion are controversial. They are also full of refined sugar and synthetic additives, such as color, preservatives, and artificial sweeteners.
COMMERCIALLY SMOKED AND CURED MEATS	Bacon, corned beef, hotdogs, luncheon meat, and smoked fish contain nitrates, which are carcinogenic. Processed meats are also very high in table salt, which dehydrates the body and causes an imbalance between sodium and potassium. Dehydration contributes to inflammation.
WHITE VINEGAR AND VINEGAR-CONTAINING FOODS	Most refined vinegars are made from grains and can promote growth of candida yeast in the intestines or directly damage the intestines.
PROCESSED OIL PRODUCTS	Highly processed oils are often chemically extracted, exposed to high temperatures, bleached, and stripped of all valuable nutrients such as vitamin E. Commercial mayonnaise, fractionated vegetable oils, hydrogenated or partially hydrogenated vegetable oils, margarine, modified vegetable oils, vegetable shortening, and salad dressings made with sugar and refined oils should be avoided completely. The processing that turns liquid oils into semisolid fats creates trans-fats (see page 86), which increase inflammation. Avoid purchasing oils in plastic containers. Buy cold-pressed, unrefined oils in dark (black, brown, deep blue, green, or purple) glass bottles and store them in a cool, dark place.

ITEM	WHY TOSS IT?
COFFEE AND REGULAR BLACK TEA	The caffeine in tea and coffee stresses the adrenal glands, leaving many people with anxiety, increased sensitivity to stress, and insomnia. Stress is the greatest enemy of the immune system.
YEAST	Don't consume baker's yeast, brewer's yeast, or other foods prepared with an active yeast. Avoid all bread and pastries. If you have a candida infection, you may need to avoid nutritional yeast as well.
DAIRY	Eliminate butter, cheese (the worst kinds are moldy cheeses, such as blue cheese, and soft varieties, such as Brie), ice cream, milk, and yogurt. Toss prepared foods with dairy ingredients, such as macaroni and cheese. If you're lactose intolerant or allergic to casein, dairy can cause inflammation.
GLUTEN GRAINS	Avoid all barley, kamut, oats, rye, spelt, and wheat, as well as the flour made from these grains, including prepared foods such as bread, cereals, candy, malt, and pasta. Gluten is one of the proteins found in some grass grains that can be very difficult to digest and can cause many sensitivity symptoms, such as back and joint pain, dark circles under the eyes, IBS, and skin disorders. Oats and barley must be tested to ensure they're tolerated, as they contain some form of gluten.
PEANUTS AND RANCID NUTS OR SEEDS	Peanuts grow underground and are often high in mold. They can be potential allergens because mold aflatoxins are harmful to the liver and immune system. Rancid nuts and seeds contain damaged oils that promote inflammation.
CORN	Corn is a potential allergen. Avoid cereal, corn bread, corn chips, crackers, and other snack foods made from corn; dextrose-sweetened foods; and sweetened drinks made with high-fructose corn syrup.
NIGHTSHADE FAMILY VEGETABLES	Eggplants, peppers (including paprika, cayenne, and jalapeño), potatoes, tobacco, tomatillos, and tomatoes may cause inflammation because they contain alkaloids that can affect nerve-muscle function, digestion, and joint flexibility. Alkaloids are especially high in the nightshade leaves, unripe fruit such as green peppers and green tomatoes, and older potatoes. Tobacco is also a nightshade plant, so smokers may be more susceptible to a sensitivity. Goji berries are part of the nightshade family and may irritate people who are sensitive to alkaloids.
PROCESSED SOY PRODUCTS	Processed soy foods such as dairy and meat substitutes (including soy burgers, cheese, ice cream, mayonnaise, meat, milk, and yogurt), soy flour, textured vegetable protein (TVP), and tofu promote inflammation in people who are sensitive or allergic to soy. The processing methods involved in producing these products increase the possibility that a person's immune system will react to this otherwise nutritious bean.

WHAT TO KEEP/WHAT TO BUY

ITEM	WHAT TO KEEP/WHAT TO BUY
NATURAL SWEETENERS	Brown rice syrup, coconut syrup, honey (raw varieties for raw dishes and unpasteurized liquid forms for cooked dishes), tree sap syrups (for example, birch, maple, etc.), stevia (liquid extract or whole-leaf powder), and yacón syrup are some suitable sweeteners to help you transition into a sugar-free lifestyle.
VARIETY OF HEALTHY OILS	Buy unrefined, cold-pressed oils in glass jars. For hot dishes and low-temperature cooking, use avocado, coconut, extra-virgin olive, grape seed, mustard seed, or sesame seed oil. For raw dressings and cool dishes, use omega-3-rich oils cold-pressed from algae, fish flesh or liver, seeds (chia, flax, hemp, perilla, pumpkin, and sacha inchi), and walnuts. After eight weeks on the MTHI plan, organic butter and ghee (clarified butter) are healthy choices when eaten in moderation for people who aren't sensitive or allergic to dairy.
FRESH VEGETABLES	Focus 50 percent of your diet on bright colors and dark green vegetables (aim for 7–10 servings a day). Eat as many low-starch greens as possible, such as broccoli, cabbage, celery, celery root, chard, dandelion, fresh herbs, kale, radish, snap pea, and zucchini. Choose beet root, carrot, Jerusalem artichoke (also called sunroot or sunchoke), kudzu root, sweet potato, taro, winter squashes, and yam as substitutes for white potatoes. If you have IBS or IBD, it's best to cook vegetables until they're tender.
DAIRY ALTERNATIVES	Use unsweetened almond milk, brown rice milk, hemp seed milk, and small amounts of coconut milk.
GLUTEN-FREE GRAINS	Amaranth, buckwheat, Job's tears, millet, quinoa, sorghum, teff, whole rice (black, brown, red, etc.), and wild rice are safe gluten-free seeds and grains. Rotate a different grain each day to avoid developing an allergy. Note: Some people are sensitive to all grains, so keep track of how you feel when you eat from this list.
MEAT	Consume free-range or organic chicken, eco-friendly fish (anchovy, Arctic char, barramundi, sardine, spring trout, tilapia, and wild line–caught Pacific salmon), emu, lamb, turkey, and wild game.
NUTS AND SEEDS	Eat fresh almond, Brazil nut, filbert (also known as hazelnut), macadamia, pecan, and walnut, as well as chia, flax, hemp, pumpkin, sesame, and sunflower seeds. Nut and seed butters are also great choices. (Those made from raw nuts and seeds are healthier than those made from toasted ingredients.)
BEANS AND LEGUMES	Adzuki, black, garbanzo (chickpea), red and white kidney, lima, mung, navy, and turtle beans, as well as lentils and peas, are good sources of protein and fiber. Soy can be eaten safely as edamame (young soybeans) or as a fermented food (examples include miso, natto, wheat-free tamari sauce, and tempeh).
SALAD DRESSING ALTERNATIVES	Lemon and lime juices make good substitutes for white vinegar. Unpasteurized apple cider vinegar sold in a glass bottle has health-promoting qualities and can be used if yeast isn't a serious concern. Unrefined organic brown rice, fruit, red wine, and umeboshi plum vinegars contain antioxidants. Avoid conventional balsamic vinegar because it contains added sugar. Enjoy lots of fresh garlic for its antifungal qualities. Experiment with herbs and spices for adding flavor.

Q AND A

Q. When on a budget, what types of fruits and vegetables are the most important to buy organically?

A. The following information was compiled by analysts from the Environmental Working Group (EWG). It's based on the results of 43,000 tests that were conducted to assess the levels of pesticides found in produce. Nearly all the data used to create these lists consider how people typically wash and prepare produce (for example, apples were washed before testing). While washing and rinsing may reduce levels of some pesticides, it doesn't eliminate them. Peeling reduces exposure, but valuable nutrients often go down the drain with the peel. The best option is to eat a varied diet, wash all produce, and choose organic, when possible, to reduce exposure to harmful chemicals. Washing fruits and vegetables with a vegetable wash, diluted vinegar, or food-grade hydrogen peroxide can help remove some toxic residues. When shopping for dried fruits, try to buy organically grown ones because you won't be able to wash these the same way you can wash fresh produce. Foods high in pesticides are listed from the most to the least contaminated, and foods low in pesticides are listed from the least to the most contaminated.

CONVENTIONAL PRODUCE GUIDE

HIGH IN PESTICIDES	LOW IN PESTICIDES
• Apples • Celery • Strawberries • Peaches • Spinach • Nectarines (imported) • Grapes (imported) • Sweet bell peppers • Potatoes • Blueberries (domestic) • Lettuce • Kale • Collard greens • Summer squash	• Onions • Sweet corn • Pineapples • Avocado • Asparagus • Sweet peas • Mangoes • Eggplant • Cantaloupe • Kiwi fruit • Cabbage • Watermelon • Sweet potatoes • Grapefruit • Mushrooms

Source: Environmental Working Group

STEP TWO—ELIMINATING PAIN TRIGGERS

Duration: 2 weeks

Now we're going to transition into a foods elimination agenda. The average time it takes to complete step two is about two weeks, but give yourself more time if necessary. You'll be cutting out refined food (white sugar, white flour, deep-fried food, and harmful fats), which will start to balance your blood sugar levels.

Most refined foods congest the body because of their lack of fiber and nutrients. Did you know that the average person in North America eats his or her weight in sugar a year? The U.S. Department of Agriculture states that this is equivalent to consuming 156 pounds of high-fructose corn syrup and white sugar in the form of breakfast cereals, ketchup, soft drinks, and cookies.

ELIMINATION SCHEDULE

DAYS 1 TO 5	DAYS 6 TO 10	DAYS 11 TO 14
Cut out fried foods, margarine, vegetable shortening, and hydrogenated or partially hydrogenated vegetable oils.	Cut out corn and corn products, such as breads, cereals, chips, crackers, muffins, nachos, tacos, tortillas, and other snack foods; avoid corn-based ingredients such as foods and drinks sweetened with dextrose or high-fructose corn syrup or soups and sauces containing corn starch.	Temporarily avoid foods that are potential allergy/inflammation triggers to figure out whether or not you're sensitive to them.
Avoid processed foods that contain food coloring and preservatives.		First eliminate the nightshade family plants (eggplant, pepper, potato, tobacco, and tomato), then peanuts, unfermented soy, and then the rest of the gluten grains.
Cut out sugar and other sweeteners, including aspartame and related sweeteners, brown sugar, cane juice, cane sugar, fructose, glucose, lactose, malt, maltose, mannitol, raw sugar, sorbitol, Sucanat, sucrose, Sweet'N Low, turbinado sugar, white sugar, yellow sugar, and candy.	Cut out wheat products, such as couscous, wheat bread, pasta, and prepared cereals.	You'll also have to avoid bananas and oranges because they're common allergens. Remember, you'll be able to test all these foods after the elimination phase is complete.
	Eliminate butter, cheese, ice cream, milk, and yogurt.	
	Eliminate alcoholic beverages, including beer, all hard liquors, and wine.	

Avoiding refined foods is the most important step you can take. To begin substituting these refined products, eat the foods you've added to your cupboard in step one and increase your daily servings of fruits and vegetables.

Aim for three fruits and seven to ten vegetable servings a day. If that sounds like too many fruits and vegetables, think again. For example, one medium carrot is equal to one serving. If you have one carrot as a snack and one celery stalk and a 2–cup (500 mL) bowl of salad as part of your lunch, then that's four servings right there. Photocopy the following table and tape it onto your fridge. This will help you determine your serving sizes as you work through step two.

FOOD SERVING GUIDE

FOOD TO MEASURE	EXAMPLE OF A SERVING	WHAT IT LOOKS LIKE
A serving of vegetables	½ cup (120 mL) broccoli	Your fist
All leafy greens	1 cup (240 mL) salad	Coffee mug
Meat, poultry, fish, or vegetarian protein	3 ounces (85 g) salmon	Deck of cards
Legumes	¾ cup (180 mL) lentils	A heaping handful
Nuts and seeds	¼ cup (60 mL) almonds	Golf ball
Pasta, rice, and cereal	¼ cup (60 mL) pasta	Lightbulb
Yogurt	¾ cup (180 mL) yogurt	Teacup
Fruit	½ cup (125 mL) berries	Baseball
Oils and fats	1 tbsp (15 mL)	Thumb tip (tip to first knuckle)

It's important to eliminate dairy in the first phase of the MTHI plan because you need to determine whether or not you're allergic to it. Don't be concerned about the lack of dietary calcium from dairy sources during these eight weeks. Fresh leafy greens, fish, nuts, sea vegetables, and seeds are excellent sources of calcium.

As you continue with this process, don't be embarrassed to literally say good-bye to unhealthy foods—talk to them, stare at them, do what you have to do! Changing your eating habits is like quitting smoking. Food is a comfort, and it can be a close friend if nothing else is working. Trust me, I know how you feel. For me, it was really hard to say good-bye to movie popcorn. As a child, I would get dropped off at the movie theater and spend hours engrossed in *Star Wars* characters while eating buckets of popcorn. Later on in life I connected joy with escape and popcorn. I got over my movie popcorn obsession by crumbling rice cakes (they have the same texture as popcorn without the jagged edges that may irritate tender intestinal tissues) and drizzling them with healthy oil, like spice-infused extra-virgin olive oil. Then I added some sea salt, a splash of apple cider vinegar, and dried dill, and presto—an easy-to-digest and satisfying movie snack was born!

Becoming creative with your food is important during this transition. Use the recipes in this book to experiment and create your own versions of your family favorites using healthier alternatives.

STEP THREE—STAYING THE COURSE

Duration: 8 weeks

This step is all about sticking to the plan on a physical and emotional level. For the next eight weeks (while using the recipes in this book), eat five times a day: three meals and two snacks, making sure to eat at least seven to ten servings of vegetables. If you think this is going to take too much time, take one day of the week to prepare a lot of your foods and snacks. Then freeze them so that they'll keep for the week. Think of it this way—you won't have to cook for the rest of the week! Make sure your grocery shopping list is always consistent with the MTHI plan. Check out the Anti-Inflammatory Food Chart on page 166. Photocopy it and post it on your fridge for quick reference.

To help keep you on track, organize a shelf of healing snacks so you know where to look for a quick bite. Always carry a snack with you, as this will help keep your blood sugar level stable. Feel free to stash some ready-made snacks in your briefcase, purse, work desk drawer, or glove box of your car. This provides you with a healthy alternative to fast food, or candy from vending machines. Challenge your taste buds with my recommended snack choices:

- Fresh fruit such as apples, pears, or blueberries

- Raw vegetable sticks such as celery, carrot, cucumber, and zucchini or fresh snap peas

- Flavored nori seaweed (found in Asian grocery stores or health-food stores; make sure it doesn't contain MSG or sugar)

- Whole-grain gluten-free crackers (baked and sugar-free)

- Dried apricots, figs, dates, and dried cranberries (apple juice sweetened); limit this snack to a few pieces of fruit to avoid blood sugar spikes and make sure the fruit isn't sprayed with sulfur

- One handful of almonds, Brazil nuts, hazelnuts, macadamia nuts, pecans, or walnuts (note: discontinue eating these if you begin to cough or have an itchy throat or mouth, chest or throat tightness, or a rash after eating)

- Honey-sweetened snack bars made with raw sesame, chia, flax, sunflower, or pumpkin seeds

- Trail mix with your favorite dried fruits (no sugar added), nuts, and seeds (try mixing 1 ounce [30 g] each of hemp seeds, dried apple-juice-sweetened cranberries, pumpkin seeds, and hazelnuts)

As you approach step four, I highly recommend you work with an allergist or naturopathic doctor who focuses on allergy testing. Allergy testing could identify any additional offending foods that might limit your progress. If you suffer from inflammatory bowel disease (IBD), your symptoms may not subside on this program. Results vary by individual, but most high-fiber carbohydrates such as whole grains and raw vegetables, simple carbohydrates such as starchy bread, and whole nuts or seeds can cause problems. During a flare-up, I suggest you support digestion by cooking foods thoroughly, pureeing everything possible, eating warm soups, and avoiding large or heavy meals.

Some people with severe digestive inflammation (for instance, patients with ulcerative colitis or Crohn's disease) may find that the menu in this book isn't strict enough. You may want to consider the Specific Carbohydrate Diet™. It's restrictive, but some people have experienced remarkable relief from their symptoms. (For more information, please read *Breaking the Vicious Cycle* by Elaine Gottschall or *Gut and Psychology Syndrome Book* by Dr. Natasha Campbell-McBride.)

Note: You should never move on from step three by bingeing on the foods you haven't eaten for a while, since you'll experience severe repercussions! Doing so will overwhelm your body with foods that you may be allergic to. As you've learned from Chapter 3, exposing your body to allergens can be very destructive and cause a lot of cell and tissue damage. When you begin to remove allergens and chemical-laden processed foods from your diet, your body has the chance to detoxify and repair tissues. However, both of these important healing steps take time. If you shock your body with a large and unexpected load of offending foods, you'll arrest your healing process and overburden your detoxifying organs.

SUCCESS TIPS FOR STEP THREE

If you have healthy digestive function, avoid eating carbohydrates on their own. Pair a starchy or sweet food with one of the following: fat (for example, nut butter with rice crackers), protein (beef with brown rice noodles), or fiber (flax seeds baked into a whole-grain flatbread or cracker). Fats, protein, and fiber all help slow down the absorption of sugars (simple carbohydrates), thereby keeping your blood sugar balanced.

Take probiotics. Many forms of inflammation begin in the digestive tract. A probiotic supplement such as acidophilus can help restore balance to this system and allow for the proper absorption of nutrients (see page 128 for more information on friendly intestinal bacteria).

Mix it up. Your body may tag common foods as allergens, so eat something different every day to avoid exacerbating allergies and to keep your meals interesting. You could also develop nutritional deficiencies if you limit your diet too strictly.

STEP FOUR—TIME TO TEST

Duration: 12 weeks

In step four we're testing foods we haven't eaten for a while, and we do this by reintroducing one new test food at a time. I think this is the hardest step because you'll want to jump back into the foods you've missed. Why are we doing this? We're figuring out which foods make us feel unwell after we've eaten them. Essentially, this is all about getting to know your body better.

Start with the healthiest foods. Bananas, oranges, red peppers, and tomatoes are good choices because they're full of nutrients. If you can tolerate cooked tomatoes, your menu items will expand widely because many world cuisines use tomatoes in their dishes. Bananas can be used to thicken and sweeten shakes and baked dishes.

After you've experimented with vegetables and fruits, try cultured dairy. Goat and sheep yogurt or live-cultured soft goat cheese can help provide the digestive tract with probiotic bacteria, which knock out problematic yeast overgrowth. Studies have shown that milk and dairy foods from small animals such as sheep or goats can help heal the digestive tract because they're easier to digest than cow's milk. At first, avoid milk from cows and high-fat cheeses because they're difficult to digest and contain certain fats that can trigger inflammation.

If you try gluten grains, reintroduce oats (which are technically free of wheat gluten if they're processed in a separate gluten-free facility), then barley and rye, as they're also relatively low in gluten. Spelt and kamut are close relatives to wheat and contain high amounts of gluten. To keep your joints mobile, reduce the amount of gluten in your diet whenever possible.

It's important for you to stay committed to step four for the full 12 weeks because it can take up to seventy-two hours to have an allergic reaction, and you need at least four days between separate food tests. This is why you need to give your body a rest after you've tested a food. The following schedule is the classic guide recommended by health practitioners for reintroducing foods.

FOOD REINTRODUCTION TESTING SCHEDULE

DAY 1	DAY 2	DAY 3	DAY 4	DAY 5	DAY 6	DAY 7	DAY 8	DAY 9
Eat 3 portions* of one test food	Avoid test food	Avoid test food	Avoid test food	Eat 3 portions* of one test food	Avoid test food	Avoid test food	Eat 3 portions* of one test food	If no negative reaction, test next food

*For portion sizes, see Food Serving Guide on page 158.

FOOD TESTING GUIDE

TYPE OF FOOD	WHEN TO REINTRODUCE	SYMPTOMS TO WATCH OUT FOR
Banana (ripe)	After 8 weeks	Hives, bowel problems
Tangerine/orange/grapefruit	After 9.5 weeks	Hives, rashes, stomach pain
Tomatoes (cooked, then raw)	After 11 weeks	Rashes, joint and stomach pain
Red peppers	After 12.5 weeks	Rashes, joint and stomach pain
Sheep yogurt and cheese	After 14 weeks	Sinus problems, dark circles under eyes
Goat yogurt and cheese	After 15.5 weeks	Sinus problems, dark circles under eyes
Ghee (clarified cow butter)	After 17 weeks	Blackheads
Mussels (eco-harvested)	After 18.5 weeks	Throat itchiness, rashes
Oats	After 20 weeks	Joint pain, fatigue, brain fog

As you reintroduce food, you might notice some physical changes, such as congestion; dark circles under your eyes; fatigue; hives; or an infection in your ears, nose, or throat. These are typical signs of an allergic reaction to food. The table above lists common symptoms that may occur when you're testing foods. This will help you identify potential food allergies, intolerances, or sensitivities. Keep in mind that it's possible to experience almost any symptom with any allergen. The reaction you experience will depend on your body, the food you're allergic to, and how strongly your body reacts to the allergen. Use the food journal provided on page 208 to keep track of what you eat, and record any symptoms that are out of the ordinary. Stop eating a food once you've confirmed that you're sensitive or allergic to it, and keep it on your list of foods to avoid for three to six months; then test it again.

STEP FIVE—BETTER CHOICES EVERY DAY
Duration: A lifetime

This is the beginning of a lifelong change. Here, you're learning how to make the MTHI plan a way of life and a daily commitment. Even if you come to the decision that this isn't the plan for you, by now I hope you're making better choices in your daily nutrition. For example, the MTHI plan might influence you to substitute sweet potatoes or yams for white potatoes more often than you did before. This is why I encourage you to keep a food journal, as it's a written record of the progress and changes you have made over time.

Aside from making you healthier, step five is about pushing the boundaries in the fight against inflammation. Don't be shy—let people know why you're on the MTHI plan. By encouraging your loved ones to join you in making healing food choices, together you can embark on a lifetime commitment to eating healthier.

QUICK TIP

Buy certified organic foods whenever possible. Organic foods don't contain pesticides, antibiotics, or hormone residues. Also, organic farming practices produce richer soil, resulting in higher vitamin and mineral content in the food. According to a March 2008 report by the Organic Center, a team of scientists concluded that organically grown plant-based foods have on average 25 percent more nutrients than conventionally grown plants.

WRAP-UP

- We need to make gradual dietary changes to avoid the typical "diet mentality," which can sabotage lifelong changes.
- It is important to get emotionally on board for the MTHI plan. The MTHI plan is broken down into five easy steps to help you gradually attain the state of health you deserve.
- In order for you to be successful in your new approach to living and eating, the first step is to replace refined and processed foods with healthier options (choosing organic whenever possible), and to remove the unhealthy foods that were once psychologically comforting.
- Change your diet slowly. Step two helps you gradually cut out refined foods over a fourteen-day period.
- Stick to step three, which includes avoiding refined food and potential allergens, for at least eight weeks. By using the recipes in this book, you can replace these foods with healthy substitutions to create tasty dishes.
- In step four, reintroduce the nutritious whole foods that you eliminated, such as dairy and tomatoes, to determine whether or not you are sensitive or allergic to them.
- Step five involves permanently incorporating your new way of eating and living into each day. Share the MTHI plan with others. By encouraging your loved ones to join you in the fight against inflammation, your healing food choices can become a lifetime commitment to eating healthier.

CHAPTER 9

THE ANTI-INFLAMMATORY FOOD CHART AND THE ANTI-INFLAMMATORY FOOD PYRAMID

The Anti-Inflammatory Food Chart

The following chart is organized into three columns to guide you in selecting foods while on the MTHI plan. This guide can also help you readjust your diet and lifestyle choices even after you complete the MTHI plan.

Green Light: These foods are generally healing and, unless you have an allergy or sensitivity to them, they can be eaten freely.

Yellow Light: These foods are more likely than green-light foods to cause allergic reactions, especially in people who tend to suffer from multiple sensitivities or inflammatory conditions. One of the easiest ways to determine whether these foods are healing or hurting you is to eliminate them completely from your diet for eight weeks. Then, slowly reintroduce them one at a time to assess how your body reacts.

Refer to page 163 for guidance on how to gradually and safely reintroduce test foods.

Red Light: Refined and processed foods or additives are highly inflammatory and should be eliminated from your diet completely and permanently. Other red-light foods are common allergens that can worsen inflammatory or sensitive conditions. These foods should be avoided for as long as possible to allow the body to heal from chronic inflammation. Follow the green healing food guidelines to replace red hurting foods.

VEGETABLES

GREEN LIGHT (HEALING)	WHAT TO DO	YELLOW LIGHT (CAUTION)
Most vegetables are healing. Artichokes, celery, cucumber, cruciferous vegetables (for example, broccoli, cabbage, collard, kale, and rapini), leafy greens, root vegetables, and squashes are excellent options. Sea vegetables (for example, dulse, nori, and wakame) are excellent sources of minerals, vitamins, essential fats, and phytonutrients.	Enjoy ripe, organic vegetables as fresh and whole as possible: raw, steamed, boiled, broiled, baked, or sautéed. Eat different-colored vegetables at every meal. Colors represent various nutrients and antioxidants (for example, chlorophyll in green kale and beta-carotene in orange yams). People who suffer from IBD may be sensitive to the high-fiber content of sea vegetables. Eat dried (flaked or powdered) sea vegetables in moderation to avoid intestinal inflammation. Thoroughly soak and soften large pieces of dry sea vegetables before eating them.	Nightshade vegetables (eggplant, hot and sweet peppers, white potato, and tomato) can be inflammatory because they contain certain alkaloids that can affect nerve-muscle function, digestion, and joint flexibility in animals and humans. Nightshade alkaloids are especially high in leaves, unripe fruit such as green tomatoes, and older potatoes. Tobacco is also a nightshade plant, so smokers may be more susceptible to a sensitivity. Corn is a common allergen and is best avoided until you know that you don't react to it.

FRUITS

GREEN LIGHT (HEALING)	WHAT TO DO	YELLOW LIGHT (CAUTION)
Most fruits are healing because they're high in minerals, vitamins, antioxidants, and fiber.	Eat organic fresh and raw fruit. Eat dried and cooked fruits in moderation. Soak dried fruits until they're plump to increase digestibility. Avoid using additional sweeteners on fruit. Choose fruits that are low in sugar, such as apple, apricot, avocado, berries, cherry, dragon fruit, fig, litchi, mangosteen, passion fruit, peach, pear, plum, pomegranate, and prune. Pineapple and papaya are good choices because they're high in the anti-inflammatory enzymes bromelain and papain, respectively. Lemon and lime support digestion, boost liver detoxification, and are natural antihistamines.	Bananas and oranges are commonly overconsumed and may cause intestinal irritation for people who are sensitive to them. Avoid these fruits unless you tolerate them well. Goji berries are part of the nightshade family and may irritate people who are sensitive to nightshade alkaloids. IBD patients should use caution when eating fruits that contain many small seeds such as berries and figs. Some IBS and IBD patients are sensitive to raw fruits. If you're prone to food-induced hives, some fruits can trigger a reaction.

WHAT TO DO	RED LIGHT (HURTING)
Avoid nightshade vegetables for 8 weeks during step three, and then reintroduce them one at a time to see if you're sensitive to them. Substitute celery root, sweet potato, taro, or yam for white potato. These substitutes aren't members of the nightshade family and contain more fiber than white potatoes. Substitute whole grains like Job's tears for corn. Avoid popcorn if you have digestive issues because the hard kernels are difficult to digest. Popped amaranth or quinoa makes a good substitute.	Steer clear of all processed and fried vegetables, such as corn chips, corn nuts, French fries, fried eggplant, potato chips, onion rings, and tempura. Avoid green, old, raw, or sprouted potatoes, as these are especially high in the inflammatory alkaloid solanine. Avoid all genetically modified (GM) vegetables (corn, potato, sugar beet, and zucchini).

WHAT TO DO	RED LIGHT (HURTING)
Avoid bananas and oranges for 8 weeks during step three, and then reintroduce them individually to test your sensitivity. If you aren't sensitive to nightshades, goji berries are highly nutritious. If you have IBD, strain fruits to avoid ingesting seeds. Small seeds may irritate inflamed intestines. Cook, and if necessary peel, fruits to soften the fiber. Some fruits such as avocado, banana, fig, and red plum contain biogenic amines that can trigger hives. If you suffer from hives, journal your reactions and avoid all offending fruits.	Avoid all genetically modified (GM) fruits such as papaya from China and Hawaii. Avoid canned fruit, especially those preserved in syrup, as well as fruit chutneys, jams, jellies, and sauces made with refined sugar.

GRAINS AND BEANS

GREEN LIGHT (HEALING)	WHAT TO DO	YELLOW LIGHT (CAUTION)
Choose gluten-free grains and pseudo-grains,[1] such as amaranth, buckwheat, kasha, Job's tears, millet, quinoa, whole rice, sorghum, teff, and wild rice. Organic beans/legumes are healthy choices unless you have an allergy or sensitivity.	Eat whole, well-cooked grains. Substitute other grains for wheat. Try teff or quinoa porridge and wild rice pilaf. Crackers and pasta made from these grains are also suitable, but should be eaten in moderation. Try lentil soup, mung bean curry, adzuki bean salad, and chickpea hummus. Bean pasta is a high-protein, gluten-free option. Eat legumes well cooked, moist, and warm to increase digestibility and minimize bloating and gas.	Gluten grains (barley, kamut, oats, rye, and spelt) may cause inflammation, even in people who may not be aware of their sensitivity to gluten.[2] Grains and legumes may be unsuitable for some IBD patients. It's best to rotate soybeans in your diet to avoid having an allergic reaction or developing a soy allergy.

FISH AND SHELLFISH

GREEN LIGHT (HEALING)	WHAT TO DO	YELLOW LIGHT (CAUTION)
Select sustainably caught fresh or frozen fish. Check the www.seachoice.org fish list to help you make an informed choice.	Eat small fish (which are shorter lived and lower on the food chain than large species) to minimize exposure to heavy metals. Choose anchovies, butterfish, herring, mackerel, sablefish, sardine, trout, or wild Pacific salmon as sources of anti-inflammatory omega-3 fats. Edible jellyfish are an excellent and ecologically sustainable source of protein.	Canned fish are heated at extremely high temperatures for sterilization and may contain plastic toxins that leach out of the can. Clams, crab, lobster, mussels, oysters, and shrimp are common allergens and may contribute to inflammation. Some farmed fish, such as catfish and tilapia, contain high levels of the pro-inflammatory fat arachidonic acid.

MEAT

GREEN LIGHT (HEALING)	WHAT TO DO	YELLOW LIGHT (CAUTION)
Healthy meat choices include bison, buffalo, lamb, llama, poultry (for example, chicken, duck, emu, ostrich, pheasant, quail, and rhea), rabbit, and wild game (for example, caribou, deer, elk, and moose).	Ensure meat is from free-range or organically raised and ethically treated animals. Choose lean cuts to reduce inflammatory fats.	Eat grass-fed beef and grass-fed pork in moderation.

1. A pseudo-grain or pseudo-cereal is a seed that's derived from a plant that isn't a true cereal grass. Pseudo-grains and pseudo-cereals are gluten free. Unlike other seeds, pseudo-grains require cooking.

2. In the United States, 1 in every 133 people has celiac disease, which causes a powerful allergic reaction to gluten.

WHAT TO DO	RED LIGHT (HURTING)
Avoid eating all gluten grains for 8 weeks during step three. Then reintroduce them, as whole grains, one at a time. After the trial, eat sprouted whole-grain bread in moderation.	Wheat is a common allergen. Avoid this grain as much as possible.
Avoid all grains, legumes, and their derivatives if you have grain- or legume-sensitive IBD.	Avoid all processed and refined grains, flour, and commercially baked foods.
Eat only organic (non-GM) soy if you have no sensitivity or allergy to it. Choose steamed young soybeans (called edamame) or fermented soy foods such as miso, natto, tempeh, and wheat-free tamari sauce.	Soybeans are so widely used in foods, beverages, and supplements that many people have developed soy allergies. Eating processed soy products will increase your risk of an allergic reaction.
	Avoid genetically modified (GM) soy and processed soy products such as soy cheese, soy burgers, and texturized vegetable protein (TVP).

WHAT TO DO	RED LIGHT (HURTING)
When fresh or frozen fish isn't available, substitute with low-sodium canned varieties. Make sure they are packed in water and are sustainably caught.	Large fish such as shark, tuna, and orange roughy aren't harvested sustainably and contain higher levels of contaminants such as mercury.
Avoid all shellfish for 8 weeks during step three. Then introduce one species at a time to see if you can tolerate it.	Mercury and other toxins can affect your nervous and immune systems and increase inflammation.
Choose omega-3-rich, sustainably caught coldwater fish over farmed fish to minimize dietary arachidonic acid intake.	

WHAT TO DO	RED LIGHT (HURTING)
Beef and pork can be inflammatory because they're potential allergens and many cuts are high in inflammatory arachidonic acid.	Avoid conventional beef, chicken, and pork (especially bacon) because they contain antibiotics and hormone residues.
	Avoid processed, smoked, and deli meats, as they usually contain carcinogenic nitrate preservatives.

DAIRY AND EGGS

GREEN LIGHT (HEALING)	WHAT TO DO	YELLOW LIGHT (CAUTION)
Most plant-based milks make suitable dairy substitutes. These are most often fortified with vitamins and minerals and can be nutritious additions to a vegan diet. Organic eggs are an excellent source of lecithin, protein, B vitamins, and minerals such as the antioxidant selenium.	Try drinking almond, hemp seed, rice, or sesame seed milk. Choose unsweetened varieties whenever possible or make your own. For a cream substitute, use diluted coconut milk in moderation. Poultry fed omega-3-rich seeds will produce eggs high in these anti-inflammatory fats. To avoid developing an allergy to chicken eggs, rotate the type of egg you eat. Try eggs from organically fed and hormone-free duck, emu, ostrich, pheasant, and quail.	Dairy is a common allergen. Milk fermented with probiotics (good bacteria) can be very nutritious and can reduce your chances of experiencing a reaction. Goat and sheep milks are easier to digest than cow milk. Conventional eggs are a common allergen.

SEASONINGS

GREEN LIGHT (HEALING)	WHAT TO DO	YELLOW LIGHT (CAUTION)
Almost all fresh herbs and spices are safe and anti-inflammatory, provided you don't have an allergy to them.	Use anti-inflammatory seasonings generously, including anise seed, basil, bay leaf, caraway seed, cardamom seed, celery seed, cilantro, cinnamon bark, clove, coriander seed, cumin seed, dill seed and leaf, fennel seed, fenugreek seed, garlic, ginger root, marjoram, mustard seed, oregano, nutmeg, parsley, rosemary, sage, savory, star anise, thyme, and turmeric.	Spicy and pungent peppers such as cayenne, chili, jalapeño, paprika, and Scotch bonnets are nightshade plants and therefore contain alkaloids that may cause intestinal inflammation or exacerbate arthritis and heart-burn/acid reflux. Black and white peppercorns may irritate the intestinal lining.

THE ANTI-INFLAMMATORY FOOD PYRAMID

HEALTHY TREATS
Servings: Occasional

SUPPLEMENTS
Servings: Daily

PROTEIN
Total Servings: 3–4 per day;
eat the following sources to meet
your protein dietary needs:

MEAT, EGGS & DAIRY
Servings: 0–2 per day

FISH
Servings: 2–6 per week

NUTS & SEEDS
(both are sources of protein and fat)
Servings: 1–3 per day

BEANS & LEGUMES
(both are sources of carbohydrate and protein)
Servings: 2–3 per day

GREEN OR HERBAL TEA
Servings: 2–4 cups per day

HEALTHY FATS & OILS
Servings: 3–5 per day

WHOLE GRAINS
Servings: 3–6 a day

FRUITS
Servings: 2–4 per day

VEGETABLES
(includes sea vegetables)
Servings: 7–10 per day

HEALTHY HERBS & SPICES
Servings: Use Generously

WATER
Servings: 6–12 per day

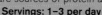

Amaranth Porridge, page 240

Jake's Muffin Max,
page 243

Apple Rice Bake, page 245

Vegetable Miso Soup,
page 259

Ginger Butternut Soup, page 263

Beet the Detox Salad, page 270

Raw Pad Thai, page 305

Kale Salad,
page 282

A Tale of Two Curries,
page 312

Collard Wraps, page 300

WHAT TO DO	RED LIGHT (HURTING)
After avoiding dairy for 8 weeks in step three, reintroduce organic goat or sheep yogurts to see if you can tolerate them. Then try organic cow dairy in moderation. Then gradually introduce cheese. Eat it in moderation or avoid it altogether. Choose varieties that are low in lactose (old Cheddar, Parmigiano-Reggiano, and Frugal) and are mold-free (cottage cheese and quark). Stick with organic eggs, and eat only a few times a week and monitor if you react to them.	Conventional dairy can be a source of xenoestrogens, antibiotics, and synthetic growth hormones.[3] Avoid processed dairy, such as ice cream that's high in saturated or trans-fats and loaded with refined sugar, artificial flavors, and artificial colors.[4] Moldy cheeses (blue, Brie, Camembert, and Gorgonzola) may contain high amounts of mold toxins that could elicit inflammatory reactions in some people. Steer clear of these cheeses, especially if you have a sensitivity to yeasts and molds.

WHAT TO DO	RED LIGHT (HURTING)
Season your food with cayenne-free curry spice blends for that flavor kick. Pungent spices such as clove, garlic, ginger, mustard, and turmeric are anti-inflammatory. Substitute black pepper with an anti-inflammatory blend of finely ground papaya and onion seeds.	In high concentrations, monosodium glutamate (MSG) is an excitatory neurotoxin that can cause chronic stimulation or death of nerve cells, including brain cells. People may experience side effects such as severe headache and irritability from exposure to MSG.[5] Artificial preservatives, sweeteners, colors, and flavoring may cause sensitivity reactions and are generally toxic to the body. Avoid all products containing artificial flavoring and other additives (including preservatives).

3. Recombinant bovine growth hormone (rBGH) isn't legally approved for use in the Canadian dairy industry. However, it's commonly injected into conventional dairy cows in the United States, and these hormone–containing dairy products are freely sold across Canada. Antibiotics are administered to conventionally raised cows in both Canada and the United States.

4. Cow's milk naturally contains small amounts of trans-fats. However, many dairy products such as ice cream may contain additional processed oils such as hydrogenated fats, which increase the amount of trans-fats present in the final product.

5. Avoid isolated and concentrated sources of monosodium glutamate (MSG) such as autolyzed yeast extract, glutamate, glutamic acid, sodium caseinate, and hydrolyzed vegetable protein. Sources include conventional bouillon cubes and powder, buffet and fast foods, flavoring (in chips, crackers, popcorn, and snack foods), packaged foods, prepared sauces and soups, restaurant food, and seasonings. Carefully check ingredient labels.

SEEDS AND NUTS

GREEN LIGHT (HEALING)	WHAT TO DO	YELLOW LIGHT (CAUTION)
Chia, flax, and perilla seeds are rich sources of omega-3 fats. Other anti-inflammatory seeds include hemp, pumpkin, sesame, and sunflower. Almond, Brazil nut, chestnut, filbert/hazelnut, macadamia nut, pecan, pine nut, and walnut are nutritious sources of protein and healthy fats, such as essential fats and vitamin E. All tree nuts are potential allergens, so be mindful to rotate all nuts to avoid overexposure.	Freshly grind chia, flax, or perilla seeds in a small grinder or food processor to maximize the freshness of the polyunsaturated fats and other vitamins. Try to avoid storing ground seeds, but if you must do so, keep them in a tightly sealed glass jar in the fridge or freezer to maintain freshness. Eat seeds and nuts raw and as fresh as possible to protect unsaturated oils and nutrients. Soak nuts in water overnight to make them more digestible.	Some whole seeds may irritate inflamed or sensitive intestines. Cashews and pistachios are healthy nuts when consumed fresh. However, they're easily contaminated with mold, especially when stored for long periods.

OILS AND FATS

GREEN LIGHT (HEALING)	WHAT TO DO	YELLOW LIGHT (CAUTION)
Mechanically cold-pressed chia seed, flax seed, hemp seed, perilla seed, algae, fish, krill, and walnut oils are excellent sources of omega-3 polyunsaturated fats. Mechanically cold-pressed almond, black currant seed, borage seed, evening primrose seed, hemp seed, pine nut, pumpkin seed, safflower seed, sesame seed, and sunflower seed oils are excellent sources of omega-6 polyunsaturated fats. Mechanically cold-pressed avocado, extra-virgin olive, and grape seed oils are rich in heart-healthy monounsaturated fats, and raw whole coconut oil has antimicrobial properties.	All oils rich in essential fats should be enjoyed raw and never cooked. Once you open the bottle, consume quickly to avoid rancidity. Store these oils in opaque glass jars in the fridge or freezer to avoid damage from heat, light, and moisture. Oils high in monounsaturated or saturated fats may be used for cooking at low temperatures (with a water or broth spritz) but are best consumed raw. Store all oils in a cool, dark place to maintain freshness.	Organic butter and ghee (clarified butter) are healthy choices when eaten in moderation by people who are not sensitive or allergic to dairy. Olive oil that isn't labeled as extra-virgin may have been blended with other cheaper oils such as chemically extracted canola, safflower, and sunflower. Oils labeled "high oleic" contain fewer polyunsaturated fats such as omega-6 fats.

WHAT TO DO	RED LIGHT (HURTING)
Soak and chew seeds thoroughly before swallowing. Seed butter, seed pastes, and seed milks are less likely to cause intestinal discomfort. Avoid or minimize your intake of cashews and pistachios. Buy nuts as fresh as possible and store them in the fridge or freezer.	If you have IBD and/or diverticulitis, all whole seeds may irritate inflamed intestines. Enjoy smooth seed butters, pastes, and milks if you can tolerate them. Avoid nuts that are rancid, pre-chopped, over-roasted, fried, and/or seasoned with sugary glazes or commercial oil and salt. Seeds and nuts that are rancid and/or heated at high temperatures contain damaged (peroxidized) oils. Peanuts are often contaminated with mold and should be avoided. Peanut butter made with hydrogenated oil is highly inflammatory.[6]

WHAT TO DO	RED LIGHT (HURTING)
Avoid dairy fats for 8 weeks in step three. Use coconut oil/butter or cacao butter when a recipe calls for saturated fat. Then slowly reintroduce organic goat and sheep ghee, to determine whether or not you can tolerate them. Introduce organic cow ghee and then cow butter after you're sure you tolerate goat and sheep dairy. Dairy can be high in saturated fats and should therefore be consumed in moderation. Use extra-virgin olive oil as often as possible. The term "extra-virgin" is regulated by the European Union but isn't recognized in other olive-producing countries such as the U.S.	Refined, processed, chemically extracted, bleached, damaged, and hydrogenated oils are toxic to every cell in your body. Almost all canola (also called rapeseed) and soybean crops are genetically modified (GM) or contaminated by GM crops and should be avoided whenever possible. If you must use canola or soybean oils, choose organic. Avoid fats and oils stored in plastic containers. Contaminants will leach out of the plastic and into the oil. Commercial dressings usually contain high amounts of sugar, white vinegar, and processed bleached oils, all of which contribute to inflammation.[7]

6. Peanuts are technically legumes. They're a type of groundnut and are rich in nutrients, including the powerful antioxidant resveratrol. Unfortunately, an increasing number of people have profound allergies to peanuts and/or to the toxic mold that commonly contaminates this food.

7. Avoid all refined and modified fats, chemically extracted and bleached oils, fried foods, hydrogenated and partially hydrogenated oils, fractionated and partially fractionated oils, margarine, and trans-fats. Read product labels carefully, as it's becoming law to list trans-fat content. Make up a fast, healthy dressing and store it in the fridge instead of using prepared products.

SWEETENERS

GREEN LIGHT (HEALING)	WHAT TO DO	YELLOW LIGHT (CAUTION)
Moderate amounts of sweeteners such as birch syrup, carob powder, coconut syrup, unrefined date sugar, raw and dry fruit, honey (raw is best), licorice root powder or syrup, *lo han kuo,* lucuma fruit powder, maple syrup, mesquite flour, rice syrup, stevia, sweet cicely leaf, tiger nut powder, vanilla, and yacón syrup are suitable choices.	Use sweeteners sparingly to avoid spikes in blood levels of insulin. Consume sweet foods with high-fiber foods to balance blood sugar. Be careful to watch portion sizes of dried fruit, as it's very concentrated in sugar. Water down fruit juice to avoid excess sugar and look for fruit-sweetened sauces and jams.	Blackstrap molasses can be a nutritious sweetener. However, because it's derived from sugar cane, which has been overconsumed, some people may have developed a sensitivity to it. Jaggery and Sucanat are unrefined dehydrated cane juice. They contain more minerals and vitamins than white sugar. Commercial agave syrup is high in fructose and can be inflammatory in people who suffer from liver disorders, fructose sensitivity, insulin resistance, or mold sensitivity. The agave syrup industry isn't ecologically sustainable. Raw, unsweetened cacao is high in nutrients, but it can be inflammatory for people who are sensitive to its stimulating alkaloids.

BEVERAGES

GREEN LIGHT (HEALING)	WHAT TO DO	YELLOW LIGHT (CAUTION)
Water is the most important liquid for health, and you must drink adequate amounts every day. Herbal teas and fresh fruit and vegetable juices can also be healing.	Drink 6 to 12 cups (1.5 to 3 L) of water (filtered or spring source) per day depending on your body size. Add a squeeze of lemon or lime for extra zing and detox support. Drink diluted coconut water, fresh fruit and vegetable juices, herbal teas, and sugar-free lemonade or limeade. Sweeten herbal teas and lemonade with stevia or raw honey. Brew teas overnight and store in the fridge to make a refreshing homemade iced tea. Read all ingredient labels to avoid sugar and artificial sweeteners in juices or iced teas. Drink mineral water and honey-sweetened herbal teas instead of soft drinks.	Freshly roasted and freshly ground coffee beans retain their potent antioxidant activity and health-promoting properties. Black and oolong teas, green tea, guarana, kola nut, and yerba maté contain caffeine, but they can also be healthy choices for people who don't suffer from adrenal exhaustion or liver congestion. These drinks are rich in antioxidants and beneficial phytonutrients. Low-thyroid patients may have to avoid green and black tea due to their high fluoride content. Some studies suggest that in small doses red wine and sake may support cardiovascular health.

WHAT TO DO	RED LIGHT (HURTING)
Avoid all sugar cane products for 8 weeks in step three of the plan to determine if you're sensitive to them. Then slowly reintroduce unrefined jaggery, Sucanat, or molasses. Avoid or minimize use of agave syrup. If possible, choose organic products that are pure, don't contain high-fructose corn syrup, and aren't processed with black mold (*Aspergillus*). Eliminate all cacao products. Then slowly reintroduce raw, unsweetened cacao seeds after 8 weeks to gauge your body's reaction. Cacao should be avoided by people who are sensitive to caffeine.	Refined cane sugar and sugar beet products suppress immune system function and promote inflammation.[8] Avoid all artificial sweeteners, such as Aspartame, saccharin, and sucralose (Splenda), which may cause tissue irritation or an inflammatory reaction. Avoid commercial chocolate that contains refined sugar or artificial sweeteners, dairy, hydrogenated oils, and artificial flavors.

8. Avoid all refined beet and cane sugars including berry (extra fine), brown, confectioner's, golden, icing, Turbinado, and white forms. Avoid confectioner's syrup, dextrose (glucose), glucose-fructose, high-fructose corn syrup, and levulose (fructose). Don't consume artificial sweeteners.

WHAT TO DO	RED LIGHT (HURTING)
If you drink coffee, moderate your consumption and drink freshly roasted and freshly ground coffee. Lightly roast a one-week supply and store it in a glass jar in the fridge or freezer. Mix it with powdered reishi mushroom or ground chicory or dandelion root to minimize caffeine intake and to support detoxification. People sensitive to caffeine should completely avoid caffeinated beverages, such as coffee, tea (black, green, oolong, and white), guarana, kola nut, and yerba maté. Generally, people with strong nerves and robust adrenal health can tolerate moderate amounts of caffeine. Avoid all alcohol for 8 weeks and reintroduce red wine or sake to see if you're sensitive to its sulfite and histamine content. If you're tolerant, keep consumption to 3 glasses or less per week.	Juices and soft drinks sweetened with sugar or artificial sweeteners like Aspartame and Sweet'N Low can cause adverse effects, such as spikes in blood levels of insulin, headaches, or allergic reactions. Preground packaged coffee is oxidized and has lost most of its health-boosting properties. Substitute roasted chicory or dandelion root tea for coffee. They taste similar to coffee yet are cleansing and not stimulating. Alcohol, especially when consumed in excess, impairs liver function, may cause fatty liver or liver cirrhosis, and can lead to metabolic disorders such as insulin resistance and diabetes. Minimize intake of alcohol to minimize liver stress long-term. Choose red wine or unfiltered sake over premixed drinks, which tend to be high in sweeteners, artificial flavors, and artificial colors.

THE ANTI-INFLAMMATORY FOOD PYRAMID

The following foods are healing and anti-inflammatory for most people. However, you should avoid any foods to which you are allergic.

WATER

Servings: 6 to 12 glasses per day (depends on activity level, body weight, and types of beverages you drink).

Healthy choices: Natural spring or filtered/purified water and unsweetened herbal tea. Avoid carbonated water—it irritates intestinal cells, hinders digestion, and causes bloating.

Reason: Proper hydration prevents and heals inflammation, balances the immune system, aids digestion, supports cardiovascular health, and promotes healthy skin. Flavor water with a spritz of lemon or lime, or unsweetened fruit juice.

VEGETABLES

Servings: 7 to 10 per day.

Healthy Options: Asparagus, beet root, cardoon, carrot, cassava root, celeriac, celery, cucumber, dark leafy greens (raw or lightly cooked amaranth greens, arugula, beet greens, bok choy, collard greens, dandelion greens, kale, kohlrabi greens, lamb's-quarters, mustard greens, nettle, pak choy, purslane, radicchio, rapini, salad greens, sheep sorrel, spinach, sweet potato greens, Swiss chard, taro greens, watercress, and wild greens), fennel bulb, globe artichoke, Jerusalem artichoke, jicama, kudzu root, leek, wood mushrooms (enoki, king oyster, maitake, oyster, shiitake, snow ear, wild mushrooms, and wood ear), nonleafy cruciferous vegetables (broccoli, Brussels sprouts, cabbage, cauliflower, daikon, kohlrabi, radish, and rutabaga), onion, parsley root, parsnip, sea vegetables, shallot, squashes (including pumpkin and zucchini), sweet potato, taro root, turnip, yacón root, and yam.

Reason: Vegetables are rich in vitamins, minerals, phytonutrients, and fiber, yet are generally low in sugar. They are an excellent choice for reducing inflammation, supporting digestion, improving regularity of bowel movements, and minimizing spikes in blood sugar. Select a range of colors, eat them raw and cooked, and choose organic and local as best you can. Most Asian mushrooms are cultivated on wood or tree stumps. Not only are they generally hypoallergenic, but many also enhance immune function and help fight intestinal yeast infections, including candida. Common button mushrooms (also known as champignon, crimini, Portobello, and white mushroom) are grown on manure and may harbor pathogens that can infect or irritate your gut.

HEALTHY HERBS AND SPICES

Servings: Unlimited amounts.

Healthy Options: Ajwain seed, allspice, anise seed, asafoetida resin, basil, bay leaf, cardamom, chive, cilantro leaf/coriander seed, cinnamon bark, clove, cumin seed, curry leaf, dill leaf and seed, fennel seed, fenugreek, garlic, ginger root, marjoram, mint, nutmeg, oregano, parsley, rosemary, sage, savory, star anise, thyme, and turmeric.

Reason: Culinary herbs and spices have been used since ancient times to support digestion, prevent food spoilage, and support probiotics. Most are either directly anti-inflammatory or help prevent inflammation by improving digestion and strengthening your immune system. Herbs and spices can be eaten raw or dried, in tea form, or as flavorful ingredients in any recipe.

WHOLE GRAINS

Servings: 0 to 6 per day.

Healthy Options: Gluten-free grains (amaranth, buckwheat, Job's tears, millet, quinoa, rice, sorghum, teff, and wild rice).

Reason: Many people experience inflammation (for example, swollen joints) from eating gluten-containing grains (barley, kamut, oat, rye, spelt, triticale, and wheat). If you have food allergies, minimize or avoid gluten. Choose well-cooked whole grains that digest slowly to avoid inflammatory spikes in blood sugar.

FRUITS

Servings: 2 to 3 per day.

Healthy Options: Apple, apricot, avocado, bilberry, blackberry, blueberry, cherry, citrus fruits, cranberry, currant, date, dragon fruit, durian, fig, gooseberry, grape, guava, kiwi, litchi, loganberry, mango, mangosteen, melons, mulberry, nectarine, papaya, peach, pear, persimmon, pineapple, plum, pomegranate, prune, raspberry, and strawberry.

Reason: Eat fruits fresh as often as possible because cooking and drying fruits increases their GI. Eat only small servings of high-GI fruits. All fruits are rich in soluble and insoluble fiber, as well as antioxidants. Choose a range of colors; fresh, seasonal, or frozen; and organic whenever possible. Use caution with citruses, especially orange, as they may irritate some people with IBS and IBD. Use caution with grapefruit and closely related citrus, such as pomello and ugli fruit, if you take prescription medication. These fruits contain a compound called naringinen, which affects how the liver metabolizes some drugs. Recent research also suggests that starfruit and possibly pomegranate may have similar effects. Consult your doctor about which fruits are safe for you to eat if you're taking prescription medications.

GREEN AND HERBAL TEA

Servings: 2 to 4 cups (500 mL to 1 liter) per day.

Healthy Options: Burdock root, catnip, chamomile, chai, dandelion leaf and root, green tea, fruit including citrus peel, hibiscus, holy basil (tulsi), lavender, mint, peppermint, rose, rooibos, and sumac.

Reason: Herbal teas hydrate, cleanse, and heal. Green tea is rich in anti-inflammatory, antioxidant tannins, known as catechins, which can help prevent formation of AGEs (page 14). Green tea should be avoided or brewed lightly for people who are sensitive to caffeine or have low thyroid function. Avoid mints if you take homeopathics. Chapter 11 gives tips on brewing for maximum flavor and therapeutic effect.

HEALTHY FATS AND OILS

Servings: 5 per day.

Healthy Options: Oils are best eaten raw and stored in a cool, dark place. Avoid frying any oil. For low-temperature cooking, use avocado, coconut, extra-virgin olive, grape seed, mustard seed, or sesame seed oil. Whole-food sources of healthy fats include avocados, nuts, seeds, and dark leafy greens. Omega-3 fats are highest in coldwater fish, some algae, ocean krill, enriched eggs, seeds (chia, flax, perilla, and sacha inchi), and walnuts. After eight weeks on the MTHI plan, organic butter and ghee (clarified butter) are healthy choices when eaten in moderation by people who aren't sensitive or allergic to dairy.

Reason: Raw healthy oils, especially omega-3s, lubricate your cells and have powerful anti-inflammatory properties. Polyunsaturated oils rich in omega-3s and omega-6s must be eaten raw and fresh to be healing. Extra-virgin olive oil is also rich in anti-inflammatory antioxidants called polyphenols. Eating healthy oils daily gives every cell in your body an "oil change" and supports tissue healing.

PROTEIN

Total Servings: 3 to 4 per day; eat from a variety of sources to meet your daily needs.

BEANS AND LEGUMES

Servings: 0 to 3 per day.

Healthy Options: Adzuki, black-eyed, common beans (varieties include anasazai, black, black turtle, borlotti, cannellini, caparrone, cranberry, great northern, green, haricot, mottled, navy, pink, pinto, red and white kidney, romano, runner, shell, snap, string, and yellow), garbanzo, lima, mung, pigeon, and soy (young edamame or fermented natto and tempeh); all lentils; and all peas.

Reason: Beans are rich in folic acid, magnesium, potassium, and soluble fiber. They have a low glycemic index and help support cardiovascular health by decreasing LDL cholesterol. Eat them well cooked on their own; in soups, salads, and curries; or puréed into spreads or dips.

SUSTAINABLY CAUGHT AND RAISED FISH

Servings: 2 to 6 per week.

Healthy Options: Anchovy, Arctic char, black cod (sablefish), herring, mackerel, salmon (especially sockeye), sardine, and trout.

Reason: These fish are rich in anti-inflammatory omega-3 fats. If you don't eat fish, take a filtered fish oil supplement, 2 to 3 grams per day. A vegan option is an algae-sourced DHA/EPA omega-3 oil. Fish is always best eaten fresh; unsalted dried, frozen, and canned are acceptable substitutes when fresh isn't available. If you eat dried fish, make sure to thoroughly soak and drain the fish several times before cooking to decrease the amount of salt. If you can source it, sun-dried, unsalted fish is a good choice. Minimize consumption of canned foods. They are heated at extremely high temperatures for sterilization and may contain high amounts of salt as well as toxins (such as plastics and heavy metals), which leach from the can. Purchase sustainably caught or raised fish and use the SeaChoice *Canada's Sustainable Seafood Guide* or the Marine Stewardship Council website (www.msc.org) as a resource.

NUTS AND SEEDS

Servings: 1 to 3 per day.

Healthy Options: Almond, apricot kernel (small, occasional amounts only), Brazil nut, chestnut, coconut,* filbert/hazelnut, macadamia nut,

---

* Coconut isn't a true nut, but a fruit. People who have tree nut allergies most often can tolerate coconut.

pecan, pine nut, and walnut; chia, flax, hemp, perilla, pumpkin, sacha inchi, sesame, and sunflower seeds.

Reason: Nuts and seeds are best eaten raw, as they're rich in anti-inflammatory fats, healing minerals, vitamin E, and protein. Soaking or sprouting increases their digestibility. Avoid rancid nuts and seeds, as they're pro-inflammatory and extremely damaging to the liver and cardiovascular system. Nuts and seeds that have been processed (including presliced or chopped) and cooked (especially at high temperatures) are more likely to contain damaged oils. Avoid moldy pistachios and cashews—only eat these fresh—and avoid peanuts because they're a common allergen and are almost always high in inflammation-causing molds.

ORGANIC EGGS, DAIRY, AND MEAT

Servings: 0 to 2 per day.

Healthy Options: Omega-3 eggs, dairy, lean meats, skinless poultry, and wild game.

Reason: Choose organic or free-range omega-3-enriched eggs (from flax seed–fed hens). After you test yourself for a dairy allergy, introduce cultured sheep and goat milk such as yogurt and kefir; then try soft cheeses and ghee (clarified butter). When reintroducing cow's milk, select from organic, grass-fed, naturally raised animals. Eat organic, cage-free poultry (use bones for making broth). Eat wild game or lean cuts of naturally raised, grass-fed beef and bison.

SUPPLEMENTS

Servings: Daily.

Healthy Options: A high-quality, full-spectrum multivitamin/mineral that includes antioxidants (vitamins A, C, E, plus mixed carotenoids, selenium, and zinc); co-enzyme Q_{10}; 2 to 3 grams of a molecularly distilled fish oil tested for contaminants, or an algae-sourced DHA/EPA oil; and 1,000 to 4,000 IU of vitamin D_3.

Note: If you suffer from an inflammatory bowel disease (IBD) and find that your symptoms do not subside on this program, you may have to eliminate some foods on the safe list. These vary by individual, but most high-fiber carbohydrates such as whole grains and raw vegetables, simple carbohydrates such as starchy bread, and whole nuts or seeds can cause problems. During a flare-up, I suggest you purée everything possible, eat warm soups, and avoid eating large or heavy meals. Cook foods for a long time to improve digestibility. To heal severe intestinal inflammation, you may want to try avoiding all sugars and starchy carbohydrates (beans, grains, and root vegetables). The Specific Carbohydrate Diet™ is restrictive, but some people have experienced remarkable relief from their symptoms. Refer to *Breaking the Vicious Cycle* by Elaine Gottschall or *Eat Well Feel Well* by Kendall Conrad.

Reason: A full-spectrum multivitamin/mineral supplement helps fill any gaps in your diet when you're unable to meet your daily requirement of micronutrients. A whole food–based supplement is best for absorption and effectiveness. Avoid supplements made of synthetic vitamins. CoQ_{10} is a powerful anti-inflammatory antioxidant, and it supports cellular metabolism and cardiovascular health.

HEALTHY TREATS

Servings: Occasional.

Healthy Options: Unsweetened dried fruit; sugar-free snacks sweetened with fruit or unrefined fruit sugars, brown rice syrup, raw honey, root syrups, stevia leaf, or tree sap syrups.

Reason: It's important to occasionally enjoy treats on the MTHI plan so you don't feel completely deprived and later face irresistible cravings for refined sweets. Dried fruit is loaded with minerals and antioxidants. Soak dried fruit in water or slice into warm whole-grain porridge to improve digestibility. Unrefined fruit sugars include sugars and syrups made from various fruits, the most common being dates.

Raw honey is packed with natural antibiotic, antifungal, and antiyeast compounds, plus enzymes, vitamins, minerals, and plant antioxidants. Whole-leaf stevia is an incredibly sweet and nutritious flavoring with a slight licorice taste (avoid stevia if you're allergic to plants in the daisy family, such as ragweed and chamomile).

"We are indeed much more than what we eat, but what we eat can nevertheless help us to be much more than we are."

—ADELLE DAVIS,

AUTHOR OF *LET'S EAT RIGHT*

CHAPTER 10

BUILDING A HEALTHY KITCHEN

As I've said earlier, there are seven billion diets for seven billion people. You must fine-tune any food plan to suit your needs and preferences. It's important to understand that the menu plan in this book is only one way you might approach your eating habits.

It's impossible to plan a menu that removes all known allergens, but I have attempted to remove the most common ones. The exceptions I have made are eggs, small amounts of fermented soy, and tree nuts, all of which are anti-inflammatory foods if you're not allergic to them. It's really unfortunate when the body tags them as an allergen. Those who have a tree nut allergy can often handle seeds that are processed in a separate facility, so seeds are often a good substitute when a recipe calls for nuts. I also have a few recipes that contain eggs; if you can't tolerate eggs, then ignore the recipe. Alternatively, if eggs are called for in a baking recipe, you can use a vegan egg substitute such as ground flax seeds (see page 244) to act as the binding agent. The most important thing to do is to start experimenting and embracing a variety of foods from around the globe that will keep your palate interested and fulfilled.

Most recipes in this menu plan yield four servings, but you may want to halve the amounts the first time you make something with unusual ingredients you've never tasted before. I intentionally chose to make the recipes this size so you would have leftovers to freeze and enjoy later when you're in a hurry. Dinner leftovers can be great for breakfast. These savory foods will balance your blood sugar far more than a sweet pastry and cup of coffee to start the day, and you'll find yourself more mentally focused, emotionally steady, and able to cope with daily stressors. The MTHI menu plan does include sweet-tasting breakfasts, but these contain more protein and healthy oils than the average conventional breakfast, and they help you avoid an early morning spike in insulin. That being said, nothing beats greens in the morning! The Japanese, for example, are the longest-living humans on Earth, and they often start the day with greens, rice, and fish.

UTENSILS FOR A HEALTHY KITCHEN

My first piece of advice is that you purchase the best equipment you can afford. Remember that you're likely preparing several meals a day and whatever you buy needs to work well and be long lasting. Secondly, but no less important, is to avoid plastic as much as possible. This includes plastic cutting boards and storage containers, since BPA (bisphenol A, a dangerous estrogen mimicker found in most plastics) leaches from plastic into your food. You also might want to eliminate nonstick coatings typically used on cookware because they are extremely toxic. (Nonstick pans contain chemicals such as perfluorooctanoic acid [PFOA] that also act as powerful estrogen mimics. They have been implicated in infertility and other hormone imbalances.) Choose pans made from safer materials like stainless steel, cast iron, glass, or titanium, or pans that are enamel coated, all of which won't leach toxins into your fabulous kitchen creations. These pans are easy to clean and dishwasher safe, with the exception of cast iron. Earthenware or glass is probably the best option for cooking in your oven.

ANTI-INFLAMMATORY SHOPPING GUIDE

Photocopy and check off what you want to shop for this week.

*Foods marked with an asterisk (*) may contain ingredients that you should avoid. Check labels for: aluminum (baking soda only), anti-caking agents, color, gluten, hydrogenated oils, MSG or related additives (page 60), refined cane sugar, refined oils, soy protein isolate, table salt, white vinegar, and/or yeast.

PRODUCE

Organic, local, all colors, in season.

Apple

Apricot

Artichoke

Asparagus

Avocado

Beans (fresh)

Green

Purple

Yellow

Beet Root and Greens

Berries

Blueberry

Blackberry

Cranberry

Raspberry

Strawberry

Broccoli

Brussels Sprouts

Burdock Root

Cabbage (green, purple, red)

Carrot

Cauliflower

Celery

Celery Root/Celeriac

Cherry

Cucumber

Fennel Bulb and Greens

Fresh Herbs

Basil

Chive

Cilantro

Dill Greens

Garlic (fresh, whole)

Ginger Root (fresh, whole)

Lemongrass

Marjoram

Mint

Oregano

Parsley

Rosemary

Sage

Savory

Tarragon

Thyme

Turmeric Root (fresh, whole)

Grape

Jerusalem Artichoke/Sunchoke

Jicama Root

Kohlrabi

Leafy Greens

Bok Choy

Collard

Dandelion

Kale

Mustard

Purslane

Spinach

Swiss Chard

Turnip

Leek

Lemon

Lettuces

Arugula

Bib

Boston

Butterhead

Mesclun Mix

Radicchio

Romaine

Lime

Mixed Asian Greens

Mango

Mushrooms

Enoki

Maitake

Oyster

Shiitake

Snow Ear

Wood Ear

Okra

Onion

Green

Red

Yellow

Peach/Nectarine

Pear

Peas (snap, snow, sweet, etc.)

Pineapple
Plum
Pomegranate
Pumpkin
Radish
Rapini
Shallot
Sprouts (beans, grains, seeds)
Sweet Potato
Squashes (all summer and winter varieties including zucchini)
Taro Root and Greens (eddoe)
Yam

SNACKS

Dried fruits with no added sugar, sulfates, or hydrogenated oils.

Apple
Apricot
Blueberry
Cherry
Cranberry
Date
Fig
Prune

PACKAGED FOODS

Buy preserves in glass jars as much as possible. Canned foods are for occasional, emergency meals. When possible, buy food in enamel-lined cans.

Anchovy
Artichoke*
Baking Powder*
Beans (canned)
    Adzuki
    Black

Fava
Garbanzo
Kidney
Mung
Pinto
Romano
Broccoli Sprout Juice
Broth (organic beef, chicken, and vegetable)
Coconut Milk
Fish Flakes (bonito)*
Herring
Kudzu Root Powder
Lentils (canned)
Olives (in olive oil)
Soup (bean or vegetable)
Protein Powder (hemp, pea, sprouted brown rice; avoid whey and soybean)
Rice Crisp Cereal*
Rice Paper
Rice Tortilla
Salmon (wild sockeye)
Sardine (in water)

NUTS & SEEDS

Whole, raw, oil-free, unsalted. Store in airtight container in fridge or freezer.

Almond
Chia Seed
Brazil Nut
Flax Seed
Hazelnut
Hemp Seed
Macadamia
Pecan
Pine Nut
Pumpkin Seed

Sesame Seed (black and white varieties)
Sunflower Seed
Walnut
Any nut and seed butters made from above.

GRAINS, BREADS, CEREALS & LEGUMES

Choose whole-grain products, not whole-wheat products.

Amaranth
Breakfast Cereals (whole grain)*
Brown Rice
Dried Beans
Flax Flatbread*
Job's Tears
Lentils
Millet
Peas
Quinoa (black, red, or white)
Sorghum
Sprouted Grain, Yeast-Free Bread (brown rice, buckwheat, millet, or quinoa)*
Teff
Whole Flour
    Almond
    Amaranth
    Arrowroot
    Bean (garbanzo, romano; avoid soybean)
    Buckwheat
    Quinoa
    Rice
    Tapioca
Whole Pasta
    Bean or Lentil
    Buckwheat

Quinoa

Sweet Potato

Wild Rice

REFRIGERATOR CASE & FROZEN FOODS

Avoid anything with carrageenan. As an isolated food additive, this complex fiber may cause intestinal irritation. Choose low- or nonfat organic dairy products with no added sugar. Pay attention to the sodium content of frozen meals and to the kind of oils used in prepared sauces and dips.

Bean Dip

Edamame (young soybeans)

Goat and Sheep Butter, Ghee, Kefir, or Yogurt (test after eight weeks on the MTHI plan)

Frozen Berries

Açai

Blueberry

Blackberry

Cranberry

Raspberry

Strawberry (organic)

Frozen Vegetables (choose a variety)

Almond, Coconut, Hemp Seed, or Rice Milk*

Miso (with live culture)

Mochi (brown rice treat)

Omega-3 Fortified Eggs

Pesto Made with Extra-Virgin Olive Oil (basil, cilantro, kale, etc.)

Tempeh (fermented soy)

BEVERAGES

Filtered or Natural Spring Water

Fruit Juice*

Tea (green and various herbal)

Vegetable Juice*

MEAT/FISH

Choose fresh or frozen to widen your selection.

Coldwater oily fish:

Arctic Char

Black Cod (sablefish, butterfish)

Haddock

Halibut

Herring

Mackerel

Salmon (fresh or frozen, wild or canned sockeye)

Sardine

Tilapia

Trout

Other Fish Not Prone to Contamination or Overfishing (refer to the SeaChoice *Canada's Sustainable Seafood Guide*)

Free-range, organic poultry:

Chicken

Cornish Hen

Duck

Goose

Emu

Ostrich

Pheasant

Quail

Rhea

Turkey

Grass-fed red meats:

Beef

Bison

Lamb

Rabbit

Venison

Wild Game (deer, moose, etc.)

CONDIMENTS, FLAVORS & OILS

Stored in glass jars:

Apple Butter

Apple Cider Vinegar (unpasteurized)

Avocado Oil

Brown Rice Vinegar

Boullion (organic beef, chicken, and vegetable)*

Coconut Oil

Chia Seed Oil

Dill Pickle (fermented)*

Extra-Virgin Olive Oil

Fermented Vegetables*

Flax Seed Oil

Grape Seed Oil

Hemp Seed Oil

Honey (raw and unpasteurized liquid)

Horseradish*

Mustard (Dijon and yellow)*

Nutritional Yeast

Peppermint Liquid Extract

Perilla Seed Oil

Pickled Ginger Root*

Pumpkin Seed Oil

Sacha Inchi Seed Oil

Salt (unrefined gray sea or pink Himalayan rock)

Sauerkraut (fermented)*

Sesame Seed Oil (raw and
toasted seed varieties)
Tamari Sauce*
Umeboshi Plum Paste
Umeboshi Plum Vinegar
Unrefined Vanilla Extract
Walnut Oil
Wasabe*

DRY HERBS AND SPICES, POWDERED AND WHOLE FORMS*

Allspice
Basil
Bay Leaf
Cardamom
Chives
Cinnamon

Clove Bud
Coriander Seed
Cumin Seed
Curry Leaf
Dill Seed
Fennel Seed
Ginger Root
Mustard Seed (black and yellow
varieties)
Nutmeg
Parsley
Poppy Seed
Rosemary
Sage
Thyme
Turmeric

SEAWEEDS

Arame
Dulse
Hijiki
Kombu
Nori
Wakame

SUPPLEMENTS/ MEDICINAL HERBS

Chlorella Powder
Slippery Elm Bark Powder
Spirulina Powder
Stevia (extract or whole-leaf
powder)
Vitamin C Crystals (corn-free,
non-GMO)
Xantham Gum

COOKING BEANS

Beans, beans, the magical fruit, the more you eat, the more you toot! If the old ditty resonates with you, it means you aren't digesting them well. Beans can be tough to digest, but they are packed with fiber, protein, and B vitamins. Soaking and cooking beans thoroughly helps break down the complex sugars (oligosaccharides such as raffinose) that can challenge your digestive system.

If flatulence is a problem for you when you eat beans, start with small amounts to allow your body to gradually increase the production of enzymes necessary to help digest them. Cook your beans until they burst or mash effortlessly to ensure that they are ready to eat. Herbs that promote the digestion of beans include ajwain seed, anise seed, asafoetida (hing) resin, basil, bay leaf, cardamom, cinnamon bark, clove, coriander seed, cumin seed, fennel seed, fenugreek seed, garlic, ginger root, marjoram, mint, star anise, winter or summer savory, and turmeric. Cooking beans with a blend of two or three of these herbs will improve digestibility—but don't mix all of these herbs in a pot with your beans! Experiment with the ones that you find tastiest and most suitable to supporting your digestion. Many people from India maintain the tradition of chewing on dried fennel seeds or drinking a cup of fennel tea at the end of a legume-based meal to aid digestion.

Getting the Perfect Bean

- Cooking time depends on whether you're using dried or fresh beans. The fresher the beans, the shorter the cooking time. Beans are tastier and less grainy when cooked slowly, so avoid pressure cooking if possible.

- Rinse beans thoroughly in cold water and discard any that are discolored or badly formed. Also remove any pebbles or small stones.

- If using dried beans, cover beans with 3 to 4 times their volume of filtered water. Soak for at least 8 hours or overnight (you can skip the soaking step for mung beans, lentils, and split peas, but make sure to rinse them). Discard the soaking water. Rinse thoroughly. For some of the longer-cooking beans, I have found that soaking them for 24 hours and changing the soaking water two or three times can decrease the cooking time.

- Both soaked dried beans and fresh beans need to be covered with 3 to 4 times their volume with fresh filtered water.

- Bring to a gentle boil. Lower heat and simmer, partially covered, to ensure that the water does not boil over. Skim off the foam that accumulates on top of the water, as it increases intestinal gas.

- Stir occasionally to avoid starch sticking to the bottom of the pot and possibly burning.

- Add more water as needed to keep the beans covered.

- Add your choice of herbs and spices. A ½ strip (about 3 inches/ 8.5 cm) of kombu (a sea vegetable) per cup (250 mL) of dried beans is also a great way to support digestion and boost mineral content. Alternatively, add 1 bay leaf per cup (250 mL) of dried beans for easier digestibility.

- Add a pinch of gray sea salt or pink rock salt only after the beans are tender (about 10 minutes before they are fully cooked), so that the beans cook all the way through.

- See the following chart for cooking times.

COOKING GUIDELINES FOR BEANS

BEANS (DRIED, 1 CUP/250 ML)	SOAKING TIME (HOURS)	WATER (CUPS/ 250 ML)	COOKING TIME	PRESSURE COOKING (WATER)	PRESSURE COOKING (TIME)
ADZUKI	6–8	3½	2 hours	1½ cups (375 mL)	45 min
ANASAZI	6–8	4	2–2½ hours	2½ cups (625 mL)	30 min
BLACK-EYED	8	4	1–1½ hours	2½ cups (625 mL)	45 min
BLACK TURTLE	6–8	4	2–2½ hours	Not recommended	N/A
CHICKPEA (GARBANZO)	Overnight	4	4 hours	2½ cups (625 mL)	60 min
CRANBERRY	12	4	3–3½ hours	Not recommended	N/A
LENTILS (BROWN, RED, ETC.)	Not recommended	2	30–60 min	Not recommended	N/A
LIMA BABY	8 or overnight	2½	1½–2 hours	2 cups (500 mL)	30 min
MUNG	8 or overnight	2½	1–1½ hours	2 cups (500 mL)	30 min
NAVY BEAN/ GREAT NORTHERN	8	3	2 hours	2½ cups (625 mL)	30 min
PEAS	Not required	3	60–70 min	Not recommended	N/A
PINTO	8	3	2½–3 hours	2½ cups (625 mL)	45–60 min
RED KIDNEY	8 or overnight	4	2–2½ hours	2½ cups (625 mL)	45 min

Quick-Soak Method for Beans

When time is limited, wash and pick over beans and put them in a stockpot. Cover with 3 inches (7.5 cm) of water. Bring to a boil for 10 minutes, remove from heat, then cover and soak for 1 hour. Discard soaking water, add fresh water, and cook until tender.

COOKING GRAINS

The Best Way to Cook Grains

- Rinse all whole grains in cold water and drain well. It's easiest to use a fine-mesh strainer for this task. Amaranth and teff are too tiny for rinsing, so skip this step for these grains.

- Bring liquid (water, meat or vegetable stock, or rice milk) to a gentle boil in a saucepan.

- Add the grain and stir, bringing the liquid back to a gentle simmer.

- Cover and reduce heat to the lowest setting possible.

- Cook until soft, but not mushy (see page 195 for recommended times).

Getting the Best Grain

- Recommended cooking times are approximate and variable because some people like eating slightly firm cooked grains.

- Don't peek inside the pot when the grains are cooking. By letting steam escape, you prolong the cooking time. Don't stir most grains unless you are fluffing them after they're done. However, amaranth and teff seeds do need to be occasionally stirred because their mineral-rich soluble fiber (mucilage) will otherwise stick to the pot.

- Make sure you cook grains in enough liquid (such as water, broth, or milk substitute) so that it doesn't boil dry while cooking (see below).

- Test the grains for readiness when the recommended cooking time has been reached. Most whole grains are much better if they're slightly chewy. However, people with a compromised digestive system and inflamed gut should eat thoroughly cooked, moist grains with enough warm cooking liquid or broth to ease digestion.

- Different grains have different characteristics. Some grains, such as Job's tears, kasha, millet, quinoa, whole-grain rice, and wild rice, won't become sticky even after cooking. Others, such as amaranth, buckwheat, sorghum, and teff, will have a more porridge-like consistency.

- Experiment! You will find that each type of grain has a number of subtypes (the color, shape, or size may vary), giving them

COOKING GUIDELINES FOR GRAINS

GRAIN (1 CUP/250 ML)	WATER (LIQUID)	COOKING TIME (APPROXIMATE)	YIELD (APPROXIMATE)
AMARANTH	2 cups (500 mL)	25–30 min	2 cups (500 mL)
BROWN RICE	2–2½ cups (500–625 mL)	35–40 min	2½ cups (625 mL)
BUCKWHEAT (AND KASHA)	2 cups (500 mL)	15–20 min	2 cups (500 mL)
JOB'S TEARS	3 cups (750 mL)	60–70 min	3 cups (750 mL)
MILLET	3 cups (750 mL)	20–25 min	3 cups (750 mL)
QUINOA (RINSED WELL)	2 cups (500 mL)	20–25 min	4 cups (1 L)
RICE (LONG, MEDIUM)	2 cups (500 mL)	40–45 min	2 cups (500 mL)
TEFF	3 cups (750 mL)	15–20 min	3 cups (750 mL)
WILD RICE (LONG, BLACK)	3½ cups (875 mL)	60–70 min	3 cups (750 mL)

different flavors and textures. Their nutritional value is usually comparable, but mineral and vitamin profiles may vary slightly.

- Lightly toasting dry grains will give them a nutty flavor. Spread the grains (unrinsed) in a skillet and heat for approximately 4 to 7 minutes over medium-low heat, stirring constantly, until the grains are golden. Then add cooking liquid and continue to cook (when adding liquid to a hot pot, be careful that it does not spatter).

- Some grains, notably buckwheat (including kasha), millet, quinoa, and teff, can be fluffed just before serving.

Specific Information on Particular Grains

Amaranth is a gluten-free ancient Aztec seed that's considered a culinary grain. A nutritional powerhouse, it packs high amounts of protein (5 g) and calcium (60 mg) per ½ cup/125 mL. It has a sticky texture when cooked, and congeals quickly as it cools. It combines well in recipes with buckwheat, millet, and brown rice. Cooked amaranth grains can also be added to baked goods or stews, and raw seeds can be popped like popcorn.

Buckwheat isn't actually a type of wheat, nor is it related to the cereal grasses. It's actually the seed of a bush fruit; therefore, it's gluten-free. Since it has such a mild taste, toasting it briefly before simmering it in liquid will perk up its flavor. Toasted buckwheat seeds are called kasha. Buckwheat has a soft texture when cooked and combines well with pasta salads, quinoa, and winter squash.

Kasha (Roasted Buckwheat) has a stronger flavor and a drier texture than raw buckwheat. It's great mixed with garlic, rice, and vegetables and other seasonings to make a pilaf. To avoid mushiness, cook 1 cup (250 mL) kasha with 1 beaten egg in a heavy saucepan over medium heat, stirring until dry. Add 2 cups (500 mL) boiling liquid. Cover, reduce heat, and simmer 20 minutes. Fluff before serving.

Job's Tears tastes like barley, and it's one of the most popular medicinal foods in China. It can be used alone or mixed in soup, and is nutritionally therapeutic for painful and stiff joints. If you suffer from joint pain and stiffness, you'll need to eat about 1 cooked cup (250 mL) a day for one to two weeks before you notice the benefits. At that point, continue to eat it twice a week for health maintenance. Job's tears is also very healing for the kidneys.

The traditional use of Job's tears may have a scientific basis. Based on experimental animal studies, Japanese scientists have isolated numerous active chemical components from Job's tears, including coixol (which is anti-inflammatory, antihistaminic, muscle relaxing, and fever reducing) and coixans (which have sugar-lowering properties that can help people with diabetes manage their blood sugar).

Millet is gluten-free and a good source of the carotenoid lutein, which helps support eye health. It's exceptionally easy to digest and therefore makes an ideal food for convalescence from an inflamed or irritated gut. It has a nutty flavor, and goes well with curried dishes, salads, and soups. You can make it into a breakfast porridge by cooking in a little extra liquid. It contains goitergens, so it may be contraindicated for people who suffer from hypothyroidism.

Quinoa is an ancient Incan seed grain related to amaranth and is loaded with nutrition. It has 50 percent more protein than wheat, and more iron and calcium than most other grains. Quinoa combines well with millet and buckwheat, and is great in soups and stews or as a side dish. Black, purple, and red quinoa varieties are richer in color and crunchier in texture, and have a stronger flavor than white quinoa. All varieties have an enjoyable texture that is unique to the grain.

Teff is a staple grain in Ethiopia, and is supercharged with iron. A 1-cup (250 mL) serving will provide 25 percent of your daily iron needs. It's also a rich source of fiber and protein. Sweet and malty in flavor, teff is one of the smallest grains in the world, which may be why its name means "lost." (Don't rinse it in a mesh strainer or you will lose it down the drain!) Lightly dry toast it before cooking for a richer flavor. The flour can be used to make pancakes and crepes, and the grain makes a great porridge.

Whole, Unpolished Rice (for example, black, brown, and red), which has only the outer hull removed, retains an impressive variety of vitamins, including B3 and E, and minerals such as magnesium, manganese, and selenium. Whole rice contains only a small amount of protein. However, it has a relatively high level of the amino acid lysine, which is the critical amino acid that our immune system uses to fight the cold sore virus. Brown rice contains four times the amount of fiber found in white rice because the bran isn't milled away. This insoluble fiber is important for maintaining a healthy digestive tract.

- Rinsing medium-grain and short-grain rice under cold water before you cook it helps release the starch that makes cooled rice sticky.

- You can pressure cook rice, but the grains won't remain separate, light, and fluffy.

- To cook basmati rice, which has a light, fluffy texture, soak it in cool water before cooking for as much time as you have permitting. Basmati retains more starch than other rice varieties, so after soaking, rinse it until the water is no longer cloudy.

- Since brown rice features an oil-rich germ (part of the husk), it's more susceptible to becoming rancid than white rice. It should therefore be stored in the refrigerator in an airtight container. Stored in this way, brown rice will keep fresh for about six months.

Wild Rice is the seed of a Native American marsh grass. It's low in calories; rich in fiber; and higher in iron, niacin, protein, and riboflavin than brown rice. It triples in volume when cooked, and a small amount will give a distinctive character to a pilaf, stuffing, salad, or soup.

MEAL PLANNING GUIDELINES

An eating plan that promotes a lifetime of good health will balance your nutritional and emotional needs. The MTHI menu was designed with both body-supporting nutrients and soul-satisfying flavors in mind to help you stick with the program. Keeping both of these aspects in balance, you'll be able to adjust with ease to the healthiest choices. You just have to take it one bite at a time. If you feel that frequent food preparation is too much for you, get into the habit of making larger batches and storing them. For example, cook enough quinoa so you can have some in the morning and then pack the rest in a Thermos so you can snack on it throughout the day.

Good Eating Habits to Establish:

- Eat your first meal within two hours of waking. Eat low-GI food.

- Eat three meals and two snacks spaced over the day to keep energy levels up.

- Instead of a sugary treat, enjoy 1 to 2 servings of fruit for dessert or as a snack.

- Make sure half of your plate is filled with vegetables. (Vegetables must be cooked if you suffer from any inflammatory bowel conditions.)

- Include 2 to 3 vegetables in every meal for a minimum of 7 servings a day. The minerals in vegetables alkalize your body, helping to reduce inflammation.

- Try to eat 35 grams of fiber a day. You can achieve this by increasing your consumption of fruit, vegetables, whole grains, legumes, and seeds. Drink plenty of fluids.

CALORIC INTAKE

Most adults need to consume between 1,800 and 3,000 calories a day. If you're eating the appropriate number of calories for your level of activity, your weight shouldn't fluctuate greatly. Women, people with a smaller build, and people with a less active lifestyle need fewer calories. Conversely, men, people with a larger build, and people with a more active lifestyle need more calories to maintain their weight.

The distribution of calories you consume should be as follows: 40 to 50 percent from carbohydrates, 20 to 30 percent from fat, and 20 to 30 percent from protein. If you have strong digestion, meaning you don't experience any burping, gas, or bloating after eating, try to include carbohydrates, fats, and proteins at each meal.

Each of us has a built-in protein-portion meter—the size of the palm of your hand! For instance, if you have a smaller palm, you need a smaller amount of protein per serving. It's really that simple. Use your palm to determine what size your protein portion should be at each meal.

Here are a few general rules for portion sizes, in case you're eating out or trying to decide when you're in the grocery aisle:

Animal Choices: 1 small chicken breast, a 3- to 4-ounce steak, 2 to 3 eggs

Vegetarian Choices: 4 ounces (120 g) of tempeh, 1 cup (250 mL) of cooked lentils or bean dip, or 2 ounces (60 g) of nuts or seeds

When choosing vegetarian options, mix grains with legumes to ensure you get a complete variety of amino acids.

Legumes include beans, lentils, and peas. There are many choices like black, kidney, navy, and pinto as well as the lesser known, but equally delicious and nutritious, cranberry and fava beans. In the pea family are black-eyed peas, chickpeas (garbanzo beans), lentils, and split peas. Legumes are often low in the essential amino acids methionine (mung beans are an exception) and tryptophan, so try to pair them with grains or seeds for a complete protein source.

Grains include amaranth, buckwheat, Job's tears, quinoa, millet, teff, whole rice, and wild rice. Many grains are low in the amino acid lysine, except amaranth, which boasts 1 gram of lysine per 100-gram serving, and quinoa, which contains 0.5 grams per 100-gram serving. Pair grains with legumes or nuts and seeds to complete the protein.

Nuts and Seeds can also be low in lysine. Almonds, pecans, and walnuts can be added as a quick meal topping or added to a bean or legume recipe to complete the protein. Delicious anti-inflammatory seeds include chia, flax, hemp, pumpkin, sacha inchi, sesame, and sunflower.

NOTE FOR VEGETARIANS

Fermented soy is allowed in this meal plan, as long as you are sure you aren't sensitive to it and don't have a thyroid imbalance (soy can reduce thyroid function). It's easy to substitute tempeh in many of the chicken or meat recipes provided. Like tofu, tempeh is made from soybeans that are ground and molded into a cake. It's a nutty, protein-rich option and is great in lunch wraps. Unlike tofu, tempeh is fermented with *Rhizopus oligosporus* yeast culture and is therefore more digestible, less likely to produce gas, and less likely to act as an allergen. The fermentation process also deactivates the various compounds present in soy and other legumes that inhibit protein and carbohydrate digestion. Natto is similarly fermented with *Bacillus subtilis* bacterial culture, and miso is fermented with various nutritional yeasts.

It's important for vegetarians to get enough protein in order to manage carbohydrate cravings and build lean muscle. If you're chronically tired, you may want to ensure you're getting enough iron and vitamin B_{12}; both are hard to obtain on a vegetarian diet and are critical nutrients for cell metabolism, energy production, blood formation, liver function, and overall optimal health.

Great vegetarian sources of iron include:

Lentils, cooked	1 cup (250 mL) = 6.6 mg
Spinach, cooked	1 cup (250 mL) = 6.4 mg
Quinoa, cooked	1 cup (250 mL) = 6.3 mg
Tempeh	1 cup (250 mL) = 4.8 mg
Lima beans, cooked	1 cup (250 mL) = 4.4 mg
Swiss chard, cooked	1 cup (250 mL) = 4.0 mg
Blackstrap molasses	1 tbsp (15 mL) = 2.6 mg

Vitamin B_{12} is found naturally in meat, milk products, and eggs, so if you are vegan, it is important to consider a B_{12} supplement. Spirulina, sea vegetables, and nutritional yeast do not contain adequate amounts of B_{12} to prevent deficiency symptoms.

Complete Protein Pairings

Food combinations that make a complete protein:

- Legumes with grains/nuts/seeds

- Dairy with grains/nuts/seeds/legumes

MODIFICATIONS TO THE MTHI PLAN

If you suffer from ileocecal valve syndrome or any inflammatory bowel disease such as ulcerative colitis, diverticulitis, ankylosing spondylitis, or Crohn's disease, you will have to make food modifications to the MTHI plan. I suggest you reduce or completely eliminate (depending on the severity of your condition) foods high in roughage such as raw foods, whole nuts and seeds, whole grains, and popcorn. You also may need to reduce starch found in beans, so consult a naturopathic doctor for guidance and specific protocols. Eat fruits and vegetables fully cooked to soften them, and avoid swallowing inedible seeds such as those in berries, tomatoes, peppers, eggplants, cucumbers, and grapes. Blend nuts and seeds into butters to ease digestion. You may need to completely avoid strawberries, raspberries, blueberries, and related fruits. Eat soupy dal (split beans and peas with the outer skins removed) instead of whole legumes. Eliminate spicy foods and avoid stimulants such as alcohol, cocoa, and caffeine. Blending your food into a hearty soup may help improve your digestion, soothe your intestines, and help calm inflamed areas.

SUGGESTED 7-DAY OMNIVORE MENU PLAN

Note: Days are interchangeable. If you are short on time, simplify a meal by eating steamed greens, squash and protein of your choice. It is very important that you rotate your food choices to avoid allergies and improve your nutrient diversity. Be brave and experiment with new foods and your taste buds will adapt quickly. Consider making meals on the weekend and freezing them into portions for fast weekend-meal choices. Wash and chop produce when you get home from shopping so vegetables become an instant snack item. There are traditional breakfast items suggested, but for faster healing, eat lunch or dinner suggestions as the first meal to ensure your blood sugar will be more balanced throughout the day.

DAY	MORNING TEA	BREAKFAST	MORNING SNACK
1	Ginger Tea	Creamy Rice Porridge with Cranberries	Celery Sticks with Nut Butter or Seed Butter
2	Burdock Tea	Pesto Omelet OR Leftover Frittata	Apple Slices with 2 tbsp (30 mL) Pumpkin Seeds
3	Morning Lemon Cleanse	Amaranth Porridge	Fruit Juice Popsicle
4	Rooibos Tea	Indian "Anda Bhurji" Eggs	Sugar Snap Peas or Jicama with Lentil Dip
5	Nettle Tea	Immune-Building Brown Rice Congee	Dried Berries with Hemp Seeds
6	Chai Tea	Flax Apple Pudding with Grain-Free Berry Muffin	Almonds and Dried Figs
7	Rosehip Tea	Warming Quinoa Porridge with Vanilla Almond Milk	Lynn's Raw Carrot Halva Balls

© 2011 JulieDaniluk.com

LUNCH	AFTERNOON SNACK	DINNER
Raincoast Sockeye Salmon Salad with Butternut Ginger Soup	Broccoli with Bean Dip	Frittata with Pesto, Sweet Potato, and Spinach and choice of Salad OR Braised Greens with Garlic
Salmon with Fennel Greens and Sautéed Baby Bok Choy	Green Shake OR 1 Organic Peach	Dijon Chicken with Sesame Burdock Sauté and Sesame Green Beans OR Shepherd's Pie with White Root Mash, Raw Gravy, and Shiitake Mushroom and Arugula Sauté
Roast Beef, Chicken, or Turkey Rollups with Vegetable Miso Soup	"Hit the Trail" Mix with Apple Sauce	Pomegranate-Poached Halibut with Beet the Detox Salad OR Slow-Cooked Swiss Steak with Root Vegetables and Cauliflower "Popcorn"
The Power Reactor Salad with Sesame Tamari Vinaigrette, Green Pea Hummus, and Sunny Flax Crackers	Walnut Halves with Ripe Pear	Ginger Zucchini Salad with Dijon Salmon Patties, Guacamole, and Sunny Flax Crackers
Dijon Salmon Patty on Amaranth Salad with Creamy Ginger Dressing	Zucchini Sticks with dip of choice	Spice-Rubbed Bison Tenderloin with Cauliflower Whip and Endive Pear Salad Fish option: 15-Minute Arctic Char with Dill Mustard Sauce
Buckwheat Soba Noodles with Cabbage and Pumpkin Seeds	Vegetable, Miso, or Chicken Broth	A Tale of Two Curries with Perfect Brown Rice and Braised Greens with Garlic
Sushi Renovation with Asian Coleslaw	Jicama Sticks	Job's Tears Chicken and Ginger Stew with Steamed Asparagus and Lemon-Parsley Sauce

SUGGESTED 7-DAY VEGAN MENU PLAN

Note: Days are interchangeable. If you're short on time, simplify a meal by eating steamed greens, squash, and protein of your choice. It's very important that you rotate your food choices to avoid allergies and improve your nutrient diversity. Be brave and experiment with new foods, and your taste buds will adapt quickly. There are traditional breakfast items suggested, but if you eat lunch or dinner suggestions as the first meal, your blood sugar will be more balanced throughout the day.

DAY	MORNING TEA	BREAKFAST	MORNING SNACK
1	Ginger Tea	Cranberry Quinoa Granola	Fresh Cherries
2	Burdock Tea	Warm and Savory Breakfast Soup	Apple Slices with Pumpkin Seeds
3	Morning Lemon Cleanse	Warming Quinoa Porridge with Vanilla Almond Milk	Sautéed Bok Choy with 1 oz (30 grams) sesame seeds
4	Chai Tea	Blueberry Hemp Smoothie with Puffed Quinoa Bars	Lynn's Raw Carrot Halva Balls
5	Rooibos Tea	Teff Porridge	Jules's Crispy Rice Squares
6	Nettle Tea	Flax Apple Pudding and Jake's Muffin Max	Zucchini Sticks with Ultimate Nut/Seed Butter
7	Rosehip Tea	Amaranth Porridge OR Dinner Leftovers	Popeye Juice

LUNCH	AFTERNOON SNACK	DINNER
Sunny Flax Crackers with Anti-Inflammatory Lentil Dip	Apple Rice Bake	Ezra's Herbed Quinoa Risotto with Kale Salad
Fast-Cooking Kichadi in a Thermos with Farmers' Market Wild Salad	The Skinny Dip	Vegetable Tempeh Stir-fry with Pecan Wild Rice Salad
Sushi Renovation with Vegetable Miso Soup	Pickle-dilly Salad	African Nut Butter Stew with Dulse Chips
Raw Pad Thai OR Buckwheat Blueberry Salad	Nectarine	Kelp Noodle Panang Curry with Cool Jicama Slaw
Cranberry Quinoa Salad with Collard Wraps	Jicama Sticks with Lime	Pesto White Bean Bowl and Roasted Fennel with Olives and Garlic
Seaweed Salad with Adzuki Millet Salad	Zippy Lentil Tapenade with Summer Squash	Sweet Potato Gratin with Dandelion Salad
Lentil Spinach Dal	Krispy Kale Chips	Shepherd's Pie with White Root Mash, Raw Gravy, and Shiitake Mushroom and Arugula Sauté

YOUR FOOD JOURNAL

By keeping a record about your feelings and food choices, you may unveil the connection between physical and emotional symptoms. Look at your emotional attachment to the foods you eat, as we are often sensitive to the very foods we crave the most.

HOW DO I FEEL TODAY? (CIRCLE ONE OF THE FOLLOWING)
☺ HAPPY/EXCITED   ☺ NEUTRAL   ☹ SAD/DEPRESSED

WHAT I ATE TODAY	PORTION SIZE	HOW DID I FEEL ABOUT EATING IT?	HOW I FELT AFTER EATING IT

ALLERGY SUBSTITUTION CHART

EGG–Where it is found	RECIPE RENOVATION	How to live without it
Baby foods • Baked foods • Bouillon/consommé • Candy (nougat, white chocolate) • Ice cream • Mayonnaise • Meringue • Pasta • Processed meats • Salad dressings • Sauces (alfredo, hollandaise, béarnaise) Derivatives to watch for include albumin, lecithin, livetin, lysozyme conalbumin, ovalbumin, ovoglobulin, ovomucin, ovomucoid, ovotransferrin, ovovitellin, simplesse, and vetellin.	**1 egg is equal to:** 1 tbsp (15 mL) of ground flax seed + 3 tbsp (45 mL) of water; whisk for 2 to 3 minutes. ¼ cup (60 mL) of applesauce or apricot purée + 2 tbsp (30 mL) of oil (add an extra ½ tsp [2.5 mL] of baking powder if you are baking to help leavening)	Some people who are allergic to chicken eggs can handle goose eggs or quail eggs. Most baked foods can be made using a flax seed binder. Note that egg replacers are often made with potato starch, so read ingredients lists carefully.
DAIRY/CASEIN–Where it is found	**RECIPE RENOVATION**	**How to live without it**
Artificial butter flavor • Baby foods • Baked foods • Breaded foods • Candy (chocolate, nougat, caramel color) • Canned fish • Flavoring • Mayonnaise • Margarine made from vegetable oil • Substitute cheese made from soy or rice (often contains whey or casein) • Medication • Processed meat • Puddings • Salad dressings • Sauces • Supplements (Homeopathics) • Sherbet Derivatives to watch for include hydrolyzed whey protein, lactose, lactalbumin, lactalbumin phosphate, lactoglobulin, lactic acid, simplesse, whey, and whey powder.	**1 cup (250 mL) of cow, goat, or sheep milk is equal to:** 1 cup (250 mL) of broth for savory recipes 1 cup (250 mL) of milk made from almond, rice, or hemp for sweet recipes (if you are baking, add 1 tbsp [15 mL] of oil to preserve richness and consistency) **1 cup (250 mL) of cow butter is equal to:** 1 cup (250 mL) of coconut butter 1 cup (250 mL) of avocado (used in cold preparations only)	Puréed sweet potatoes or yams, mashed butternut squash, coconut milk, or toasted nuts can make most recipes taste creamy. You won't miss the cheese when you top a meal with avocado or seeds.

NUTS–Where they are found	RECIPE RENOVATION	How to live without them
Alcohol (Frangelico, Amaretto) • Asian foods • Baked foods • Baking mixes • Battered or fried foods • Candy • Cereals • Chili • Crackers • Ice cream • Milk formula • Nut butters • Pesto • Sauces and gravies • Soups Watch food labels for hydrolyzed plant protein, hydrolyzed vegetable protein, natural flavorings, and vegetable fat. Make sure food labels specify nut-free processing facilities.	**½ cup (125 mL) of ground nuts is equal to:** ½ cup (125 mL) of ground seeds ½ cup (125 mL) of nut-free granola or crunchy cereals for toppings and texture in baked foods **1 tbsp (15 mL) of nut butter is equal to:** 1 tbsp (15 mL) of butter made from hemp, pumpkin, sesame (tahini), or sunflower seeds or soybeans	Snack on nut-free bars, trail mix made with seeds, fresh fruit, and crunchy vegetables such as carrots and celery. Make your own seed butter (see my Ultimate Nut-Seed Butter recipe on page 343).
SOY–Where it is found	**RECIPE RENOVATION**	**How to live without it**
Baby foods • Baked foods • Canned fish • Chocolates (cream centers) • Cooking oils • Ice cream • Margarine • Mayonnaise • Meat products • Natural flavors • Protein bars • Protein powders • Powdered meal replacements • Sauces (Asian, gravy, soy, Worcestershire) • Seasoned salt • Shortening • Stabilizers • Thickeners Derivatives to watch for include hydrolyzed vegetable or plant protein, natural and artificial flavoring, textured vegetable protein (TVP), vegetable gum, and vegetable starch.	**1 cup (500 mL) of soybeans is equal to:** 1 cup (500 mL) of any other bean or lentil ¾ cup (185 mL) of soaked nuts or seeds **1 cup (500 mL) of soy milk is equal to:** 1 cup (500 mL) of dairy or nondairy milk **1 tbsp (15 mL) of tamari sauce is equal to:** 1 tbsp (15 mL) of vegetable or beef broth and a pinch of salt **1 tbsp (15 mL) of miso paste is equal to:** 1 bouillon cube 1 tsp (5 mL) of umeboshi plum paste	Beans, lentils, nuts, and seeds are a great protein source and give a "meaty" texture to vegetarian dishes. Experiment with almonds, amaranth, hemp seeds, and quinoa. Create Asian flavors using fresh ginger root, rice vinegar, sesame oil, and umeboshi plum paste.

WHEAT/GLUTEN–Where it is found	RECIPE RENOVATION	How to live without it
Baby foods • Baked foods • Baking mixes • Beer • Breaded foods • Candy (chocolate bars, licorice) • Cereals (sweetened with malt) • Flavored coffees and teas • Fried foods • Imitation seafood and bacon • Sauces (Asian, gravy, soy) • Malted milk shakes • Medications/supplements • Pastas • Processed meats • Snack foods • Soups (stews and stocks) Derivatives to watch out for include bulgur, couscous, durum, einkorn, emmer, enriched/white/whole wheat flour, farina, gluten, graham flour, high-gluten/protein flour, kamut, seitan, semolina, spelt (dinkel, farro), triticale (a cross between wheat and rye), *Triticum aestivum* (summer wheat), and wheat berry/bran/flour/germ/starch.	**3 cups (750 mL) of wheat flour is equal to:** 2 cups (500 mL) brown rice flour (finely ground) ⅔ cup (170 mL) arrowroot starch ⅓ cup (85 mL) tapioca flour Mixing different gluten-free flours helps to make baked goods taste closer to wheat flour. You can purchase premixed gluten-free flour blends, but be careful to avoid corn and potato starch.	Stock up on healthy gluten-free cereals, pasta, and snacks. Bring them with you when you are on the go so you can eat what you want when you want it. Choose foods made with fiber-rich amaranth, beans, buckwheat, flax seeds, rice bran, sorghum, and wild rice.
FISH/SEAFOOD–Where it is found	**RECIPE RENOVATION**	**How to live without it**
Chinese, Indian, Indonesian, Japanese, Thai, and Vietnamese foods • Caesar salad • Fried foods (French fries and chicken nuggets are often cooked in the same oil as fish or shellfish) • Imitation crab • Omega-3 oil supplements • Worcestershire sauce	Beans, nuts, eggs, and lean meats are the best replacement for fish on your plate. **1 tbsp (15 mL) of fish sauce is equal to:** 1 tbsp (15 mL) of tamari sauce **1000 mg salmon oil supplement is equal to:** 1 tsp (5 mL) of borage seed or algae-based omega-3 oil	Breaded and broiled tempeh can double as fish sticks. Lean meats will keep your baked sweet potato or yam company. Homemade vegetable sushi makes a fun snack. Thinly pounded poultry and soy-based substitutes can mimic the texture of fish in your favorite recipes.

211

PART THREE

THE RECIPES:
FAST HEALTHY FOOD &
DECADENT SLOW FOOD

"We cannot work, we cannot think, unless our stomach wills so . . . After a cup of tea . . . it says to the brain, 'Now rise, and show your strength . . . see, with a clear eye, into Nature, and into life.'"

—JEROME K. JEROME, *THREE MEN IN A BOAT*

(*TO SAY NOTHING OF THE DOG*)

CHAPTER 11

LIQUID HEALING

In the MTHI program, I strongly encourage you to try a different tea every day. In the end, your taste buds will appreciate the herbs' healing effects and their natural fruity, woodsy, and spicy flavors. Before you take your first sip of tea, keep the following in mind:

- Try long brews for roots and leaves—this will boost the tea's potency.

- Delicate flowers and leaves should not be boiled, as this can reduce their medicinal properties. A longer steeping time, 10 minutes up to 2 hours, will yield a stronger tea with more beneficial properties. Serve steeped tea hot or iced. If you wish, add sweetener, lemon, or spices to taste.

- Avoid steeping caffeinated tea (black, green, or white) in water that's too hot or for longer than 7 minutes, as this will result in a bitter, unsavory brew and higher caffeine content. Consider steeping for 3 to 7 minutes, depending on how strong you like your tea.

Note: Consult your health practitioner if pregnant or nursing to establish which teas are safe for you and your baby.

HEALING TEAS

Herbal teas are healing, hydrating, and soothing. Making your own fresh teas from whole plant parts can be very rewarding, and fresh teas usually have stronger healing properties and are less expensive than prepackaged tea bags. Flowers, leaves, nonwoody stems, and other soft plant parts can be steeped, whereas resins, roots, seeds, woody stems, and other hard parts must be decocted (see page 218). Powdered or finely shredded roots can also be infused. All teas can be prepared in 1-liter mason jars and stored in the refrigerator for ease of use.

INFUSIONS (EXTRACTS PREPARED BY SOAKING THE LEAVES OF A PLANT IN LIQUID)

Infusion is a method of preparing teas that involves pouring hot water over plant matter (such as dried leaves or berries) and steeping, which means soaking plant matter in liquid for a period of time and then removing the plant matter before consumption.

Basic Instructions

1. Place 1 tsp (5 mL) of herbs per cup (250 mL) of water into a teapot or mug and pour filtered water (just off the boil) over top.

2. Infuse for 3 to 7 minutes to suit your taste. To increase the healing properties of the tea, cover it while it steeps. If the tea is uncaffeinated, then stir occasionally to assist the brewing process. Strain before drinking.

CRANBERRY ROSE HIP HERBAL TEA

This combination of rose hips and cranberry is a perfect fit. Both rose hips and cranberries are high in vitamin C, which supports the immune system. The acidity of the berries stops bacteria from attaching to the walls of the bladder, helping to prevent bladder infections.

Rose hips are the fruits that form at the base of the rose flower. They contain a whopping 1,700 mg of vitamin C per 100 g of dried rose hip. Rose hips are often included in herbal blends (especially with hibiscus), but they taste fabulous on their own. This tea has a tangy, tart flavor and a pinkish color.

1 tbsp (15 mL)	dried rose hips
4 cups (1 L)	filtered water, just off the boil
¼ cup (60 mL)	pure cranberry juice
½ tsp (2.5 mL)	stevia whole-leaf powder OR ¼ tsp (1 mL) stevia extract

Place rose hips in a teapot. Pour in boiled filtered water and cranberry juice. Add stevia to taste.

Makes 4 cups (1 L).

NETTLE GREEN TEA

Green tea contains high concentrations of catechin polyphenols, which stimulate fat metabolism and promote thermogenesis—a process whereby the body generates heat by burning fuels such as fat. Green tea may even be good for your teeth. It is a rich source of natural fluoride, containing up to 400 ppm. The tea plant extracts fluoride from the soil in which it grows. Fluoride can disrupt thyroid function, so if you have hypothyroidism, then consider avoiding green tea.

Nettle is a fantastic source of potassium, calcium, and magnesium, which can give you the energy you need for exercise. Nettle has a gentle grassy flavor and when infused overnight, turns an intense emerald green.

Place 3 tea bags or 1 tbsp (15 mL) of dried nettle leaves into a pot or cup and pour 1 L (4 cups) of boiling filtered water over. Infuse for at least 20 minutes. Place 1 green tea bag into the existing teapot and infuse for an additional 3 minutes or less to maximize antioxidant, and minimize caffeine, content. Serve hot or iced. Add sweetener, lemon, or other spices to taste.

Makes 4 cups (1 L).

QUICK TIP

For a fast kidney cleanse, add a nettle tea bag to your water bottle and let it infuse overnight.

ROOIBOS TEA

Rooibos is becoming more popular in Western countries because it contains high level of antioxidants such as aspalathin and nothofagin, lacks caffeine, and has low tannin levels (compared to fully oxidized black tea). The flavor of rooibos tea is often described as sweet (without sugar added) and slightly nutty. The resulting brew is a reddish-brown color, explaining why rooibos is sometimes referred to as "red tea."

Place 3 tea bags of rooibos tea or 3 tsp (15 mL) of dried leaf and rooibos bark into a pot and pour 4 cups (1 L) of boiling filtered water over. Infuse for at least 20 minutes. A longer steeping time, up to 2 hours, will yield a stronger tea with more beneficial properties. Serve hot or iced. Add sweetener or lemon to taste, or steep with a peppermint tea bag for a more refreshing taste.

Makes 4 cups (1 L).

TULSI (HOLY BASIL) AND CHAMOMILE TEA

Modern scientific research confirms that tulsi (holy basil) reduces stress, enhances stamina, relieves inflammation, lowers cholesterol, eliminates toxins, protects against radiation, prevents gastric ulcers, lowers fevers, improves digestion, regulates blood pressure and blood sugar, and provides a rich supply of antioxidants and other nutrients. Tulsi is especially effective in supporting the heart, blood vessels, liver, and lungs.

Chamomile can help you fall asleep if you drink it before bed, but don't hesitate to sip it throughout the day. Its relaxing effects do not interfere with activities such as driving a car or completing difficult tasks. Chamomile is an ideal choice for people with ulcers or other stomach problems aggravated by anxiety. It's also recommended for muscle pain that results from stress. If you are experiencing muscle twitching, chamomile tea can help.

Place 2 tea bags of tulsi tea or 2 tsp (10 mL) of dried tulsi leaves and 2 tsp (10 mL) chamomile flowers (or 2 chamomile tea bags) into a pot and pour 6 cups (1.5 L) of boiling filtered water over. Infuse for at least 20 minutes. The tea must steep in hot water in a covered pot or teapot for at least 15 minutes. A longer steeping time, such as 2 hours, will yield a stronger tea with more beneficial properties. Serve hot or iced. If desired, add sweetener or lemon to taste, or steep with a peppermint tea bag.

Makes 6 cups (1.5 L).

DECOCTIONS (THE ESSENCE OF ROOTS AND BARK EXTRACTED BY HEATING OR BOILING)

Decoction is a method of making teas that involves placing plant matter in a pot with water, boiling the mixture for a set amount of time, and then straining the mixture before consumption.

Basic Instructions

1. Place 1 tsp (5 mL) of herbs per cup (250 mL) of water into a pot and bring to a gentle boil.

2. Simmer for 7 to 10 minutes. To increase the healing properties of the tea, keep it covered.

Delicate flowers and leaves should not be boiled, as this can reduce their medicinal properties. A longer steeping time, such as 15 to 20 minutes, yields a stronger tea with more beneficial properties. Serve steeped tea hot or iced. If you wish, add sweetener, lemon, or spices to taste.

Makes 1 cup (250 mL).

LICORICE TEA

Licorice root is a wonderfully sweet way to nourish the body. It contains glycyrrhizin and glycyrrhizic acid, both of which are anti-inflammatory. Licorice root tea calms the stomach lining, relieves exhausted adrenals, and nourishes nerves while providing an energy kick. Unlike caffeine, licorice is safe to use in the evening.

Place 2 one-inch (2.5 cm) pieces of whole licorice root in 4 cups (1 L) of water. Bring to a boil and simmer for 10 to 15 minutes.

Alternatively, place 1 tbsp (15 mL) of shredded licorice root in a teapot. Add 4 cups (1 L) of freshly boiled water. Steep for 15 minutes.

Makes 4 cups (1 L).

GINGER TEA

It is no surprise that Japan—where ginger root is used liberally—is home to the longest-living people in the world! Enjoy ginger root tea whenever your stomach is upset or when you're experiencing sore joints. If you're in a rush, you can use a tea bag, but it's a good idea to stock your fridge (or freezer) with fresh ginger root, as it is more effective.

2 inches (5 cm)   ginger root
4 cups (1 L)   filtered water

Finely chop ginger root and steep in boiling filtered water for at least 20 minutes. Consider steeping it overnight—a long infusion maximizes the transfer of the active ingredients into the liquid.

Makes 4 cups (1 L).

GINSENG TEA

Get to the root of fatigue with ginseng. According to naturopathic doctor Patrizio Nardini, "The active ingredients called ginsenosides work on the pituitary-adrenal axis, increasing resistance to stress, boosting metabolism, and increasing stamina." Unlike stimulants, ginseng optimizes hormonal balance and gives you sustained energy throughout the day.

Ginseng tea is slightly sweet at first taste, but may have a bit of a bitter aftertaste. It is often mixed with chrysanthemum tea and sweetened with raw honey.

Boil 4 cups (1 L) of water, add 8 to 10 ginseng slices, and simmer for 20 minutes. Strain and cool.

Makes 4 cups (1 L).

GINGER CHAI

This drink is anti-inflammatory and calming without making you drowsy. I recommend you have it to alleviate brain fog or an upset tummy. This is my all-time favorite fall and winter beverage. It is naturally warming and comforting.

4 cups (1 L)	unsweetened almond milk
4 cups (1 L)	Ginger Tea (see recipe on page 219)
½ tsp (2.5 mL)	cinnamon
½ tsp (2.5 mL)	stevia whole-leaf powder OR ¼ tsp (1 mL) stevia extract OR 1–2 tsp (5–10 mL) unpasteurized liquid honey
⅛ tsp (0.5 mL)	nutmeg
⅛ tsp (0.5 mL)	ground cloves

Combine all ingredients in a 3-quart (3 L) saucepan and simmer for 5 minutes.

Makes 8 cups (2 L).

BURDOCK TEA

Burdock (also known as gobo) is a root used in Japanese cuisine. It not only tastes great, but also is a strong liver detoxifier and hormone-balancing herb. The liver is the major calorie-burning organ in the body and regulates fat metabolism. When operating efficiently, the liver burns body fat and provides an exit route for fat from the body via bile. Burdock contains a carbohydrate called inulin, which supports healthy intestinal flora (however, it may irritate people who suffer from IBD). If fresh burdock is unavailable, use 1 tbsp (15 mL) of dried chopped root. Similar in flavor to boiled asparagus, burdock is a pleasant addition to soups and salads. Make the tea as suggested below and then marinate the fresh burdock pieces in lemon juice to be used in your favorite dish anytime.

12 inches (30 cm) burdock root

4 cups (1 L) filtered water

Slice the burdock into dime-sized pieces. Bring to a boil and simmer for 15 minutes. Drink the tea once it has cooled to a comfortable sipping temperature. Store leftover tea in a glass jar in the fridge. And don't worry—it's natural for it to turn bright green!

Makes 4 cups (1 L).

CHAI: RED, WHITE, AND GREEN

Popularized in India, spiced chai is a great source of antioxidants and nutrients that support digestion. Often served with milk and honey, chai can be served hot or cool. Traditional blends use a mixture of sweet and zesty spices such as cinnamon, ginger root, cardamom, and cloves. Each of these ingredients heals digestion and, as a result, reduces inflammation.

7 cups (1.75 L)	water
1 tbsp (15 mL)	fennel or anise seed
6	green cardamom pods
12	cloves
1	cinnamon stick
¼ inch (0.5 cm)	ginger root, sliced thinly
2 tbsp (30 mL)	green, white, or rooibos tea
6 tbsp (75 mL)	raw honey
1 cup (250 mL)	almond or rice milk

In a saucepan, combine first 6 ingredients (water and spices) in a pan, cover, and bring to a medium boil for 5 minutes. Turn off heat and steep for 10 minutes. Add tea and bring to a boil again, simmering for 5 minutes. Strain out spices and tea. Add honey and almond milk to taste.

Makes 8½ cups (2.25 L).

JUICES AND SMOOTHIES

Liquid meals can be powerful tools for nourishing your cells and cleansing your whole system. Here are some recipes for my favorite cleansing juices and strengthening smoothies.

223

MORNING LEMON CLEANSE

This recipe is an adaptation of Stanley Burroughs's Master Cleanse. Even if you aren't doing a formal cleanse, this beverage has benefits; it could be used occasionally throughout the entire MTHI plan to gently cleanse the body of toxins.

Drink this mixture before breakfast to help improve liver function and digestion. The classic Master Cleanse calls for maple syrup and cayenne and is consumed daily for forty days. I prefer to use a sweetener that is lower on the glycemic index, such as raw honey, and a cleansing spice that is less irritating to the intestines, such as turmeric. Choose organic, vine-ripened citrus whenever possible. Note: It is important that you consult a holistic practitioner for advice during a cleanse.

2 tbsp (30 mL)	lemon or lime juice (2 tbsp is the equivalent to the juice of ½ a lemon or 1 lime)
1 tbsp (15 mL)	raw honey OR 10 drops stevia extract liquid
⅛–¼ tsp (0.5–1 mL)	turmeric (gradually increase the amount used)
2 cups (500 mL)	filtered warm water

Combine the juice, honey, and turmeric with water in a large mug.

Makes 2 cups (500 mL).

CLEANSING GINGER LEMONADE

In herbal medicine, ginger root promotes the elimination of intestinal gas as well as relaxing and soothing the intestinal tract. Both the lemon and the ginger root are rich sources of antioxidants that inhibit inflammation.

2 inches (5 cm)	ginger root
4 cups (1 L)	filtered water
2 tbsp (30 mL)	organic lemon juice
1 tsp (5 mL)	whole stevia leaf, ground OR ½ tsp (2.5 mL) powdered stevia OR 20 drops of liquid stevia

Finely chop ginger root and steep in freshly boiled water for at least 20 minutes. Consider steeping it overnight, as a long infusion maximizes the transfer of the active ingredients into the liquid. Add lemon juice and stevia, and stir. Serve hot or cold for a refreshing and revitalizing treat.

Makes 4 cups (1 L).

PURIFIER JUICE

Many people have already discovered the powerful healing effects of juicing. Juicing fresh organic vegetables and fruit provides a concentrated source of vitamins, minerals, and enzymes. You might be hesitant to try vegetable juices, but it is quite common to develop a taste for and then a craving for them! The energy boost from drinking vegetable juices is also very similar to what you get from drinking coffee, but without the negative side effects. If you don't own a juicer, make the Green Shake on page 226. The greens in this recipe help balance the sugars from the carrots and apples. Because carrots are naturally high in sugar, it is important to dilute this juice with filtered water.

3 organic carrots

2 organic apples

½ organic cucumber

1 organic celery stalk

1 small bunch organic Swiss chard

Wash all produce in filtered water. Chop ingredients into small pieces so they fit easily into a juicer and add 1 cup (250 mL) filtered water. Juice the vegetables, stir, and drink immediately. Vegetable juice oxidizes quickly, so share the juice or store in a glass container and consume within 8 hours.

Makes 4 cups (1 L).

POPEYE CARROT JUICE

This juice packs a nutritional punch. The combination of carrots, spinach, and parsley provides an excellent source of antioxidants and is great for internal cleansing.

3 to 4	carrots
4 oz (125 g)	package fresh spinach, washed
4 cups (1 L)	fresh loose spinach
½ cup (125 mL)	flat-leaf parsley
1 medium	apple or pear
2 to 3	celery stalks
1 cup (250 mL)	filtered water
to taste	lemon, freshly squeezed

Juice all vegetables, leaving the celery for last. Stir in filtered water. Add lemon juice, if using.

Makes 4 cups (1 L).

Note: Vegetable juice oxidizes quickly, so share the juice or store in a glass container and consume within 8 hours.

GREEN SHAKE

For those who struggle to consume 5 to 7 daily servings of the vegetables necessary for repairing inflammation, a greens supplement is very important. If you mix the greens powder into juice, be sure to dilute the beverage with water to avoid spiking your blood sugar levels. Chlorella and spirulina are the two most popular forms of blue-green algae and are found in most health-food stores. They contain dozens of critical nutrients such as B vitamins and amino acids.

Note: If this is your first green drink, you may experience minor temporary side effects (headaches, loose stools, and blemishes) due to positive nutritional changes. Although unpleasant, these are signs that your body is getting rid of toxins.

½ cup (125 mL)   unsweetened berry or cherry juice
½ cup (125 mL)   filtered water
1 tsp (5 mL)   spirulina or chlorella powder

Pour the juice and water into a 2-cup (500 mL) glass jar (with a tight-fitting lid). Add the spirulina or chlorella powder, screw on the lid, and shake well to combine.

Makes 1 cup (250 mL).

PROTEIN HIGHLIGHT: SPIRULINA

Spirulina is a microscopic blue-green algae (also known as cyanobacteria) that flourishes in freshwater and saltwater. Its use as a food dates back to ancient civilizations, including the Kamen-Bornu and Baguirmi kingdoms of central Africa (near present-day Chad) and the Aztecs of South America.

Spirulina contains an unusually high amount of protein, between 55 and 77 percent by dry weight (depending on the source). It is a complete protein that contains all essential amino acids (though with reduced amounts of methionine, cysteine, and lysine when compared to the proteins of meat, eggs, and milk). It is, however, superior to typical plant protein, such as that of legumes.

Spirulina is rich in healing oils including a variety of omega-3 and omega-6 fats. In addition, spirulina contains vitamins B_1, B_2, B_3, B_6, C, D, and E and folic acid. It's a rich source of potassium and also contains calcium, chromium, iron, magnesium, manganese, selenium, and zinc.

FLAX-TO-THE-MAX SHAKE

I love this shake because it is thick, creamy, and green! Flax seeds provide fiber, protein, and omega-3s. Avocado provides anti-inflammatory omega-9 fat (which strengthens your cardiovascular system) and vitamin B_6 (which helps your liver maintain estrogen balance). Spirulina and chlorella boost energy.

2 tbsp (30 mL)	finely ground flax seed or flax protein powder
2 cups (500 mL)	filtered water
3 tbsp (45 mL)	raw honey OR 4 succulent Medjool dates, pitted
¼ tsp (1 mL)	cinnamon
½ medium	avocado (ripe)
1 tsp (5 mL)	spirulina or chlorella powder

OPTIONAL ADDITION:

1 tbsp (15 mL)	lemon juice

Combine all ingredients in a blender and blend until smooth.

Makes 2½ cups (625 mL).

BLUEBERRY HEMP SMOOTHIE

This is a fun and easy breakfast on the run. Blueberries and hemp seeds are both great inflammation fighters. Blueberries contain antioxidant anthocyanins and phenols. Using a test called ORAC (Oxygen Radical Absorbance Capacity), the USDA Human Nutrition Research Center on Aging reported that blueberries help protect the vascular and nervous systems, and especially the brain, from free radical–induced aging. Hemp provides healing omega-3 fats and a special omega-6 fat (called gamma-linolenic acid, abbreviated GLA), which helps to balance hormones.

2 tbsp (30 mL)	hemp seeds
1 cup (250 mL)	fresh or frozen blueberries
1 cup (250 mL)	unsweetened almond or hemp milk
1 tbsp (15 mL)	raw honey
1 tsp (5 mL)	pure vanilla extract
½ tsp (2.5 mL)	cinnamon

Combine all ingredients in a blender and blend until smooth.

Makes 2½ cups (625 mL).

VANILLA ALMOND MILK

If almond milk is not available at your local health-food store, it's easy to make in your kitchen blender. Almonds are a rich source of magnesium. Recent studies confirm that dates and raw honey nourish the nervous system and stimulate immune function. You can substitute hazelnuts for almonds for variety.

2 cups (500 mL)	filtered water for rinsing almonds
¾ cup (185 mL)	raw almonds
3 cups (750 mL)	filtered water
1 tbsp (15 mL)	pure vanilla extract
1	pitted Medjool date OR 1 tbsp (15 mL) raw honey

Soak the almonds in 2 cups (500 mL) filtered water in a jar in the refrigerator overnight. Drain water and rinse almonds. Blend the soaked almonds with 3 cups (750 mL) filtered water until smooth (approximately 2 minutes).

Strain the mixture into a large bowl, pressing with the back of a spoon to extract as much liquid as possible. (Refrigerate or freeze the almond pulp for later use—it can be added to porridge or soup for a nutty flavor.)

Return the almond milk to the blender, add the vanilla and date or raw honey, and blend until smooth. This milk will last in the refrigerator for about 3 to 5 days. Shake well before using.

Makes 3½ cups (875 mL).

LEGEND FOR THE RECIPES IN THIS BOOK

 The recipe is free of eggs and egg products.

 The recipe is free of soy and its derivatives.

 The recipe is free of dairy and its derivatives. Nut, seed, and rice milks are used as substitutes.

 The recipe is free of tree nuts. If you do not see this symbol and would like the recipe to be nut-free, consider substituting a seed instead.

 The recipe has a GI score of 55 or less on the glycemic index. The glycemic index (GI) is a system of measuring how fast a carbohydrate triggers a rise in circulating blood sugar. The higher the index number, the faster the blood sugar increases. A list of glycemic values for common foods is provided on page 92.

 The recipe is gluten-free. If you suffer from inflammatory bowel disease, ankylosing spondylitis, or irritable bowel syndrome, you may need to avoid certain forms of starch present in gluten-free grains. Be sure to keep a record of your progress and consult a health practitioner for a more individualized plan.

 The recipe has more than 70 percent raw ingredients. Raw nuts, seeds, and produce are very nutritious, but must be minimized for patients with inflammatory bowel disease. If you suffer from a digestive disorder, you may want to steam produce and soak nuts or seeds to assist digestion.

CHAPTER 12

MEALS TO BEGIN THE DAY

Remember the above quote when trying the following recipes. The size of your culinary world will expand if you have the courage to try some healing cuisine!

IMMUNE-BUILDING BROWN RICE CONGEE WITH CHICKEN OR FISH

Congee is a rice porridge commonly served for breakfast in Asia. Made with one part rice to about sixteen parts liquid, congee is easy to digest and tones the body, so it is often given to weak or frail people. This is an excellent soup when you are feeling cold, weak, or generally unwell. A slow cooker works well to prepare this, and you can cook it all day (8 hours) if you choose. If you do, use about 2 cups (500 mL) more water. This recipe optionally includes astragalus root, an herb native to China and available at health-food stores. It is thought to relieve weakness and fatigue and to enhance stamina and immunity. Chicken stock makes the best-tasting congee, but if you do not have any on hand, you can use filtered water. Adding unpasteurized miso at the end provides a rich flavor and probiotic boost.

INGREDIENTS:

8 cups (2 L)	chicken or vegetable stock or filtered water
½ cup (125 mL)	short-grain brown rice
6 oz (170 g)	chicken breast OR 2 large white fish fillets,
	chopped into small pieces
½ tsp (2.5 mL)	gray sea salt or pink rock salt
1 tbsp (15 mL)	miso, dissolved in 2 tbsp (30 mL) of water
3	green onions (scallions), finely chopped
2 tbsp (30 mL)	finely grated ginger root
1½ tsp (7.5 mL)	toasted sesame oil (¼ tsp/1 mL per serving)

OPTIONAL ADDITIONS:

4 cups (1 L)	red chard, kale, or spinach, chopped
¼ cup (60 mL)	dried and sliced astragalus root

DIRECTIONS:

1. Combine the stock or water, rice, chicken, astragalus (if using), and sea salt in the largest stockpot you have, or in a slow cooker set on high.

2. Bring to a simmer over medium heat.

3. Turn the heat as low as possible. (Place the pan on a diffuser if you have one.) If using a slow cooker, turn it down to a simmer.

4. Cook for 4 to 8 hours (you might start this in the evening, cooking it overnight in a slow cooker so the congee is ready when you wake up). Turn off the heat and stir in the miso mixture. Fold in leafy greens, if using, and allow to wilt.

5. Serve in deep bowls topped with the green onions, grated ginger root, and sesame oil.

Makes 6 servings.

GRAIN-FREE BERRY MUFFINS

I just love a breakfast muffin that is satisfying but not too sweet. This moist muffin is more of a scone and offers wonderful anti-inflammatory magnesium and antioxidants. The high amount of cinnamon balances blood sugar.

INGREDIENTS:

2½ cups (625 mL)	almond flour
1 tsp (5 mL)	baking soda
½ tsp (2.5 mL)	gray sea salt or pink rock salt
1 tbsp (15 mL)	cinnamon
½ cup (125 mL)	extra-virgin olive oil
3 large	organic eggs
½ cup (125 mL)	unpasteurized liquid honey
1 tbsp (15 mL)	pure vanilla extract
1 cup (250 mL)	blueberries or raspberries, fresh or frozen

DIRECTIONS:

1. Preheat the oven to 300°F (150°C). Line a standard 12-cup muffin tin with paper liners.

2. In a medium bowl, whisk together the almond flour, baking soda, salt, and cinnamon. Add the oil, eggs, honey, and vanilla to the dry ingredients and stir until the batter is smooth. Using a silicone spatula, gently fold in the blueberries just until they are evenly distributed throughout the batter.

3. Divide batter between muffin cups. Bake the muffins on the center rack for 35 minutes, rotating the pan after 15 minutes. A toothpick inserted into the center of the muffin should come out clean.

4. Let the muffins stand for 15 minutes, then transfer to a wire rack and let cool completely. Store the muffins in an airtight container at room temperature for up to 3 days.

Makes 12 muffins.

TEFF PORRIDGE

Teff, a very nutritious ancient African grain, is easy to digest and will leave you feeling satisfied for the whole morning. It is gluten-free and also very low on the allergy scale because it has rarely been used in Western diets. Teff has a nutty flavor and is high in iron. Eating this delicious alternative to oatmeal is especially important for women during their menstrual period when they lose iron and are more susceptible to anemia.

If you are unable to find teff in your local health-food store, this recipe can also be made with quinoa.

INGREDIENTS:

1 cup (250 mL)	whole-grain teff
3 cups (750 mL)	filtered water
2 tsp (10 mL)	cinnamon
¼ tsp (1 mL)	ground cloves
1	large apple, chopped
¼ tsp (1 mL)	gray sea salt or pink rock salt
½ cup (125 mL)	walnuts, almonds, or hemp seeds
2 tbsp (30 mL)	raw honey (or to taste)
to taste	unsweetened almond milk (for serving)

DIRECTIONS:

1. Set a heavy 2-quart (2 L) saucepan over medium heat. Add the teff, stirring frequently for 3 to 6 minutes until the grains give off a mild, toasted aroma and begin to pop. (You will see little white dots of popped grain, but may not hear the popping.)

2. Take the pan off the heat and, standing back to avoid spatters, add the water and spices. Stir well to combine.

3. Turn the heat to low-medium, then cover and simmer for 10 minutes, stirring often to prevent the grains from sticking to the bottom.

4. Add the chopped apple and salt. Stir and heat for a few minutes. Add nuts or seeds before serving.

5. Serve warm with a drizzle of raw honey and almond milk.

Makes 3 to 4 servings.

PESTO OMELET

This wonderful omelet celebrates the flavors of Italy. It's both super-high in protein and deeply satisfying. The onions and oregano in the seasoning contain phytonutrients that protect the olive oil from being damaged from cooking heat. The broccoli and carrot provide lots of healing vitamin A and fiber, which are beneficial for the digestive system.

INGREDIENTS:

1 tbsp (15 mL)	extra-virgin olive oil
1 tsp (5 mL)	Italian herb blend (basil, marjoram, oregano, rosemary, sage, savory, and/or thyme)
4 tbsp (60 mL)	chopped red onion
4 tbsp (60 mL)	finely grated carrot
½ cup (125 mL)	broccoli, chopped finely
4 large	organic eggs
2 tbsp (30 mL)	dairy- and nut-free pesto (store-bought or see page 278)
pinch	gray sea salt or pink rock salt

OPTIONAL ADDITIONS:

2 tbsp (30 mL)	black beans
½ cup (125 mL)	chopped fresh basil
6	olives, chopped

DIRECTIONS:

1. Lightly coat a medium cast-iron sauté pan with olive oil and add Italian herb blend and onion.

2. Heat pan over medium-low heat and add carrot and broccoli. Spritz liberally with filtered water or broth to ensure the oil doesn't overheat. Sauté for about 3 to 4 minutes or until vegetables are just tender.

3. In the meantime, whisk the eggs until they are foamy and light.

4. Pour eggs over the vegetables, cover, and cook for about 2 minutes or until eggs are almost set.

5. Distribute pesto and black beans (if using) evenly over eggs.

6. Fold omelet in half and add more pesto for color. Cook 2 minutes longer over low heat. Season with salt. Garnish with basil and olives, if using.

Makes 2 servings. If you're cooking for one, consider packing the second serving for an afternoon snack at work.

WARMING QUINOA PORRIDGE

This hot cereal takes just a few minutes to prepare. The spices are all wonderful for soothing the digestive tract and reducing inflammation. Feel free to use whatever fruits and spices you have on hand. Rolled quinoa is similar to rolled oats in texture but has much smaller flakes. By rolling the grain flat, it cooks in a fraction of the time. This cereal is perfect for a portable meal—simply boil the water and pour it into a wide-mouth Thermos, add all the remaining ingredients, and enjoy when you get to your destination. For extra creaminess, serve with almond or coconut milk.

INGREDIENTS:

2 cups (500 mL)	filtered water
¾ cup (185 mL)	rolled quinoa flakes
1 tsp (5 mL)	cinnamon
½ tsp (2.5 mL)	cardamom powder
¼ tsp (1 mL)	nutmeg
¼ tsp (1 mL)	turmeric
1 tbsp (15 mL)	raw honey OR 5 drops stevia extract liquid
⅛ tsp (0.5 mL)	gray sea salt or pink rock salt
½ cup (125 mL)	apple, diced
½ cup (125 mL)	blueberries (if frozen, add before quinoa to thaw)
¼ cup (60 mL)	chopped almonds or hemp seeds

DIRECTIONS:

1. Boil the water in a small saucepan. Add the rolled quinoa and stir for 2 to 3 minutes.

2. Remove from heat and mix in the spices, raw honey, apple and blueberries, and almonds.

Makes 2 servings.

CREAMY RICE PORRIDGE WITH CRANBERRIES

Most rice pudding recipes stimulate insulin release quickly because they are made with white rice and sugar. The short-grain brown rice in this dish not only is rich in B vitamins and fiber but also has an extra-creamy texture. You can replace the cranberries with dried blueberries or black cherries for variety, or omit them altogether if desired. This dish is so tasty that it can be eaten as a treat as well as a sound breakfast.

INGREDIENTS:

3 cups (750 mL)	almond milk (water can be substituted if needed)
1 cup (250 mL)	short-grain brown rice
1 tsp (5 mL)	lemon zest
pinch	gray sea salt or pink rock salt
⅓ cup (85 mL)	dried cranberries (apple juice sweetened)
1 tsp (5 mL)	cinnamon (or to taste)
1 tsp (5 mL)	pure vanilla extract
¼ cup (60 mL)	coconut milk (optional)
½ cup (125 mL)	hemp seeds OR 2 oz (60 g) rice protein powder
2 tbsp (30 mL)	raw honey (optional)

GARNISH:

1 tbsp (15 mL)	nuts and seeds

DIRECTIONS:

1. Over high heat, bring almond milk, rice, lemon zest, and salt to a boil in an uncovered pot.

2. Reduce heat to low and simmer, stirring occasionally, for 45 minutes.

3. Add cranberries and cinnamon. Cook on low for another 15 minutes or until rice is tender and liquid is absorbed. The rice should be very creamy.

4. Stir vanilla into pudding. Simmer for 2 minutes. Remove from heat.

5. Fold coconut milk and hemp seeds into pudding.

6. If desired, sweeten with a drizzle of honey or extra cinnamon, or add crunch with nuts or seeds.

Makes 4 servings.

AMARANTH PORRIDGE

Amaranth is an ancient grain dating back hundreds of years to the Aztec culture in Mexico. It offers unusually high levels of protein (higher than most other grains). Amaranth contains a whopping 20 grams of fiber per serving, higher than wheat, corn, rice, or soybeans. It is a gluten-free grain with a great nutty flavor and a smooth creamy texture when cooked. This is one of my favorite comfort-food breakfasts!

INGREDIENTS:

⅔ cup (175 mL)	whole-grain amaranth
2 cups (500 mL)	filtered water
¼ cup (60 mL)	hemp seeds or pumpkin seeds
1 tbsp (15 mL)	raw honey
1 tsp (5 mL)	cinnamon
½ cup (125 mL)	blueberries or dried cranberries (apple juice sweetened)
1	medium pear, chopped

DIRECTIONS:

1. Amaranth's sticky consistency calls for a cast-iron or titanium surface to minimize heavy cleanup. If you don't have a natural nonstick skillet, you can use a heavy 2-quart (2 L) saucepan, but make sure to stir the porridge frequently to avoid sticking.

2. Combine the amaranth and water in a skillet with a tight-fitting lid.

3. Bring to a boil, cover, and turn down to low heat. Simmer for 25 to 30 minutes, stirring once every 10 minutes to ensure the grains don't stick to the pot, until the liquid is completely absorbed.

4. Remove from heat and add the seeds, raw honey, and cinnamon, stirring well. Divide the hot cereal between two bowls (or put one portion in a sealable container for the next day), and top with blueberries and pear.

Makes 2 servings.

WARM AND SAVORY BREAKFAST SOUP

The Japanese start their day with something savory, which helps to keep their blood sugar balanced throughout the day to reduce cravings. Try to eat lunch and dinner menu items (which are typically higher in protein) for breakfast as often as you can, since they can prevent insulin spikes and slow destructive inflammatory reactions in the body. They will also improve mood, which is critical for healing.

INGREDIENTS:

4½ cups (1.1 L)	filtered water
3 cups (750 mL)	chopped leeks
1½ cups (375 mL)	finely chopped black kale or broccoli
1 cup (250 mL)	cooked adzuki or black beans
¼ cup (60 mL)	arame seaweed
2 cups (500 mL)	enoki mushrooms
2 tsp (10 mL)	minced ginger root
4 tbsp (60 mL)	miso

DIRECTIONS:

1. Bring water to a boil in a medium saucepan.

2. Add vegetables, beans, seaweed, mushrooms, and ginger root and simmer for 10 minutes until vegetables are soft but still bright green.

3. Turn off the heat and add miso, stirring until dissolved.

Makes 4 servings.

Note: Don't let miso boil—boiling kills its healthy bacteria (probiotics) and reduces its therapeutic properties.

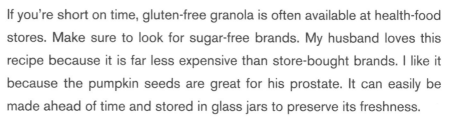

CRANBERRY QUINOA GRANOLA

If you're short on time, gluten-free granola is often available at health-food stores. Make sure to look for sugar-free brands. My husband loves this recipe because it is far less expensive than store-bought brands. I like it because the pumpkin seeds are great for his prostate. It can easily be made ahead of time and stored in glass jars to preserve its freshness.

INGREDIENTS:

⅓ cup (85 mL)	organic apple butter
3 tbsp (45 mL)	tahini (or substitute another nut butter if unavailable)
½ tsp (2.5 mL)	pure vanilla extract
4 tbsp (60 mL)	unpasteurized liquid honey (or to taste)
2 cups (500 mL)	rolled quinoa
2 tsp (10 mL)	cinnamon
½ tsp (2.5 mL)	nutmeg
½ tsp (2.5 mL)	cardamom
1 tbsp (15 mL)	flax seed protein powder
¾ cup (185 mL)	chopped hazelnuts
½ cup (125 mL)	pumpkin seeds
½ cup (125 mL)	dried cranberries, apple juice sweetened
½ cup (125 mL)	dried blueberries, apple juice sweetened

DIRECTIONS:

1. Preheat oven to 275°F (135°C).

2. Combine the wet ingredients in a bowl, and stir.

3. Stir the dry ingredients, except hazelnuts, pumpkin seeds, and dried berries, into the wet mixture. Stir it all together and spread onto unbleached parchment–lined baking sheet.

4. Break up large clumps to ensure even cooking.

5. Bake for 45 minutes to 1 hour, stirring every 15 minutes to ensure even browning, until the granola is starting to crisp.

6. Remove the granola from the oven and stir in the hazelnuts, pumpkin seeds, and dried berries. Cool granola completely on the pan before transferring to an airtight container. It will get crunchy as it cools.

Makes 4 cups (1 L).

Note: Consider doubling this recipe! Store in an airtight container and use within two weeks. Freeze for longer storage.

JAKE'S MUFFIN MAX

These muffins taste so good and fresh that you'll be fooled into thinking they contain some of the ingredients you are avoiding on the MTHI plan. My friend Jake created these muffins for his son who is on a gluten-free diet. Because the healthy whole-grain quinoa is mixed with the light arrow-root flour, the muffins have a consistency that is close to regular flour. The xanthan gum adds springiness to the muffin, which otherwise is lost when using gluten-free grains. Coconut sugar is extracted from the nectar of coconut flowers and is much lower on the glycemic index, making it a good choice for healing. It is found in many health-food stores.

INGREDIENTS:

2 portions	vegan egg substitute (see next page)
½ cup (125 mL)	coconut oil
¾ cup (185 mL)	coconut sugar
½ tsp (2.5 mL)	pure vanilla extract
2 cups (500 mL)	grated apple
½ cup (125 mL)	quinoa flakes
½ cup (125 mL)	coconut flour
½ cup (125 mL)	sorghum flour

½ cup (125 mL)   arrowroot flour

1¼ tsp (6 mL)   xanthan gum

2 tsp (10 mL)   baking powder (aluminum- and gluten-free can be
found in a health-food store)

1¼ tsp (6 mL)   baking soda

½ tsp (2.5 mL)   cinnamon

½ tsp (2.5 mL)   nutmeg

½ tsp (2.5 mL)   gray sea salt or pink rock salt

¾ cup (185 mL)   blueberries, fresh or frozen

¾ cup (185 mL)   raspberries, fresh or frozen

To make vegan egg substitute: Use 1 tbsp (15 mL) ground flax and 3 tbsp (45 mL) water for each egg. Gently warm in a saucepan over low heat and stir continuously for a couple of minutes until mixture thickens into the gelatinous consistency of an egg. Allow to cool.

DIRECTIONS:

1. Preheat the oven to 350°F (175°C) and line a 12-cup muffin tin with paper liners.

2. In a large bowl, mix together the egg substitute, oil, coconut sugar, and vanilla. Add the apples and stir to combine.

3. In a separate bowl, whisk together all of the dry ingredients. Add the dry ingredients to the wet, and stir until just combined. Stir in the blueberries and raspberries. Do not overmix or the muffins will be dense.

4. Spoon the batter into the muffin tin. Bake for 30 to 40 minutes, until puffed and golden brown. A toothpick inserted into the center of a muffin should come out clean.

Makes 12 muffins. Store the muffins in an airtight container.

APPLE RICE BAKE

This is a great way to use up leftover brown rice from dinner. You can also use leftover millet or quinoa for variety. This makes a nutritious breakfast loaded with B vitamins and energy-packed minerals. It tastes like rice pudding and apple pie in one. Yummy!

INGREDIENTS:

2 cups (500 mL)	cooked brown rice
1 cup (250 mL)	almond milk (or rice milk, if unavailable)
½ cup (125 mL)	almonds or hazelnuts, chopped
2 tsp (10 mL)	cinnamon
1 tbsp (15 mL)	pure vanilla extract
3 tbsp (45 mL)	unpasteurized liquid honey
½ tsp (2.5 mL)	nutmeg
1 tsp (5 mL)	ginger root
½ tsp (2.5 mL)	turmeric
2 cups (500 mL)	apple, chopped but unpeeled (about 2 large apples)
1 tsp (5 mL)	psyllium husk powder (optional—adds extra fiber)
3 large	organic eggs, whisked OR 3 egg substitutes (see recipe, page 244)
pinch	gray sea salt or pink rock salt

DIRECTIONS:

1. Use a fork to mix all ingredients together in a large mixing bowl.

2. Pour into a 11 × 7 × 2–inch baking dish and bake at 350°F (175°C) for 35 to 45 minutes. If using egg substitute, bake 15 minutes longer.

Makes 8 servings.

FLAX APPLE PUDDING

This breakfast is not only tasty, but also incredibly healthy! The apples each contain 5 grams of fiber, including pectin, which is very beneficial for cleansing the gallbladder. Flax is one of the highest sources of soluble fiber, which cleanses the colon and reduces cholesterol. Flax seeds contain up to 800 times more active lignans (plant estrogens found in the outer husk) than other plant sources. Studies have shown that these powerful antioxidants may reduce the risk of hormone-sensitive cancers, such as breast and prostate cancers. Slippery elm bark powder is an exceptionally healing herb that soothes inflammation in the stomach and small intestine. It has a slightly sweet taste and a smooth, silky texture.

Note: If you choose to grind your own flax seeds in a coffee grinder, set it to extra fine for a smooth result. Occasionally, I like to replace the flax seeds in this recipe with ground chia seeds for variety.

INGREDIENTS:

3	medium apples (unpeeled), cored and diced
½ cup (125 mL)	filtered water
2 tbsp (30 mL)	flax protein powder or finely ground flax seeds
1 tsp (5 mL)	pure vanilla extract
½ tsp (2.5 mL)	cinnamon

OPTIONAL TOPPINGS:

1 tsp (5 mL)	slippery elm bark powder + 2 tbsp (30 mL) filtered water
1 tbsp (15 mL)	chopped almonds
1 tbsp (15 mL)	shredded coconut
to taste	unsweetened almond milk (for serving)

DIRECTIONS:

1. Bring the apples and water to a boil in a medium saucepan, then cover and reduce heat to a simmer for 10 minutes until the apples are soft and mushy. If you plan to use slippery elm bark powder

as a topping, add an extra 2 tablespoons (30 mL) of water before cooking apples.

2. Remove from heat; mix in the flax protein powder or flax seeds, vanilla, and cinnamon until smooth.

3. Portion into a breakfast bowl (or two). Top with slippery elm bark powder, chopped almonds and/or shredded coconut, and almond milk.

Makes 2 small servings or 1 very large serving.

ANDA BHURJI (INDIAN SCRAMBLED EGGS)

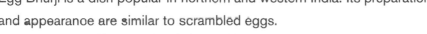

Egg Bhurji is a dish popular in northern and western India. Its preparation and appearance are similar to scrambled eggs.

Curry contains a powerful healing herb called turmeric that appears to protect the delicate blood vessels in the brain from the plaque that is responsible for reduced brain function. Researchers have found a correlation between the high consumption of turmeric and low rates of Alzheimer's disease among South Asians. By adding turmeric to the oil at the beginning, you protect the oil from oxidation and remove the turmeric's bitterness.

INGREDIENTS:

1 tbsp (15 mL)	extra-virgin olive oil
½ tsp (2.5 mL)	cumin
½ tsp (2.5 mL)	turmeric
½ cup (125 mL)	onions, sliced
1 cup (250 mL)	zucchini, into ½-inch (1 cm) dice
½ cup (125 mL)	diced asparagus
½ tsp (2.5 mL)	gray sea salt or pink rock salt

½ tsp (2.5 mL)	coriander
½ tsp (2.5 mL)	cinnamon
4 large	organic eggs
½ cup (125 mL)	fresh cilantro leaves, chopped

DIRECTIONS:

1. Warm oil in skillet on medium-low heat and add cumin seed and turmeric powders. Stir for a few seconds.

2. Add the onions and cook for 2 minutes.

3. Add the zucchini and asparagus and cook 3 to 4 minutes.

4. Add the salt, coriander, and cinnamon.

5. Stir and cook for 2 minutes.

6. Whisk eggs in a small bowl and pour into pan. Add cilantro and stir until the eggs are cooked.

Makes 2 servings.

> *"Soup is cuisine's kindest course. It breathes reassurance; it steams consolation; after a weary day it promotes sociability. Soup is the song of the hearth . . . and the home."*
>
> —LOUIS P. DEGOUY, *THE SOUP BOOK*

CHAPTER 13

SOUPS AND SIDES

ROASTED FENNEL WITH OLIVES AND GARLIC

Roasting brings out fennel's sweet side. Fennel is rich in vitamin C, potassium, and fiber, and is very easy to digest. The green fronds can be tough when roasted. I like them, but remove them if you prefer soft-roasted fennel. Olives are rich in the polyphenol phytonutrient hydroxytyrosol, which is being researched for breast cancer prevention. The spices protect the olive oil from potential heat damage.

INGREDIENTS:

3	medium-sized fennel bulbs (5 inch/12 cm in diameter)
¼ cup (60 mL)	extra-virgin olive oil
6	large cloves garlic, coarsely chopped
1 tbsp (15 mL)	fresh thyme, chopped
to taste	gray sea salt or pink rock salt
½ cup (125 mL)	pitted kalamata olives, halved

DIRECTIONS:

1. Preheat oven to 350°F (175°C).

2. Trim fennel, then cut each bulb vertically into 8 wedges.

3. Combine fennel, olive oil, garlic, and thyme in a large bowl. Toss to coat.

4. Spread fennel on a baking sheet. Sprinkle with salt and roast for 15 minutes.

5. Using tongs, turn wedges over. Continue to roast until tender, about 20 minutes.

6. Sprinkle olives over fennel and roast for about 8 minutes or until fennel begins to lightly brown at edges.

7. Transfer to a bowl. Serve warm or at room temperature. This recipe can be made up to a day ahead.

Makes 8 servings.

SESAME GREEN BEANS

Ginger root, turmeric, sesame seed, and extra-virgin olive oil all boast anti-inflammatory properties. Unrefined sesame oil contains an antioxidant called sesamol, which protects it from becoming rancid. Sesamol is also antifungal. A Harvard Medical School study showed that mice with damaged intestines recovered much faster on a diet rich in sesame oil. Sesame seeds also contain the highest total phytosterol content (about 400 mg per 100 g). Plant sterols reduce cholesterol, enhance the immune response, and decrease the risk of certain cancers.

INGREDIENTS:

3 cups (750 mL)   green beans (trimmed)

DRESSING:

2 tbsp (30 mL)   chia, flax, perilla, or sacha inchi seed oil

1   garlic clove

2 tbsp (30 mL)   toasted sesame seed oil

1 tbsp (15 mL)   tamari (wheat-free)

1   lemon, juiced

½ tsp (2.5 mL)   turmeric

¼ cup (60 mL)   black or brown sesame seeds (garnish)

DIRECTIONS:

1. Water-sauté the green beans with 1 inch (2.5 cm) of water (a technique whereby you "sauté" the beans in water instead of oil, briefly blanching and rotating them, which preserves the vitamins in the beans while speeding up cooking time). Keep moving them around to cook evenly for 5 to 7 minutes. (Alternatively, you can steam the beans.)

2. Mix dressing ingredients (except sesame seeds) in a glass jar and set aside.

3. Remove beans from the water (which can be saved and used later as vegetable broth if desired) and place them in a serving bowl.

4. Pour the dressing over the beans, sprinkle with sesame seeds, and toss to coat evenly. Serve warm or cool. Refrigerated, the beans will keep for up to 3 days.

Makes 4 to 6 servings.

JICAMA STICKS

This vegetable tastes like water chestnut, apple, and potato combined. It's crisp and has a crunch that is deeply satisfying. Its sweet flavor comes from the inulin, a fiber also known as fructooligosaccharide, which helps to feed the probiotic bacteria in the digestive tract. It's one of my favorite snacks and is only 45 calories per cup.

INGREDIENTS:

1 large jicama
½ cup (125 mL) lemon juice

DIRECTIONS:

1. Peel the jicama and chop into ½ × 4–inch (1 cm × 10 cm) sticks.

2. Soak pieces in lemon juice and chill. Enjoy right out of the fridge.

Makes 4 cups (1 L).

PESTO SWEET POTATO MASH

At one of our first romantic dinners, this recipe won the heart (and stomach!) of my husband. It's a super-fast recipe that wows every time. Sweet potato isn't a nightshade vegetable and is lower on the glycemic index than white potatoes, making it a great anti-inflammatory comfort food. Sweet potato has more than double the amount of fiber of two white potatoes of the same size. It's also a great source of vitamin B_6, a critical nutrient for supporting hormone balance.

253

INGREDIENTS:

2 lb (900 g)	sweet potatoes or yams, diced into ½-inch (1 cm) cubes
4	garlic cloves, peeled and chopped
½ cup (125 mL)	dairy- and nut-free pesto (store-bought or see page 278)
¼ tsp (1 mL)	gray sea salt or pink rock salt

DIRECTIONS:

1. Put the sweet potatoes and garlic in a large saucepan and add cold water to just cover.

2. Bring to a boil over high heat. Reduce heat to medium-low. Simmer, covered, for 20 to 25 minutes, until potatoes are tender. Drain off the cooking water (storing it in a glass jar for sweet vegetable broth later).

3. Mash roughly with a potato masher, then stir in the pesto and salt.

Makes 4 to 6 servings.

DULSE CHIPS

Dulse is packed with an abundance of trace minerals that rebuild the nerves and immune system. Dulse is also rich in phytonutrients that reduce the body's inflammatory response. If you are missing potato chips, the crispiness of dulse may help satisfy your cravings. You can also crush dulse into flakes after toasting or grind it in a saltshaker to give salads and soups an intense salty flavor with a balanced mineral profile. Be mindful of portion size if on a sodium-reduced diet.

INGREDIENT:

40 g package   dulse strips

DIRECTIONS:

1. Preheat the oven to 300°F (150°C).

2. Spread the dulse evenly on a cookie sheet.

3. Bake for 10 to 12 minutes, until crispy. Be sure it dries out completely to give desired texture.

Makes 2 cups (500 mL). Dulse chips will keep indefinitely in an airtight container.

CAULIFLOWER WHIP

Puréed cauliflower has the same texture as mashed potatoes. It tastes great as a side dish or as a late-afternoon snack. Cauliflower is an excellent source of B vitamins, vitamin C, and fiber. By serving this instead of mashed potatoes, you not only reduce the potential for inflammation, but also slash calories (1 cup/250 mL of mashed potato contains 200 calories whereas the same serving of mashed cauliflower contains 100 calories).

INGREDIENTS:

2 cups (500 mL)	filtered water
1	small head of cauliflower (3–4 cups or 1 L)
¼ cup (60 mL)	chia, flax, or hemp seed oil
1 tsp (5 mL)	gray sea salt or pink rock salt (or to taste)
1 tsp (5 mL)	lemon juice

CURRY OPTION:

½ tsp (2.5 mL)	coriander
½ tsp (2.5 mL)	cumin
2	garlic cloves, minced
¼ tsp (1 mL)	turmeric

DIRECTIONS:

1. Cut the cauliflower into 3-inch (7.5 cm) florets. Place them in a large pot with the small amount of water. Cover and turn the heat to high.

2. Bring to a boil and then turn down to simmer, allowing the cauliflower above the surface of the water to be steamed for 6 to 8 minutes or until soft when pierced with a knife. This cooking method preserves more of the nutrients.

3. Remove from heat and drain. Transfer the cooked cauliflower, oil, salt, lemon juice, and garlic and spices, if using, into a food processor or blender and purée until very smooth.

Makes 2 cups (500 mL).

LENTIL SPINACH DAL

Garam masala is the most aromatic and fragrant of all Indian spice blends. Compared to store-bought garam masala, a fresh homemade spice blend tastes better and has a more potent healing effect.

INGREDIENTS:

4 cups (1 L)	filtered water
1 cup (250 mL)	chana dal (a yellow lentil also known as cholar dal), rinsed well
1 tsp (5 mL)	turmeric
pinch	gray sea salt or pink rock salt (or to taste)
10 oz (285 mL)	frozen spinach OR 2 cups (500 mL) fresh spinach, chopped
1 tbsp (15 mL)	extra-virgin olive oil
1 tsp (5 mL)	cumin seeds
1 cup (250 mL)	onion, chopped
3	garlic cloves, chopped
2 tsp (10 mL)	coriander
1 tsp (5 mL)	Julie's Garam Masala (see page 257)
4 tbsp (60 mL)	lemon juice
garnish	fresh cilantro

DIRECTIONS:

1. Bring the water to a boil in a large pot and add the dal. Lower the heat to medium, add the turmeric and salt, and simmer for 35 minutes. After 20 minutes, uncover pot and skim off lentil foam with a spoon.

2. Add the spinach and cook for 4 to 5 minutes until the spinach is tender.

3. About 10 minutes before the dal is ready, gently heat the oil in a skillet and then add the cumin seeds. As they start to pop, add the onions and sauté until translucent.

4. Add the garlic, coriander, and garam masala and cook, stirring, for 2 minutes.

5. Add the dal mixture and lemon juice. Stir and heat through.

6. Garnish with cilantro and serve.

Makes 6 servings.

JULIE'S GARAM MASALA

INGREDIENTS:

2 tbsp (30 mL)	cumin seeds
2 tbsp (30 mL)	coriander seeds
2 tbsp (30 mL)	cardamom seeds
1 stick (3 in/5 cm)	cinnamon, broken into small pieces
1 tsp (5 mL)	whole cloves
1 tsp (5 mL)	freshly grated nutmeg
½ tsp (2.5 mL)	saffron or safflower petals (optional)

DIRECTIONS:

1. Place cumin, coriander, cardamom, cinnamon, and cloves in a spice mill or coffee grinder and grind to a powder. Stir in nutmeg and saffron.

Makes ½ cup (125 mL).

SUNNY FLAX CRACKERS

Omega-3 fats in flax seeds act as essential building blocks for cell membranes and help reduce inflammation. Both turmeric and ginger root are powerful anti-inflammatory spices, making this the ultimate cracker choice for healing. It may seem like a lot of work to make your own crackers, but this recipe takes only a few minutes of prep time. To prepare these crackers, you will need a dehydrator or an unbleached parchment-lined baking sheet. If using an oven, double the recipe to reduce the number of times you have to use your oven.

INGREDIENTS:

1 cup (250 mL)	flax seeds
1 cup (250 mL)	sunflower seeds
2 cups (500 mL)	filtered water (used to soak the seeds only)
2	lemons, juiced OR 4 tbsp (60 mL) lemon juice
1 tsp (5 mL)	raw honey OR 3 drops stevia extract liquid
1 tbsp (15 mL)	minced fresh ginger root
1 tsp (5 mL)	turmeric
1 tsp (5 mL)	gray sea salt or pink rock salt

DIRECTIONS:

1. Place the flax and sunflower seeds in a glass jar and then pour in the water. Soak overnight. (If you're in a hurry, you can make the crackers with just a 30-minute soak, but the flax will not sprout in that time. Otherwise, the recipe tastes about the same.)

2. In the morning (or 6 to 8 hours later), drain off the remaining liquid. Do not rinse. The stickiness of the wet seeds glues the recipe ingredients together.

3. Put the flax mixture in a food processor fitted with the S-blade, along with lemon juice, honey, spices, and salt. Blend until mixture is uniform.

4. Spread the mixture evenly onto your dehydrator fruit-roll trays or onto an 18 × 13 × 1–inch (40 × 30 × 2 cm) baking sheet lined with unbleached parchment paper.

5. If using a dehydrator, set at 115°F (45°C) for about 12 hours.

6. If using an oven, use the lowest setting and crack the door open with something heatproof, like a ball of tinfoil or a wooden spoon, to allow the moisture to escape. It will take anywhere from 3 hours (if you have a convection oven) to 8 hours (if you have an older oven) to dehydrate. Be sure not to cook the flax seeds or you will damage the delicate oil. The flax seeds should not change color. When the cracker separates easily from the tray and is stiff, it is ready.

7. When nice and dry, break into big pieces. Transfer to an airtight container and store in a dry place.

Makes 24 to 36 crackers.

VEGETABLE MISO SOUP

Miso is a fermented soybean paste made with rice. Nori is a paper-thin sheet of seaweed, often used to wrap sushi, and can be found at Asian markets or health-food stores. Seaweeds are a good source of magnesium, which acts as a natural relaxant, and help prevent migraine headaches and reduce the severity of asthma symptoms. Because miso settles, be sure to stir the soup before eating. The optional bonito (fish) flakes add a rich flavor to this recipe. If on a sodium-reduced diet, use half the miso and a salt-free vegetable stock.

INGREDIENTS:

4 cups (1 L)	vegetable or fish stock or filtered water
2¼ cups (560 mL)	filtered water (divided)
4 oz (120 g)	tempeh, cut into ¼-inch (0.5 cm) cubes
1 cup (250 mL)	sliced shiitake mushrooms
1	carrot, sliced
2 cups (500 mL)	broccoli florets
⅓ cup (85 mL)	miso

OPTIONAL ADDITIONS:

1 tbsp (15 mL)	bonito flakes
1 sheet	nori

DIRECTIONS:

1. In a large saucepan, combine the stock and 2 cups (500 mL) of water and bring to a boil.

2. Stir in the tempeh and mushrooms. Reduce heat to medium-low and simmer for 10 minutes.

3. Add the carrot and broccoli and cook for about 5 minutes or until the broccoli is al dente. Remove the soup from heat.

4. Dissolve the miso (and bonito flakes, if using) in the remaining ¼ cup (60 mL) of water, then whisk the miso mixture into the pot.

5. If using the nori, use scissors to cut sheet into 3 × ¼–inch (8 cm × 5 mm) strips and add to the top of the soup as a garnish. Serve hot.

Makes 6 cups (1.5 L) or about 4 servings.

BRAISED GREENS WITH GARLIC

This recipe is fantastic with any type of greens (Swiss chard, kale, collards, rapini, or mustard greens). Swiss chard has broad, slightly crinkly glossy leaves and wide stems that are usually white or red, but sometimes yellow, pink, or multicolored. When cooked, the leaves taste similar to spinach but are a little more tart. Swiss chard contains an incredible amount of fiber and phytonutrients. Just 1 cup (250 mL) has 110 percent of your daily value of vitamin A, and 305 percent of vitamin K, and is only 35 calories!

INGREDIENTS:

1 large bunch	leafy greens
2 tbsp (30 mL)	extra-virgin olive oil
2	garlic cloves, minced
pinch	gray sea salt or pink rock salt

OPTIONAL ADDITION:

1 tbsp (15 mL)	dairy- and nut-free pesto (store-bought or see page 278)

DIRECTIONS:

1. Set a large pot of salted filtered water to high heat.

2. To clean greens, plunge them into plenty of cold water. Swirl them around to loosen and remove any dirt. Keep the greens immersed (pushed under the water) for 1 minute, then lift them out of water and drain. You can use a salad spinner to dry them or just blot them on a clean dishtowel. Trim any dry or ragged ends, then roughly chop to desired size. To prepare the greens well ahead of serving time, wrap them in a towel and refrigerate in a sealed bag for up to 24 hours.

3. Place greens in boiling water and cook for 3 minutes. Drain and transfer to a bowl of cold water to stop the cooking process, and then drain again.

4. To finish, place a large skillet over medium heat, and add the oil. Spritz liberally with filtered water or broth to ensure the oil doesn't overheat. Add the garlic and sauté until translucent, about 20 seconds. Add the greens, and sprinkle with the sea salt. Sauté greens, stirring for 3 to 5 minutes. Toss with pesto before serving if you want to add extra zip.

Makes 4 servings.

SESAME BURDOCK SAUTÉ

Burdock (also called gobo) is one of the most powerful healers in the Japanese diet. The name might be unfamiliar to you, but you may have experienced the plant's burrs catching onto your clothes while walking through the woods. Burdock is often found in health-food stores or Asian grocery stores. It has been used traditionally to cleanse the liver, lymph, and kidneys. Combined with anti-inflammatory sesame oil, this recipe is among the true healing dishes. Consider serving it with any fish or lentil dish.

Tip: To prepare burdock, scrub the skin under running water with a brush. Do not peel burdock root, as most of the nutrients are right below the surface of the skin. Using the julienne cut (commonly called for in burdock recipes) results in matchstick-sized pieces of the root.

INGREDIENTS:

    1 tbsp (15 mL)   toasted sesame oil

    1 cup (250 mL)   julienned burdock root

    1 cup (250 mL)   vegetable or chicken broth, or filtered water (divided)

    1 cup (250 mL)   julienned carrots

    1 tbsp (15 mL)   tamari (wheat-free)

DIRECTIONS:

1. In a medium or large skillet or wok, add sesame oil, generous spritzes of filtered water or broth, and burdock. Sauté for 3 minutes over medium heat.

2. Add ½ cup (125 mL) of the broth, bring to a boil, cover, and continue to cook for 5 minutes.

3. Add the carrot, tamari, and the remaining broth. Bring to a boil again, then cook over medium heat for another 5 minutes until vegetables are tender.

Makes 3 servings.

GINGER BUTTERNUT SOUP

This is a wonderful soup when you're feeling under the weather—the beta-carotene helps to protect the lungs when fighting a cold or flu. Squash is one of the first foods offered to babies—a good indication that it's easy to digest. Ginger root is a great reliever of nausea and is a warming herb. If you need to speed up this dish, you can add canned lentils and shave 15 minutes off the cooking time. Use only 8 cups (2 L) of cooking liquid if you choose to use canned lentils.

INGREDIENTS:

2 cups (500 mL)	finely chopped onions
1 tbsp (15 mL)	extra-virgin olive oil
2	garlic cloves, minced
10 cups (2.5 L)	filtered water or vegetable stock
7 cups (1.75 L)	butternut squash, peeled and diced
1 cup (250 mL)	lentils, red split
1 tbsp (15 mL)	minced fresh ginger root OR ½ tsp (2.5 mL) powdered ginger root

1 tsp (5 mL)   ground cinnamon

¼ tsp (1 mL)   ground nutmeg

3 tbsp (45 mL)   tahini

1 tsp (5 mL)   gray sea salt or pink rock salt (or to taste)

OPTIONAL ADDITIONS:

¼ cup (60 mL)   pumpkin or squash seeds, roasted

½ cup (125 mL)   minced fresh parsley or watercress

1 tsp (5 mL)   turmeric

DIRECTIONS:

1. In a large soup pot over medium-low heat, cook the onion in the oil about 2 to 3 minutes, until the onions are translucent.

2. Stir in the garlic, then add the water or stock. Add squash and lentils.

3. Cover and bring to a boil over high heat. Uncover pot and skim off lentil foam with a spoon. Reduce heat and simmer until the squash and lentils are tender, about 40 minutes.

4. Using a blender, food processor, or immersion blender, purée the squash mixture along with the spices, tahini, and salt.

5. Serve hot, garnished with roasted pumpkin or squash seeds and parsley or watercress, if desired.

Makes 6 servings.

STEAMED ASPARAGUS WITH LEMON PARSLEY SAUCE

Asparagus is packed with selenium, an important mineral for your immune system. It can be served warm or cool, making it the perfect side dish for both lunch at work and dinner.

INGREDIENTS:

1 lb (450 g)	asparagus, trimmed
1 cup (250 mL)	Lemon Parsley Sauce (page 266)
1 tbsp (15 mL)	capers (optional)

DIRECTIONS:

1. Place the asparagus in a stovetop steamer over 1 inch (2.5 cm) of water. Cover and turn heat to high. Steam for 7 minutes, or until al dente.

2. Remove from heat and rinse the asparagus under cold water to stop the cooking process.

3. Transfer the asparagus to a clean dishtowel and pat dry.

4. Arrange the asparagus on a serving dish and toss with the sauce and capers.

5. Allow to marinate for a few minutes before serving. A longer marination time will result in a richer flavor.

Makes 4 servings.

LEMON PARSLEY SAUCE

INGREDIENTS:

1 tbsp (15 mL)	any omega-3-rich oil (try chia, flax, perilla, or sacha inchi seed or lemon-flavored fish oil)
2 tbsp (30 mL)	chicken or vegetable broth
½ cup (125 mL)	parsley, chopped
2 tbsp (30 mL)	tamari (wheat-free)
2 tbsp (30 mL)	lemon juice

DIRECTIONS:

1. Mix all the ingredients in a blender or food processor until smooth. If you don't have access to a blender, then you can mix it in a mason jar, but the sauce will not be as creamy.

2. Transfer to a glass jar with a tight-fitting lid and store in the refrigerator.

Makes 1 cup (250 mL).

SAUTÉED BABY BOK CHOY

Smaller heads of bok choy have mild crunchy stems and spinach-like leaves that are more tender than the larger variety. Bok choy is an incredible source of calcium—1 cup (250 mL) contains the same amount as half a cup of milk. This recipe can also be made with rapini. With thin stalks, serrated leaves, and clusters of floral buds, rapini (also known as broccoli rabe) is very tender and tastes slightly bitter. Bitter foods stimulate bile flow, which is good for liver and gallbladder health.

INGREDIENTS:

1 tbsp (15 mL)	extra-virgin olive oil
1 tsp (5 mL)	powdered ginger root OR 1 tbsp (15 mL) finely chopped fresh ginger root
1 tsp (5 mL)	garlic, chopped
4 cups (1 L)	baby bok choy (or 1 bunch rapini)
¼ cup (60 mL)	filtered water
1 tbsp (15 mL)	tamari (wheat-free) OR 1 tsp (5 mL) umeboshi plum paste
to taste	gray sea salt or pink rock salt

DIRECTIONS:

1. Gently heat the oil, ginger root, garlic, and bok choy in a large wok or skillet over medium-high heat. Spritz liberally with filtered water or broth.

2. Stir-fry until slightly wilted, then add the water. Cover the wok and steam for 2 minutes or until the bok choy is tender-crisp.

3. Uncover the wok and continue to cook until liquid is reduced to about a spoonful. Add tamari and salt to taste, and stir.

Makes 2 servings.

CAULIFLOWER "POPCORN"

The idea of cauliflower popcorn was inspired by the golden edges and buttery taste of the cauliflower in this simple dish. Nutritional yeast is not a live yeast and therefore does not throw off the delicate digestive balance of the gut in the same way that live brewer's yeast (found in alcohol) does. It is one of nature's richest sources of B vitamins, providing energy and nourishment to the nervous system. Nutritional yeast is available in many health-food stores and grocery stores with health-food sections.

INGREDIENTS:

4 cups (1 L)	cauliflower (1 large head)
2 tbsp (30 mL)	extra-virgin olive oil
pinch	gray sea salt or pink rock salt (or to taste)
1 tbsp (15 mL)	nutritional yeast

DIRECTIONS:

1. Preheat oven to 350°F (175°C).

2. Trim the head of cauliflower, discarding the core and thick stems. Cut florets into pieces about the size of Ping-Pong balls.

3. In a large bowl, whisk together the olive oil and salt, then add the cauliflower pieces and toss thoroughly.

4. Line a baking sheet with unbleached parchment, if you have it, for easy cleanup, then spread the cauliflower pieces on the sheet and sprinkle evenly with nutritional yeast.

5. Roast for 1 hour, turning 3 or 4 times, until most of each piece has turned golden.

Makes 4 cups (1 L).

WHITE ROOT MASH

Standard mashed potatoes are high in the inflammatory chemical solanine but, luckily, you can easily substitute other healthy white root vegetables. This recipe uses celery root but can be interchanged or mixed with young white turnip, or Jerusalem artichokes (sunchokes). Serve as a side dish or as a topping for Shepherd's Pie (page 332).

269

INGREDIENTS:

2 cups (500 mL)	filtered water
4 cups (1 L)	diced celery root or white turnip or Jerusalem artichoke
6 tbsp (90 mL)	chia, flax, perilla, or pumpkin seed oil, divided
½ tsp (2.5 mL)	gray sea salt or pink rock salt

GARNISH:

1 tsp (5 mL)	cilantro

DIRECTIONS:

1. Simmer celery root and water in a medium saucepan for 8 to 10 minutes or until the cubes are tender. Drain well.

2. Add 5 tablespoons (75 mL) oil and salt and process in a food processor with the S-blade until smooth.

3. Scoop into a large bowl and garnish with chopped cilantro and remaining 1 tbsp (15 mL) oil.

Makes 2 servings.

> *"Cooking is at once child's play and adult joy. And cooking done with care is an act of love."*
>
> —CRAIG CLAIBORNE, *A KITCHEN PRIMER*

CHAPTER 14

SALADS, SAUCES, DIPS, AND DRESSINGS

BEET THE DETOX SALAD

Beets, carrots, and apples have all been traditionally used for liver detoxification. Beets contain betaine, which supports liver health while also decreasing homocysteine in the blood. High homocysteine levels are linked with cardiovascular disease. Beets are also a good source of iron, which carries oxygen in the blood. Carrots are rich in beta-carotene, which the body converts into vitamin A. Vitamin A encourages cell turnover plus boosts the immune system by increasing the number of infection-fighting cells, natural killer cells, and helper T-cells. Apple flavonoids provide antioxidant protection, preventing unwanted inflammation; help prevent excessive clumping of blood platelets; help regulate blood pressure; and prevent overproduction of fat in the liver. You might want to try this salad when you have had something that did not agree with you the day before and you want to get back on track. It also adds color and appeal to any main course.

INGREDIENTS:

1	large beet, coarsely grated
1	large carrot, coarsely grated
1	large apple, diced
2 tbsp (30 mL)	almonds, chopped
2 tbsp (30 mL)	flax, hemp, perilla, or pumpkin seed oil
2 tbsp (30 mL)	lemon juice
4 cups (1 L)	mixed greens

OPTIONAL ADDITIONS:

2 tbsp (30 mL)	fresh dill or parsley, finely chopped
2	garlic cloves, minced
¼ tsp (1 mL)	gray sea salt or pink rock salt

DIRECTIONS:

1. Toss all ingredients, except the mixed greens, together in a large bowl. Mix in optional additions if using. You can make the dressing up to 2 days in advance and refrigerate.

2. Divide mixed greens between 4 plates and top with apple mixture.

Makes 4 side servings.

CRANBERRY QUINOA SALAD

Quinoa is an ancient grain that is a good source of protein. It is also rich in vitamins B_2 and E, copper, iron, magnesium, manganese, potassium, zinc, and fiber. This recipe makes a great portable salad.

INGREDIENTS:

2 cups (500 mL)	cooked quinoa (see page 308)
½ cup (125 mL)	hemp seeds
1 cup (250 mL)	chopped parsley
1	coarsely grated carrot
3 tbsp (45 g)	pumpkin seeds
3 tbsp (45 g)	dried cranberries (apple juice sweetened)

DRESSING:

2 tbsp (30 mL)	hemp seed oil
2 tbsp (30 mL)	lemon juice
½ tsp (2.5 mL)	umeboshi plum paste
1 tsp (5 mL)	raw honey OR 3 drops stevia extract liquid
¼ tsp (1 mL)	gray sea salt or pink rock salt

DIRECTIONS:

1. Combine all salad ingredients in a large bowl.

2. Combine all dressing ingredients in a small glass jar with a tight-fitting lid, and shake well.

3. Toss the salad and dressing and serve immediately.

Makes 6 servings.

HONEY MUSTARD DRESSING

This dressing is really fast and simple and tastes great on any greens. Both olive and hemp seed oils are immune boosting. By using natural mustard and raw honey, you avoid the white vinegar and sugar found in many commercial honey mustard dressings. Look for natural mustard in your health-food store; it contains apple cider vinegar rather than refined white vinegar.

INGREDIENTS:

½ cup (125 mL)	chia, flax, or hemp seed or walnut oil
1 tbsp (15 mL)	raw honey
¼ cup (60 mL)	natural mustard
pinch	gray sea salt or pink rock salt

DIRECTIONS:

1. Place all ingredients in a small glass jar with a tight-fitting lid, and shake well to combine. Stores well for a week in the fridge.

Makes ¾ cup (185 mL).

SEAWEED SALAD

Seaweed has over sixty trace minerals that help to nourish every part of the body. It is high in iodine, one of the most valuable minerals for metabolism, since it helps thyroid function. Calcium-rich hijiki and arame are easier for Westerners to get used to because they are sliced into thin ribbons, which create a more delicate texture.

INGREDIENTS:

2 cups (500 mL)	arame or hijiki (seaweed, cut into thin strips)
4 cups (1 L)	filtered water
1 cup (250 mL)	cucumber, quartered and chopped
½ cup (125 mL)	green onion, chopped
½ cup (125 mL)	fresh parsley, chopped
2 tbsp (30 mL)	toasted sesame or flax, hemp, or perilla seed oil
½ cup (125 mL)	julienned or coarsely grated carrots
¼ cup (60 mL)	lemon juice
2 tbsp (30 mL)	tamari (wheat-free)

DIRECTIONS:

1. Rinse the seaweed well.

2. Place seaweed and water in a small pot and bring to a boil for 5 minutes. If you suffer from digestive problems, it is best to turn off the heat after 5 minutes and let the mixture soak for 2 to 3 hours.

3. Drain and place seaweed in a large mixing bowl.

4. Add the remaining ingredients to the seaweed and toss well. This salad keeps for days in the fridge.

Makes 4 servings.

GUACAMOLE

Avocado is a rich source of anti-inflammatory omega-9 fat. Unlike most fruits, avocados start to ripen only after they are picked. To avoid bruised ones, buy a firm avocado and store it in a paper bag at room temperature to speed ripening. Undisturbed, it will ripen in two to five days. You can add an apple to the bag to hurry the process. A ripe avocado yields to gentle pressure but is still somewhat firm. If your avocado is ripe before you're ready to eat it, put it into the refrigerator, where it should keep for a few days.

INGREDIENTS:

2	medium avocados
1 tbsp (15 mL)	minced red onion
1 tbsp (15 mL)	lime juice
1	garlic clove, minced
pinch	gray sea salt or pink rock salt
5	green olives, chopped (optional)

DIRECTIONS:

1. Place all ingredients in a medium bowl and mash with a fork. Serve immediately with Sunny Flax Crackers (page 258).

Makes 1½ cups (375 mL).

SESAME TAMARI VINAIGRETTE

The toasted seed and apple cider flavors of this dressing go well with Asian-style salads or meals, and apple cider vinegar aids digestion. Try drizzling the vinaigrette over grilled chicken breast, too.

INGREDIENTS:

¼ cup (60 mL)	unsweetened berry juice
¼ cup (60 mL)	apple cider vinegar
2 tbsp (30 mL)	tamari (wheat-free)
1 tbsp (15 mL)	toasted sesame oil
1 tbsp (15 mL)	raw honey
1 tsp (5 mL)	finely grated ginger root

DIRECTIONS:

1. Whisk all ingredients in a small bowl until the honey is incorporated.

2. Pour over salad or transfer to a jar and store in the fridge until needed.

Makes ¾ cup (185 mL).

GINGER ZUCCHINI SALAD

The sesame seeds and ginger root in this recipe are a super duo for fighting inflammation and add an Asian flavor to the salad greens. Create the zucchini and carrot ribbons with a vegetable peeler to let them soak up the tasty dressing.

INGREDIENTS:

3	small zucchini, cut into wide ribbons
1	large carrot, cut into wide ribbons
50 g package	natural pickled ginger root OR 1 tbsp (15 mL) fresh ginger root, chopped
1 tbsp (15 mL)	toasted sesame oil
1 tbsp (15 mL)	chia, flax, hemp, perilla, or sacha inchi seed oil
1 tbsp (15 mL)	black sesame seeds
1 tsp (5 mL)	raw honey
12 oz (400 mL)	adzuki or pinto beans, drained and rinsed

DIRECTIONS:

1. Toss all ingredients in a large bowl until mixed.

2. Divide between 2 plates and enjoy.

Makes 2 servings.

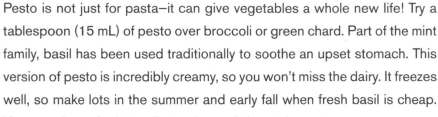

DAIRY-FREE PESTO

Pesto is not just for pasta—it can give vegetables a whole new life! Try a tablespoon (15 mL) of pesto over broccoli or green chard. Part of the mint family, basil has been used traditionally to soothe an upset stomach. This version of pesto is incredibly creamy, so you won't miss the dairy. It freezes well, so make lots in the summer and early fall when fresh basil is cheap. You can also substitute cilantro for an Asian-style pesto.

INGREDIENTS:

2 cups (500 mL)	fresh basil leaves (tightly packed)
¾ cup (185 mL)	extra-virgin olive, walnut, or flax or perilla seed oil
½ cup (125 mL)	raw sunflower seeds
2 to 6	garlic cloves (depending on size of cloves and your preference)
½ tsp (2.5 mL)	gray sea salt or pink rock salt (or to taste)
2 tsp (10 mL)	lemon juice

DIRECTIONS:

1. Combine all ingredients in a food processor using the S-blade, and blend until smooth. Use immediately, or store in a jar in the fridge for up to 2 weeks, or in the freezer for up to 6 months.

Makes 2 cups (500 mL).

PICK-A-DILLY SALAD

The silica in cucumber is an essential component of healthy connective tissues found in muscles, tendons, ligaments, cartilage, and bone. Cucumbers are a very good source of vitamin C, an important nutrient for building collagen in the skin. Because cucumbers are part of the melon family, this salad is best eaten on its own to ensure proper digestion. Melons quickly ferment, which can cause gastric distress for people with poor digestive health.

INGREDIENTS:

2   English cucumbers

DRESSING:

½ cup (125 mL)   apple cider vinegar

1 tbsp (15 mL)   raw honey

3 tbsp (45 mL)   fresh dill OR 1 tbsp (15 mL) dried dill

1 tsp (5 mL)   mustard seeds, brown or golden

1   garlic clove, peeled and chopped

½ tsp (2.5 mL)   gray sea salt or pink rock salt

2 tbsp (30 mL)   chia or flax seed oil

DIRECTIONS:

1. Slice cucumber thinly using a food processor or mandoline. Place cucumbers in a large bowl.

2. Combine dressing ingredients, pour over cucumber, and toss to coat evenly.

3. Enjoy immediately or store in the fridge for up to 2 days.

Makes 6 side salads.

ANTI-INFLAMMATORY LENTIL DIP

This dip features ingredients that are especially beneficial for the immune system. The garlic contains allicin, a powerful antibiotic and antifungal compound. This dip can be used as a home remedy to help speed recovery from respiratory infections. The whole recipe boosts immunity: lentils provide iron; almonds provide sterols; hemp seeds provide omega-3 fats; lemon juice provides vitamin C; and the garlic, basil, and turmeric are antibiotic! If left for a few days, the garlic flavor in this dip deepens nicely. Serve with Sunny Flax Crackers (page 258) or with "dippable" vegetables such as carrots, zucchini, snap peas, celery, or jicama.

INGREDIENTS:

16 oz (475 mL)	canned lentils, drained OR 2 cups (500 mL) cooked lentils
1 cup (250 mL)	almond butter or finely chopped walnuts
2 tbsp (30 mL)	hemp seed oil
1	large garlic clove
½ cup (125 mL)	fresh basil OR 2 tbsp (30 mL) dairy- and nut-free basil pesto (store-bought or see page 278)
⅓ cup (85 mL)	lemon juice
1 tsp (5 mL)	lemon zest
1 tsp (5 mL)	turmeric
¼ tsp (1 mL)	gray sea salt or pink rock salt (or to taste)

OPTIONAL ADDITION:

2	drops stevia extract liquid

DIRECTIONS:

1. Process all ingredients in a food processor fitted with the S-blade until very smooth.

Makes 3 cups (750 mL).

RAINCOAST SOCKEYE SALMON SALAD

This salad contains some great nutritional powerhouses. Just 4 ounces (140 g) of sockeye salmon contains a whopping 1,500 mg of omega-3 fats, which are converted to anti-inflammatory resolvins by the body. Resolvins, unlike anti-inflammatory drugs, do not have negative side effects on our digestive or cardiovascular systems. Unfortunately, recent statistics indicate that nearly 99 percent of people do not eat enough omega-3 fats to maintain good health. Look for wild, sustainably caught fish, as it is lower in toxins than farmed fish. Celery contains vitamin C and other phytonutrients that help lower cholesterol. Celery coumarins have also been shown to help prevent some types of cancer.

INGREDIENTS:

2 cups (500 mL)	mixed salad greens
5	black olives (stored in olive oil, not salt brine)
1 cup (250 mL)	jicama or apple, thinly sliced
1 cup (250 mL)	celery stalks, chopped fine
1	green onion, sliced in thin rounds
5 oz (160 g)	wild sockeye salmon
1 tbsp (15 mL)	dairy- and nut-free pesto (store-bought or see page 278)
1 cup (250 mL)	sunflower sprouts

DIRECTIONS:

1. Mound the mixed greens on your plate.

2. Scatter the olives and jicama or apple slices over the greens.

3. In a small bowl, gently mix the celery, green onion, salmon, and pesto together.

4. Portion the fish mixture over the bed of greens and top with the sunflower sprouts.

Makes 1 large serving.

KALE SALAD

If I could pick one vegetable to eat for life, it would be kale. An excellent source of vitamin A, vitamin C, and manganese, kale is also a very good source of fiber, calcium, vitamin B$_6$, and potassium. I feel it has so much to offer that I find myself eating it four to five times a week.

Dinosaur kale (also known as black kale, cavolo nero, Tuscan kale, or Lacinato kale) is a member of the brassica family, which includes cabbages. This slightly spicy and dark variety of kale is the easiest to clean because it is not as curly. I love that it is one of the last vegetables found locally in cool climates before winter sets in. Its flavor actually improves after the first frost.

INGREDIENTS:

6 cups (1.5 L)	dinosaur kale, chopped
½	lemon
pinch	dried basil
pinch	gray sea salt or pink rock salt
1 tbsp (15 mL)	extra-virgin olive or chia, flax, or hemp seed oil
2 tbsp (30 mL)	red onion, minced
2 tbsp (30 mL)	green onion, chopped (about 1 whole onion)
1 small	cucumber, thinly sliced
1	garlic clove, minced
¼ cup (60 mL)	chopped kalamata olives

DIRECTIONS:

1. Wash kale and cut into small strips.

2. Lightly steam the kale for 5 to 7 minutes in a steamer basket. Transfer to a large bowl and add lemon, basil, salt, and oil. Toss.

3. Add the remaining ingredients and mix well.

Makes 4 servings.

ASIAN COLESLAW

This salad is packed with indole-3-carbinol (I3C), a phytonutrient that has proven anticancer properties. Daikon, a spicy radish from Japan, is high in vitamin C and helps to support the digestion of fats. To julienne vegetables such as carrots, cut thin, 1-inch (2.5 cm) strips that resemble matchsticks.

INGREDIENTS:

2 cups (500 mL)	shredded red cabbage
1 cup (250 mL)	thinly sliced daikon radish
1 cup (250 mL)	julienned carrots
4 cups (1 L)	shredded napa cabbage
½ cup (125 mL)	black sesame seeds

DRESSING:

¼ cup (60 mL)	lemon juice
1 tbsp (15 mL)	rice syrup or raw honey
1 tsp (5 mL)	minced fresh ginger root
1 tbsp (15 mL)	toasted sesame oil
⅓ cup (85 mL)	flax, hemp, perilla, or pumpkin seed oil

DIRECTIONS:

1. Mix salad ingredients.

2. In a small glass jar, shake all dressing ingredients.

3. Pour dressing over salad and toss to combine.

Makes 8 to 10 servings.

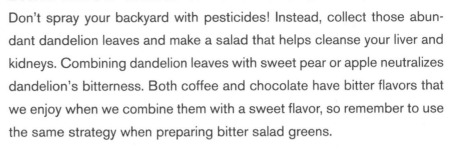

DANDELION SALAD WITH TAHINI DRESSING

Don't spray your backyard with pesticides! Instead, collect those abundant dandelion leaves and make a salad that helps cleanse your liver and kidneys. Combining dandelion leaves with sweet pear or apple neutralizes dandelion's bitterness. Both coffee and chocolate have bitter flavors that we enjoy when we combine them with a sweet flavor, so remember to use the same strategy when preparing bitter salad greens.

INGREDIENTS:

2 cups (500 mL)	chopped dandelion greens
1 medium	pear or apple, chopped
1–2 tsp (5–10 mL)	freshly grated ginger root
2 tbsp (30 g)	pumpkin seeds

DRESSING:

½ cup (125 mL)	tahini
¼ cup (60 mL)	lemon juice
¼ cup (60 mL)	extra-virgin olive, walnut, or flax seed oil
2 tbsp (30 mL)	filtered water
1 tsp (5 mL)	raw honey or up to 1 tbsp (15 mL) to taste
1 tbsp (15 mL)	tamari (wheat-free) OR 1 tsp (5 mL) umeboshi plum paste, if sensitive to soy

DIRECTIONS:

1. In a medium bowl, combine salad ingredients.

2. In a small bowl, combine dressing ingredients.

3. Pour dressing over salad and toss to combine.

Makes 2 to 4 servings.

FARMERS' MARKET SALAD

Spinach is rich in a flavonoid called kaempferol. Researchers measured the flavonoid intake of 66,940 women enrolled in the Nurses Health Study between 1984 and 2002. The study revealed that women with the most kaempferol in their diets reduced the risk of developing ovarian cancer by 40 percent, compared to women eating the least kaempferol-rich foods.

INGREDIENTS:

2 cups (500 mL)	arugula, chopped
2 cups (500 mL)	spinach, chopped
1 cup (250 mL)	pea shoots
1 cup (250 mL)	apple slices
½ cup (125 mL)	fresh blueberries, washed
½ cup (125 mL)	pecans, chopped, or pumpkin seeds

DRESSING:

¼ cup (60 mL)	flax, hemp, or perilla seed oil
2 tbsp (30 mL)	apple cider vinegar
1 tsp (5 mL)	Dijon mustard
1 tsp (5 mL)	raw honey
¼ tsp (1 mL)	gray sea salt or pink rock salt
¼ cup (60 mL)	finely chopped wild leeks or spring onion

DIRECTIONS:

1. In a large bowl, layer all the green ingredients.

2. Top with the apples, blueberries, and pumpkin seeds.

3. Whisk all of the dressing ingredients together and serve over salad.

Makes 4 servings.

BUCKWHEAT BLUEBERRY SALAD

Despite the name, buckwheat is not related to wheat and is gluten-free. High in iron, manganese, magnesium, and zinc, buckwheat is a healthy addition to any soup, granola, or side dish. The pigments in blueberries contain strong anti-inflammatory properties. The essential fats in the dressing also help balance hormones and reduce inflammation.

INGREDIENTS:

1 cup (250 mL)	buckwheat kernels
2½ cups (625 mL)	filtered water
½ cup (125 mL)	hemp seeds
1 cup (250 mL)	chopped cilantro
1½ cups (375 mL)	grated zucchini
1 cup (250 mL)	fresh blueberries

DRESSING:

⅓ cup (85 mL)	walnut or flax or hemp seed oil
¼ cup (60 mL)	apple cider vinegar or lemon juice
¼ tsp (1 mL)	gray sea salt or pink rock salt (or to taste)
2 tsp (10 mL)	raw honey
2 tbsp (30 mL)	mint, freshly chopped

DIRECTIONS:

1. Put the buckwheat kernels into a saucepan and heat the kernels until they begin to take on a golden color.

2. In a separate pot, bring water to a boil. Add kernels and simmer for about 15 minutes without stirring. Remove from heat and allow to cool, then fluff.

3. Combine buckwheat with all salad ingredients.

4. Whisk together dressing ingredients, pour over salad, and toss.

Makes 8 servings.

RAW GRAVY

This amazing sauce makes seemingly boring vegetables sing. Make a double recipe and store in your fridge for a few days—the garlic and ginger root keep it fresh. You can replace tamari with 1 tsp (5 mL) umeboshi plum paste, a Japanese healing plum that kills unwanted microbes in the gut.

INGREDIENTS:

¼ cup (60 mL)   miso

¼ cup (60 mL)   extra-virgin olive or chia, flax, or hemp seed oil

¼ cup (60 mL)   filtered water

¼ cup (60 mL)   tahini

1 tbsp (15 mL)   tamari (wheat-free)

1 tbsp (15 mL)   minced garlic

1 tbsp (15 mL)   grated ginger root

¼ cup (60 mL)   lemon juice

OPTIONAL, IF EXTRA SWEETNESS IS DESIRED:

1 tsp (5 mL)   raw honey OR 5 drops stevia extract liquid

DIRECTIONS:

1. Process all ingredients in a blender until smooth.

Makes 1½ cups (375 mL).

THE SKINNY DIP

Wouldn't it be great if your vegetable dip contained more than two servings of vegetables? This one does! Spinach boasts energizing B vitamins, magnesium, and iron. The fat in this dip helps the absorption of lutein and zeazanthin, which studies suggest combat macular degeneration, the leading cause of blindness.

INGREDIENTS:

10 oz (285 mL) frozen chopped spinach, thawed OR 6 cups (1.5 L) fresh spinach, blanched and drained

⅔ cup (175 mL) sliced water chestnuts, drained

1 tbsp (15 mL) fresh dill

½ lime, juiced

2 green onions, chopped

½ garlic clove, crushed

½ cup (125 mL) extra-virgin olive or flax or hemp seed oil

1 tbsp (15 mL) whole-grain natural mustard

½ tsp (2.5 mL) gray sea salt or pink rock salt

DIRECTIONS:

1. To reduce the water in the spinach, squeeze out all moisture by placing the thawed spinach in the center of a clean dishtowel and pressing down to remove as much moisture as possible. (If you skip this step, your dip will be runny.) If using fresh, wash greens well, then bring a pot of water to a boil and quickly blanch the fresh spinach for 1 minute. Drain well, squeezing out excess moisture.

2. Place the water chestnuts, dill, lime juice, green onions, and garlic in a food processor with the S-blade and process mixture until finely chopped. Add the spinach and process for another 10 seconds.

3. Add the oil, mustard, and salt, then process until smooth.

4. Refrigerate for at least 1 hour before serving to allow flavors to blend.

Make 4 servings.

POPPY SEED DRESSING

One tbsp (15 mL) of poppy seeds contains the same amount of calcium as ½ cup (125 mL) of milk.

INGREDIENTS:

1 tsp (5 mL)	poppy seeds
2 tbsp (30 mL)	walnut or chia, flax, hemp, or sacha inchi seed oil
1 tsp (5 mL)	apple cider vinegar
1 tsp (5 mL)	Dijon mustard
½ tsp (2.5 mL)	raw honey
1 tbsp (15 mL)	minced onion (optional)
⅛ tsp (0.5 mL)	gray sea salt or pink rock salt (or to taste)

DIRECTIONS:

1. Heat a small skillet over medium-low heat.

2. Add poppy seeds and gently toast, stirring until fragrant, about 1 minute.

3. Transfer to a small glass jar that has a tight-fitting lid and let cool.

4. Add remaining ingredients and shake until blended.

Makes 2 servings.

CURRIED HONEY-LIME DRESSING

Limes were used by the British Navy to prevent scurvy due to their vitamin C content. This earned the British the often pejorative nickname of "limeys"—even as their citrus consumption conferred a tremendous advantage in the early days of sea travel and trade.

INGREDIENTS:

1	lime, zested and juiced
½ cup (125 mL)	natural or homemade mayonnaise
1 tbsp (15 mL)	raw honey
½ tsp (2.5 mL)	finely grated fresh ginger root
¼ tsp (1 mL)	cumin
¼ tsp (1 mL)	turmeric
½ tsp (2.5 mL)	gray sea salt or pink rock salt
1	small garlic clove, minced
¼ cup (60 mL)	chopped cilantro

DIRECTIONS:

1. Mix all ingredients and serve.

Makes ¾ cup (185 mL).

COOL JICAMA SLAW

Jicama is a tasty vegetable from Mexico that has the combined flavor of apple, water chestnut, and potato. It makes a great side dish because it is extremely low in calories (80 per cup).

Alternative: If you can't find jicama at a store near you, try using an Asian pear instead. It has the same texture and tastes wonderful in this salad. If you are sensitive to tree nuts, try hemp seeds instead.

INGREDIENTS:

1 large	English cucumber, seeded and julienned
½ lb (225 g)	jicama, peeled and julienned
2 medium	carrots, peeled and julienned
⅓ cup (85 mL)	chopped fresh cilantro leaves
⅓ cup (85 mL)	lemon juice
2 tbsp (30 mL)	extra-virgin olive or flax, perilla, or pumpkin seed oil
½ cup (125 mL)	walnut
pinch	gray sea salt or pink rock salt

DIRECTIONS:

1. In a mixing bowl, combine the cucumber, jicama, carrots, cilantro, lemon juice, oil, and walnuts. Season with salt and toss gently.

2. Serve immediately or refrigerate for up to 3 days.

Makes 4 servings.

ALMOND AMARANTH SALAD WITH CREAMY GINGER DRESSING

Amaranth is a seed grain with a fantastic nutty flavor and one of the highest protein-to-carbohydrate ratios of any grain. The salty flavor of the dulse flakes is a nice contrast to the pear, and its iodine content supports the thyroid gland. This recipe was inspired by Brendan Brazier and his great book *The Thrive Diet.*

INGREDIENTS:

¼ cup (60 mL)	whole-grain amaranth
4 cups (1 L)	mixed leafy greens
½ cup (125 mL)	hemp seeds
1 cup (250 mL)	pear, chopped
½ cup (125 mL)	snow peas, sliced in half lengthwise
1 tsp (5 mL)	dulse flakes

DIRECTIONS:

1. To make fresh popped amaranth, preheat a skillet on the stove on high. Put a spoonful of amaranth into the skillet and shake or stir the seeds for 20 seconds until they start to pop like popcorn. Remove the popped amaranth to prevent it from burning and then repeat process until all the amaranth is popped. You can buy pre-popped amaranth, but it's often stale. The process is fun and fills the house with a wonderful nutty fragrance.

2. Divide the mixed greens between two bowls.

3. Divide the hemp seeds, pear, and snow peas between the two bowls, then top each bowl with popped amaranth.

4. Dust the salads with dulse flakes and serve.

Makes 2 servings.

CREAMY GINGER DRESSING

The nutritional yeast in this recipe is brimming with B vitamins, and the ginger root is a powerful anti-inflammatory herb.

INGREDIENTS:

¼ cup (60 mL)	chia, flax, hemp, perilla, or pumpkin seed oil
2 tbsp (30 mL)	apple cider vinegar
2 tbsp (30 mL)	tahini
2 tbsp (30 mL)	filtered water
2 tsp (10 mL)	grated fresh ginger root
2 tsp (10 mL)	nutritional yeast
¼ tsp (1 mL)	gray sea salt or pink rock salt

DIRECTIONS:

1. Whisk together all ingredients. Serve over salad.

Makes ⅔ cup (175 mL).

ARUGULA RAINBOW SALAD

Turn this fresh and colorful salad into a quick main dish by doubling the recipe and topping each portion with 3 ounces (90 g) of chicken breast.

INGREDIENTS:

2 cups (500 mL)	arugula, torn into large pieces
1½ cups (375 mL)	broccoli florets
1 cup (250 mL)	coarsely grated carrot
½ cup (125 mL)	radish, finely diced
1 tbsp (15 mL)	red onion, minced
3 oz (90 g)	cooked chicken breast (optional)

DIRECTIONS:

1. Place arugula, broccoli, carrot, radish, and onion in a medium bowl.

2. Top with dressing of choice.

Makes 2 salads.

PECAN WILD RICE SALAD

Both wild and brown rice have a rich, nutty flavor that complements the sweet cranberries and tart lemon. Pecans provide heart-healthy mono-unsaturated fats and sterols that can lower LDL (bad) cholesterol.

INGREDIENTS:

1 cup (250 mL)	wild rice or brown rice (or a mix of both)
2⅓ cups (585 mL)	filtered water (or use liquid amount suggested on rice package)
½ tsp (2.5 mL)	gray sea salt or pink rock salt
19 oz (560 mL)	can of green lentils, rinsed and drained
½ cup (125 mL)	dried cranberries (apple juice sweetened)

½ cup (125 mL)	chopped pecans
¼ cup (60 mL)	sliced green onions
1 tbsp (15 mL)	lemon juice
2 tbsp (30 mL)	chia, flax, hemp, perilla, or sacha inchi seed oil
1 tsp (5 mL)	raw honey or rice syrup
1 tsp (5 mL)	lemon zest

DIRECTIONS:

1. Combine rice, water, and salt and cook for 55 to 60 minutes (see note below).

2. In a medium bowl, mix cooked rice, lentils, cranberries, pecans, and green onions together.

3. In a separate jar, mix lemon juice, oil, honey, and lemon zest.

4. Add dressing to rice mixture and mix thoroughly just before serving,

Makes 4 to 6 servings.

TO COOK RICE:

Typically, brown rice is cooked with a 1:2 ratio of rice to water. Wild rice is cooked with a 1:3 ratio of wild rice to water. To cook a mixture of wild and brown rice, use a ratio of 1 cup (250 mL) of rice to 2⅓ cups (585 mL) of water. Bring rice, ½ teaspoon (2.5 mL) salt, and water to a boil. Cover, reduce heat to low, and simmer for 55 to 60 minutes. Do not stir or uncover. Remove from stove and let stand, covered, for 10 minutes. Uncover, fluff with a fork, and let cool to almost room temperature.

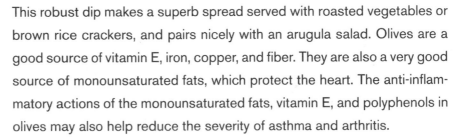

ZIPPY LENTIL TAPENADE

This robust dip makes a superb spread served with roasted vegetables or brown rice crackers, and pairs nicely with an arugula salad. Olives are a good source of vitamin E, iron, copper, and fiber. They are also a very good source of monounsaturated fats, which protect the heart. The anti-inflammatory actions of the monounsaturated fats, vitamin E, and polyphenols in olives may also help reduce the severity of asthma and arthritis.

INGREDIENTS:

2⅓ cups (585 mL)	cooked green lentils (or canned), rinsed and drained
1 cup (250 mL)	pitted olives (kalamata are a great choice)
⅓ cup (85 mL)	walnut or flax, hemp, or perilla seed oil
1	large garlic clove, coarsely chopped
½ cup (125 mL)	chopped fresh parsley or cilantro
2 tbsp (30 mL)	capers, rinsed and drained
1 tsp (5 mL)	lemon zest
¼ cup (60 mL)	lemon juice

DIRECTIONS:

1. Process lentils, olives, oil, and garlic in a food processor. Add parsley, capers, lemon zest, and juice. Pulse on and off until combined.

2. Transfer to a bowl, cover, and refrigerate.

Makes 3 cups (750 mL). Will keep for up to 1 week.

GREEN PEA DIP

This sweet dip boasts the calcium and B vitamins needed for a healthy nervous system. Because sweet peas are easier to digest than chickpeas, they're great for anyone who suffers from digestive troubles.

INGREDIENTS:

3 cups (750 mL)	frozen or fresh green peas
1	garlic clove, sliced
½ tsp (2.5 mL)	cumin
1 tsp (5 mL)	gray sea salt or pink rock salt
3 tbsp (45 mL)	fresh lemon juice
3 tbsp (45 mL)	chia, flax, hemp, perilla, or sacha inchi seed oil
½ cup (125 mL)	sliced fresh flat-leaf parsley

OPTIONAL ADDITIONS:

1 tsp (5 mL)	extra-virgin olive oil
½ tsp (2.5 mL)	ground sumac

DIRECTIONS:

1. Process thawed or fresh peas with all other ingredients in a food processor until smooth.

2. Spoon pea mixture into a serving bowl. Chill in the fridge for 1 hour.

3. Drizzle with a little oil and sprinkle with sumac (if using) just before serving.

Makes 3 cups (750 mL).

ADZUKI MILLET SALAD

By mixing a bean with a grain, you create a dish that is a complete protein—an excellent vegetarian replacement for meat that is extremely low in saturated fat. Millet is a gluten-free grain that is a good source of most B vitamins. A ½-cup (125 mL) serving provides more than 20 percent of your daily requirement for iron, magnesium, and zinc.

INGREDIENTS:

3 cups (750 mL)	filtered water
1 cup (250 mL)	millet
2 tbsp (30 mL)	extra-virgin olive oil
½ cup (125 mL)	chopped red onion
3	garlic cloves, chopped
½ cup (125 mL)	diced carrot
½ cup (125 mL)	chopped celery
1 tbsp (15 mL)	grated ginger root
1 cup (250 mL)	small broccoli florets
1 cup (250 mL)	cooked adzuki beans
½ cup (125 mL)	diced green onion
⅓ cup (85 mL)	fresh cilantro or basil, packed

OPTIONAL ADDITION:

¼ cup (60 mL)	chopped hazelnuts (filberts)

DRESSING:

2 tbsp (30 mL)	apple cider vinegar
1 tbsp (15 mL)	raw honey
2 tbsp (30 mL)	tamari (wheat-free) OR 2 tsp (10 mL) umeboshi plum paste
4 tbsp (60 mL)	flax or hemp seed oil

DIRECTIONS:

1. Bring millet and water to a boil, cover, then turn heat to low and simmer for 25 minutes, or until all liquid is absorbed. Let stand for 5 to 10 minutes to cool before transferring to a large mixing bowl. Fluff with a fork.

2. Heat oil in a cast-iron skillet over medium heat. Spritz liberally with filtered water or broth to ensure the oil doesn't overheat. Add onion, garlic, carrot, celery, ginger root, and broccoli and sauté for 5 to 7 minutes.

3. Remove pan from heat and add adzuki beans, green onion, and cilantro.

4. Whisk together all dressing ingredients and toss with millet, vegetables, and beans.

Makes 8 servings.

COLLARD WRAPS

This recipe is delicious in either a collard leaf or a sheet of nori. Nori seaweed is a good source of iodine and excellent for thyroid function. Like kale, collards are a member of the brassica family, along with broccoli and cauliflower, which are known cancer fighters. Collard leaves are smooth in texture and relatively broad, making them the perfect substitute for a tortilla. This is a great recipe for entertaining. You can keep the filling in the fridge and stuff them when you are ready to enjoy the leftovers.

INGREDIENTS:

½ head	cauliflower, finely chopped
4	medium carrots, chopped
1	beet, peeled and chopped
3	green onions (white parts only), thinly sliced
to taste	gray sea salt or pink rock salt
1 tsp (5 mL)	turmeric
5 tbsp (75 mL)	lemon juice or apple cider vinegar
1 tsp (5 mL)	mustard seeds
1¼ tsp (6 mL)	cumin
¼ tsp (1 mL)	coriander
¼ tsp (1 mL)	mustard powder
½ cup (125 mL)	cilantro, packed
6 tbsp (90 mL)	walnut or flax, hemp, or perilla seed oil
12	collard leaves

DIRECTIONS:

1. Pulse half the cauliflower, carrots, and beet in a food processor until ricelike. Transfer to a mixing bowl. Repeat with the remaining cauliflower, carrots, and beet.

2. Toss vegetables with remaining ingredients, except collard leaves.

3. Scoop a heaping tablespoon of the mixture on top of each collard leaf, roll up, and enjoy!

Makes 12 wraps (4 to 6 servings).

Ezra's Herbed Quinoa
Risotto, page 324

Shepherd's Pie, page 332

Pick-a-Dilly Salad,
page 279

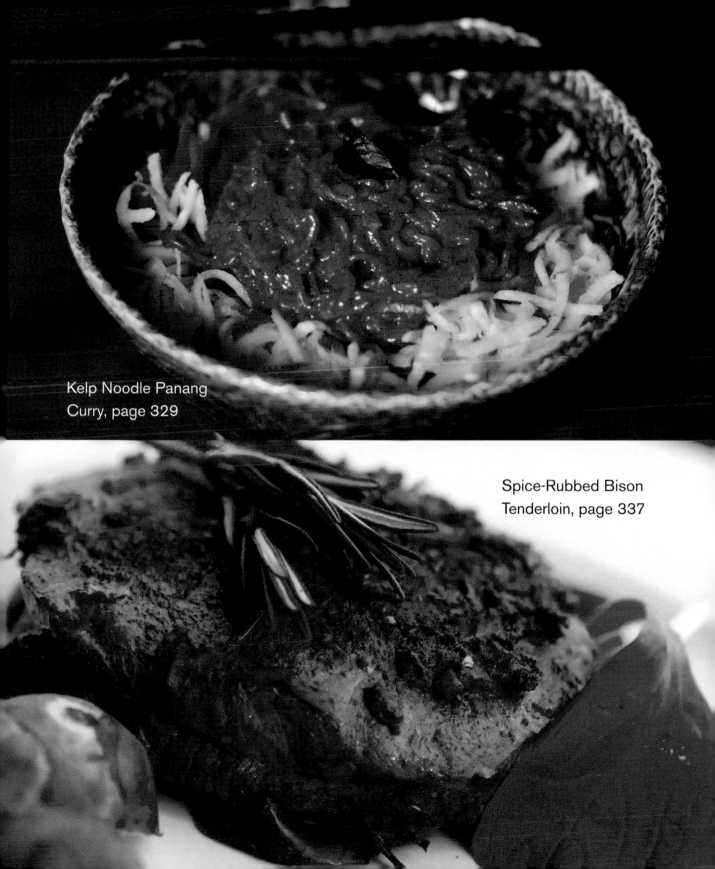

Kelp Noodle Panang
Curry, page 329

Spice-Rubbed Bison
Tenderloin, page 337

Asian Coleslaw,
page 283

Krispy Kale Chips,
page 363

Halva Balls, page 358

Key Lime Pie,
page 360

Cinnamon Baked Apples, page 347

Almond Butter Pears,
page 349

Stuffed Sailors,
page 351

Berry Pie, page 341

ENDIVE PEAR SALAD

Besides giving this salad a satisfying crunch, walnuts are a rich source of omega-3 fats as well as vitamins, minerals, protein, and antioxidants.

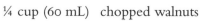

INGREDIENTS:

1	firm Bartlett pear (red or green)
3 cups (750 mL)	butterhead lettuce (Bibb or Boston), torn into bite-sized pieces
2 cups (500 mL)	purple endive, torn into bite-sized pieces
¼ cup (60 mL)	chopped walnuts

DRESSING:
(This recipe makes more than is needed for this salad.)

3 tbsp (45 mL)	vegetable broth or filtered water
3 tbsp (45 mL)	walnut or flax, hemp, perilla, or pumpkin seed oil
2 tbsp (30 mL)	green onion (finely chopped)
1½ tbsp (22.5 mL)	apple cider vinegar
½ tsp (2.5 mL)	Dijon mustard
¼ tsp (1 mL)	gray sea salt or pink rock salt
1 tsp (5 mL)	dried basil or 1 tbsp (15 mL) fresh basil (optional)

DIRECTIONS:

1. Whisk the broth, oil, green onion, vinegar, mustard, salt, and basil, if using, in a small bowl.

2. Just before serving, cut the pear into 16 slices.

3. Place in a large bowl and add 1 tbsp (15 mL) of the dressing. Toss to coat. Add the lettuce, endive, and half the dressing. Toss again. Store remaining dressing.

4. Divide among 4 plates and top with the walnuts.

Makes 2 entrée-sized servings or 4 side servings.

THE POWER REACTOR SALAD

This meal-sized salad features turkey, which is loaded with the relaxing and repairing amino acid tryptophan. Red onions are very rich in chromium, a trace mineral that helps cells respond to insulin. This salad's high fiber content will help you feel full and satisfied.

INGREDIENTS:

6 cups (1.5 L)	mixed salad greens
1 cup (250 mL)	coarsely grated carrots
2 tbsp (30 mL)	minced red onion
1 cup (250 mL)	sunflower sprouts
¼ cup (60 mL)	Sesame Tamari Vinaigrette (page 276)
1	medium apple, chopped
4 slices	roasted turkey breast, sliced
¼ cup (60 mL)	pine nuts

DIRECTIONS:

1. Toss the greens, carrots, onions, sprouts, and vinaigrette in a large bowl until the vegetables are evenly coated with the dressing.

2. Divide between 2 plates.

3. Divide the apple slices, turkey, and pine nuts between the 2 plates, placing them on top of the salad.

Makes 2 large entrée-sized servings or 4 side salads.

HEMP GINGER DRESSING

Hemp seeds contain anti-inflammatory omega-3 fats. They also contain 11 g of protein per 2 tbsp (30 mL).

INGREDIENTS:

2 tbsp (30 mL)	hemp seeds
1 tbsp (15 mL)	raw honey
1 tbsp (15 mL)	chopped ginger root
2 tbsp (30 mL)	filtered water
1 tsp (5 mL)	chopped garlic
1 tsp (5 mL)	lemon juice
1 tsp (5 mL)	gray sea salt or pink rock salt

DIRECTIONS:

1. Process all ingredients in a blender until smooth.

Makes ½ cup (125 mL).

SHIITAKE MUSHROOM AND ARUGULA SAUTÉ

Shiitake mushrooms contain the active compound lentinan, which has the ability to strengthen the immune system. Lentinan is a polysaccharide that has also been shown to have anticancer activity. The amount of *L*-ergothioneine, a powerful antioxidant, is 40 times higher in shiitake mushrooms than in wheat germ.

INGREDIENTS:

2 tbsp (30 mL)	extra-virgin olive oil
2 cups (500 mL)	fresh shiitake mushrooms, sliced
¼ cup (60 mL)	vegetable stock
2	garlic cloves, minced
1 cup (250 mL)	chopped onion
½ tsp (2.5 mL)	gray sea salt or pink rock salt
9 cups (2.25 L)	loosely packed arugula
1 tsp (5 mL)	toasted sesame oil (optional)

DIRECTIONS:

1. In a large cast-iron skillet, heat oil over medium heat.

2. Add onion and salt and sauté until translucent. Add mushrooms and garlic.

3. Cook, stirring occasionally, for up to 7 minutes, until onions and mushrooms are golden and tender.

4. Reduce heat to medium-low. Add vegetable stock.

5. Gradually add arugula, and cook, stirring gently, for 1 to 2 minutes, until all is incorporated and leaves have wilted.

6. Drizzle with sesame oil. Serve immediately.

Makes 2 servings.

Tip: Add shiitake mushrooms to your other soups and stews to boost immune function year-round.

> *"All I ask of food is that it doesn't harm me."*
>
> —MICHAEL PALIN
>
> (*MONTY PYTHON'S FLYING CIRCUS*)

CHAPTER 15

MAIN MEALS

RAW PAD THAI

This raw dish is packed with detoxifying vegetables. Zucchini makes a wonderful substitute for noodles and boasts only 25 calories per cup (250 mL). Cabbage and cauliflower both contain indole-3-carbinol (I3C), which helps to balance hormones by reducing excess estrogen in the body. Almonds are high in omega-9 and vitamin E, and make a great substitute for the typical peanut sauce.

INGREDIENTS:

I	medium zucchini
I	large carrot
I	green onion, chopped
½ cup (125 mL)	shredded purple cabbage
½ cup (125 mL)	cauliflower florets
½ cup (125 mL)	mung bean sprouts or radish sprouts (spicy)

SAUCE:

2 tbsp (30 mL)	tahini
2 tbsp (30 mL)	almond butter
1 tbsp (15 mL)	lime or lemon juice
2 tbsp (30 mL)	tamari (wheat-free)
1 tbsp (15 mL)	raw honey
¼ tsp (1 mL)	garlic, minced
½ tsp (2.5 mL)	ginger root, grated

DIRECTIONS:

1. Use a spiralizer (or mandoline, or vegetable peeler) to create noodles from the carrots and zucchini. Place them in a large mixing bowl and top with the vegetables.

2. Whisk sauce ingredients in a bowl. The sauce will be thick, but will thin out after it's mixed with the vegetables.

3. Pour the sauce over the noodles and vegetables, and toss. This dish tastes even better the next day once the flavors have had a chance to blend.

Makes 4 servings.

SLOW-COOKED SWISS STEAK

This is my mother-in-law Linda's recipe. As a busy mom who taught in a classroom all day, she used to get this dish started in the morning in a slow cooker, knowing that when she came home after work, she could rely on this healthy, ready-to-eat, no-fuss dinner to please her kids. Being from northern Canada, my husband fondly remembers this dish being made from lean moose meat.

You can use any lean red meat in this dish (for example, goat or venison) and feel good about the fact that it contains less arachidonic acid than fatty cuts. (Arachidonic acid can cause inflammation in the body. See page 87 for more details.) The long cooking time results in meat that is incredibly tender. All the orange vegetables are a rich source of vitamin A, which helps to rebuild skin and the lining of the lungs and digestive tract. Serve this stew with a fresh salad or steamed green vegetables. When you have finished 8 weeks of the program and are ready to introduce tomatoes, try adding 3 cups (750 mL) of stewed tomatoes and cut back on the vegetable broth by 2 cups.

INGREDIENTS:

2.2 lb (1 kg)	lean beef roast, cut into 1-inch (2.5 cm) steaks
6 cups (1.5 L)	chicken, beef, or vegetable stock
3	medium sweet potatoes or yams, cut into 2-inch (5 cm) pieces (approximately 4 cups/1 L)
2 cups (500 mL)	chopped onions
2 cups (500 mL)	carrots, cut into 2-inch (5 cm) pieces
2 cups (500 mL)	Jerusalem artichokes (sunchokes) or parsnips, cut into 2-inch (5 cm) pieces
¼ cup (60 mL)	lemon juice
3	garlic cloves, chopped
¼ cup (60 mL)	parsley flakes OR ½ cup (125 mL) fresh parsley
1 tbsp (15 mL)	dried basil

2 tsp (10 mL)   rosemary

1 tsp (5 mL)   oregano

1 tsp (5 mL)   thyme

½ tsp (2.5 mL)   gray sea salt or pink rock salt

DIRECTIONS:

1. Preheat a large saucepan or Dutch oven on medium heat. Lower heat to medium-low and gently brown beef roast about 1 minute each side. Alternatively, you could cook this in a slow cooker by adding all the ingredients at once and letting it stew for 5 to 6 hours.

2. Add all remaining ingredients. Bring to a boil, and then reduce heat to low.

3. Simmer for 3 hours, checking once an hour to stir and to ensure the stew is simmering. If the heat is too high, you may run out of liquid. Add more if required, because the broth is the best part. To finish the dish, stir in the lemon juice, and serve hot. The flavor of this stew improves with time.

Makes 4 servings.

COOKING QUINOA

1 cup (250 mL)   quinoa

1¾ cups (435 mL)   filtered water

1. Rinse the quinoa in a fine-mesh strainer under cold running water.

2. Place the quinoa in a small saucepan with the water and bring to a boil. Reduce heat to low, cover, and simmer for 15 minutes. Do not stir. When all the liquid is absorbed, remove from heat and fluff with a fork.

Makes 2½ cups (625 mL).

PESTO WHITE BEAN BOWL

This perfect vegan dish was created by fellow nutritionist and cookbook author Jae Steele and featured in her great book *Get It Ripe*. She writes, "This meal-in-a-bowl is quick to put together and tastes great at room temperature for lunch or dinner out of the house. Both white beans and quinoa are great sources of protein, calcium, magnesium, and fiber. The raw bok choy and pesto add a nice freshness to the meal. Feel free to grate in a clove of garlic if that's your kind of thing, or add any other vegetables on hand, like grated carrot."

INGREDIENTS:

1½ cups (325 mL)	cooked cannellini or navy beans
	(or one 14 oz/400 g can, drained and rinsed)
¼ cup (125 mL)	dairy- and nut-free pesto (store-bought or see page 278)
¼ tsp (1 mL)	gray sea salt or pink rock salt
2 cups (500 mL)	cooked quinoa (see page 308), brown rice, or millet
4 cups (1 L)	baby bok choy, chopped, or organic baby spinach
2 tbsp (30 mL)	flax seed or extra-virgin olive oil
	(optional, depending on how oily the pesto is)

DIRECTIONS:

1. Gently mix the white beans with the pesto and salt in a bowl.

2. Divide the quinoa between 2 dishes. Top with the bok choy, and then the pesto bean mixture. Drizzle with the oil and season with salt to taste.

Makes 2 servings.

DIJON SALMON PATTIES

Using rice crackers or rolled quinoa instead of bread crumbs in this recipe makes it easier to digest and prevents you from feeling bloated. Serve these patties with a large green salad. You can also skip making the patties, omitting the egg and crackers/quinoa, and instead serve the salmon mixture over a bed of salad greens.

INGREDIENTS:

1 tbsp (15 mL)	extra-virgin olive oil, divided
½ cup (125 mL)	finely chopped red onion
¼ cup (60 mL)	finely chopped celery (optional)
1 lb (450 g)	canned salmon, drained and flaked
2	organic egg whites OR 1 whole organic egg
¾ cup (185 mL)	crushed rice crackers (about 20 crackers) or rolled quinoa, divided
1 tbsp (15 mL)	dried dill OR ¼ cup (60 mL) fresh chopped dill
1 tbsp (15 mL)	mustard seed, whole

DIRECTIONS:

1. Add 1 teaspoon (5 mL) of oil to a small skillet over medium heat. Spritz liberally with filtered water or broth to ensure the oil doesn't overheat.

2. Add the onion and celery and sauté for 4 minutes, or until tender.

3. In a medium-sized bowl, combine the onion mixture with the salmon, egg, ½ cup (125 mL) of the crushed rice crackers or rolled quinoa, dill, and mustard.

4. Divide the salmon mixture into 4 equal portions, using your hands to shape each into a ½-inch-thick patty.

5. Put the remaining ¼ cup (60 mL) of crushed rice crackers or rolled quinoa on a plate. Coat each patty with 1 tablespoon (15 mL) of crushed crackers.

6. Cover and chill the patties for 20 minutes.

7. Heat the remaining 2 teaspoons (10 mL) of olive oil in the same skillet over medium heat. Cook the patties for 5 minutes on each side, until lightly browned.

8. Serve hot.

Makes 4 servings.

ALLERGY-REDUCING TIP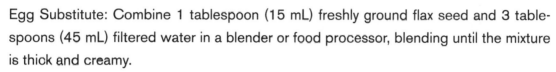

Egg Substitute: Combine 1 tablespoon (15 mL) freshly ground flax seed and 3 tablespoons (45 mL) filtered water in a blender or food processor, blending until the mixture is thick and creamy.

A TALE OF TWO CURRIES

I invented this recipe for my nephew's birthday because half of the party guests were vegetarian and the other half wanted chicken. You can try it either way, depending on your mood or dietary needs. Any fresh, local, seasonally available vegetables can be used, as the curry sauce goes well with anything. At the height of summer, try to use green and purple beans, zucchini, or carrots—or whatever local farmers are harvesting at the time. Visit your favorite farmers' market, experiment with the produce, and have fun!

Curry is traditionally served with rice. If you have good digestion, rice is a nice way to soak up the rich sauce.

INGREDIENTS:

3 cups (750 mL)	chopped onions (about 3 medium bulbs)
1 tbsp (15 mL)	extra-virgin olive oil
2 tbsp (30 mL)	chopped garlic
2.2 lb (1 kg)	chicken thighs, skinned OR three 14 oz (400 mL) cans black beans
3 cups (750 mL)	carrots, sliced into coins
2 cups (500 mL)	chopped kale
1 tbsp (15 mL)	minced ginger root
1 tbsp (15 mL)	turmeric
½ tbsp (7.5 mL)	cinnamon
½ tbsp (7.5 mL)	ground coriander
1 tsp (5 mL)	gray sea salt or pink rock salt
2 cups (500 mL)	chicken or vegetable stock
½	lemon or 1 medium lime, zested and juiced
2 cups (500 mL)	cauliflower or broccoli, cut into 2-inch (5 cm) pieces
½ cup (125 mL)	coconut milk
¼ cup (60 mL)	tahini

OPTIONAL ADDITIONS:

¼ cup (60 mL) dried cranberries (apple juice sweetened)

1 pineapple core (cut into fine slices—the texture is just like water chestnut; tip: serve the rest of the pineapple for dessert)

8-inch piece lemongrass

DIRECTIONS:

1. In a large saucepan or Dutch oven, sauté the onions in the oil over medium-low heat until soft, about 7 minutes. Spritz liberally with filtered water or broth to ensure the oil doesn't overheat.

2. Add the garlic and sauté a few minutes more, being careful not to brown or burn it. Keep it gently toasted and golden. Then add chicken and brown for 5 minutes.

3. Add carrots, kale, spices, salt, and stock and gently simmer over low heat for 20 to 25 minutes.

4. Add the broccoli or cauliflower and lemon or lime zest and simmer for another 5 minutes, or until the vegetables are al dente. If you prefer a tangy curry, add more citrus zest.

5. Stir in the lemon or lime juice, coconut milk, and tahini and mix thoroughly.

Note: If you're short on time, you can skip browning the chicken, or consider investing in a slow cooker. Just wait to add the coconut milk until right at the end, mixing it in just before you serve it.

Makes 7 or 8 servings.

JOB'S TEARS CHICKEN AND GINGER STEW

This is one of my most healing recipes. Job's tears is a gluten-free grain that tastes like barley. It's used in Asia as a remedy for painful and stiff joints. The active phytonutrients in Job's tears, including coixol, are anti-inflammatory, antihistaminic, and muscle relaxing.

INGREDIENTS:

2.2 lb (1 kg)	fresh chicken breast, skinless and boneless
5 quarts (5 L)	chicken broth
1 cup (250 mL)	Job's tears, soaked overnight and drained
2 tbsp (30 mL)	unpasteurized apple cider vinegar
2 tbsp (30 mL)	minced fresh ginger root
2 cups (500 mL)	chopped onions
2 cups (500 mL)	diced carrots or parsnips
1 cup (250 mL)	chopped burdock root
1 tbsp (15 mL)	parsley flakes OR 2 tbsp (30 mL) fresh parsley
1 tbsp (15 mL)	chopped basil
½ tsp (2.5 mL)	gray sea salt or pink rock salt (or to taste)
1½ cups (375 mL)	chopped green beans
1 cup (250 mL)	sliced fresh shiitake mushrooms, stems removed
½ cup (125 mL)	chopped scallions, cilantro, or additional parsley (garnish)

DIRECTIONS:

1. Cut chicken into bite-sized pieces. Place the chicken in a stockpot with the broth, Job's tears, cider vinegar, and ginger root. Bring to a rolling boil, then reduce the heat to low, cover, and simmer for 1 hour.

2. Add the onions, carrots or parsnips, burdock root, herbs, and salt. Bring to a boil again, then cover and simmer for another 30 minutes.

3. Add the green beans and mushrooms and simmer for a final 10 minutes, or until beans are tender. Remove from heat.

4. Serve hot in individual bowls. Garnish with chopped scallions, cilantro, or parsley.

OPTIONAL TOPPING:

Add a dash of toasted sesame oil to each bowl before serving to add a potent nutty flavor.

Makes 6 to 8 servings.

BUCKWHEAT SOBA NOODLES WITH CABBAGE AND PUMPKIN SEEDS

Cabbage contains anticarcinogenic nutrients that prevent some cancer-causing substances, which are broken down in the liver, from regrouping and recirculating in the bloodstream. These same nutrients have also been shown to help with the liver's elimination of other toxins. Traditionally, Japanese soba noodles are made with buckwheat (a relative of the rhubarb plant) and contain no gluten. However, modern commercial varieties are often made with a combination of buckwheat and wheat flour, so look for gluten-free brands. Buckwheat has a nutty flavor and pairs wonderfully with pumpkin seeds.

INGREDIENTS:

1 head	green or purple cabbage
1 tbsp (15 mL)	extra-virgin olive oil
1 cup (250 mL)	thinly sliced onion
1 cup (250 mL)	julienned carrot
1 tsp (5 mL)	gray sea salt or pink rock salt, divided
½ package (113 g)	100 percent buckwheat soba noodles
2	garlic cloves, minced

DRESSING:

1 tbsp (15 mL)	raw honey (or to taste)
2 tbsp (30 mL)	miso
1 tbsp (15 mL)	toasted sesame oil
½ cup (125 mL)	pumpkin seeds
½ tsp (2.5 mL)	umeboshi plum paste (optional)

DIRECTIONS:

1. Quarter the cabbage, cutting through the core. Remove and discard tough outer leaves. Cut away and discard the hard white core from each quarter. Slice each quarter crosswise into thin strips until you have about 3 cups (750 mL). Set aside.

2. Heat the olive oil in a large skillet over medium-low heat. Spritz liberally with filtered water or broth to ensure the oil doesn't over-heat. When the oil is warm, add the onion and sauté until tender, about 5 minutes.

3. Add the cabbage, carrots, and salt, stirring until cabbage is well coated. Reduce heat to medium-low. Cover and cook, stirring occasionally, until cabbage is very tender, about 20 minutes.

4. Meanwhile, bring 4 quarts (4 L) of filtered water to a boil in a large pot. Add the noodles and ½ tsp (2.5 mL) salt, or to taste. Boil until al dente, about 6 minutes.

5. Meanwhile, whisk dressing ingredients together, and set aside.

6. Drain the noodles and rinse under warm running water.

7. Toss noodles with the vegetable mixture and dressing. Divide among 4 bowls, topping each with pumpkin seeds.

Makes 4 servings.

SWEET POTATO FRITTATA

Whole eggs have inositol and choline, which are vital nutrients for brain function. The iron in spinach boosts immunity and prevents fatigue. If you don't want leftovers, just halve the recipe.

INGREDIENTS:

1 tsp (5 mL)	extra-virgin olive oil
1 cup (250 mL)	sliced red onion
2 cups (500 mL)	baby spinach
1 cup (250 mL)	thinly sliced sweet potato
12 large	organic eggs
¼ cup (60 mL)	filtered water
¼ tsp (1 mL)	gray sea salt or pink rock salt
1½ tbsp (22.5 mL)	dairy- and nut-free basil pesto (store-bought or see page 278)
½ cup (125 mL)	arame, soaked for 15 minutes
as desired	fresh herbs, chopped

317

DIRECTIONS:

1. Preheat the oven to 350° F (175° C). Use the olive oil to grease a 10 × 14–inch (23 cm × 30 cm) baking pan.

2. Layer onion, spinach, and sweet potato in the bottom of a casserole dish.

3. Whisk eggs, water, salt, and pesto in a medium-sized bowl until well blended.

4. Pour mixture over vegetables in casserole dish. Top with arame and herbs, if using.

5. Cook for 30 minutes, or until eggs are set.

Makes 6 servings.

AFRICAN NUT BUTTER STEW

This stew is truly a one-pot meal. All your nutritional needs are met in this dish, which is so rich and creamy that it will leave you feeling deeply satisfied. The brown rice and beans combine to make a complete vegetarian protein. If time allows, consider soaking the beans and brown rice overnight for easier digestion and reduced cooking time. The tiger nut powder adds a subtle sweetness to the stew. It's a good source of chromium and calcium, both of which help to stabilize blood sugar levels and prevent cardiovascular inflammation. Freeze leftovers so you have a healthy meal when you're short on time. This stew pairs nicely with Dulse Chips (page 254).

INGREDIENTS:

1 cup (250 mL)	chopped onion
2	garlic cloves, minced
4 cups (1 L)	vegetable stock, divided
2 cups (500 mL)	diced sweet potato or yam
1½ cups (375 mL)	white beans (canned or cooked)
½ cup (125 mL)	brown rice
¼ tsp (1 mL)	gray sea salt or pink rock salt
¼ cup (60 mL)	almond butter
2 cups (500 mL)	chopped kale
2 tbsp (30 mL)	lemon juice
1 tbsp (15 mL)	tamari (wheat-free)
1 tbsp (15 mL)	raw honey
1 tbsp (15 mL)	grated fresh ginger root

OPTIONAL ADDITIONS:

¼ cup (60 mL)	tiger nut powder
1 cup (250 mL)	extra vegetable stock

DIRECTIONS:

1. In a large saucepan or Dutch oven, water-sauté the onion and garlic in 2 tbsp (30 mL) of the vegetable stock over medium heat for 3 to 5 minutes.

2. Add the remaining stock, sweet potato or yam, white beans, brown rice, and salt. Cover and let simmer for 45 minutes.

3. When the rice is completely cooked, scoop ½ cup (125 mL) liquid from the stew into a small bowl and whisk together with the almond butter to make a paste.

4. Add the almond butter paste to the pot along with the kale. Stir and cook for 5 minutes. Turn off heat.

5. Add the lemon juice, tamari, honey, ginger root, and tiger nut powder, if using, and stir again. Note that if you opt to include tiger nut powder, you should increase the amount of broth in the recipe by 1 cup (250 mL). Serve hot.

Makes 8 servings.

SUSHI RENOVATION

This recipe is brimming with immune-building, detoxifying ingredients. Selenium, found in shiitake mushrooms, is an important antioxidant for fighting cancer. The brown rice and quinoa give this sushi a lower glycemic index than conventional sushi.

INGREDIENTS:

1 cup (250 mL)	short-grain brown rice
½ cup (125 mL)	quinoa
3 cups (750 mL)	filtered water, divided
+ 2 tbsp (30 mL)	
½ cup (125 mL)	fresh sliced shiitake mushrooms
1 cup (250 mL)	vegetable broth
2 tbsp (30 mL)	brown rice vinegar
6 sheets	nori, 6 × 8 inches (15 × 20 cm) each
½ cup (125 mL)	grated carrot
½ cup (125 mL)	cucumber with peel, cut into matchsticks
½	grated daikon radish
1 tbsp (15 mL)	toasted sesame seeds (garnish)
1 tbsp (15 mL)	pickled ginger root
1 tsp (5 mL)	tamari (wheat-free)
2 tbsp (30 mL)	pickled ginger root
1 tbsp (15 mL)	natural wasabi

DIRECTIONS:

1. Add water, brown rice, and quinoa to a pot cover and bring to a boil. Then reduce heat to low and simmer for 55 to 60 minutes. Do not stir.

2. Meanwhile, in a separate pot, boil shiitake mushrooms in broth for 5 minutes.

3. When grains are done, remove the lid and drape a clean dishtowel over the pot for 10 minutes while they cool.

4. Transfer grains to a bowl and fluff using a fork or wooden paddle.

5. In a small bowl, make sushi vinegar by combining brown rice vinegar with 2 tbsp (30 mL) water. Slowly pour vinegar over grains.

6. On a sushi mat, lay out a sheet of nori. Leaving a 1-inch (2.5 cm) border at the top and bottom, cover sheet with grains. Evenly distribute fillings between the 6 nori sheets horizontally across the center of the sheets. Be careful not to overfill.

7. Run a wet finger across the top flap of the nori sheet to ensure a good seal, and roll the mat with a firm squeeze. Run a wet finger along the seam to seal the roll securely.

8. Cut into 1-inch (2.5 cm) slices with a sharp knife and garnish with sesame seeds.

9. Serve with pickled ginger root, wheat-free tamari, and wasabi.

Makes 36 pieces.

SALMON WITH FENNEL GREENS

Fresh fennel and fennel seeds flavor this elegant main course. Fennel contains anethole, a phytonutrient that has been shown to reduce inflammation. The omega-3 fats, such as EPA (eicosapentaenoic acid), found in salmon are anti-inflammatory, and they support cardiovascular health by preventing platelets from sticking together, thus improving blood flow. A 4-ounce (120 g) serving of salmon contains one-third of your daily recommended value of omega-3 fats.

INGREDIENTS:

¼ cup (60 mL)	extra-virgin olive oil
2 tbsp (30 mL)	minced white onion
½ tsp (2.5 mL)	gray sea salt or pink rock salt
2 tbsp (30 mL)	chopped fennel greens, divided
1 tbsp (15 mL)	fresh dill OR 1 tsp (5 mL) dried dill
1 tsp (5 mL)	fennel seeds
1	large fennel bulb (quartered, then cut lengthwise into ¼-inch [0.5 cm] slices)
¼ cup (60 mL)	vegetable stock or filtered water
two 7 oz (200 g)	salmon fillets
1 tbsp (15 mL)	raw honey or maple syrup
2 tbsp (30 mL)	lemon juice

OPTIONAL ADDITION:

¼ cup (60 mL)	fresh dill (garnish)

DIRECTIONS:

1. In a small bowl, mix the oil, onion, salt, fennel greens, and dill. Set aside.

2. Gently toast the fennel seeds in a large cast-iron or titanium skillet over medium-low heat until fragrant, stirring constantly for about 1½ minutes. Transfer the seeds to a small bowl and let cool.

3. Add 1 tbsp (15 mL) of the oil mixture to the same skillet and sauté over medium–low heat until onions are translucent. Spritz liberally with filtered water or broth to ensure the oil doesn't overheat. Add the sliced fennel bulb and stock. Cover and cook until al dente, about 5 minutes.

4. Uncover the skillet add the cooled fennel seeds.

5. Place the salmon fillets on top of the fennel, cover, and cook for 5 minutes.

6. Turn the salmon over. Coat it with the rest of the oil mixture. Cover and continue cooking until the salmon is opaque in the center, about 3 minutes longer.

7. In a small bowl, mix together the honey and lemon, and then add it to the skillet along with the remaining tablespoon of chopped fennel greens. Stir to heat through.

8. Divide the fennel mixture between 2 plates. Top with the salmon and spoon remaining sauce over top. Garnish with fresh dill.

Makes 2 servings.

EZRA'S HERBED QUINOA RISOTTO

Asparagus is an excellent source of vitamin K, as well as numerous B vitamins, including folate, B_1, B_2, B_3, and B_6. It's also high in vitamins A and C, iron, manganese, potassium, and fiber. Quinoa and other whole grains are a rich source of magnesium, a mineral that acts as a cofactor for more than 300 enzymes, including those involved in insulin secretion and glucose metabolism. Spring garlic scapes are the flower stalks that spring out of the garlic bulb. They're rich in allum, which can help protect against osteoarthritis.

Chef Ezra Title, my co-host on the TV show *Healthy Gourmet*, created this incredibly healthy recipe. To learn more about Ezra, visit his website at www.chezvousdining.ca.

INGREDIENTS:

1 tsp (5 mL)	extra-virgin olive oil
1 cup (250 mL)	diced onion
3	spring garlic scapes (stalks), chopped
1 cup (250 mL)	quinoa
¼ cup (60 mL)	unpasteurized apple cider vinegar
2 cups (500 mL)	chicken or vegetable stock
½ tsp (2.5 mL)	gray sea salt or pink rock salt
¼ cup (60 mL)	canned puréed squash or pumpkin
12	asparagus spears, chopped
¼ bunch	parsley, chopped
5	basil leaves, chopped
¼ bunch	chives, chopped
5	green onions, chopped (garnish)

DIRECTIONS:

1. Add olive oil, onions, and spring garlic into a small, shallow pot. Spritz liberally with filtered water or broth to ensure the oil doesn't overheat. Sauté on medium–low until translucent, approximately 2 minutes.

2. Stir in quinoa, coating it with the oil. Turn heat to medium-high and add apple cider vinegar to the pot, stirring constantly.

3. Once the vinegar has evaporated, add stock and salt. Cover and bring to a simmer, cooking on low for approximately 10 minutes, and stirring occasionally.

4. Add asparagus spears and simmer for another 5 minutes.

5. When quinoa is cooked, add squash purée and fresh herbs.

6. Garnish with green onion and serve immediately.

Makes 6 servings.

15-MINUTE ARCTIC CHAR WITH DILL MUSTARD SAUCE

Eating Arctic char is one of the healthiest dietary choices you can make. It has a special omega-3 fat called DHA (docosahexaenoic acid), which not only reduces inflammation, but also helps to keep moods positive and memory sharp. You can use salmon or trout in this recipe if Arctic char isn't available.

INGREDIENTS:

1 tsp (5 mL)	unpasteurized liquid honey
1 tbsp (15 mL)	chopped fresh dill or tarragon OR 1 tsp (5 mL) dried dill or tarragon
1 tbsp (15 mL)	natural Dijon mustard
⅓ cup (85 mL)	chicken broth
4 tbsp (60 mL)	fresh lemon juice, divided
4 medium	Arctic char fillets
4 tbsp (60 mL)	extra-virgin olive oil, divided
to taste	gray sea salt or pink rock salt
3	garlic cloves, minced

DIRECTIONS:

1. To make the sauce, whisk together honey, herbs, mustard, chicken broth, and 2 tbsp (30 mL) of lemon juice in a bowl. Set aside.

2. Preheat broiler on high. Place a stainless steel skillet (be sure the handle is also stainless steel) or cast-iron pan 6 inches below the broiler for about 10 minutes to get it very hot.

3. While the pan preheats, marinate char with 2 tbsp (30 mL) fresh lemon juice, 2 tbsp (30 mL) olive oil, and salt.

4. Using an oven mitt, carefully pull pan out from under heat and place char on hot pan. Return to broiler. Keep in mind that the fish is cooking rapidly on both sides, so it will be done very quickly, usually in approximately 7 minutes depending on thickness. Test with a fork for readiness. It will flake easily when it's cooked. Char tastes best when it's still pink inside. Place skillet contents on a serving dish and set aside.

5. Using the same skillet, add remaining 2 tbsp (30 mL) olive oil and garlic, spritz liberally with filtered water or broth to ensure the oil doesn't overheat, and gently sauté until tender, about 1 minute. Avoid browning the garlic. Add the reserved sauce and cook on medium until it reduces and thickens. Pour over the fish and serve.

Makes 4 servings.

SWEET POTATO GRATIN

This is an adaptation of a Mollie Katzen recipe by my friend and fellow nutritionist Cathy Hayashi. Be sure to thinly slice the sweet potatoes so they'll cook properly and release enough starch to thicken and set the gratin. Slicing the spinach into ribbons helps disperse the flavor throughout.

INGREDIENTS:

1	large garlic clove, minced
2 tsp (10 mL)	freshly grated lime peel
3 tbsp (45 mL)	fresh lime juice
3 tbsp (45 mL)	chopped cilantro
1 tsp (5 mL)	dried thyme
1½ tsp (7.5 mL)	gray sea salt or pink rock salt
14 oz (400 mL)	coconut milk
½ cup (125 mL)	filtered water
4 cups (1 L)	sweet potatoes, peeled, halved, then sliced thinly
2 cups (500 mL)	cooked brown rice
15 oz (415 mL)	cooked black beans OR 1½ cups (375 mL) cooked chicken, chopped into small pieces
4 cups (1 L)	fresh spinach leaves, sliced into ribbons

TOPPING:

¾ cup (185 mL)	quinoa flakes
2 tsp (10 mL)	fresh thyme OR ½ tsp (2.5 mL) dried thyme
¼ tsp (1 mL)	cumin
¼ tsp (1 mL)	gray sea salt or pink rock salt
1 tbsp (15 mL)	extra-virgin olive oil

DIRECTIONS:

1. Preheat oven to 350°F (175°C). Combine the garlic, lime peel and juice, cilantro, thyme, salt, water, and coconut milk in a 2-cup (500 mL) measuring cup.

2. Pour one-third of this mixture into a 9 × 13–inch (20 × 30 cm) baking pan.

3. Layer half of the sweet potatoes on the bottom, followed by half of the rice, half of the black beans or chicken, and half of the spinach.

4. Pour another third of the coconut milk mixture over this layer and repeat layering with the remaining sweet potatoes, rice, beans or chicken, and spinach.

5. Pour remaining coconut milk mixture to cover the entire dish.

6. Combine all topping ingredients and sprinkle over the gratin.

7. Bake, uncovered, for about 60 minutes, rotating the pan in the oven after 30 minutes to ensure uniform baking.

8. When the sweet potatoes are tender and the topping is crisp, remove from the oven and let sit for 2 to 3 minutes to firm up before serving.

Makes 8 servings.

KELP NOODLE PANANG CURRY

This recipe was created to satisfy a craving for panang curry (also called phanaeng curry), which is a mild Malaysian and Thai curry made with coconut milk. Unlike the traditional recipe, this one isn't fried—it's raw—but it still has a sweet tangy flavor that's very true to the original. I used kelp noodles in place of wheat noodles. Kelp noodles are made from seaweed and have only 6 calories per serving. Daikon radish is a rich source of potassium and vitamin C.

INGREDIENTS:

Sauce:

2 tbsp (30 mL)	flax seed oil
2 tbsp (30 mL)	extra-virgin olive or hemp oil
2 tsp (10 mL)	turmeric
1 tsp (5 mL)	cinnamon
1 tsp (5 mL)	cumin
1 tsp (5 mL)	cardamom
1 tsp (5 mL)	mustard powder
¼ cup (60 mL)	fresh cilantro leaves OR 2 tbsp (30 mL) cilantro pesto
2 tbsp (30 mL)	ground almonds or almond butter
2 tbsp (30 mL)	unpasteurized liquid honey
1 tbsp (15 mL)	lemon juice
1 tsp (5 mL)	dulse flakes
1 tsp (5 mL)	gray sea salt or pink rock salt
4 tbsp (60 mL)	raw coconut butter (with coconut meat in it; available at health-food stores)

Noodles:

1 package	kelp noodles
¼	carrot, grated
¼	zucchini or daikon radish, grated
¼	yellow (summer) squash, grated

DIRECTIONS:

1. Process the sauce ingredients in a food processor until smooth.

2. Rinse noodles with water, then cut to desired length and place into a large bowl.

3. Pour sauce over the noodles, add the grated vegetables, and combine until well mixed. You can enjoy this dish raw or warmed gently in a saucepan for 5 minutes. If you warm the dish, make sure to drizzle the flax seed onto the dish before serving—flax seed oil should never be heated.

Makes 4 servings.

FAST-COOKING KICHADI IN A THERMOS

This is a wonderful recipe when you want a fresh detoxifying stew. It's a fantastic meal-on-the-go because it cooks while you're in transit, although it also makes a delicious at-home meal. I discovered this cleansing recipe while studying with yoga instructor Matthew Remski on a 28-day Ayurvedic detox retreat. I ate only berries and cleansing stews called kichadi, yet felt satisfied because of the nutritional balance in the kichadi. The spices in this dish are very healing to the digestive tract. By rotating the type of vegetables you use, you can keep this stew interesting—experiment for a different lunch every time.

INGREDIENTS:

4 cups (1 L)	filtered water
1 cup (250 mL)	chopped spinach
½ cup (125 mL)	grated carrot
½ cup (125 mL)	quinoa
½ cup (125 mL)	split mung beans

1 tsp (5 mL)	grated fresh ginger root
1 tsp (5 mL)	turmeric
¼ tsp (1 mL)	cumin
¼ tsp (1 mL)	gray sea salt or pink rock salt

OPTIONAL ADDITIONS:

1 tbsp (15 mL)	minced garlic
½ cup (125 mL)	grated parsnip
½ cup (125 mL)	chopped collards
1 tbsp (15 mL)	extra-virgin olive oil
1 tbsp (15 mL)	miso paste or vegetable boullion

DIRECTIONS:

1. In a medium saucepan over high heat, bring all the ingredients (except the oil and miso, if using) to a rapid boil and stir.

2. Lower heat to medium, cover, and simmer for 10 minutes.

3. Transfer stew to a large (4-cup/1 L) wide-mouth stainless steel or glass-lined Thermos.

4. Add the oil and miso, screw on lid, and shake well.

5. Leave stew to cook in the Thermos for at least 1 hour (2 hours is best).

6. Stir well before serving.

Tip: Consider buying a canning funnel with a 2-inch (5 cm) opening to guide the fluid into the Thermos and avoid spills.

Makes 2 servings.

SHEPHERD'S PIE

You can use whichever fresh vegetables you have on hand to make this recipe. I love making this dish in the fall when produce is abundant at the local farmers' market. A vegetarian version can be made by substituting lentils for the meat. The first three ingredients can be replaced with sweet potato, yam, or the White Root Mash found on page 269.

INGREDIENTS:

2 cups (500 mL)	skinned and diced celery root
2 cups (500 mL)	diced Jerusalem artichokes
2 cups (500 mL)	skinned and diced turnip
2 tbsp (30 mL)	extra-virgin olive oil (plus 2 tbsp/30 mL if making lentil version)
1 lb (450 g)	ground bison or turkey OR 2 cups (500 mL) cooked lentils
2 cups (500 mL)	chopped onions
2	garlic cloves, minced
1 tsp (5 mL)	cumin
1 tsp (5 mL)	gray sea salt or pink rock salt
3 tbsp (45 mL)	Italian herb blend (basil, marjoram, oregano, rosemary, sage, savory, and/or thyme)
1 cup (250 mL)	chopped carrots
1 cup (250 mL)	diced sweet potato or yam
1 cup (250 mL)	chopped celery
1 cup (250 mL)	sweet peas
2 cups (500 mL)	chopped fresh spinach
½ cup (125 mL)	kasha (toasted buckwheat)
¼ cup (60 mL)	fresh sage OR 1 tsp (5 mL) dry sage

DIRECTIONS:

1. Boil celery root, Jerusalem artichoke, and turnip in 3 cups (750 mL) of water until soft. Drain and mash with 2 tbsp (30 mL) olive oil. Set aside.

2. Brown the bison meat in a large pot over medium-low heat with onion, garlic, cumin seed, salt, and herbs. (If making the lentil version, heat 2 tbsp/30 mL olive oil over medium-low heat with onion, garlic, cumin seed, salt, and herbs before adding the lentils.) Spritz liberally with filtered water or broth to ensure the oil doesn't overheat.

3. Add the carrots, sweet potato or yam, celery, peas, spinach, kasha, and sage. If cooking the lentil version, add ¾ cup (185 mL) of vegetable broth. Stir well and cook for 8 minutes.

4. Transfer to a 9 × 13–inch (20 cm × 30 cm) baking dish. Top with the mashed white root vegetables.

5. Bake at 350°F (175°C) for 20 minutes. Move to the top rack position and broil on low for 5 minutes or until nicely browned.

7. Serve hot or allow to set in the fridge overnight.

Makes 6 to 8 servings.

DIJON CHICKEN

This is a fast, healthy meal that tastes great as leftovers the next day. The coconut milk contains lauric acid, which helps to boost the immune system. The mustard seeds in the Dijon mustard are a good source of selenium, a nutrient shown to help reduce the severity of asthma, decrease some of the symptoms of rheumatoid arthritis, and help prevent cancer. Turmeric has been shown to have powerful anti-inflammatory effects. Using skinless chicken reduces the amount of saturated fat in the recipe.

INGREDIENTS:

8 (2.2 lb/1 kg)	skinless chicken thighs
2 tbsp (30 mL)	extra–virgin olive oil
1 tsp (5 mL)	turmeric
½ tsp (2.5 mL)	gray sea salt or pink rock salt
¼ cup (60 mL)	vegetable or chicken broth
2 cups (500 mL)	red onion, sliced
¼ cup (60 mL)	natural Dijon mustard
cup (85 mL)	coconut milk
2 tbsp (30 mL)	unpasteurized liquid honey
1 tbsp (15 mL)	Italian herb blend (basil, marjoram, oregano, rosemary, sage, savory, thyme) or herbes de Provence (basil, fennel, lavender, savory, thyme)

DIRECTIONS:

1. Drizzle the oil over the chicken thighs and sprinkle with turmeric and salt. Spritz liberally with filtered water or broth to keep meat moist and ensure the oil doesn't overheat. Cook in a large cast-iron or stainless steel skillet over medium heat for 5 to 7 minutes, turning every couple of minutes until golden on all sides.

2. Add the onion and continue to cook, stirring occasionally, for 3 to 5 minutes, until the onion has softened.

3. Spread the mustard evenly over the chicken pieces using a spoon or brush.

4. Cook for 15 minutes, or until the chicken is cooked through and no longer pink in the center. Remove from the skillet and set aside.

5. Pour the coconut milk and honey into the skillet. Warm gently and stir for 2 to 3 minutes, until the sauce has thickened slightly.

6. Arrange the chicken thighs on a shallow serving dish and pour the sauce over and around the chicken. Adjust seasonings to taste.

7. Garnish with the herbs and serve immediately.

Makes 4 servings.

ROAST BEEF, CHICKEN, OR TURKEY ROLL-UPS

These roll-ups are so easy and tasty, you'll start relying on them as you would a sandwich. You can turn these roll-ups into sandwiches by using toasted gluten-free bread instead of lettuce. Try alternating between turkey or chicken slices, as rotating your protein sources lessens the likelihood that you will develop a sensitivity to any one protein. If you like your roll-ups spicy, try adding a dash of natural horseradish or wasabi.

INGREDIENTS:

10 thin slices	lean organic roast beef, chicken, or turkey breast
1 tbsp (15 mL)	natural mustard
5 leaves	Boston, Bibb, or Romaine lettuce
½ cup (125 mL)	cucumber slices
¼ cup (60 mL)	avocado slices

DIRECTIONS:

1. Place 2 thin slices of roast beef, chicken, or turkey inside 1 large lettuce leaf.

2. Spread with mustard, add additional vegetables, and roll tightly.

3. Serve immediately.

Makes 5 rolls.

SPICE-RUBBED BISON TENDERLOIN

Bison are raised on the open range, where they get a chance to eat lots of omega-3-rich grasses. All of the spices in this recipe have powerful anti-inflammatory action and also help with digestion. Consider taking a protein digestive enzyme supplement with this meal if you're adjusting to eating meat and your stomach is having a tough time.

Note: If you're unable to source bison, you can substitute organic or grass-fed beef tenderloin.

INGREDIENTS:

2 sprigs	fresh rosemary (remove and chop leaves, discard stem)
2 tbsp (30 mL)	minced garlic
1 tsp (5 mL)	cinnamon
2 tsp (10 mL)	coriander seeds (lightly dry-toasted and ground)
2 tsp (10 mL)	cumin seeds (lightly dry-toasted and ground)
½ tsp (2.5 mL)	allspice
1 tsp (5 mL)	minced fresh ginger root
½ tsp (2.5 mL)	gray sea salt or pink rock salt
four 6-ounce (180 g)	bison tenderloin fillets

DIRECTIONS:

1. Combine the rosemary, garlic, spices, ginger root, and salt in a small bowl and set aside.

2. Place the bison on a 12 × 12–inch (30 cm × 30 cm) glass baking dish and coat both sides with the spice mix.

3. If using the oven, preheat the broiler on low and then place the fillets under the broiler, 6 inches (15 cm) from the heat. If using a grill pan on the stove, use medium-low heat. Spritz liberally with filtered water or broth to keep the meat moist and to ensure the spices don't burn.

4. Broil or grill for 4 to 6 minutes on each side depending on how well done you like it. Check the meat often to prevent overcooking.

5. Remove from the oven or grill and allow to rest for a few minutes before serving.

Makes 4 servings.

POMEGRANATE-POACHED HALIBUT

When life finds me blindingly busy, I pull out this five-minute-prep-time recipe to save my sanity. Halibut is a popular white fish choice, but you can use any kind of white fish, fresh or frozen. Other excellent choices include tilapia, basa, cod, and haddock. I suggest serving this with Beet the Detox Salad (page 270) on a bed of greens.

INGREDIENTS:

2	red onions, finely sliced
eight 3 oz fillets	halibut (use 2 per person)
(90 g)	
1 cup (250 mL)	pomegranate juice

SAUCE:

½ cup (125 mL)	mayonnaise
¼ cup (60 mL)	natural mustard
1 tsp (5 mL)	nutritional yeast

DIRECTIONS:

1. Preheat the oven to 350°F (175°C).

2. Place the fish fillets on top of the onions in a large flat glass or stainless steel dish and pour the pomegranate juice over. Bake for 8 minutes for fresh fish, or 12 minutes for frozen.

3. Meanwhile, whisk together the sauce ingredients in a small bowl.

4. Remove baking dish from oven and turn broiler to low. Portion a tablespoon (15 mL) of sauce on each piece of fish and return to the oven.

5. Broil until sauce begins to thicken, about 5 minutes. Place fish on a serving platter and pour onions and cooking sauce over top. Serve hot.

Makes 4 servings.

VEGETABLE TEMPEH STIR-FRY

This is a great example of what you can do with tempeh if you don't want to rely on meat for protein. Tempeh contains more protein than tofu and is also more flavorful.

INGREDIENTS:

1 tbsp (15 mL)	extra-virgin olive oil
1 cup (250 mL)	onion, sliced
4	garlic cloves, chopped
2 tbsp (30 mL)	minced fresh ginger root
3 cups (750 mL)	thin asparagus, cut into 2-inch (5 cm) lengths
1 medium	zucchini, sliced
4 oz (115 g)	tempeh, cut into ½-inch (1 cm) cubes
1 tbsp (15 mL)	tamari (wheat-free)
2 tbsp (30 mL)	lemon juice
to taste	gray sea salt or pink rock salt
1 tsp (5 mL)	sesame seeds

DIRECTIONS:

1. Add oil and onion to a wok or 10-inch (22 cm) stainless steel skillet. Spritz liberally with filtered water or broth to ensure the oil doesn't overheat and cook over medium-low heat for about 2 to 3 minutes, stirring constantly.

2. Add garlic, ginger root, asparagus, and zucchini and continue to cook for another 2 to 3 minutes, stirring constantly.

3. Add tempeh, tamari, and lemon juice; cover and cook on low for about 2 minutes, or until vegetables are tender-crisp.

4. Season with salt and sprinkle with sesame seeds. Serve immediately.

Makes 2 servings.

> *"Vegetables are a must on a diet. I suggest carrot cake, zucchini bread and pumpkin pie."*
>
> —JIM DAVIS

CHAPTER 16

TREATS

BERRY PIE

Raspberries and blueberries are loaded with salicylic acid, the same heart disease–fighting and pain-numbing compound found in aspirin. However, unlike aspirin, which can increase inflammation, berries are deliciously anti-inflammatory. I created this dish with my nephew Kaydn in mind, as he's on kidney dialysis and must stay on a nourishing low-sodium diet. Look for apple juice sold in a glass jar, as the canned juice often contains toxic heavy metals and plastics leached from the can.

INGREDIENTS:

2 cups (500 mL)	apple juice
¼ cup (60 mL)	agar flakes
¼ cup (60 mL)	arrowroot flour or kudzu root powder
¾ cup (185 mL)	unpasteurized liquid honey
4 cups (1 L)	blueberries
1 cup (250 mL)	crushed pecans
1 cup (250 mL)	raspberries

DIRECTIONS:

1. Bring apple juice and agar to a gentle boil in an uncovered pot.

2. As soon as the juice comes to a boil, turn heat to medium and cook for 3 minutes to dissolve the agar. Meanwhile, whisk the arrowroot flour or kudzu powder into the honey in a medium-sized bowl.

3. When agar is fully dissolved, pour the honey and arrowroot/kudzu mixture into the pot. Whisk until thick, about 2 minutes. Remove from heat. Add blueberries and mix well.

4. Line a 10-inch (25 cm) pie plate with crushed pecans. Pack down nuts with a spoon as much as possible before adding pie filling. The nuts will form the bottom of the pie but won't stick together like a traditional piecrust. Pour blueberry mixture into pie plate and top with fresh raspberries for garnish. Refrigerate for 2 hours until set.

Makes 8 to 12 servings.

GENEVA'S GINGER COOKIES

When my grandma Geneva started juicing and eating healthfully in the 1950s, she was a follower of health pioneers such as Paul Bragg. This recipe is inspired by ginger root, her favorite anti-inflammatory spice; Geneva has spent countless kitchen hours baking the most amazing goodies with it!

INGREDIENTS:

½ cup (125 mL)	almond butter
2 tsp (10 mL)	cinnamon
2 tsp (10 mL)	ground ginger
2 cups (500 mL)	almond flour
1 tbsp (15 mL)	ground flax meal
6 tbsp (90 mL)	unpasteurized liquid honey

1 tsp (5 mL)   pure vanilla extract

as desired   slivered almonds for decoration

DIRECTIONS:

1. Preheat the oven to 350°F (175°C).

2. Place all the ingredients into a bowl and stir to thoroughly combine.

3. Roll the dough by hand into 1-inch (2 cm) balls and lightly press down with a fork. Decorate with slivered almonds.

4. Place the cookies on a baking sheet lined with unbleached parchment paper.

5. Bake 10 to 12 minutes, or until golden. The cookies will crisp as they cool.

6. Store in an airtight container.

Makes 24 cookies.

ULTIMATE NUT/SEED BUTTER

INGREDIENTS:

1 cup (250 mL)   nuts or seeds

pinch   gray sea salt or pink rock salt

2 tbsp (30 mL)   raw honey (or to taste)

¼ cup (60 mL)   almond or avocado oil

1 tsp (5 mL)   pure vanilla extract

DIRECTIONS:

1. Process the nuts or seeds in a food processor until powderlike.

2. Add the salt, honey, oil, and vanilla and continue blending until moist and butterlike. Be patient, as it takes time to bring out the oil in certain nuts such as almonds.

Makes ¾ cup (185 mL).

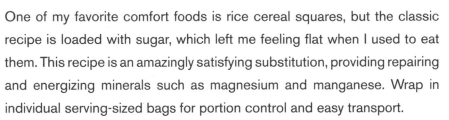

JULE'S CRISPY RICE SQUARES

One of my favorite comfort foods is rice cereal squares, but the classic recipe is loaded with sugar, which left me feeling flat when I used to eat them. This recipe is an amazingly satisfying substitution, providing repairing and energizing minerals such as magnesium and manganese. Wrap in individual serving-sized bags for portion control and easy transport.

INGREDIENTS:

1 tsp (5 mL)	avocado, hazelnut, or pumpkin seed oil
1 cup (250 mL)	rice syrup
½ cup (125 mL)	hazelnut butter
½ cup (125 mL)	tahini
½ tsp (2.5 mL)	gray sea salt or pink rock salt
1 tbsp (15 mL)	pure vanilla extract
4 cups (1 L)	crispy brown rice cereal
⅔ cup (175 mL)	raw or roasted hazelnuts, chopped

OPTIONAL INGREDIENTS:

¼ cup (60 mL)	protein powder (choose hemp seed, sprouted brown rice, or pea protein)
⅓ cup (85 mL)	shredded dried coconut
½ cup (125 mL)	hemp seeds
1 tsp (5 mL)	cinnamon

DIRECTIONS:

1. Lightly oil a 9 × 13–inch (23 × 33 cm) pan. Set aside.

2. In a saucepan over low heat, combine rice syrup, hazelnut butter, and tahini until softened.

3. Remove from heat. Add salt, vanilla, and protein powder if using. Stir well.

4. Fold in cereal, hazelnuts, and other optional ingredients, stirring until well mixed. Press into lightly oiled pan.

5. Slice into squares and chill in the refrigerator for 1 hour.

6. Store in the fridge or freezer in a glass container fitted with an airtight plastic lid to maintain freshness and prevent crumbling.

Makes 12 squares.

FIG AND DATE SQUARES

I just love fig and date squares, but the high sugar and flour content of conventional squares leaves me feeling blue. I came up with this recipe for a gluten- and sugar-free version. Both figs and dates provide valuable B vitamins and minerals such as magnesium, all of which are essential for nerve health. Just avoid eating more than one piece at a time because they're quite sweet.

FILLING INGREDIENTS:

⅔ cup (175 mL)   dried figs

⅔ cup (175 mL)   pitted dates

1 tbsp (15 mL)   lemon juice

1 tbsp (15 mL)   raw honey

1 tbsp (15 mL)   psyllium husk

TOPPING INGREDIENTS:

4   large pitted dates, chopped

½ cup (125 mL)   pecans

½ cup (125 mL)   almonds

⅓ cup (85 mL)   shredded dried coconut

½ tsp (2.5 mL)   cinnamon

pinch   gray sea salt or pink rock salt

DIRECTIONS:

1. Process filling ingredients in a food processor until they form a paste. Set aside.

2. For the topping, process all ingredients until just coarsely chopped.

3. Press half of the topping crumble into the bottom of an 8 × 8–inch (20 × 20 cm) square baking pan.

4. Evenly spread all of the fig and date filling over top, and sprinkle with the remaining crumble.

5. Press layers together with the back of a spoon to about 1 inch (2.5 cm) thick.

6. Cut into squares and serve immediately, or store in an airtight container in the refrigerator.

Makes 9 squares.

CINNAMON BAKED APPLES

This dish is an easy substitute for apple pie, as all the spices used are the same as those in a traditional apple pie recipe. These baked apples are so nutritious that you can eat them as a special breakfast treat. Your house will smell wonderfully as they cook in the oven. This recipe is also lovely for the winter holidays.

INGREDIENTS:

½ cup (125 mL)	various nuts and/or seeds
¼ cup (60 mL)	dried cranberries (apple juice sweetened)
2	dates, pitted and chopped
1 tsp (5 mL)	grated fresh ginger root
1 tsp (5 mL)	cinnamon
½ tsp (2.5 mL)	nutmeg
¼ tsp (1 mL)	ground cloves
4	apples
¼ cup (60 mL)	unpasteurized liquid honey
1 cup (250 mL)	apple juice or cider

DIRECTIONS:

1. Preheat the oven to 325°F (160°C).

2. Mix nuts or seeds, cranberries, dates, ginger root, and spices in a bowl.

3. Don't peel the apples, since most of the fiber and nutrients are in the skin. Being careful not to cut through the bottom of the apple; cut out the core.

4. Stuff each apple with the nut/seed mixture, then drizzle with honey and place in an 8 × 8–inch (20 × 20 cm) square baking dish.

5. Pour the juice around the fruit to keep it moist.

6. Bake for 30 to 35 minutes, until the fruit is soft. Serve warm.

Makes 4 servings.

KEY LIME MACAROONS

In the days when I had very few options for "treats," these macaroons were a welcome diversion. This recipe has a pinch of vitamin C and lime zest for a tangy antioxidant flare, but you can also make a classic macaroon by omitting these two ingredients. Make sure to buy corn-free, non-GMO vitamin C crystals to minimize your risk of an allergic reaction.

INGREDIENTS:

6	organic eggs, whites only
⅛ tsp (0.5 mL)	gray sea salt or pink rock salt
2½ tsp (12.5 mL)	pure vanilla extract
¾ cup (185 mL)	unpasteurized liquid honey
3 cups (750 mL)	unsweetened finely shredded coconut

OPTIONAL ADDITIONS:

1 tbsp (15 mL)	grated lime zest
½ tsp (2.5 mL)	vitamin C crystals (ascorbic acid)

DIRECTIONS:

1. Preheat the oven to 250°F (120°C). Line 2 cookie sheets with unbleached parchment paper.

2. In an electric mixer, beat the egg whites and the salt on medium speed until stiff peaks form.

3. Gently fold in the vanilla, honey, coconut, and lime zest and vitamin C crystals, if using, until combined thoroughly.

4. Place heaping tbsp (15 mL) of coconut batter 1 inch (2.5 cm) apart on the cookie sheets.

5. Bake for 50 to 55 minutes, then cool for up to 3 hours to create a chewy center and crispy edges.

Makes 24 macaroons.

ALMOND BUTTER PEARS

This dessert is one of my all-time favorites. Choose slightly firm pears, as they will retain their shape better when cooked. Pears contain rich amounts of pectin, a soluble fiber that cleanses the liver and bowel. One pear contains 4.5 grams of fiber, which is more than the average bowl of cold cereal! By blending almonds in the food processor, you are creating your own almond butter at a fraction of the cost of what you'd buy in a store.

INGREDIENTS:

½ cup (125 mL)	almonds or sunflower seeds
¼ cup (60 mL)	dried cranberries (apple juice sweetened)
1 tsp (5 mL)	cinnamon
1 tsp (5 mL)	grated fresh ginger root
¼ tsp (1 mL)	cardamom
¼ tsp (1 mL)	ground cloves
¼ cup (60 mL)	unpasteurized liquid honey
4	pears
1 cup (250 mL)	litchi, berry or pear juice

DIRECTIONS:

1. Preheat the oven to 350°F (175°C).

2. Process the nuts or seeds, cranberries, spices, and honey in a blender or food processor until smooth.

3. Cut unpeeled pears in half and scoop out the core.

4. Divide the nut/fruit mixture between the 8 pear halves and place them in an 8 × 8–inch (20 × 20 cm) square baking dish.

5. Pour the juice around the fruit to keep it moist.

6. Bake for 30 minutes, until fruit is tender. Serve warm.

Makes 4 servings.

APPLE BERRY QUINOA CRISP

Quinoa is a perfect food for anyone recovering from an injury because it's an amazing source of manganese and magnesium, both of which are important cofactors for metabolizing anti-inflammatory omega-3 fats. Manganese nourishes the ligaments and magnesium reduces muscle pain, making these minerals a pain-fighting duo. Unlike most other grains and seed-grains, quinoa is also a good source of lysine. Lysine is an essential amino acid that helps fight the cold sore virus, and it supports tissue growth and repair. This dessert is so healthy that you can even enjoy the leftovers for breakfast because the nuts and seeds are great sources of morning protein and essential fats.

INGREDIENTS:

4 cups (1 L)	chopped apples (about 8 apples, depending on size)
2 cups (500 mL)	frozen wild blueberries
1 cup (250 mL)	apple or berry juice
1 tsp (5 mL)	cinnamon

TOPPING:

1 cup (250 mL)	ground almonds
½ cup (125 mL)	rolled quinoa flakes
½ cup (125 mL)	hazelnuts, chopped
½ cup (125 mL)	pecans, chopped
½ cup (125 mL)	pumpkin or sunflower seeds
2 tsp (10 mL)	cinnamon
1 tsp (5 mL)	ground ginger
1 tsp (5 mL)	nutmeg
½ tsp (2.5 mL)	gray sea salt or pink rock salt
½ cup (125 mL)	unpasteurized liquid honey
¼ cup (60 mL)	coconut oil
¼ cup (60 mL)	hemp seeds (garnish)

DIRECTIONS:

1. Preheat the oven to 250°F (120°C).

2. In an 8-cup (2 L) casserole dish, mix the chopped apples, frozen berries, juice, and cinnamon.

3. Combine the almonds, quinoa flakes, nuts, seeds, spices, and salt in a large bowl. Add the honey and oil, and stir until just mixed.

4. Spread topping over the fruit.

5. Bake for 1 hour and 20 minutes, until topping begins to lightly brown. Serve warm. Top with hemp seeds if desired.

Makes 8 servings.

STUFFED SAILORS

This recipe was created for a type 2 diabetic who continued to eat a whole box of raspberry cookies in one sitting, despite his condition. He's an avid sailor, so I thought it would be fun to create a dessert that looked like his sailboat. I wanted to make sure he could enjoy sweet treats without causing further damage to his pancreas and cardiovascular system. Dates were a natural, perfect choice because they're full of healing, metabolism-boosting B vitamins. The trick is to eat just one or two of these sailboat dates because they're also naturally high in sugar. This recipe calls for Medjool dates, which are the sweetest and chewiest variety widely available in North America. Young gingko leaves, which should be harvested in the spring, are tender and tangy because they're high in vitamin C. They're also excellent cardiovascular tonics that help to improve cell oxygenation and nourishment, especially in the brain. Because of this property, ginkgo is a traditional medicine that has been scientifically proven to improve mental function. If you don't have access to ginkgo trees, substitute wood sorrel, which is also rich in vitamin C and supports cardiovascular health.

INGREDIENTS:

12	Medjool dates
¼ cup (60 mL)	hemp or pumpkin seed butter
½ tsp (2.5 mL)	cinnamon
¼ tsp (1 mL)	ginger
2 tbsp (30 mL)	tiger nut powder
24	whole pecans
24	whole fresh raspberries

OPTIONAL ADDITION:

24	young, whole gingko or wood sorrel leaves, freshly picked

DIRECTIONS:

1. Carefully cut dates in half and remove pits. Shape date to look like the hull of a sailboat. Place cut-side up on a plate.

2. To make filling, combine seed butter, spices, and tiger nut powder into a bowl and mix thoroughly. Spoon 1 teaspoon (5 mL) of filling onto each date half.

3. Press a pecan on one end of each boat and gently place a raspberry on the other end.

4. Fold each gingko leaf in half, pierce with a toothpick, and insert into the center of the filling so it resembles a sail. If using wood sorrel, simply place the leaf stem into the filling without the toothpick.

5. Chill for a few minutes before serving.

Makes 24 pieces.

"HIT THE TRAIL" MIX

This is a great recipe to make every couple of weeks. It's full of magnesium, anti-inflammatory omega-3 fats and plant sterols that balance the immune system. Brazil nuts are an excellent source of cancer-fighting selenium. Dr. Brian Wansink and his team at Cornell University have demonstrated that you're less likely to eat more than the recommended handful of trail mix if it's divided into portions. Check out his amazing book, *Mindless Eating: Why We Eat More Than We Think*, for more details.

INGREDIENTS:

½ cup (125 mL)   Brazil nuts

1 cup (250 mL)   dried cranberries (apple juice sweetened)

½ cup (125 mL)   dried blueberries or cherries (apple juice sweetened)

½ cup (125 mL)   hemp seeds

1 cup (250 mL)   macadamia nuts

½ cup (125 mL)   pine nuts

½ cup (125 mL)   pumpkin seeds

DIRECTIONS:

Mix all ingredients in a large bowl. Portion ⅓-cup (85 mL) servings into small sealable bags for an easy snack on the run.

Makes 5 cups (1.25 L).

GINGER LEMONADE ICE POPS

It's no surprise that Japan, where ginger root is used liberally, is home to the longest-living people in the world. Enjoy ginger root tea whenever your stomach is upset or when you're experiencing sore joints. If you're in a rush, you can use a tea bag, but it's always a good idea to stock your fridge (or freezer) with fresh ginger root. In herbal medicine, ginger root is used to relieve inflammation in the digestive tract and to relax and soothe the throat. Both lemon and ginger root are rich sources of antioxidants that inhibit inflammation.

FIRST MAKE A STRONG GINGER ROOT DECOCTION:

¼ cup (60 mL)   ginger root, grated

4 cups (1 L)   filtered water

DIRECTIONS:

Finely chop ginger root and steep with freshly boiled water for at least 20 minutes. Consider steeping it overnight—a long infusion maximizes the transfer of the active ingredients into the liquid.

TO MAKE THE POPSICLES:

4 cups (1 L)   strong ginger root tea

4 tbsp (60 mL)   organic lemon juice

3 tbsp (45 mL)   raw honey OR 30 drops liquid stevia

1. Stir ginger root tea, lemon juice, and raw honey or stevia together.

2. Pour into ice-pop makers and freeze for at least 2 hours.

Makes 6 to 8 pops.

THE BEST CARROT CAKE EVER

This is my mom's recipe, so it's true comfort food to me! I've made different versions for every birthday in my family since I realized that my joint and digestive pain was caused by intolerance to gluten and sugar. This cake not only tastes great but also delivers a medicinal dose of cinnamon. You may be shocked by the 7 tsp (35 mL) used in the recipe, but if you divide the cake into 14 pieces, then each piece has ½ tsp (2.5 mL) of cinnamon. This amount of cinnamon, if taken on a daily basis, has been shown to reduce glucose, triglyceride, and cholesterol levels by 10 to 30 percent. This is one of the only desserts that make me feel fantastic. I hope you enjoy it, too. Try replacing some of the cranberries with pecans if you prefer crunch.

INGREDIENTS:

⅔ cup (175 mL)	unpasteurized liquid honey
¼ cup (60 mL)	softened coconut oil
2 large	organic eggs OR 3 servings vegan egg substitute (see page 244)
½ cup (125 mL)	organic applesauce
2 tsp (10 mL)	pure vanilla extract
2½ cups (625 mL)	almonds (to make flour)
7 tsp (35 mL)	cinnamon
1 tsp (5 mL)	nutmeg
1 tsp (5 mL)	allspice
½ tsp (2.5 mL)	ground cloves
1 tsp (5 mL)	ground ginger
1 tsp (5 mL)	baking powder (aluminum- and gluten-free can be found in a health-food store)
½ tsp (2.5 mL)	gray sea salt or pink rock salt
2 cups (500 mL)	finely grated carrots, packed well
¾ cup (185 mL)	dried cranberries (apple juice sweetened)
1	organic lemon, zested

DIRECTIONS:

1. Preheat the oven to 350°F (175°C). Line a 10 × 3–inch (23 × 7 cm) round glass baking dish with unbleached parchment paper. A little coconut oil on the bottom of the dish will help keep your parchment paper tacked down. Smooth the paper and fold the sides to fit the round dish.

2. In a large mixing bowl, blend together honey, coconut oil, eggs, applesauce, and vanilla.

3. Process almonds in a food processor on high speed until they've become a fine meal that can be used as flour.

4. In a separate bowl, mix the almond flour, spices, baking powder, and salt. Add the grated carrots, cranberries, and lemon zest.

5. Add the honey mixture to the flour mixture, stirring until well blended.

6. Pour the cake batter into the prepared pan. Bake for 45 minutes. A wooden toothpick or skewer inserted into the center should come out clean. Allow to cool for 20 minutes before slicing and serving.

Makes 14 slices.

MOM'S SWEET POTATO PIE

This is a staple in our house. As our dietary needs have changed, the ingredients keep getting healthier, but the same great flavor comes through because of all the spices. You can purchase a gluten-free crust or simply serve it without a crust as we do in my mother's house.

INGREDIENTS:

2 cups (500 mL)	baked sweet potato or yam
3	organic eggs or vegan egg substitute (see page 244)
1 cup (250 mL)	filtered water
¾ cup (185 mL)	unpasteurized liquid honey (or less, if you prefer)
1 tbsp (15 mL)	cinnamon
½ tsp (2.5 mL)	nutmeg
½ tsp (2.5 mL)	allspice
1 tsp (5 mL)	pure vanilla extract
1	gluten-free prepared piecrust (optional)

DIRECTIONS:

1. Preheat the oven to 350°F (175°C).

2. Mix all of the ingredients in a mixing bowl until smooth.

3. Pour into a piecrust or small, lightly oiled soufflé cups.

4. Bake for about 40 minutes in the soufflé cups or about 50 to 55 minutes for the whole pie, until a knife inserted into the center of the pie comes out clean.

Makes 6 to 8 servings.

LYNN'S RAW CARROT HALVA BALLS

This light-tasting dessert is from my wonderful sister Lynn, who has taught me a great deal about cooking and is one of the few people who eats cleaner than I do. Her anti-inflammatory diet has saved her from severe arthritic pain and colitis. Lynn rarely eats dessert, but she came up with this wonderful treat for her big family of five boys! In her words, "It finishes your meal on a delicate note." In the boys' words, "It's really addictive." The tahini is rich in sterols that help to balance the immune system. The spices aid digestion and reduce inflammation.

INGREDIENTS:

1 cup (250 mL)	pecans
1 tsp (5 mL)	whole cardamom seed
2 cups (500 mL)	finely grated carrot
¼ cup (60 mL)	raw tahini
¼ cup (60 mL)	raw honey
½ tsp (2.5 mL)	pure vanilla extract
1 tsp (5 mL)	cinnamon
½ tsp (2.5 mL)	gray sea salt or pink rock salt
½ cup (120 mL)	coconut, finely shredded and unsweetened, divided

DIRECTIONS:

1. In a food processor, grind pecans to a fine meal.

2. In a spice grinder or with a mortar and pestle, grind cardamom seed. If you don't have a spice grinder, then ground cardamom will work but is not as flavorful. Grate the carrots using a food processor with the fine grating screen or use the fine side of a box grater.

3. Place carrot, tahini, honey, vanilla, cinnamon, ground cardamom, salt, ground pecans, and all but 2 tbsp (30 mL) of the finely shredded coconut into a large mixing bowl and mix well.

4. Pour remaining coconut on a plate and roll 1 tsp (5 mL) of the halva ball mixture in it.

5. Refrigerate halva balls until ready to serve.

Makes 24 balls.

PUFFED QUINOA BARS

This recipe is healthy enough to be a breakfast bar on days when you don't have time to eat a sit-down meal. The cinnamon and seeds nicely balance the higher glycemic index of the rice syrup and quinoa. You can stick with the classic vanilla flavor or make a St. Patrick's Day treat with a snap of mint!

INGREDIENTS:

½ cup (125 mL)   almond or hazelnut butter

½ cup (125 mL)   brown rice syrup

1 tsp (5 mL)   pure vanilla extract

¼ cup (60 mL)   finely chopped dried cherries (or other unsweetened dried fruit)

¼ cup (60 mL)   chia seeds, ground

½ cup (125 mL)   hemp seeds

3 cups (750 mL)   puffed quinoa

2 tsp (10 mL)   cinnamon powder

¼ tsp (1 mL)   gray sea salt or pink rock salt

FOR OPTIONAL MINT FLAVOR, ADD:

1 tsp (5 mL)   mint extract

½ tsp (2.5 mL)   spirulina powder (for color and B vitamins)

DIRECTIONS:

1. Mix nut butter, brown rice syrup, and vanilla liquid ingredients in a large bowl.

2. Add dry ingredients and mix well with a wooden spoon. It will take some time, so be patient and keep mixing.

3. Pack ½ inch (1 cm) deep in an 9 × 13–inch (23 × 33 cm) pan lined with unbleached parchment paper. Place in the fridge for 30 minutes to set.

4. Cut into bars and package in airtight container to maintain freshness.

Makes 24 bars.

KEY LIME PIE

This pie is the ultimate healthy gourmet treat. You'll wish you could turn back time with the last bite of this pie—proof that nutritious food can taste good. Avocados are packed with vitamin B_6, which supports your liver in metabolizing and balancing certain hormones such as estrogen. It's the perfect nonchocolate rescue for PMS.

INGREDIENTS:
Crust:

1 cup (250 mL)	unsweetened shredded coconut
1 cup (250 mL)	walnuts
¼ tsp (1 mL)	gray sea salt or pink rock salt
½ cup (125 mL)	pitted Medjool dates

Filling:

3	firm avocados
3 tbsp (45 mL)	lime juice
1 tsp (5 mL)	lime zest

½ cup (125 mL)   raw honey

pinch   gray sea salt or pink rock salt

as desired   kiwi or lime slices

DIRECTIONS:

1. Process the coconut, walnuts, and salt in a food processor until coarsely ground.

2. Add the dates and process until the mixture resembles bread crumbs and begins to clump together.

3. Press into the bottom and sides of a 9-inch (23 cm) pie plate using the back of a spoon or your fingers.

4. Place the crust in the freezer for 15 minutes.

5. Process all the filling ingredients in a food processor until smooth.

6. Pour the filling into the piecrust. Set in fridge for 20 minutes.

7. Garnish with fresh slices of kiwi fruit or thin slices of lime.

Makes 8 servings.

TOASTED PUMPKIN SEEDS

I was inspired to create this recipe when I was asked to create a 100-mile diet menu and realized that pumpkin seeds aren't commercially produced and sold locally, even though I live in "pumpkin central" near Niagara Falls, Ontario. The pickle juice I use is made in Brantford, Ontario. You may think the ingredients make a strange combo, but the result is a perfect blend of garlicky, sour, and salty flavors with a fantastic crunch. Both squash and pumpkin seeds are rich in zinc, a critical nutrient for the immune system and omega-3 metabolism. This recipe makes a great snack anytime you have a hankering for something salty and crunchy. The seed shell and sterols in the pumpkin seed flesh help to protect the oils from heat damage.

INGREDIENTS:

¾ cup (185 mL)   fresh seeds (about the amount that comes out of a
medium-sized squash or pumpkin)

2 tbsp (30 mL)   dill pickle juice (from sugar-free, naturally fermented
pickles) OR 1 tbsp (15 mL) tamari (wheat-free)

DIRECTIONS:

1. Scoop the seeds out of the squash or pumpkin. Carefully remove flesh from each seed. Rinse and drain well.

2. Heat a cast-iron or titanium pan over medium-high heat. Lower heat before adding seeds. Place seeds in hot pan and dry roast until you hear a popping sound (about 3 to 4 minutes). Stir to avoid burning the seeds.

3. Pour the dill pickle juice (or soy sauce, if you prefer) into the hot pan, making sure to move your hand away quickly to avoid getting a steam burn.

4. Using a wooden spoon, stir the seeds until all the liquid evaporates.

5. Transfer to a bowl and let cool. Store in a mason jar.

Makes ¾ cup (185 mL).

KRISPY KALE CHIPS

Kale chips make a perfect replacement for potato or corn chips when you're having a craving. One serving (2 cups/500 mL) of these crispy delights gives you 300 mg of calcium, or the equivalent of a full cup (250 mL) of milk. Kale has lower levels of oxalic acid than spinach, which allows its calcium to be more bioavailable than the calcium in spinach. Ensure that the cashews you buy are fresh.

INGREDIENTS:

2   bunches green curly kale (20 cups/5 L), washed, large stems removed, torn into bite-sized pieces

"Cheese" Coating:

1 cup (250 mL)   fresh cashews, soaked 2 hours

1 cup (250 mL)   sweet potato, grated

1   lemon, juiced (about 4 tbsp/60 mL)

2 tbsp (30 mL)   nutritional yeast

1 tbsp (15 mL)   raw honey

½ tsp (2.5 mL)   gray sea salt or pink rock salt

2 tbsp (30 mL)   filtered water

DIRECTIONS:

1. Place kale in a large mixing bowl.

2. Process remaining ingredients in a blender or food processor until smooth.

3. Pour over kale and mix thoroughly with your hands to coat the kale. (You want this mixture to be really glued onto the kale.)

4. Place kale onto unbleached parchment paper and dehydrate for 6 hours at 115°F (45°C). You'll need to use 2 trays. If you don't own a dehydrator, set your oven to 150°F (65°C) and dehydrate for 2 hours. At the one-hour point, turn over leaves to ensure even drying.

5. Remove and store in a dry airtight container.

Makes about 8 cups (2 L).

COCONUT ICE CREAM

This recipe is quick and easy to make. I have to hide it deep in the freezer at my house, otherwise it doesn't last long!

INGREDIENTS:

1½ cups (375 mL) coconut milk

⅓ cup (85 mL) raw honey

2 tsp (10 mL) peppermint or pure vanilla extract

1 tbsp (15 mL) coconut oil

⅓ cup (85 mL) macadamia nuts

DIRECTIONS:

1. Process all ingredients in a blender or food processor until smooth.

2. Pour the mixture into an ice-cream maker and process according to the manufacturer's directions. (It should be ready in about 20 to 25 minutes, or when it looks like it's really thick.)

3. You can eat it fresh out of the ice-cream maker, or ripen it by freezing for another hour or two.

Note: If you don't own an ice-cream maker, pour the mixture into a freezer-safe container and freeze for 20 minutes. Shake vigorously and return to freezer. Repeat this process until you reach your desired consistency.

Makes about 2½ cups (625 mL).

RESOURCES

Preferred Nutrition Inc.
Hormone-, inflammation-, and
immune-balancing supplements
153 Perth Street
Acton, ON L7J 1C9
1-888-826-9625
www.pno.ca

**Natural Factors Nutritional
Products Ltd.**
High-quality supplements
1550 United Boulevard,
Coquitlam, BC, V3K 6Y2
1-604-777-1757
www.naturalfactors.com

Bob's Red Mill
Organic gluten-free grains and beans
13521 SE Pheasant Court
Milwaukie, OR 97222
1-503-654-3215
www.bobsredmill.com

Fresh Hemp Foods Ltd.
Top-quality hemp seed products
69 Eagle Drive
Winnipeg, MB R2R 1V4
1-204-953-0233
www.manitobaharvest.com

Eden Foods, Inc.
Noodles, beans, sauces, seeds, rice
syrup, and dried fruit
701 Tecumseh Road
Clinton, MI 49236
1-517-456-7854
www.edenfoods.com

Raincoast Trading
Sustainable fish products
9398 Alaska Way
Delta, BC V4C 4R8
1-604-582-8268
www.raincoasttrading.com

Acropolis Organics
Organic olive oil
6 Curity Avenue, Unit 6
Toronto, ON M4B 1X2
1-416-429-5111
www.acropolisorganics.com

Weleda
Organic skin care
1 Closter Road
P.O. Box 675
Palisades, NY 10964
1-800-241-1030
www.weleda.com

Food For Life
Gluten-free bread and tortillas
Box 1434
Corona, CA 92878
1-951-279-5090
www.foodforlife.com

Bio-K International Inc.
Scientifically proven probiotics
Parc Scientifique
495 boul. Armand-Frappier
Laval, QC H7V 4B3
1-450-978-2465
www.biokplus.com

Ascenta Health Ltd.
High-quality fish oil
4-15 Garland Avenue
Dartmouth, NS B3B 0A6
1-866-224-1775
www.ascentahealth.com

Sahana Ayurvedic Products
Top-quality organic herbs and spices
5764 Monkland Avenue, Suite 471
Montreal, QC H4A 1E9
1-514-369-8175
www.arayuma.com

Mary's Organic Crackers
Gluten-free crackers, snacks, and
cookies
P.O. Box 965
Gridley, CA 95948
1-530-846-5100
www.marysorganiccrackers.com

TallGrass Distribution Ltd
Supplier of oils, probiotics, and organic
body care
40 E 5th Avenue
Vancouver, BC V5T 1G8
1-604-709-0101
www.tallgrass.biz

Look for a provincial food co-op in
your area from which you can buy
healthy foods directly. For example:

Ontario Natural Food Co-op
Organic food manufacturer and
distributor
5685 McLaughlin Road
Mississauga, ON L5R 3K5
1-905-507-2021
www.onfc.ca

Look for a local health-food store in your area with great staff who can guide you to healthy choices. For example:

The Big Carrot Natural Food Market
348 Danforth Avenue
Toronto, ON M4K 1N8
1-416-466-2129
www.thebigcarrot.ca

For a detailed glossary, extended reference section, and further information about how to heal inflammation, check out www.juliedaniluk.com. The Meals That Heal Inflammation Online Course explores in depth the concepts outlined in this book.

ACKNOWLEDGMENTS

First and foremost, I would like to thank my husband, Alan Smith, who makes my life elegant and organized. He is the rock that I have built my life on, and I am grateful every day for his endless support. His recipe editing, food styling, and technical skills made this book possible. The fact that he started binding it by hand to ensure people could access it is a testament to his selfless dedication.

To my substantive editor, Daniela Rambaldini, who gave the project precision and clarity. Her conscientiousness elevated this book to stand the test of time. She had the strength and wisdom to keep digging for facts to ensure every claim is truthful and accurate. Her scope of knowledge is unparalleled, and many insightful additions to the text are due to her generosity. Her friendship is one of my greatest treasures.

To my sister Lynn Daniluk, my Gemini twin, who mirrors back to me many lessons every day. Lynn taught me how to cook by intuition, but the greatest gift of all is how her personal integrity has touched every page of this book. She was the very first editor of the self-published version of *Meals That Heal Inflammation* and has contributed hundreds of hours to this book by way of editing, formatting, and writing advice.

To senior editor, Pamela Murray, who edited MTHI for the Random House edition. She has been incredibly kind, accessible, and masterful in the refinement of *Meals That Heal Inflammation*. I am so grateful for her flexible nature and patience. Both traits contributed to a very joyful process.

To my literary agent, Rick Broadhead, who championed MTHI. He reached out and inspired me to write a book eight years ago and has worked tirelessly to build, nurture, and protect it.

To my brother and yoga instructor, Shambunata Saraswati (Steven Daniluk), who has given me the tools to relax and heal. I owe him for my flexibility and peace of mind. One of his greatest contributions is the understanding that in reality there is light. The object casting the shadow of darkness is the misunderstanding and fear in the mind.

To the researchers who made written contributions. Emily Kennedy, Dr. Jennie Brand-Miller, Jean Kim, Nikki Yeh, and Aldi Llogori—all helped to investigate and clarify information. It was a relief to realize that community can transform a long voyage into a fun ride.

To my mother, Elaine, who bravely took me off all refined food when I was eight years old and changed my life forever. Her caring allowed me to function in school, and I owe my ability to learn to her tenacity.

To my grandmother Geneva, who practiced detoxification in the 1950s before the health-food movement existed. She taught our family to see food as a tool for powerful rejuvenation.

To my father, Neil, who instilled in me a wonderful work ethic. I am grateful for his honest feedback as my unofficial recipe tester. I am also grateful for his teaching that every day is an opportunity to be positive and to give something back.

To my amazing group of copy editors, proofreaders, and recipe creators/testers: Deirdre Molina, Karen Rolfe, Liba Berry, Elena Radic, Margaret Reffell, Morgan Yew, Tory Healy, Linda Smith, Evis Lasku, Jae Steele, Joan Morris, Lisa Tai, Jeff Woods, Maureen Kirkpatrick, Darren Dumas, Tanya Scata, Ezra Title, Jake Rubin, and Mary Catherine

Pittis. Without them this book would still be a scribble in my kitchen notebook.

To my expert advisers: Dr. Suzanna Ivanovics, Dr. Zoltan Rona, Kate Kent, Dr. Kate Wharton, Colin Campbell, Cathy Hayashi, Dr. Mubina Jiwa, Ursula Buck, Dr. Patricha McCord, Romy Croitoru, Paul McConvey, Megan MacMillan, Brett Hawes, Anthony Dipasquale, and Dr. Richard Dodd. Their contributions give this book depth and a wider perspective.

To my former manager, Martin Robertson, who was the creative director of this project since its conception. He was a source of strength and inspiration in the early days, and I miss him. I am grateful that he guided me through this process.

To the talented potters showcased in the food photography: Elaine Daniluk, Glenn Gangnier, and Dale Mark. Their beautiful handmade pottery created a wonderful accent to the food.

To Deane Parkes, Brenda Parkes, the talented team at Preferred Nutrition, and all the members of The Big Carrot Natural Food Market. Your support over the years has been a huge gift, and I am very blessed to be part of your community.

REFERENCES

Introduction

Appel, L.J. 2008. *Circulation.* 118(3): 214–215.

Ebringer, A. 1992. *Rheumatic Diseases Clinics of North America.* 19(1): 105–121.

Ezz El-Arab, A.M., *et al.* 2006. *BMC Complementary and Alternative Medicine.* 6: 6.

Gracey, M., and M. King. 2009. *The Lancet.* 374(9683): 65–75.

MacDonald, T.T., and G. Monteleone. 2005. *Science.* 207(5717): 1920–1925.

Chapter 1

Brownlee, M. 2001. *Nature.* 414(6865): 813–820.

Colbin, A. 1996. *Food and Healing.* Ballantine Books. NY, NY.

Dodd, R., BSc, ND. Pers. Comm. www.naturalpath-cancerclinic.com. Mississauga, ON.

Fleming, A. 1929. *British Journal of Experimental Pathology.* 779(8): 226–236.

Fukami, K., *et al.* 2004. *Kidney International.* 66(6): 2137–2147.

Inman, R.D., and H.S. El-Gabalawy. 2009. *Clinical and Experimental Rheumatology.* 27(Suppl. 55): S26–S32.

Kiecolt-Glaser, J.K., *et al.* 2002. *Psychosomatic Medicine.* 64(1): 15–28.

Landrigan, P.J., *et al.* 1999. *Environmental Health Perspectives.* 107(Suppl. 3): 431–437.

Nigro, J., *et al.* 2006. *Endocrine Reviews.* 27(3): 242–259.

Phillips, T.M. 2000. *Journal of Exposure Analysis and Environmental Epidemiology.* 10(Suppl. 6): 769–775.

Poulain, M., *et al.* 2004. *Experimental Gerontology.* 39(9): 1423–1429.

Robles, T.F., *et al.* 2005. *Current Directions in Psychological Science.* 14(2): 111–115.

Walton, J.D. 1983. *Journal of the Royal Society of Medicine.* 76(12): 998–1010.

Chapter 2

Adam, T.C., and E.S. Epel. 2007. *Physiology and Behavior.* 91(4): 449–458.

Adams, S.G. Jr., *et al.* 1994. *Journal of Behavioral Medicine.* 17(5): 459–476.

Berthoud, H.R. 2008. *Neurogastroenterology and Motility.* 20 (Suppl. 1): 64–72.

Cajochen, A., *et al.* 2003. *Journal of Neuroendocrinology.* 15 (4): 432–437.

Chandrashekar, J., *et al.* 2006. *Nature.* 444(7117): 288–294.

Clays, E., *et al.* 2005. *Journal of Occupational and Environmental Medicine.* 7(9): 878–883.

Davidson, R.J., *et al.* 2003. *Psychosomatic Medicine.* 65(4): 564–570.

Diego, M.A., *et al.* 1998. *International Journal of Neuroscience.* 96(3–4): 217–224.

Dunn, A.L., *et al.* 2005. *American Journal of Preventative Medicine.* 28(1): 1–8.

Emmons, R. 2007. *Thanks!* Houghton Mifflin Co. NY, NY.

Feingold, B.F. 1974. *Why Your Child is Hyperactive.* Random House. NY, NY.

Frusztajer, N.T., and J.J. Wurtman. 2009. *The Serotonin Power Diet.* Rodale Press. Emmaus, PA.

Furness, J.B., *et al.* 1999. *Gastrointestinal and Liver Physiology.* 277(5): G922–G928.

Hayashi, T., and K. Murakami. 2009. *Life Sciences*. 85(5–6): 185–187.

Hayashi, T., et al. 2006. *Psychotherapy and Pyschosomatics*. 75(1): 62–65.

Jang, H-J., et al. 2007. *Proceedings of the National Academy of Sciences*. 104(38): 15069–15074.

Kabat-Zinn, J. 1990. *Full Catastrophe Living*. Delacorte Press. NY, NY.

Lindemann, B. 2001. *Nature*. 413(6852): 219–225.

Lutz, A., et al. *Proceedings of the National Academy of Sciences*. 101(46): 16369–16373.

Mann, N. 2000. *European Journal of Nutrition*. 39(2): 71–79.

McGinnis, W.R., et al. 2008. *Alternative Therapies in Health and Medicine*. 14(2): 40–50.

Murray, M.T., and J. Pizzorno. 1998. *Encyclopedia of Natural Medicine*. Revised 2nd ed. Prima Publishing. Roseville, CA.

Pfeiffer, C.C. 1987. *Nutrition and Mental Illness*. Healing Arts Press. Rochester, VT.

Rozengurt, E., and C. Sternini. 2007. *Current Opinion in Pharmacology*. 7(6): 557–662.

Shi, P., et al. 2003. *Molecular Biology and Evolution*. 20(5): 805–814.

Sorlie, P.D., et al. 2000. *Archives of Internal Medicine*. 160(13): 2027–2032.

Srinivasan, V., et al. 2005. *Neurotoxicity Research*. 7(4): 293–318.

Vanderhaeghe, L.R. 2001. *Healthy Immunity*. Macmillan Canada. Toronto, ON.

Vanderhaeghe, L.R. 2001. *The Immune System Cure*. Prentice Hall. Scarborough, ON.

Walling, A. 2006. *Journal of the American Academy of Nurse Practitioners*. 18(4): 135–143.

Walsh, W.J., et al. 2004. *Physiology & Behavior*. 82(5): 835–839.

Yim, V.W.C., et al. 2009. *Journal of Alternative and Complementary Medicine*. 15(2): 187–195.

Chapter 3

Arrieta, M.C., et al. 2006. *Gut*. 55(10): 1512–1520.

Bateson-Koch, C. 1994. *Allergies: Disease in Disguise*. Alive Books. Burnaby, BC.

Bischoff, S., and S.E. Crowe. 2005. *Gastroenterology*. 128(4): 1089–1113.

Brostoff, J., and S.J. Challacombe. 2002. *Food Allergy and Intolerance*. 2nd ed. W.B. Saunders. Philadelphia, PA.

Cerutti, A., and M. Rescigno. 2008. *Immunity*. 28(6): 740–750.

Colbin, A. 1996. *Food and Healing*. Ballantine Books. NY, NY.

Dattner, A.M. 2010. *Clinics in Dermatology*. 28(1): 34–37.

David, T.J. 2000. *British Medical Bulletin*. 56(1): 34–50.

Donnet-Hughes, A., et al. 2008. Pp. 355–362. In: *Nutrition in Pediatrics*. D. Duggan, et al. (eds.). 4th ed. BC Decker. Hamilton, ON.

Duygu, O., and E. Mete. 2008. *Current Opinion in Pulmonary Medicine*. 14(1): 9–12.

Emsley, J., and P. Fell. 2001. *Was It Something You Ate?* Oxford University Press. NY, NY.

Haas, E.M. 2006. *Staying Healthy with Nutrition*. 21st Century ed. Celestial Arts. Berkeley, CA.

Haas, E.M., and C. Stauth. 2001. *The False Fat Diet*. Random House. NY, NY.

Heo, H.J., and C.Y. Lee. 2004. *Journal of Agricultural and Food Chemistry*. 52(25): 7514–7517.

Isolauri, E., et al. 2002. *Gut*. 50(Suppl. 3): iii54–iii59.

List, B.A., and K.J. Vonderhaar. 2010. *MCN*. 35(6): 325–329.

Liu, Z., et al. 2005. *Acta Paediatrica*. 94(4): 386–393.

MacDonald, T.T., and G. Monteleone. 2005. *Science*. 307(5717): 1920–1925.

Maes, M., and J.C. Leunis. 2008. *Neuroendocrinology Letters*. 29(6): 101–109.

Majamaa, H., et al. 1996. *Clinical and Experimental Allergy*. 26(2): 181–187.

Mantovani, A. 2005. *Nature*. 435(7043): 752–753.

Matsen, J. 1987. *Eating Alive*. Crompton Books. Vancouver, BC.

Murray, M.T. 1994. *Arthritis*. Prima Publishing. Rockland, CA.

Murray, M.T., and J. Pizzorno. 1998. *Encyclopedia of Natural Medicine*. Revised 2nd ed. Prima Publishing. Roseville, CA.

Park, Y.W., et al. 2006. *Small Ruminant Research*. 68(1–2): 88–113.

Peterson, S., et al. 2006. *Food and Chemical Toxicology*. 44(9): 1474–1484.

Pfeiffer, C.C. 1987. *Nutrition and Mental Illness*. Healing Arts Press. Rochester, VT.

Rapp, D.J. 1991. *Is This Your Child?* William Morrow and Company Inc. NY, NY.

Rapp, D.J. 1988. *Journal of the American Medical Association*. 260(3): 341–342.

Sarjeant, D. 1999. *Hard to Swallow*. Alive Books. Burnaby, BC.

Schmidt, M.A., and T. Dimon. 2004. *Childhood Ear Infections*. North Atlantic Books. Berkeley, CA.

Sigthorsson, G., et al. 1998. *Gut*. 43(4): 506–511.

Vaclavik, V., and E.W. Christian. 2007. *Essentials of Food Science.* 3rd ed. Springer Science. NY, NY.

Van de Perre, P. 2003. *Vaccine.* 21(24): 3374-3376.

Vanderhaeghe, L.R. 2001. *Healthy Immunity.* Macmillan Canada. Toronto, ON.

Vanderhaeghe, L.R. 2001. *The Immune System Cure.* Prentice Hall. Scarborough, ON.

Vesterlund, S., *et al.* 2006. *Microbiology.* 152(6): 1812–1826.

Yong, L.C. 1997. *Experimental and Toxicologic Pathology.* 49(6): 409–424.

Chapter 4

Ardies, C.M. 2003 *Integrative Cancer Therapies.* 2(3): 238–246.

Bäckhed, F., *et al.* 2005. *Science.* 307(5717): 1915–1920.

Bahekar, A.A., *et al.* 2007. *American Heart Journal.* 154(5): 830–837.

Baker, B.S., *et al.* 2008. *Giornale Italiano di Dermatologia e Venerologia.* 143(2): 105–117.

Béliveau, R., and D. Gingras. 2005. *Foods That Fight Cancer.* McClelland & Stewart. Toronto, ON.

Biltagi, M.A., *et al.* 2009. *Acta Paediatrica.* 98(4): 737–742.

Cantin, E.M., *et al.* 1995. *Journal of Virology.* 69(8): 4898–4905.

Clays, E., *et al.* 2005. *Journal of Occupational and Environmental Medicine.* 7(9): 878–883.

Cuvelier, C., *et al.* 1987. *Gut.* 28(4): 394–401.

Dogan, B., *et al.* 2008. *International Journal of Dermatology.* 47(9): 950–952.

Folts, J.D. 2002. *Advances in Experimental Medicine and Biology.* 505: 95–111.

Gao, J.X., *et al.* 2008. *Respirology.* 13(4): 528–536.

Gershoff, S. 1996. *The Tufts University Guide to Total Nutrition.* 2nd ed. HarperCollins. NY, NY.

Gillum, R.F. 2004. *Journal of the National Medical Association.* 96(11): 1470–1476.

Hashimoto, S., *et al.* 2008. *Allergology International.* 57(1): 21–31.

Higdon, J.V., *et al.* 2007. *Pharmacological Research.* 55(3): 224–236.

Holick, M.F. 2007. *New England Journal of Medicine.* 357(3): 266–281.

Holick, M.F. 2004. *American Journal of Clinical Nutrition.* 80(6): 1678S–1688S.

Hsu, H.Y., *et al.* 1995. *Journal of Biological Chemistry.* 270(33): 19630–19637.

Hsu, J.C., *et al.* 2006. *Biochemical Pharmacology.* 72(12): 1714–1723.

Hulisz, D. 2004. *Journal of the American Pharmacists Association.* 44(5): 594–603.

Hyöty, H. 2002. *Annals of Medicine.* 34(3): 138–147.

Itzhaki, R.F., and M.A. Wozinak. 2004. *Journal of Neuroimmunology.* 156(1): 1–2.

Itzhaki, R.F., and M.A. Wozniak. 2006. *Progress in Lipid Research.* 45(1): 73–90.

Itzkowitz, S.H., and X. Yio. 2004. *Gastroenterology and Liver Physiology.* 287(1): G7–G17.

Jun, H.S., and J.W. Yoon. 2003. *Diabetes/Metabolism Research and Reviews.* 19(1): 8–31.

Kähkönen, M.P., *et al.* 2003. *Journal of the Science of Food and Agriculture.* 83(14): 1403–1411.

Kähkönen, M.P., *et al.* 2001. *Journal of Agriculture and Food Chemistry.* 49(8): 4076–4082.

Kalhoff, H. 2003. *European Journal of Clinical Nutrition.* 57(Suppl. 2): S81–S87.

Kallio, P., *et al.* 2008. *American Journal of Clinical Nutrition.* 87(5): 1497–1503.

Kamer, A.R., *et al.* 2008. *Alzheimer's & Dementia.* 4(4): 242–250.

Karamanolis, D.G., and I. Krylagkitsis. 2004. *Annals of Gastroenterology.* 17(3): 234–236.

Kochhar, K.P. 1999. *Journal of Orthomolecular Medicine.* 14(4): 210–218.

Kummerow, F.A. 2009. *Atherosclerosis.* 205(2): 458–465.

Lila, M.A. 2004. *Journal of Biomedicine and Biotechnology.* 2004(5): 306–313.

Liu, S., *et al.* 2002. *American Journal of Clinical Nutrition.* 75(3): 492–498.

Lugasi, A., *et al.* 2003. *Acta Biologica Szegediensis.* 47(1–4): 119–125.

Maggio-Price, L., *et al.* 2006. *Cancer Research.* 66(2): 828–838.

Mickleborough, T.D., *et al.* 2005. *Medical Science in Sports and Exercise.* 37(6): 904–914.

Mickleborough, T.D., *et al.* 2001. *European Journal of Applied Physiology.* 85(5): 450–456.

Murray, M.T., and J. Pizzorno. 1998. *Encyclopedia of Natural Medicine.* Revised 2nd ed. Prima Publishing. Roseville, CA.

Norris, J.M., *et al.* 2007. *Journal of the American Medical Association.* 298(12): 1420–1428.

Owen, C.M., *et al.* 2001. *British Journal of Dermatology.* 145(6): 886–890.

Prasad, A.S., *et al.* 2007. *American Journal of Clinical Nutrition.* 85(3): 837–844.

Qi, L., and F.B. Hu. 2007. *Current Opinion in Lipidology.* 18(1): 3–8.

Quigley, E.M.M. 2010. *Pharmacological Research.* 61(3): 213–218.

Riccioni, G., et al. 2007. *Annals of Clinical and Laboratory Sciences.* 37(1): 96–101.

Richardson, S.J., et al. 2009. *Diabetologia,* 52(6): 1143–1151.

Schmidt, M.A., and T. Dimon. 2004. *Childhood Ear Infections.* North Atlantic Books. Berkeley, CA.

Smith, G.R., and S. Missailids. 2004. . *Journal of Inflammation.* 1:3.

Telfer, N.R., et al. 1992. *Archives of Dermatology.* 128(1): 39–42.

Thabane, M., and J.K. Marshall. 2009. *World Journal of Gastroenterology.* 15(29): 3591–3596.

Thune, I., et al. 1997. *New England Journal of Medicine.* 336(18): 1269–1275.

Tuffaha, A., et al. 2000. *Clinics in Chest Medicine.* 21(2): 289–300.

van der Werf, N., et al. 2007. *Diabetes/Metabolism Research and Reviews.* 23(3): 169–183.

Vanderhaeghe, L.R. 2001. *Healthy Immunity.* Macmillan Canada. Toronto, ON.

Vanderhaeghe, L.R. 2001. *The Immune System Cure.* Prentice Hall. Scarborough, ON.

Verdu, E.F., et al. 2007. *Canadian Journal of Gastroenterology.* 21(7): 435–455.

Walboomers, J.M., et al. 1999. *Journal of Pathology.* 189(1): 12–19.

Wozniak, M.A., et al. 2009. *Journal of Pathology.* 217(1): 131–138.

Zhao, G., et al. 2005. *Journal of Dermatology.* 32(2): 91–96.

Chapter 5

Allport, S. 2006. *The Queen of Fats.* University of California Press. Berkeley, CA.

Anderson, S.D. 2006. *Current Opinion in Allergy and Clinical Immunology.* 6(1): 37–42.

Anderson, S.D., and E. Daviskas. 2000. *Journal of Allergy and Clinical Immunology.* 106(3): 453–459.

Arnaud, M.J. 2003. *European Journal of Clinical Nutrition.* 57(Suppl. 2): S88–S95.

Baker, B.S., et al. 2008. *Giornale Italiano di Dermatologia e Venerologia.* 143(2): 105–117.

Balch, P.A. 2000. *Prescription for Nutritional Healing.* Avery Publishers. NY, NY.

Barclay, W.R., et al. 1994. *Journal of Applied Phycology.* 6(2): 123–129.

Batmanghelidj, F. 2003. *Water: For Health, For Healing, For Life.* Warner Books. NY, NY.

Beattie, J., et al. 2005. *Current Nutrition and Food Science.* 1(1): 71–86.

Bedani, A., and T.D. DuBose. 1995. Pp. 69–103. In: *Fluid, Electrolyte and Acid Base Disorders.* A.I. Arieff and R.A. DeFronzo (eds.). Churchill Livingstone. NY, NY.

Benzie, I.F.F. 2000. *European Journal of Nutrition.* 39(2): 53–61.

Biltagi, M.A., et al. 2009. *Acta Paediatrica.* 98(4): 737–742.

Bouby, N., and S. Fernandes. 2003. *European Journal of Clinical Nutrition.* 57(Suppl. 2): S39–S46.

Bourre, J.M. 2005 *Journal of Nutrition, Health and Aging.* 9(1): 31–38.

Boyd Eaton, S. and S. Boyd Eaton III. 2000. *European Journal of Nutrition.* 39(2): 67–60.

Brand-Miller, J., and K. Foster-Powell. 2008. *The New Glucose Revolution Shopper's Guide to GI Values 2008.* Da Capo Press. Philadelphia, PA.

Bruning, P.F., et al. 1992. *International Journal of Cancer.* 52(4): 511–516.

Brynes, A.E., et al. *British Journal of Nutrition.* 89(2): 207–218.

Burdge, G. 2004. *Current Opinion in Clinical Nutrition and Metabolic Care.* 7(2): 137–144.

Burk, R.F. 2002. *Nutrition in Clinical Care.* 5(2): 75–79.

Campbell, N.R., et al. 1994. *Clinical and Investigative Medicine.* 17(6): 570–576.

Chan, A.C. 1993. *Canadian Journal of Physiology and Pharmacology.* 71(9): 725–731.

Clandinin, M.T., et al. 1991. *FASEB Journal.* 5(13): 2761–2769.

Colbin, A. 1996. *Food and Healing.* Ballantine Books. NY, NY.

Cole, G.M., et al. 2005. *Neurobiology of Aging.* 26(Suppl. 1): S133–S136.

Conlin, P.R., et al. 2000. *American Journal of Hypertension.* 13(9): 949–955.

Connor, K.M., et al. 2007. *Nature Medicine.* 13(7): 868–873.

Cordain, L. 1999. In: Evolutionary Aspects of Nutrition and Health. A.P. Simopoulos (ed.). *World Review of Nutrition and Dietetics.* 84: 19–73.

Cordain, L., et al. 2000. *British Journal of Nutrition.* 83(3): 207–217. Davis, T.A., et al. 2006. *Journal of the American Chemical Society.* 128(46): 14987–14904.

Dogan, B., et al. 2008. *International Journal of Dermatology.* 47(9): 950–952.

Erasmus, U. 1993. *Fats That Heal Fats That Kill.* Alive Books. Burnaby, BC.

Fallon, S. 2001. *Nourishing Traditions*. New Trends Publishing. Washington, D.C.

Foster-Powell, K., *et al.* 2002. *American Journal of Clinical Nutrition*. 76(1): 5–56.

Frank, J., *et al.* 2002. *Journal of Agriculture and Food Chemistry*. 50(25): 7226–7230.

Gawain, S. 2002. *Developing Intuition*. New World Library. Novato, CA.

Graci, S. 2001. *The Food Connection*. MacMillan Canada. Toronto, ON.

Gu, Y-H., and M.A. Belury. 2005. *Cancer Letters*. 220(1): 21–28.

Guech-Ongey, M., *et al.* 2005. *International Journal of Cardiology*. 111(1): 98–103.

Hasturk, H., *et al.* 2007. *Journal of Immunology*. 179(10): 7021–7029.

Hibbeln, J.R. 1998. *Lancet*. 351(9110): 1213.

Hiramaya, S., *et al.* 2004. *European Journal of Clinical Nutrition*. 58(3): 467–473.

Hsing, A.W., *et al.* 2003. *Journal of the National Cancer Institute*. 95(1): 67–71.

Hyöty, H. 2002. *Annals of Medicine*. 34(3): 138–147.

Jump, D.B., *et al.* 1999. *Prostaglandins, Leukotrienes and Essential Fatty Acids*. 60(5–6): 345–349.

Keller, U., *et al.* 2003. *European Journal of Clinical Nutrition*. 57(Suppl. 2): S69–S74.

Kellogg, J.H. 1923. *The Natural Diet of Man*. Modern Medicine Publishing Company. Battle Creek, MI.

Kidd, P.M. 2007. *Alternative Medicine Review*. 12(3): 207–227.

Knobler, H., *et al.* 1999. *Q Journal of Medicine*. 92(2): 73–79.

Labow, B.I., and W.W. Souba. 2000. *World Journal of Surgery*. 24(12): 1503–1513.

Langlands, S.J., *et al.* 2004. *Gut*. 53(11): 1610–1616.

Leiper, J.B., *et al.* 2003. *European Journal of Clinical Nutrition*. 57(Suppl. 2): S30–S38.

Levrat, M., *et al.* 1991. *Journal of Nutrition*. 121(11): 1730–1737.

Lila, M.A. 2004. *Journal of Biomedicine and Biotechnology*. 2004(5): 306–313.

Logan, A.C. 2004. *Lipids in Health and Disease*. 3: 25.

Machlin, L.J., and A. Bendich. 1987. *FASEB Journal*. 1(6): 441–445.

Mann, N. 2000. *European Journal of Nutrition*. 39(2): 71–79.

Manz, F., and A. Wentz. 2003. *European Journal of Clinical Nutrition*. 57(Suppl. 2): S10–S18.

Matsumoto, H., *et al.* 2002. *Journal of Agricultural and Food Chemistry*. 50(18): 5034–5037.

Mickleborough, T.D., *et al.* 2005. *Medical Science in Sports and Exercise*. 37(6): 904–914.

Mickleborough, T.D., *et al.* 2001. *European Journal of Applied Physiology*. 85(5): 450–456.

Murray, M.T., and J. Pizzorno. 1998. *Encyclopedia of Natural Medicine*. Revised 2nd ed. Prima Publishing. Roseville, CA.

Nettleton, J.A. 1991. *Journal of the American Dietetic Association*. 91(3): 331–337.

Neu, J. 2001. *Journal of Nutrition*. 131: 2585S–2589S.

Neu, J., *et al.* 2002. *Current Opinion in Clinical Nutrition and Metabolic Care*. 5(1): 69–75.

Newsholme, P. 2001. *Journal of Nutrition*. 131(Suppl. 9): 2515S–2522S.

Nikfar, S., *et al.* 2008. *Diseases of the Colon and Rectum*. 51(12): 1775–1780.

Nilsson, A.C., *et al.* 2008. *Journal of Nutrition*. 138(4): 732–739.

Ooi, V.E.C., and F. Liu. 2000. *Current Medical Chemistry*. 7(7): 715–729.

Pieri, C., *et al.* 1994. *Life Sciences*. 55(15): PL271–PL276.

Pietta, P.G. 2000. *Journal of Natural Products*. 63(7): 1035–1042.

Pittas, A.G., *et al.* 2006. *Obesity*. 14(12): 2200–2209.

Pollan, M. 2008. *In Defense of Food*. Penguin Books. NY, NY.

Potter, P.C., *et al.* 1991. *Archives of Disease in Childhood*. 66(2): 216–219.

Powell, S.R. 2000. *Journal of Nutrition*. 130(Suppl. 5): 1447S–1454S.

Ramirez-Tortosa, M.C., *et al.* 2004. *British Journal of Nutrition*. 91(6): 943–950.

Rasi, A., *et al.* 2007. *International Journal of Dermatology*. 26(11): 1155–1159.

Reeds, P.J., and D.G. Burrin. 2001. *Journal of Nutrition*. 131(Suppl. 9): 2505S–2508S.

Rimando, A.M., *et al.* 2004. . *Journal of Agriculture and Food Chemistry*. 52(15): 4713–4719.

Ritz, P., *et al.* 2003. *European Journal of Clinical Nutrition*. 57(Suppl. 2): S2–S5.

Rostan, E.F., *et al.* 2002. *International Journal of Dermatology*. 41(9): 606–611.

Seaman D.R. 1998. *Clinical Nutrition for Pain, Inflammation and Tissue Healing*. NutraAnalysis Inc. Hendersonville, NC.

Sears, B. 2005. *The Anti-Inflammation Zone*. HarperCollins. NY, NY.

Seguin, R., and M.E. Nelson. 2003. *American Journal of Preventive Medicine*. 25(3): 141–149.

Shirreffs, S.M. 2003. *European Journal of Clinical Nutrition*. 57(Suppl. 2): S6–S9.

Shoelson, S.E., *et al.* 2006. *Journal of Clinical Investigation.* 116(7): 1793–1801.

Simopoulos, A.P. 2009. In: A Balanced *Omega-6/Omega-3* Fatty Acid Ratio, Cholesterol and Coronary Heart Disease. A.P. Simopoulos and F. de Meester (eds.). *World Review of Nutrition and Dietetics.* 100: 1–21.

Simopoulos, A.P. 2004. *Biological Research.* 37(2): 263–277.

Simopoulos, A.P. 2000. *Poultry Science.* 79(7): 961–970.

Simopoulos, A.P. 1999. *American Journal of Clinical Nutrition.* 70(3): 506–509.

Simopoulos, A.P. 1999. *Prostaglandins, Leukotrienes and Essential Fatty Acids.* 60(5–6): 421–429.

Smith, A.J., and L. Shaw. 2003. *European Journal of Clinical Nutrition.* 57(Suppl. 2): S75–S80.

Song, Y., *et al.* 2009. *Journal of Nutrition.* 139(9): 1626–1631.

Spiller, R. 2008. *Alimentary Pharmacology and Therapeutics.* 28(4): 385–396.

Stuchl'k, M., and S. Žák. 2002. *Biomedical Papers.* 146(2): 3–10.

Svobodová, A., *et al.* 2008. *Biofactors.* 33(4): 249–266.

Tilg, H., and A.R. Moschen. 2008. *Trends in Endocrinology and Metabolism.* 19(10): 371–379.

Urosevic, N., and R.N. Martins. 2008. *Journal of Alzheimer's Disease.* 13(4): 421–435.

Uusitalo, L., *et al.* 2008. *American Journal of Clinical Nutrition.* 88(2): 458–464.

Valyi-Nagi T., and T.S. Dermody. 2005. *Histology and Histopathology.* 20(3): 957–967.

van der Hulst, R.R.W.J., *et al.* 1993. *The Lancet.* 341(8857): 1363–1365.

Vanderhaeghe, L.R. 2001. *Healthy Immunity.* Macmillan Canada. Toronto, ON.

Vanderhaeghe, L.R. 2001. *The Immune System Cure.* Prentice Hall. Scarborough, ON.

Verdu, E.F., *et al.* 2007. *Canadian Journal of Gastroenterology.* 21(7): 435–455.

Virtanen, S.M., and M. Knip. 2003. *American Journal of Clinical Nutrition.* 78(6): 1053–1067.

Wannamethee, G., *et al.* 2006. *American Journal of Clinical Nutrition.* 83(3): 567–574.

Watson, B. 2002. *Renew Your Life.* Renew Life Press. Clearwater, FL.

Wilson, M-M.G., and J.E. Morley. 2003. *European Journal of Clinical Nutrition.* 57(Suppl. 2): S24–S29.

Woods, V.B., *et al.* 2005. *Occasional Publication No. 4.* Agri-Food and Biosciences Institute. Global Research Unit. Belfast, Northern Ireland.

Yunsook, L., *et al.* 2004. *Journal of Nutrition.* 134(4): 811–816.

Zaher, H., *et al.* 2007. *Indian Journal of Dermatology.* 52(4): 184.

Zara-Stone, S., *et al.* 2007. *Molecular Nutrition and Food Research.* 51(6): 675–683.

Zhao, G., *et al.* 2005. *Journal of Dermatology.* 32(2): 91–96.

Ziegler, T.R., *et al.* 2000. *Current Opinion in Clinical Nutrition and Metabolic Care.* 3(5): 355–362.

Chapter 6

Benjamin, B.E. 2007. *Listen to Your Pain.* Penguin Books. NY, NY.

Brien, S., *et al.* 2009. *Evidence-Based Complementary and Alternative Medicine.* 2011 (Article ID 528403): 1–10.

Buck, U., RMT. Pers. Comm. Chester Avenue Massage Therapy. Toronto, ON.

Campbell, C., Personal Trainer, Nutritional Coach. Pers. Comm. www.myodesign.com. Toronto, ON.

Craig, R.P. 1975. *Injury.* 6(4): 313–316.

Davey, L.J., PT, MScPT, MSc, CAFCI. Pers. Comm. Toronto Physiotherapy. www.torontophysiotherapy.ca. Toronto, ON.

Deoora, T.K. 2004. *Healing Through Cranial Osteopathy.* Frances Lincoln. London, UK.

Dupler, D. 2006. Acupuncture. In: *The Gale Encyclopedia of Medicine.* 3rd ed. J.L. Longe (ed.). Gale. Detroit, MI.

Greene, E. 2006. Massage therapy. In: *The Gale Encyclopedia of Medicine.* 3rd ed. J.L. Longe (ed.). Gale. Detroit, MI.

Kabat-Zinn, J. 2005. *Full Catastrophe Living.* 15th ed. Random House Publishing. NY, NY.

Kent, K., Dipl. Ac, CH (NCCAOM). Pers. Comm. www.katekenttcm.com. Toronto, ON.

Kolt, G.S., and L. Snyder-Mackler (eds.). 2007. *Physical Therapies in Sport and Exercise.* Elsevier Health Sciences. Philadelphia, PA.

Masarsky, C. 2008. *Dynamic Chiropractic.* 26(14): 34.

McCord, P., DC. Pers. Comm. Total Body Chiropractic Therapy Clinic. w.totalbodychiro.com. Toronto, ON.

Pearl, B., and G.T. Moran. 1986. *Getting Stronger.* Random House. NY, NY.

Polsdorfer, J., and M.D. Ricker. 2006. Osteopathy. In: *The Gale Encyclopedia of Medicine.* 3rd ed. J.L. Longe (ed.). Gale. Detroit, MI.

Satyanda, S. 1981. *Yoga and Kriya.* K.L. Bhargava & Co. Impression House. Mumbai, Maharashtra, India.

Seguin, R., and M.E. Nelson. 2003. *American Journal of Preventive Medicine.* 25(3): 141–149.

Solan, M. 2009. *Natural Health.* 39(6): 78–79.

Tiran, D., and S. Mack. 2000. *Complementary Therapies for Pregnancy and Childbirth.* 2nd ed. Elsevier Health Sciences. Philadelphia, PA.

Walker, B. 2007. *The Anatomy of Sports Injuries.* North Atlantic Books. Berkeley, CA.

Chapter 7

Arrieta. M.C., *et al.* 2006. *Gut.* 55(10): 1512–1520.

Bäckhed, F., *et al.* 2005. *Science.* 307(5717): 1915–1920.

Barbara, G., *et al.* 2008. *Journal of Clinical Gastroenterology.* 42(Suppl. 3): S214–217.

Beausoleil, M., *et al.* 2007. *Canadian Journal of Gastroenterology.* 21(11): 732–736.

Beck, L. 2001. *Leslie Beck's Nutrition Encyclopedia.* Penguin Canada. Toronto, ON.

Belleme, J., and J. Belleme. 2007. *Japanese Foods That Heal.* Tuttle Publishing. North Clarendon, VT.

Beltz, B.S., *et al.* 2007. *Neuroscience Letters.* 415(2): 154–158.

Boesten, R.J., and W.M. de Vos. 2008. *Journal of Clinical Gastroenterology.* 42(Suppl. 3, Pt. 2): S163–S167.

Brandtzaeg, P., *et al.* 1999. *Immunology Today.* 20(6): 267–277.

Colbin, A. 1996. *Food and Healing.* Ballantine Books. NY, NY.

Cuvelier, C., *et al.* 1987. *Gut.* 28(4): 394–40.

Gottschall, E.G. 1994. *Breaking the Vicious Cycle.* Kirkton Press, Kirkton, ON.

Graci, S. 2001. *The Food Connection.* MacMillan Canada. Toronto, ON.

Greene, J.D., and T.R. Klaenhammer. 1994. *Applied and Environmental Microbiology.* 60(12): 4487–4494.

Guarner, F., and J. Malagelada. 2003. *The Lancet.* 361(9356): 512–519.

Hart, A.L., *et al.* 2004. *Gut.* 53: 1602–1609.

Hill, M.J. 1997. *European Journal of Cancer Prevention.* 9(Suppl. 1): S43–S45.

Hooper, L.V., and J.I. Gordon. *Science.* 292(5519): 1115–1118.

Isolauri, E., *et al.* 2002. *Gut.* 50(Suppl. 3): iii54–iii59.

Jensen, B. 1999. *Dr. Jensen's Guide to Better Bowel Care.* Avery. NY, NY.

King, B.J. 2003. *The Fat Wars Action Planner.* Wiley Press. Toronto, ON. Klaenhammer, T.R., *et al.* 2008. *Journal of Clinical Gastroenterology.* 42(Suppl. 3, Pt. 2): S160–S162.

Knobler, H., *et al.* 1999. *Q Journal of Medicine.* 92(2): 73–79.

Langlands, S.J., *et al.* 2004. *Gut.* 53: 1610–1616.

Lee, J.S., *et al.* 2009. *World Journal of Gastroenterology.* 15(15): 1869–1875.

Lenoir-Wijnkoop, I., *et al.* 2007. *Nutritional Review.* 65(11): 469–489.

Levine, J., *et al.* 1995. *Clinical Infectious Diseases.* 21(4): 881–886.

Lewis, S.J., and K.W. Heaton. 1999. *American Journal of Gastroenterology.* 94(8): 2010–2116.

Lin, H.C. 2004. *Journal of the American Medical Association.* 292(7): 852–858.

Lombardo, L. 2008. *Minerva Gastroenterologica e Dietologica.* 54(3): 287–293.

MacDonald, T.T., and G. Monteleone. 2005. *Science.* 307(5717): 1920–1925.

Massacand, J.C., *et al.* 2008. *PLoS ONE.* 3(7): e2588.

Matsen, J. 1987. *Eating Alive.* Crompton Books. Vancouver, BC.

Mengheri, E. 2008. *Journal of Clinical Gastroenterology.* 42(Suppl. 3, Pt. 2): S177–S178.

Mimura, T., *et al.* 2004. *Gut.* 53(1): 108–114.

Mohamadzadeh, M., *et al.* 2005. *Proceedings of the National Academy of Sciences.* 102(8): 2880–2885.

Murray, M.T., and J. Pizzorno. 1998. *Encyclopedia of Natural Medicine.* Revised 2nd ed. Prima Publishing. Roseville, CA.

Ouwehand, A., *et al.* 2002. *European Journal of Nutrition.* 41(Suppl. 1): I/32–I/37.

Pregliasco, F., *et al.* 2008. *Journal of Clinical Gastroenterology.* 42(Suppl. 3, Pt. 2): S224–S233.

Rimoldi, M., *et al.* 2005. *Nature Immunology.* 6(5): 507–514.

Singh, J., *et al.* 1997. *Carcinogensis.* 18(4): 833–841.

Taylor, J.R., and D. Mitchell. 2007. *The Wonder of Probiotics.* St. Martin's Press. NY, NY.

Vaclavik, V., and E.W. Christian. 2007. *Essentials of Food Science.* 3rd ed. Springer Science. NY, NY.

Vanderhaeghe, L.R. 2001. *Healthy Immunity.* Macmillan Canada. Toronto, ON.

Vanderhaeghe, L.R. 2001. *The Immune System Cure.* Prentice Hall. Scarborough, ON.

Vesterlund, S., *et al.* 2006. *Microbiology.* 152(6): 1812–1826.

Watson, B. 2002. *Renew Your Life.* Renew Life Press. Clearwater, FL.

Watson, B., and L. Smith. 2003. *Gut Solutions.* Renew Life Press. Clearwater, FL.

Zeuzem, S. 2000. *International Journal of Colorectal Diseases.* 15(2): 59–82.

Chapter 8

Beauchamp, G.K., *et al.* 2005. *Nature.* 437(7055): 45–46.

Belleme, J., and J. Belleme. 2007. *Japanese Foods That Heal.*

Tuttle Publishing. North Clarendon, VT.

Borek C. 2006. *Journal of Nutrition.* 136(Suppl. 3): 810S–812S.

Breaky, J., *et al.* 2001. Pp. 87–97. In: *Food Additives.* 2nd ed. A.L. Branen, *et al.* (eds.). Marcel Dekker. NY, NY.

Brien, S., *et al.* 2004. *Evidence-based Complementary and Alternative Medicine.* 1(3): 251–257.

Bukovská, A., *et al.* 2007. *Mediators of Inflammation.* 2007(Article ID 23296): 1–9.

Chainy, G.B., *et al.* 2000. *Oncogene.* 19(25): 2943–2950.

Chen, J., *et al.* 2008. *Nutrition and Cancer.* 60(1): 43–50.

Chobotova, K., *et al.* 2010. *Cancer Letters.* 290(2): 148–156.

Choi, D.W., and S.M. Rothman. 1990. *Annual Review of Neuroscience.* 13(1): 171–182.

Conrad, K. 2006. *Eat Well, Feel Well.* Random House. NY, NY.

Das, U.N. 2002. *Nutrition.* 18(9): 786–789.

Deutsch, L. 2007. *Journal of the American College of Nutrition.* 26(1): 39–48.

Farkas, D., and D.J. Greenblatt. 2008. *Expert Opinion on Drug Metabolism and Toxicology.* 4(4): 381–393.

Feingold, B.F. 1975. *American Journal of Nursing.* 75(5): 797–803.

Gottschall, E.G. 1994. *Breaking the Vicious Cycle.* Kirkton Press, Kirkton, ON.

Grzanna, R., *et al.* 2005. *Journal of Medicinal Food.* 8(2): 125–132.

Hidaka, M., *et al* 2006. *Drug Metabolism and Disposition.* 34(3): 343–345.

Hidaka, M., *et al.* 2004. *Drug Metabolism and Disposition.* 32(6): 581–583.

Holt, P.R., *et al.* 2005. *Digestive Diseases and Science.* 50(11): 2191–2193.

Kharazmi, A., and K.A.J. Winther. 1999. *Immunopharmacology.* 7(4): 377–386.

Kim, H., *et al.* 2006. *Drug Metabolism and Disposition.* 34(4): 521–523.

Kochhar, K.P. 1999. *Journal of Orthomolecular Medicine.* 14(4): 210–218.

Krop, J.J. 2002. *Healing the Planet, One Patient at a Time.* Kos Publishing. Toronto, ON.

Kultétyová, I., *et al.* 1998. *Neuroendocrinology.* 67(6): 412–420.

Lugasi, A., *et al.* 2003. *Acta Biologica Szegediensis.* 47(1–4): 119–125.

Malanin, G., and K. Kalimo. 1989. *Clinical and Experimental Allergy.* 19(5): 539–543.

McCall, A., *et al.* 1979. *Neurobehavioral Toxicity.* 1(4): 279–283.

McDowell, L.R. 2003. *Minerals in Animal and Human Nutrition.* 2nd ed. Elsevier Health Sciences. Philadelphia, PA.

Murray, M.T. 1995. *The Healing Power of Herbs.* Random House. NY, NY.

Nagao, T., *et al.* 2005. *American Journal of Clinical Nutrition,* 81(1): 122–129.

Nicoll, R., and M.Y. Henein. 2009. *International Journal of Cardiology.* 131(3): 408–409.

Olney, J.W., and L.G. Sharpe. 1969. *Science.* 166(3903): 386–388.

Pravst, I., *et al.* 2010. *Critical Reviews in Food Science and Nutrition.* 50(4): 269–280.

Rangan, C., and D. Barceloux. 2009. *Disease-a-Month.* 55(5): 292–311.

Rimando, A.M., *et al.* 2004. *Journal of Agriculture and Food Chemistry.* 52(15): 4713–4719.

Said, H.M. 2009. *Journal of Nutrition.* 139(1): 158–162.

Sarjeant, D. 1999. *Hard to Swallow.* Alive Books. Burnaby, BC.

Schlosser, E. 2001. *Fast Food Nation.* Houghton Mifflin, Boston, MA.

SeaChoice. *Canada's Sustainable Seafood Guide.* www.seachoice.org

Singh S., *et al.* 2007. *Indian Journal of Experimental Biology.* 45(5): 403–12.

Spolaore, P., *et al.* 2006. *Journal of Bioscience and Bioengineering.* 101(6): 201–211.

Staggs, G., *et al.* 2004. *Journal of Food Composition and Analysis.* 17(6): 767–776.

Stuchl'k, M., and S. Žák. 2002. *Biomedical Papers.* 146(2): 3–10.

Takaki, I., *et al.* 2008. *Journal of Medicinal Food.* 11(4): 741–746.

Thomson, M., *et al.* 2002. *Prostaglandins, Leukotrienes, and Essential Fatty Acids.* 67(6): 475–478.

Torbergsen, A.C., and A.R. Collins. 2000. *European Journal of Nutrition.* 39(2): 80–85.

Vaclavik, V., and E.W. Christian. 2007. *Essentials of Food Science.* 3rd ed. Springer Science. NY, NY.

Varzakas, T.H., *et al.* 2010. Pp. 409–456. In: *Applied Food Chemistry.* F.Yildiz (ed.). CRC Press. Boca Raton, FL.

Wannamethee, G., *et al.* 2006. *American Journal of Clinical Nutrition.* 83(3): 567–574.

Winther, K., E. Rein, and A. Kharazmi. 1999. *Immunopharmacology.* 7(1): 63–68.

Zhang, J-W., *et al.* 2007. *Journal of Pharmacy and Pharmaceutical Sciences.* 10(4): 496–503.

Chapter 9

Benbrook, C., *et al.* 2008. *State of Science Review.* March: 1–8.

Breaky, J., *et al.* 2001. Pp. 87–97. In: *Food Additives.* 2nd ed. A.L. Branen, *et al* (eds.). Marcel Dekker. NY, NY.

Choi, D.W., and S.M. Rothman. 1990. *Annual Review of Neuroscience.* 13(1): 171–182.

Conrad, K. 2006. *Eat Well, Feel Well.* Random House. NY, NY.

Feingold, B.F. 1975. *American Journal of Nursing.* 75(5): 797–803.

Gottschall, E.G. 1994. *Breaking the Vicious Cycle.* Kirkton Press. Kirkton, ON.

Environmental Working Group. Shopper's Guide to Pesticides. www.foodnews.org.

Food and Nutrition Board, Institute of Medicine. 2005. *Dietary Reference Intakes for Energy, Carbohydrate, Fiber, Fat, Fatty Acids, Cholesterol, Protein, and Amino Acids.* National Academy Press. Washington, DC.

Haenlein, G.F.W. 2004. *Small Ruminant Research.* 51(2): 155–163.

Jandal, J.M. 1996. *Small Ruminant Research.* 22(2): 177–185.

Krop, J.J. 2002. *Healing the Planet, One Patient at a Time.* Kos Publishing. Toronto, ON.

Kultétyová, I., *et al.* 1998. *Neuroendocrinology.* 67(6): 412–420.

Malanin, G., and K. Kalimo. 1989. *Clinical and Experimental Allergy.* 19(5): 539–543.

McCall, A., *et al.* 1979. *Neurobehavioral Toxicity.* 1(4): 279–283.

Mitchell, A.E., *et al.* 2007. *Journal of Agricultural and Food Chemistry.* 55(15): 6154–6159.

Mozaffarin, D., *et al.* 2004. *American Journal of Clinical Nutrition.* 79(4): 606–612.

Munro, I.C., *et al.* 1998. *Food and Chemical Toxicology.* 36(12): 1139–1174.

Murray, M.T., and J. Pizzorno. 1998. *Encyclopedia of Natural Medicine.* Revised 2nd ed. Prima Publishing. Roseville, CA.

Nair, M.K., *et al.* 2005. *Journal of Dairy Science.* 88(10): 3488–3495.

Olney, J.W., and L.G. Sharpe. 1969. *Science.* 166(3903): 386–388.

Park, Y.W., *et al.* 2007. *Small Ruminant Research.* 68(1–2): 88–113.

Pastorello, E.A., *et al.* 1989. *Journal of Allergy and Clinical Immunology.* 84(4, Pt. 1): 475–483.

Rangan, C., and D. Barceloux. 2009. *Disease-a-Month.* 55(5): 292–311.

Sarjeant, D. 1999. *Hard to Swallow.* Alive Books. Burnaby, BC.

Schlosser, E. 2001. *Fast Food Nation.* Houghton Mifflin, Boston, MA.

Vaclavik, V., and E.W. Christian. 2007. *Essentials of Food Science.* 3rd ed. Springer Science. NY, NY.

Chapter 10

Bondesson, M., *et al.* 2009. *Reproductive Toxicology.* 28(4): 563–567.

Cherng, J.M., *et al.* 2008. *Food Chemistry.* 106(3): 944–950.

Ezz El-Arab, A.M., *et al.* 2006. *BMC Complementary and Alternative Medicine.* 6: 6.

Gilliland, F.D., and J.S. Mandel. 1996. *American Journal of Industrial Medicine.* 29(5): 560–568.

Jeppesen, P.B., *et al.* 2002. *Phytomedicine.* 9(1): 9–14.

Lee, S.W., *et al.* 2010. *Food Chemistry.* 118(3): 681–685.

Manthey, F.A., *et al.* 2002. *Journal of Agricultural and Food Chemistry.* 50(6): 1668-1671.

Murkovic, M., and W. Pfannhauser. 2000. *European Journal of Lipid Science and Technology.* 102(10): 607-611.

Prentice, J. 2006. *Full Moon Feast.* Chelsea Green Publishing. White River Junction, VT.

Tsai, P.J., *et al.* 2007. *Food and Chemical Toxicology.* 45(3): 440–447.

Tsai, T.H., *et al.* 2005. *Journal of Food Science.* 70(1): C93–C97.

Chapter 11

Bedani, A., and T.D. DuBose. 1995. Pp. 69–103. In: *Fluid, Electrolyte and Acid Base Disorders.* A.I. Arieff and R.A. DeFronzo (eds.). Churchill Livingstone. NY, NY.

Ferrara, L., *et al.* 2001. *Il Farmaco.* 56(5–7): 397–401.

Fujisawa, Y., *et al.* 2000. *Microbiology and Immunology.* 44(9): 799–804.

Hoffman, D. 2003. *Medical Herbalism.* Healing Arts Press. Rochester, VT.

Howell, A.B., *et al.* 2005. *Phytochemistry.* 66(18): 2281–2291.

Lin, S.C., *et al.* 2002. *Journal of Biomedical Science.* 9(5): 410–409.

Meoli, A.L., *et al.* 2005. *Journal of Clinical Sleep Medicine.* 1(2): 173–187.

Murray, M.T. 1995. *The Healing Power of Herbs.* Random House. NY, NY.

Nagao, T., *et al.* 2005. *American Journal of Clinical Nutrition,* 81(1): 122–129.

Prakash, P., and N. Gupta. 2005. *Indian Journal of Physiology and Pharmacology.* 49(2): 125–131.

Sidhu, K., *et al.* 2007. *Journal of Human Ecology.* 21(2): 113–116.

Snijman, P.W., *et al.* 2007. *Genetic Toxicology and Environmental Mutagenesis.* 631(2): 111–123.

Tokusoglu, Ö., and M.K. Ünal. 2003. *Food Chemistry and Toxicology.* 68(4): 1144–1148.

Winther, K., *et al.* 1999. *Immunopharmacology.* 7(1): 63–68.

Yoo, K.M., *et al.* 2008. *Food Chemistry.* 106(3): 929–936.

Chapter 12—Chapter 16

Adachi, M., *et al.* 2007. *International Journal of Food Properties.* 10(2): 375–384.

Ahamed, N.T., *et al.* 1998. Pp. 61–70. In: *Food and Nutrition Bulletin.* N.S. Scrimshaw (ed.). United Nations University Press. Tokyo, Japan.

Ayadi, M.A., *et al.* 2009. *Food and Chemical Toxicology.* 47(10): 2613–2619.

Ayaz, F.A., *et al.* 2005. *Journal of Agricultural and Food Chemistry.* 53(21): 8116–8122.

Badreldin, H.A., *et al.* 2005. *Phytotherapy Research.* 19(5): 369–375.

Barceloux, D.G. 2008. Pp. 77–83. In: *Medical Toxicology of Natural Substances.* D.G. Barceloux (ed.). John Wiley and Sons. Hoboken, NJ.

Bedani, A., and T.D. DuBose. 1995. Pp. 69–103. In: *Fluid, Electrolyte and Acid Base Disorders.* A.I. Arieff and R.A. DeFronzo (eds.). Churchill Livingstone. NY, NY.

Belleme, J., and J. Belleme. 2007. *Japanese Foods That Heal.* Tuttle Publishing. North Clarendon, VT.

Bergsson, G., *et al.* 2001. *Antimicrobial Agents and Chemotherapy.* 45(11): 3209–3212.

Block, K.I., and M.N. Mead. 2003. *Integrative Cancer Therapies.* 2(3): 247–267.

Borek C. 2006. *Journal of Nutrition.* 136(Suppl. 3): 810S–812S.

Boyer, J., and R.H. Liu. 2004. *Nutrition Journal.* 3(1): 5.

Brazier, B. 2007. *The Thrive Diet.* Da Capo Press. Philadelphia, PA.

Burtin, P. 2003. *Electronic Journal of Environmental, Agricultural and Food Chemistry.* 2(4): 498–503.

Chavali, S.R., *et al.* 2001. *Clinical Care Medicine.* 29(1): 140–143.

Chen, H.H, *et al.* 2011. *Journal of Agriculture and Food Chemistry.* 59(12): 6444–6452.

Colbin, A. 1996. *Food and Healing.* Ballantine Books. NY, NY.

Conner, B. A. 2005. *Clinical Infectious Diseases.* 41(Suppl. 8): S577–S586.

Coskuner, Y., *et al.* 2002. *Journal of the Science of Food and Agriculture.* 82(6): 625-631.

Cover, C.M., *et al.* 1998. *Journal of Biological Chemistry.* 273(7): 3838–3847.

Craig, S.A.S. 2004. *American Journal of Nutrition.* 80(3): 539–549.

D'Andrea, A.C. 2008. *Economic Botany.* 62(4): 547–566.

Daniel, E.M., *et al.* 1989. *Journal of Food Composition and Analysis.* 2(4): 338–349.

Dinkova-Kostova, A.T., *et al.* 2007. *Cancer Epidemiology and Biomarkers Prevention.* 16(4): 847–851.

Eckert, G.P. 2010. *Frontiers in Pharmacology.* 1(138): 1-10.

Erasmus, U. 1993. *Fats That Heal, Fats That Kill.* Alive Books. Burnaby, BC.

Fabiani, R., *et al.* 2008. *Journal of Nutrition.* 138(8): 1411–1416.

Fahey, J.W., *et al.* 2002. *Proceedings of the National Academy of Sciences.* 99(11): 7610–7615.

Fallon, S. 2001. *Nourishing Traditions.* New Trends Publishing. Washington, D.C.

Flower, R.J., and M. Perretti. 2005. *Journal of Experimental Medicine.* 201(5): 671–674.

Garg, M.L., *et al.* 2003. *Journal of Nutrition.* 133(4): 1060–1063.

Glew R.H., *et al.* 2006. *Plant Foods for Human Nutrition.* 61(2): 51–56.

Griffith, R.S., *et al.* 1981. *Chemotherapy.* 27(3): 209–213.

Griffith, R.S., *et al.* 1978. *Dermatologica.* 156(5): 257–267.

Griffith, R.S., *et al.* 1987. *Dermatologica.* 175(4): 183–190.

Haas, E.M. 2006. *The New Detox Diet.* Celestial Arts. Berkeley, CA.

Harnly, J.M., *et al.* 2006. *Journal of Agricultural Food and Chemistry.* 54(26): 9966–9977.

Hlebowicz, J., *et al.* 2007. *American Journal of Clinical Nutrition.* 85(6): 1552–1556.

Hlebowicz, J., *et al.* 2009. *American Journal of Clinical Nutrition.* 89(3): 815–821.

Hoffman, D. 2003. *Medical Herbalism.* Healing Arts Press. Rochester, VT.

Horne, S. 2006. *Journal of Herbal Pharmacotherapy.* 6(2): 93–100.

Hu, G., and P.A. Cassano. 2000. *American Journal of Epidemiology.* 151(10): 975–981.

Johanningsmeier, S.D., *et al.* 2005. *Journal of Food Science.* 70(5): S343–S349.

Khan, A., *et al.* 2003. *Diabetes Care.* 26(12): 3215–3218.

Kuo, Y.H., *et al.* 2009. *Journal of Ethnopharmacology.* 122(1): 28–34.

Lampe, J.W. 1999. *American Journal of Clinical Nutrition.* 70(3): 465S–490S.

Lau, F.C., *et al.* 2005. *Neurobiology of Aging.* 26(Suppl. 1): S128–S132.

Lim, G.P., *et al.* 2001. *Journal of Neuroscience.* 21(21): 8370–8377.

Lin, S.C., *et al.* 2002. *Journal of Biomedical Science.* 9(5): 410–409.

Lu, Y., *et al.* 2011. *Hepatobiliary and Pancreatic Diseases International.* 10(3): 303–307.

Maga, J.A. 1994. *Food Reviews International.* 10(4): 385–418.

Maggs, D.J., *et al.* 2000. *American Journal of Veterinary Research.* 61(12): 1474–1478.

Mateljan, G. 2006. *The World's Healthiest Foods.* George Mateljan Fdn. Seattle, WA.

McCune, M.A., *et al.* 1984. *Cutis.* 34(4): 366–373.

Meng, Q., *et al.* 2000. *Journal of Nutrition.* 130(12): 2927–2931.

Montaut, S., *et al.* 2010. *Phytochemistry.* 71(1): 6–12.

Nagao, A., *et al.* 1999. *Bioscience, Biotechnology, and Biochemistry.* 63(10): 1787–1790.

Nair, M.K., *et al.* 2005. *Journal of Dairy Science.* 88(10): 3488–3495.

Nardini, P., ND. Pers. comm. Inspired Life Health Centre. www.inspiredlife.ca. Toronto, ON.

Ogbolu, D.O., *et al.* 2007. *Journal of Medicinal Food.* 10(2): 384–387.

Pomin, V.H., and P.A.S. Mourão. 2008. *Glycobiology.* 18(12): 1016–1027.

Powell, J.J., 2005. *British Journal of Nutrition.* 94(5): 804–812.

Qin, B., *et al.* 2004. *Hormone and Metabolic Research.* 36(2): 119–125.

Regula, J., and M. Siwulski. 2007. *Acta Scientiarum Polonorum Technologia Alimentaria.* 6(4): 135–142.

Riby, J.E., *et al.* 2000. *Biochemistry.* 39(5): 910–918.

Ringman, J.M., *et al.* 2005. *Current Alzheimer's Research.* 2(2): 131–136.

Rodriguez, T.S., *et al.* 2002. *Phytomedicine.* 9(8): 687–693.

Russell, W.R., *et al.* 2009. *Food Chemistry.* 115(1): 100–104.

Scheider, E. 2001. *Vegetables from Amaranth to Zucchini.* William Morrow. NY, NY.

Scheier, L. 2001. *Journal of the American Dietetic Association.* 101(12): 1406–1408.

Shukitt-Hale, B., *et al.* 2008. *Journal of Agricultural and Food Chemistry.* 56(3): 636–641.

Stark, A.H., and Z. Madar. 2006. *Nutrition Reviews.* 60(2): 170–176.

Steele, J. 2008. *Get It Ripe.* Arsenal Pulp Press. Vancouver, BC.

Sugui, M.M., *et al.* 2003. *Food and Chemical Toxicology.* 41(4): 555–560.

Talalay, P., *et al.* 2007. *Proceedings of the National Academy of Sciences.* 104(44): 17500–17505.

Tankersley, R.W. 1964. *Journal of Bacteriology.* 87(3): 609–613.

Tenda, E.T., *et al.* 2009. *Indonesian Journal of Agriculture.* 2(1): 6–10.

Thein, D.J., and W.C. Hurt. 1984. *Oral Surgery, Oral Medicine and Oral Pathology.* 58(6): 659–666.

Tsi, D., and B.K.H. Tan. 2000. *Life Sciences.* 66(8): 755–767.

U.S. Department of Agriculture. 2009. *USDA National Nutrient Database.* Release 22. www.ars.usda.gov/ba/bhnrc/ndl.

Utsunomiya, T., *et al.* 2003. *Hepato-gastroenterology.* 50(53): 1609–1613.

Wang, H., *et al.* 1999. *Journal of Natural Products.* 62(2): 294–296.

Wansink, B. 2006. *Mindless Eating.* Bantam Dell. NY, NY.

Winkler, B.S., *et al.* 1999. *Molecular Vision.* 3(5): 32–58.

Wood, R. 1999. *The New Foods Encyclopedia.* Penguin Books. NY, NY.

Zhang, Y., *et al.* 1994. *Proceedings of the National Academy of Sciences.* 91(8): 3147–3150.

SUBJECT INDEX

RECIPES INDEX

ABOUT THE AUTHOR

Julie Daniluk, R.H.N., is a leading nutritionist and the co-host of *Healthy Gourmet,* a reality cooking show. Julie has appeared on *The Dr. Oz Show, The Right Fit,* and *The Marilyn Denis Show.* For twelve years, she was the cooperative owner and the Chief In-Store Nutritionist for one of Canada's largest health-food stores, The Big Carrot Natural Food Market. She lives in Toronto.

Website: **www.juliedaniluk.com**

Hay House Titles of Related Interest

YOU CAN HEAL YOUR LIFE, the movie, starring Louise Hay & Friends
(available as a 1–DVD program and an expanded 2–DVD set)
Watch the trailer at: **www.LouiseHayMovie.com**

THE SHIFT, the movie, starring Dr. Wayne W. Dyer
(available as a 1–DVD program and an expanded 2–DVD set)
Watch the trailer at: **www.DyerMovie.com**

• • •

THE BODY ECOLOGY DIET:
Recovering Your Health and Rebuilding Your Immunity,
by Donna Gates (with Linda Schatz)

THE HUNTER/FARMER DIET SOLUTION:
Do You Have the Metabolism of a Hunter or a Farmer? Find Out . . .
and Achieve Your Health and Weight-Loss Goals!,
by Mark Liponis, M.D.

RAW BASICS:
Incorporating Raw Living Foods into Your Diet Using Easy
and Delicious Recipes,
by Jenny Ross

RECIPES FOR HEALTH BLISS:
Using NatureFoods & Lifestyle Choices to Rejuvenate Your Body & Life,
by Susan Smith Jones, Ph.D.

THE SPARKPEOPLE COOKBOOK:
Love Your Food, Lose the Weight,
by Meg Galvin (with Stepfanie Romine)

VEGETARIAN MEALS FOR PEOPLE-ON-THE-GO:
101 Quick & Easy Recipes,
by Vimala Rodgers

All of the above are available at your local bookstore,
or may be ordered by contacting Hay House (see next page).

• • •

We hope you enjoyed this Hay House book.
If you'd like to receive our online catalog featuring additional information on
Hay House books and products, or if you'd like to find out
more about the Hay Foundation, please contact:

Hay House, Inc., P.O. Box 5100, Carlsbad, CA 92018-5100
(760) 431-7695 or (800) 654-5126
(760) 431-6948 (fax) or (800) 650-5115 (fax)
www.hayhouse.com® • **www.hayfoundation.org**

• • •

Published and distributed in Australia by:
Hay House Australia Pty. Ltd., 18/36 Ralph St., Alexandria NSW 2015 •
Phone: 612-9669-4299 • *Fax:* 612-9669-4144 • www.hayhouse.com.au

Published and distributed in the United Kingdom by:
Hay House UK, Ltd., Astley House, 33 Notting Hill Gate, London W11 3JQ •
Phone: 44-20-3675-2450 • *Fax:* 44-20-3675-2451 • www.hayhouse.co.uk

Published and distributed in the Republic of South Africa by:
Hay House SA (Pty), Ltd., P.O. Box 990, Witkoppen 2068 •
Phone/Fax: 27-11-467-8904 • www.hayhouse.co.za

Published in India by:
Hay House Publishers India, Muskaan Complex, Plot No. 3, B-2, Vasant Kunj, New Delhi 110 070 •
Phone: 91-11-4176-1620 • *Fax:* 91-11-4176-1630 • www.hayhouse.co.in

• • •

Take Your Soul on a Vacation

Visit **www.HealYourLife.com**® to regroup, recharge, and reconnect
with your own magnificence. Featuring blogs, mind-body-spirit news,
and life-changing wisdom from Louise Hay and friends.

Visit **www.HealYourLife.com** today!